OVERTURNED

RHETORIC, LAW, AND THE HUMANITIES

OVERTURNED

The Rhetoric of Overruling in the United States Supreme Court

CLARKE ROUNTREE

THE UNIVERSITY OF ALABAMA PRESS
Tuscaloosa

The University of Alabama Press
Tuscaloosa, Alabama 35487-0380
uapress.ua.edu

Typeface: Arno Pro

Cover photos by: © thatinchan- stock.adobe.com and © jonbilous - stock.adobe.com

Cover design: Sandy Turner Jr.

Cataloging-in-Publication data is available from the Library of Congress.
ISBN: 978-0-8173-2218-2 (cloth)
ISBN: 978-0-8173-6180-8 (paper)
E-ISBN: 978-0-8173-9538-4

For John R. Lyne, my friend and mentor for forty years

Contents

Tables

Acknowledgments

THIS PROJECT BEGAN MORE THAN thirty years ago after I heard President George H. W. Bush pledge to appoint justices to the US Supreme Court who would reconsider *Roe v. Wade*. (Ironically, his father, Senator Prescott Bush, helped to found the organization that became Planned Parenthood.) That political promise made me wonder how the high court could justify reversing itself. Overrulings undercut the credibility of the court—and that's all they have to support their decisions—by saying "We were wrong in the past" while implying "But trust us this time to get it right!" I decided to embark on a book-length study of the Supreme Court's overruling rhetoric. My institution at the time, Indiana University at Kokomo, generously supported my award of a $7,000 UROC Grant from a Multicampus Research Support Fund to begin the study, as well as granting me summer support for initial work on the project.

I needed that support because I wanted to look at every overruling in the court's history—about 300 decisions overruling about 350 precedents. To accomplish that, I needed access to a legal database (which was very expensive at the time) and an assistant to do the tedious work of downloading these cases, along with relevant law review articles, and to help me organize them. To put the timeline for this beginning in perspective, I purchased a cutting-edge 7200-baud modem for downloading!

I did initial work before I left Kokomo for a job at my undergraduate alma mater, the University of Alabama in Huntsville. In my new assistant professor position I received three years' credit toward tenure, making the completion of a book project in time a questionable endeavor. After earning tenure, I must confess, I became distracted by other interesting issues in legal and political rhetoric, publishing dozens of essays and six books. For example, after the shocking decision in *Bush v. Gore* ending the 2000 presidential election, I worked for five years on a five-hundred-page book showing the flaws in the conservative court's decision in the case. More recently I worked with a Finnish colleague to edit an international volume on national leaders' rhetoric in the Syrian immigration crisis.

But I never completely gave up on this book project. In the past few years, I wrote, presented, and published papers on the subject, often employing undergraduate and graduate students to help me flesh out this research. The last student assistant, Stuart Howe, helped get me over the line with his excellent help researching the background of many of these cases. And, as usual, I had the advice and forbearance of colleagues, friends, and my wife, Jennie, as I grappled with these cases. I also had a very supportive editor at the University of Alabama Press, along with the advisory board, who allowed me to publish this book in the series that I started and for which I still serve as series editor, Rhetoric, Law, and the Humanities. I particularly would like to thank the anonymous reviewers who helped me identify the strengths and weaknesses of my initial draft, and to improve its arguments and readability.

It is ironic that I should finish this book just after *Roe v. Wade* was overturned. My shock at this development and at the Roberts court's cavalier attitude toward overruling led me to devote considerable space at the end of this volume to this troubling decision and what it portends. As sad as this development is, I suppose it provides a fitting bookend to the beginning and completion of this project. And, hopefully, it makes my final arguments about the high bar that ought to be set for overruling timely and relevant.

OVERTURNED

CHAPTER 1

Judicial Rhetoric and Overruling in the US Supreme Court

ON MARCH 7, 2002, PRESIDENT George W. Bush took time during a fundraising trip to Atlanta to quietly sign the Bipartisan Campaign Reform Act (BCRA), also known as the McCain-Feingold Act for its two lead sponsors, Senator John McCain (R-Arizona) and Russ Feingold (D-Wisconsin). Passing the act was a Herculean effort that took years of negotiating and considerable political courage, especially on the part of McCain, whose party generally opposed the bill (hence, Bush's low-key signing of it).[1]

The efforts of McCain and Feingold began seven years earlier with a joint editorial in 1995 calling for reform to address the growing problem of "soft money," in-kind contributions from corporations and interest groups that circumvented limits on direct cash contributions to candidates. They managed to get a bill before Congress in 1998, though it was defeated by Senate Republicans.[2] By the 2000 elections, soft money contributions had grown to half a billion dollars. The BCRA of 2002 sought to eliminate soft money contributions and also addressed the problem of "electioneering communications," which were used by interest groups as a loophole in existing laws to indirectly attack or support political candidates. It disallowed such communications within thirty days of primary elections and sixty days of general elections. Opponents of the law issued legal challenges as soon as it went into effect following the 2002 elections.[3] The law survived the first attacks but would receive a death blow in 2010 from a split decision of the United States Supreme Court in *Citizens United v. Federal Election Commission*.[4]

The case involved a nonprofit corporation, Citizens United, which had distributed a documentary through movie theaters and DVDs suggesting that

Hillary Clinton was unfit for the presidency. The corporation wanted to offer the film on-demand as the primary elections approached; that effort was found by a lower court to violate the BRCA's rules for falling inside the thirty-day limit for electioneering communications near elections. The Supreme Court accepted an appeal from Citizens United, and Justice Kennedy wrote an opinion on behalf of the five most conservative members of the court supporting the group.[5] Instead of a narrow ruling on the particular facts of the case (such as the thirty-day limit), the majority expanded the decision to address the broad issue of corporate rights to free speech under the First Amendment. It gutted the BRCA on the grounds that the law abridged the First Amendment rights of corporations. It rejected the government's argument that it had an interest in preventing political corruption or the appearance of corruption, stating: "This Court now concludes that independent expenditures, including those made by corporations, do not give rise to corruption or the appearance of corruption. That speakers may have influence over or access to elected officials does not mean that those officials are corrupt. And the appearance of influence or access will not cause the electorate to lose faith in this democracy" (314). Later in the opinion, Kennedy supported this remarkable conclusion by limiting "corruption" to quid pro quo corruption, such as direct vote buying, noting that no examples of such corruption were included in the extensive record of an earlier case (360).

That earlier case, *McConnell v. Federal Election Commission*, followed on the heels of the passage of the BCRA and referenced Congress's one hundred thousand pages documenting the problems with soft money.[6] For example, it included testimony from former Senator Dale Bumpers (D-Arkansas) who admitted: "Candidates whose campaigns benefit from [phony 'issue ads'] greatly appreciate the help of these groups. In fact, Members will also be favorably disposed to those who finance these groups when they later seek access to discuss pending legislation."[7] In reaching its decision the majority overruled *McConnell*, as well as a 1990 case, *Austin v. Michigan Chamber of Commerce*, that upheld bans based on a speaker's corporate identity.[8]

Justice Stevens wrote a lengthy and scathing dissent rejecting the majority's reasoning. He was especially upset about the court's overruling of *Austin* and *McConnell*: "In the end, the Court's rejection of Austin and McConnell comes down to nothing more than its disagreement with their results. Virtually every one of its arguments was made and rejected in those cases, and the majority opinion is essentially an amalgamation of resuscitated dissents. The only relevant thing that has changed since Austin and McConnell is the composition of this Court" (414). Stevens complained that in overruling these precedents, the majority "strikes at the vitals of *stare decisis*," or more precisely, *stare decisis et non quieta movere*—the principle of abiding by precedents and not disturbing settled points. Stevens notes that this principle is "'the means by which we ensure that the law will not merely change erratically, but will develop in a principled and intelligible fashion' that 'permits society to presume that bedrock principles are founded in the law rather than in the proclivities of individuals.'"[9]

A week after the decision was announced, with five members of the high court sitting on the front row of the House chamber in the Capitol, President Barack Obama criticized the court's ruling in his State of the Union address, noting: "With all due deference to the separation of powers, last week, the Supreme Court reversed a century of law that I believe will open the floodgates for special interests—including foreign corporations—to spend without limit in our elections." Justice Alito silently mouthed for the camera, "Not true."[10] Communication scholar Stephen A. Smith called *Citizens United* "the most controversial 5-4 decision of the Court in the decade since *Bush v. Gore*, the case ending the contested presidential election." He added that "it was arguably the most counter-majoritarian opinion of the last two decades."[11]

THE PROBLEM OF OVERRULING

Citizens United throws into sharp relief a central rhetorical concern for the United States Supreme Court: how to justify the court's exercising of its unprecedented powers. The case reminds us that a bare majority of five of nine judges with lifetime appointments—with *one judge tipping the balance*—may, with the stroke of a pen, undo years of work by our elected officials, even when policymakers are attempting to address a significant political concern of the electorate. It cautions us that, regardless of the popularity of a law and its perceived importance, a handful of men and women (in this case, only men) can decide that the interest of purported constitutional fidelity trumps practical concerns; in this case, those practical concerns strike at the heart of our democratic system and perpetuate cynicism about electoral processes because of influence thought to be purchased with direct and indirect campaign contributions. Indeed, a year after the decision, Stan Greenberg found that "voters feel ever more estranged from government."[12] By 2012 President Obama's predictions had come true, as the number of campaign advertisements from outside groups skyrocketed from 3 percent of the total to two-thirds of the total—that is, those groups were buying twice as much advertising as the candidates themselves![13]

The exercise of such extraordinary power has been justified historically by the assumption that judges are not mere politicians in black robes supporting their own personal preferences, but decision-makers who are constrained by the law and legal reasoning. And, even though legal scholars began questioning that pretense almost a century ago, we should not be surprised to still find that "the Supreme Court speaks in a 'priestly voice' that positions them as middle-men between us and the law, that they characterize themselves as interpreters rather than creators of law, that they imply that they are chained to judicial logic rather than free to craft arguments from a rich well of rhetorical resources, that they pretend to be above normal human biases, and that they insist that what they assert about the law *is* the law. In short, the Supreme Court employs a rhetoric that pretends not to be rhetorical, and characterizes their own motives in deciding cases as severely circumscribed by the law."[14]

But *Citizens United* features not just an exercise of the ominous power of judicial review, but the Supreme Court's overruling of its own prior decisions. That is, just as it deploys this ominous power, it reminds us that it is fallible, that what it determined before is incorrect. Yet, *this time,* the majority implicitly suggests, they got it *right.* Justice Stevens has an alternative explanation for the change in law: because *who* is on the court is more important than *rules and principles of law;* that the overruling of recent precedents derives from a change in court personnel.

As this case and the book that follows suggests, overruling decisions are among the most rhetorically awkward actions in which the high court engages. As the court itself has recently reiterated, the principle of stare decisis is "a foundation stone of the rule of law" and, as such, it is "a doctrine that demands respect in a society governed by the rule of law."[15] Despite its centrality to the rule of law, the court does not always adhere to the doctrine, as *Citizens United* illustrates. Indeed, *Citizens United* is one of almost 300 cases in the court's history that have overruled more than 350 precedents, making such overrulings common enough for a genre of overruling opinions to have developed.[16] This book examines how the court has responded to the recurrent situation of abandoning its former decisions while maintaining its status as an impartial institution. It provides a rhetorical history of overruling in the Supreme Court. Most of the chapters delve into the particulars of some notable cases to go beyond generic considerations and demonstrate how unique challenges in different cases shaped the discourse of overruling. For example, the analysis will show differences in overrulings based upon the historical period in which the court is overruling, the type of case overruled (e.g., constitutional cases versus statutory and common-law cases), the age of the overruled precedent, and other variables (such as changes of personnel on the court leading to the reversal).

This chapter will begin by considering how judicial decision-making has been conceived, first by legal scholars and more recently by rhetoric scholars; the latter view judicial decisions as a species of persuasive communication. I note particularly the relevance of precedent in various conceptions of judicial decision-making.

This introductory matter lays the groundwork for a consideration of overruling rhetoric in the Supreme Court. Chapter 2 provides an overview of the history of overruling in the United States Supreme Court, noting especially how political, economic, and social forces have given rise to periods of frequent overrulings, shaping the perception of them and the justifications offered by the court for reversing itself. Chapter 3 begins a series of extended case studies with an examination of two nineteenth-century cases involving admiralty law and congressional authority to make printed money a legal currency. Chapter 4 looks at overruling cases involving statutory interpretations, which are rarer and unique in their concerns, including cases from 1844, 1917, and 1978. Chapter 5 looks at the period labeled the "Revolution of 1937," when the high court stopped killing New Deal legislation suspiciously after Franklin Roosevelt threatened to pack the court and went on a spree of overrulings that led many commentators to lament the demise of stare decisis. Chapter 6 looks at three cases protecting and expanding the rights of minorities: the flag salute case of *West Virginia v. Barnette,* the racial segregation case of *Brown v. Board of Education,* and the gay rights case of *Lawrence v. Texas*. Chapter 7 scrutinizes *Dobbs v. Jackson Women's Health Organization,* the controversial decision in 2022 that overturned the right to abortion announced in *Roe v. Wade,* comparing and contrasting that case with the cases and overruling practices covered in the earlier chapters. That case and other overruling cases by the Roberts court suggest a troubling development in the high court's overruling practices.

CONCEPTIONS OF JUDICIAL DECISION-MAKING

Theories about what judges are doing, or ought to be doing, when they decide cases can be usefully framed by a temporal continuum of concerns that define the judicial duty. Judges must be concerned with the past, the present, and the future; that is, with following the law (past), doing justice in the case before them (present), and laying down precedents that contribute to a better future, by providing rules to fairly resolve similar cases in the future and to promote good outcomes for society. Legal theories that describe or recommend effective or proper decision-making speak to these three temporal concerns, usually stressing one over the others. Legal theories that ignore one or more of these temporal concerns have been critiqued on that basis, though they often argue that the trade-off is worthwhile, as I will show.

When judges look to the past they must be concerned about following preexisting law. For natural law theorists, this might be law handed down from God, though usually it comes to decision-makers through the intercession of human reason said to be given by God. Some natural law theorists leave God out of the equation and stress an idealized *reason* as the source of law. This law-to-be-followed is indistinguishable from morals; thus, Aquinas could assert that a bad law is no law at all. He had faith that legal propositions were self-evident and could provide starting points for deducing the proper outcome for a given case.[17] We see application of this principle to the 1657 British case of *Giddings v. Brown,* which held that law repugnant to "fundamental law" is void.[18]

In this theory judicial decisions have precedential value only to the extent that they provide evidence of what this natural law is. That is, "judges discover rather than create the law."[19] William Blackstone endorsed this *declaratory theory of law,* insisting that it was the duty of courts "not . . . to pronounce a new law, but to maintain and expound the old one [and] . . . if it be found that the former decision is manifestly absurd and unjust, it is declared not that such a sentence was *bad law,* but that it was *not law.*"[20] Because Blackstone was the most important legal writer in the eighteenth century, "the declaratory theory . . . was in ascendancy at the time of the Constitutional Convention."[21]

The declaratory theory enjoyed a long life as a description of the *common law*—law created by judges since "time immemorial," relying on customs and usages to decide cases in the absence of specific, "positive" laws handed down by legislatures. Conceptions of judicial decisions as mere evidence of the law supports overturning erroneous statements of the law. We find Justice Story relying on this view in the 1842 case of *Swift v. Tyson,* where he claims: "In the ordinary use of language it will hardly be contended that the decisions of Courts constitute laws. They are, at most, only evidence of what the laws are; and are not of themselves laws."[22] In a 1917 Supreme Court case, Justice Oliver Wendell Holmes Jr. famously complained about such conceptions of the common law as, in his words, a "brooding omnipresence in the sky."[23] As late as 1935, Albert Kocourek noted that "despite the expressed disapproval of eminent writers, the prevailing doctrine is that of the declaratory theory."[24] A 1940 commentator called it "one of our most interesting, and persistent theories as to the nature of law."[25]

One of the reasons for declaratory theory's persistence is its usefulness in justifying ostensible changes in the law. If a court overrules a precedent, it can simply say that the prior decision was mistaken in understanding the law; thus, an overruling is not a *change in law* so much as a *return to the true law.* Thus, Blackstone admitted that precedents may be overturned "where the former determination is evidently contrary to reason; much more if it be contrary to the divine law." Although he thought precedents should be followed unless they are "flatly absurd or unjust," he noted that when precedents are overturned, "the subsequent judges do not pretend to make a new law, but to vindicate the old one from misrepresentation."[26]

The declaratory theory also was used by some to deny that a single precedent was controlling because, as Kent noted in his *Commentaries on American Law,* "even a series of decisions are not always conclusive evidence of what is law."[27] That position was repeated in an 1841 New York Supreme Court case, which declared that "it is going quite too far to say that a single decision of any court is absolutely conclusive as precedent."[28] As late as 1886, H. Campbell Black could claim in the *American Law Register* that "a single decision upon any given point of law is not regarded as conclusive as a precedent in the same degree that a series of decisions upon that point would be."[29]

Of course, the primary problem with natural law is its assumption that reason will inform the judge what the law requires in a given case, that its "preexistence" will be evident and its relevance to a given case plain. The problem with this assumption was succinctly stated by King James I, who proclaimed: "Reason is too large. Find me a precedent and I will accept it."[30] Indeed, early leading challengers to natural law were the imperative legal theories of Jeremy Bentham and John Austin, who looked to the "sovereign" (whether a king or a legislature) to find what the law was to be followed. Justice Holmes invokes this view, in his attack on natural law's "brooding omnipresence in the sky," offering alternatively "the articulate voice of some sovereign or quasi sovereign that can be identified."[31] But it would be H. L. A. Hart who most fully developed the theory known as legal positivism in his seminal 1958 essay, "Positivism and the Separation of Law and Morals."[32] Concerned about the clarity of law and the separation of powers that left lawmaking to the legislature, the legal positivists separated law and morals, holding that even morally bad laws were laws. They called for judges to rely on "positive law" in ascertaining what the law is in a given case, including constitutions, statutes, and even prior judicial decisions.

Hart admits that "in applying legal rules someone must take the responsibility of deciding that words do or do not cover some case in hand with all the practical consequences involved in this decision."[33] Legal skeptics, to whom I will turn, shortly, latch on to this problem to suggest that the legal positivist judge will face unclear cases (in the "penumbra" of the law) where she must effectively legislate, "making law" to fill the gaps where rules are unclear.[34] Hart concedes that, but insists that the rules typically are clear enough so that "to be occupied with the penumbra is one thing, to be preoccupied with it another."[35] He suggests that "we must decide the penumbral cases rationally by reference to social aims," bringing in future concerns to supplement legal positivism's heavy reliance on the past.[36]

Obviously following precedent is important to legal positivists, so long as it is consonant with law laid down by constitution writers and legislators. Indeed, if those with legislative power find that the courts have misunderstood the law which they, as sovereign, have laid down, they may change those laws or constitutions to correct judicial misunderstanding.

The legal theorists to whom Hart's seminal essay responded look more to the future than to the past to support judicial decisions. The legal realists were skeptical of those who claimed to be shackled by the past, whether to natural or positive law. Indeed, Karl Llewellyn describes the legal realists as sharing a "distrust of traditional legal rules and concepts insofar as they purport to *describe* what either courts or people are actually doing"; instead, the judicial opinion that purports to follow such rules and concepts engages in an after-the-fact rationalization "intended to make the decision seem plausible, legally decent, legally right, to make it seem, indeed, legally inevitable."[37] Since the law is in flux, and its rules and principles do little to bind judicial decisions, the legal realists embraced "the conception of law as a means to social ends and not as an end in itself; so that any part needs constantly to be examined for its purpose, and for its effect, and to be judged in light of both and of their relation to each other."[38]

Obviously, if the legal realists were skeptical about rules and principles binding decisions, they did not believe that precedents were constraining either, especially to the extent that prior decisions address social conditions that have changed and require new approaches. Their focus on future consequences of decisions led them to downplay the past.

A more recent, conservative counterpart of the legal realists is the law and economics movement that grew out of the University of Chicago Law School in the 1970s. Like legal realists, "law and economics scholars scoff at traditional foundationalist views of law, such as natural rights theories, and they view legal norms largely in instrumental terms."[39] They seek to use law to create efficiencies, using economic models, under the assumption that legal rules may be used to "induce efficient behavior."[40] As Gary Minda notes: "For these practitioners, judging becomes an exercise in cost-benefit analysis, transaction cost reduction, risk assessment, and wealth maximization. Such an economic perspective places the judge in the role of the 'social engineer' with the distinctive purpose of shaping rights and liabilities in the name of efficient resource allocation."[41]

Legal pragmatism, which had a renaissance in the 1990s, could be added as yet another future results-oriented philosophy which holds "that formalist methodologies are intellectual mirages due to both the wiggle room they usually offer and the epistemic limitations in law they usually fail to recognize," while recommending that "judges should reject pious conceptualizations ('fundamental rights,' 'democracy,' etc.) and legal 'foundationalism'—originalism, 'active liberty,' moral philosophy, etc.—in contemplating their proper roles, and instead embrace their inevitable roles as de facto policy makers. Pragmatists seek to refocus modern judging away from abstract, high-sounding 'distractions' such as 'fidelity' and 'judicial restraint,' and toward the concrete social consequences of adjudication."[42] Many other examples of future-oriented legal theories might be offered, but this should suffice to demonstrate the popularity of the future in legal theories since the retreat of formalism and legal positivism.[43]

Ronald Dworkin, perhaps the preeminent legal theorist of the past half century, rejects both legal positivism and legal realism (and, other future-oriented, utilitarian forms of legal philosophy) for condoning "judicial lawmaking" (which legal positivism requires when the rules do not tell a judge what to do) since, unlike legislatures whose legislation can be checked through the ballot box, the work of most judges has no such check.[44] In short, these are theories that lack political legitimacy. He also rejects legal positivism's insistence that bad laws are still laws, not because he would have judges ignore them but because he would require judges to read them in light of the legal system as a whole (i.e., laws, constitutions, precedents) in a way that supports moral principles.[45] For Dworkin, a moral principle is "a standard that is to be observed, not because it will advance or secure an economic, political or social situation deemed desirable"—the goal of the future-oriented legal philosophies discussed above—"but because it is a requirement of justice or fairness or some other dimension of morality."[46]

Although Dworkin supports a form of natural law to the extent that that includes "any theory which makes the content of law sometimes depend on the correct answer to some moral question," his theory is among the most balanced in terms of past, present, and future considerations, though arguably the nexus for past and future is joined in a concern for the present.[47] Dworkin believes a judge must treat the laws and precedents of his jurisdiction *as if* they form a "seamless web" whose coherence is undergirded by the moral principles it embodies.[48] The consideration of that law—statutes, constitutions, common law, and precedents—supports a past orientation. But the emphasis on principles in yielding this coherent view of the law speaks strongly to the individual rights which his seminal book warns us to "tak[e] . . . seriously," making present justice central. Further, in actively constructing a given jurisdiction's past, he also implies a future-oriented maintenance or constitutive function of judicial decision-making.[49]

Dworkin's particular concern for justice in the present case is conveyed at the beginning of his chapter on "hard cases" ("when a particular lawsuit cannot be brought under a clear rule of law"), where he explains: "I shall argue that even when no settled rule disposes of the case, one party may nevertheless have a right to win. It remains the judge's duty, even in hard cases, to discover *what the rights of the parties are*, not to invent new rights retrospectively."[50] One cannot say, exactly, that these rights are preexistent in the same way a legal positivist can point to a preexistent legal rule, as Dworkin explains: "Political rights are creatures of both history and morality: what an individual is entitled to have, in civil society, depends upon both the practice and the justice of its political institutions. So the supposed tension between judicial originality and institutional history is dissolved: judges must make fresh judgments about the rights of the parties who come before them, but these political rights reflect, rather than oppose, political decisions of the past."[51] To the extent that Dworkin's theory requires a judge to make *fresh* judgments about the rights of parties in original cases, his approach lessens the certainty of the law. However, his theory cannot be said to ignore the past, since Dworkin's judge not only looks at immediately relevant laws and precedents but the legal system *as a whole* in understanding it as a seamless web of law promoting good moral principles.

JUDICIAL OPINIONS AS RHETORICAL

The foregoing review of major philosophies of judicial decision-making highlights a number of important considerations for judicial opinions as rhetorical, that is, as *addressed to concrete audiences for the purpose of persuasion*. First, judges may utilize one of these approaches to the law to justify or explain their decisions, either explicitly or implicitly. Alternatively, we can see the source of some assumptions operative in judicial decision-making and appreciate that there may be influence at work. For example, supporters of the Revolution of 1937 (which finally found the high court supporting New Deal initiatives to address the Great Depression) worked in the heyday of legal realism and often overruled precedents in favor of pragmatic considerations for the social good. Or we can understand the position of constitutional "originalists," who share much in common with the legal positivists, such as an adherence to an understanding of this primary law whether it is morally good or not in order that the "sovereign" be recognized as the proper source of law.

Second, these theories, considered together, highlight some of the strengths and weaknesses of various approaches to decision-making in their preference for past, present, or future considerations. Slavishly following past law can cause problems for the present and the future, though it benefits from making law clear and conceding lawmaking authority to the legislature. A case often cited by legal scholars highlights these trade-offs. In the nineteenth-century New York case of *Riggs v. Palmer*, a grandson who stood to inherit his grandfather's fortune killed his grandfather to prevent him from changing his will after he remarried.[52] Statutes governing inheritance in New York were clear about how one determines inheritance and the legislature had made no provisions for such a contingency. The court, pained at the injustice of letting the convicted murderer inherit his grandfather's estate, strained in justifying its decision to withhold the inheritance, while a dissenting justice—no doubt an early legal positivist—said there was nothing to be done because the law was so clear and it was up to the legislature to fix the law for the future.

Third, these theories stress different sources of political legitimacy for judicial decision-making. The natural law theorists can point to the alignment of decisions with God's will or with reason. Legal positivists can note that they leave the sovereign in charge of lawmaking. Legal realists and other skeptical utilitarians, who have the toughest time justifying judicial power, at least can point to the adaptation of law to changing social needs. And Dworkin can show that respecting rights and grounding decisions in moral principles is good for the individual and for the legal system.

As I have noted elsewhere, the ideal judicial decision will effectively address the past, present, and future, "show[ing] unequivocally (1) that prior cases, long-accepted legal principles, legislative statutes, administrative regulations, state and federal constitutions, and their authors (whose intentions are invoked) require the decision; (2) that the decision yields the greatest justice in the instant case (given characterizations of litigants as deserving of legal reward or punishment); and (3) that the decision creates the fairest and most efficacious results in the long run, providing clear direction and a just outcome for all foreseeable cases like it."[53] This book focuses on cases that appear to dismiss the past by overruling prior decisions. We should not be surprised to find overruling judges either showing that they are not really ignoring past law but actually supporting it, or else justifying the dismissal of the past in light of present considerations (as occurred in the court deciding against the grandson in *Riggs*) or future considerations, such as a clearer or better law and utilitarian benefits.

The rhetorical functions of judicial opinions are implicated in the concerns of various legal theories for past, present, and future. Those functions include justification, showing that good reasons support the outcomes of judicial decisions. As Josina M. Makau notes: "At the heart of the philosophy underlying the judicial function in Western civilization generally and the American body politic specifically is the composite audience's shared belief that reasonableness must govern Supreme Court deliberations."[54] If judicial opinions are written well, Michael R. Hagan notes, "they help assure the public and other courts that decisions are not based on pure whim or prejudice. They show that there are rationales for decisions."[55]

The overall style of judicial opinions supports the idea that they are reasonable; judicial style suggests that the writer has a particular set of rhetorical commitments, commitments which Gerald B. Wetlaufer attributes to the rhetoric of law more generally: "These include commitments to a certain kind of tough-mindedness and rigor, to relevance and orderliness in discourse, to objectivity, to clarity and logic, to binary judgment, and to the closure of controversies. They also include commitments to hierarchy and authority, to the impersonal voice, and to the one right (or best) answer to questions and the one true (or best) meaning of texts. Finally, the rhetoric of our discipline reveals our commitment to a particular conception of the rule of law."[56]

If judicial discourse works to bolster the personae of the judges as reasonable and objective, it also "*creates* audience perceptions and *shapes* audience opinions . . . from their characterization of the facts to their creation of new rules."[57] It accomplishes this work through the strategic use of language, metaphors, and narratives; the construction of persons and actions; the arrangement of the opinion; appeals to pathos; the selection (or omission), framing, and construction of legal issues and their support through arguments, evidence, laws, constitutions, regulations, precedents, scholarly sources, rulings of other courts, and hypothetical cases.[58]

In addition to revealing the strategic choices of judicial opinion writers, rhetorical and legal scholars have demonstrated how judicial opinions serve to support the status quo through a hegemonic ideology, particularly a patriarchal, racist, or economic ideology.[59] More than any other writer, James Boyd White has explained the constitutive power of legal discourse in creating a legal culture that, he suggests, must be cultivated properly to ensure it is a good one.[60]

Despite the fact that legal and rhetorical scholars for decades have revealed the wide range of rhetorical choices available to judicial opinion writers in deciding and explaining their decisions, judicial rhetoric typically serves to hide those choices. It is a rhetoric that pretends not to be rhetorical.[61] Indeed, as Marin Roger Scordato explains, judicial opinion writers put on the face of the legal formalist: "Despite the [legal] realist revolution and its full acceptance by most law professors, the overwhelming majority of published trial court memoranda and appellate court opinions in this country continue to present themselves in traditional formalist terms. While perhaps not as aggressively deterministic in tone as fifty or seventy-five years ago, the written published products of our courts, with relatively few exceptions, continue to offer their holdings as the result of a distinctive legal analysis and not an explicit balancing of social costs and benefits."[62]

Judges write like legal formalists not because they embrace a traditional view of law but because they must perform the role of the judge as tied to the law, constrained by the case at hand and concerned for the future. Scordato insists that they are responding to "powerful practical incentives to present their decisions in largely formalist terms. They may be justifiably concerned that an explicitly instrumentalist presentation of their analysis and conclusions would risk a lessening in the respect granted to their decisions by the parties in the instant case. Moreover, they may fear that an explicit and widespread embrace by the courts of the instrumentalist paradigm would eventually result in a serious questioning of, and ultimate challenge to, the legitimacy of their authority."[63]

As I already have noted, given the enormous power wielded by courts—especially the United States Supreme Court—legitimacy has to be a concern. However, a review of the audiences of Supreme Court decisions reveal rhetorical needs beyond legitimacy. Indeed, the high court's audiences press harder for a careful reflection upon the consequences of the justices' rhetoric in respecting the past, providing a reasonable outcome for the present and thinking more about the future than almost any other rhetors.

AUDIENCES OF SUPREME COURT OPINIONS

As many commentators have noted, the rhetorical task faced by a Supreme Court opinion writer is complicated by its consideration of various audiences. As Golden and Makau explain, the Supreme Court addresses "a composite of particular audiences. Different from a universal audience in its particularization, but similar to this ideal in its composition, this audience provides a substantive challenge to the Court. . . . This special composite audience is made up of parties directly affected by the case, lawyers, Supreme Court justices, lower court justices, legislators, administrators, legal scholars, and other educated members of the body politic [which] create a group whose interests and shared expectations the Justices cannot ignore."[64] This section considers at length the challenges these different audiences pose for the judicial writer.

Justices of the Court as Audience

The first audience considered by a Supreme Court justice writing an opinion for the court consists of the other members of the court. As Golden and Makau note:

> As they write their opinion explicating and justifying their decisions, Justices must phrase their arguments in such a way that they will, first of all, win the approval of other Justices holding the majority view. If successful, they may even gain the support, or at least the respect, of those Justices who plan to author minority opinions. During the evolution of this step, the Justices interact freely with each other both orally and in writing. That considerable persuasion takes place in these encounters has been well documented. "I myself," observed Justice Jackson, "have changed my opinion after reading the opinions of other members of the Court. And I am as stubborn as most. But I sometimes wind up not voting the way I voted in Conference because the reasons of the majority didn't satisfy me."[65]

Ulrich adds that a majority opinion writer may "need to tone down a position to gain the adherence of other judges."[66] Judge Thurman Arnold explains the ambiguity in some judicial decisions as the outcome of compromise, because a judge "would have to put in something which he believes created an ambiguity in order to avoid provoking a dissent or a concurring opinion which would create even more ambiguity since the Court would be unanimous only on the result. [An observer] would find that men can sometimes agree on a result, but rarely on all of the reasons for that result, and that attempts to spell out reasons may be futile."[67] Percival Jackson suggests more generally that the judge should "weigh his words with an ambit of discretion so that he may secure agreement from his fellow."[68]

In addition to tending to their words, judges must ensure that they "adequately respond to each other's arguments [and] . . . work on justification through effective modification" in light of those arguments.[69] Even if an opinion writer does not win over her colleagues, she may take the sting out of concurring opinions and dissents by showing that she has considered counterarguments.

Opinion writers also address themselves in the future. Majority opinion writers tell future courts who read their decisions, "What we have determined here is the law—a precedent, which according to our customary practices, has a presumption of correctness and should be followed unless someone carries the burden of proving it wrong."[70] They usually try to make clear the legal principle to be drawn from the decision, the *holding*, and its rationale, though as Edward H. Levi has demonstrated, later courts may alter their understanding of previous holdings in light of the unique demands of later cases.[71] In a larger sense, judges often try to control the way future courts interpret their words and actions. As I have argued previously: "Judges have to think about how their own motives may be construed by future courts and lawyers. Speculations about future interpretations may lead opinion writers to emphasize the particular facts of the case before the court (suggesting that they were determinative), to display a concern that other courts might try to take the principle underlying its ruling too far (suggesting that those courts should not do so), to offer multiple grounds for a decision (suggesting that many reasons support the court's decision), and so forth."[72]

In some cases, the court is less than subtle. For example, in the election-ending decision in *Bush v. Gore*, the conservative majority stopped the recounting of ballots in Florida and invoked equal protection to decide in favor of George W. Bush. Equal protection has not been a favorite constitutional principle of conservatives, and the per curiam decision sought to limit its use as a precedent in the future by concluding: "The recount process, in its features here described, is inconsistent with the minimum procedures necessary to protect the fundamental right of each voter in the special instance of a statewide recount under the authority of a single state judicial officer. Our consideration is limited to the present circumstances, for the problem of equal protection in election processes generally presents many complexities."[73] These "complexities" were exaggerated, since the idea of ensuring that all recounted ballots are judged by the same standard for determining whether they register as a vote is fairly simple.[74]

In other cases, the high court addresses itself in a sophisticated form of rhetoric that sets the stage for moving the law in a new direction over time, building upon precedents that make incremental changes that are more acceptable than achieving a change in law in one fell swoop. This is difficult because it is not clear how a particular decision will be received and shaped in an unforeseen future or what possible cases might arise that provide an opportunity to extend a particular direction in the law. In any case, as I have discussed in my consideration of a theory I call *rhetorical consequentialism,* such future possibilities undoubtedly capture the interests of justices who believe their vision of society is preferable and perhaps partially realizable given the right lineup of legal cases.[75]

Majority opinion writers also often discuss issues that are not directly relevant to deciding a case. Such dicta are not binding but may provide greater context for interpreting the court's thinking in reaching the decision and may provide statements about hypothetical cases, legal processes, society, and so forth that writers may find quotable in later cases. They also may include opinions about alternative interpretations of the law, particularly those of dissenting and concurring opinions, to shape understandings of those positions.

Nonmajority opinions speak to the future as well, as Chief Justice Hughes explains: "A dissent in a court of last resort is an appeal to the brooding spirit of the law, to the intelligence of a future day, when a later decision may possibly correct the error into which the dissenting judge believes the court to have been betrayed."[76] Justice Cardozo agrees that "the dissenter speaks to the future," though he notes that the tone is different, because "his voice is pitched in a key that will carry through the years."[77] Indeed, the dissenting justice—by the time she is firmly a dissenter from a decision—need not worry about attracting others to her cause, ensuring she is supporting the court's legitimacy, or setting down clear law for others to follow. Thus, the dissenter may speak in a different "key," as Erin J. Rand notes Justice Ruth Bader Ginsburg did in the reproductive rights case of *Burwell v. Hobby Lobby,* where her dissent was described as a "fiery," "scathing," a "sharply-worded (and badass) reproach" that "excoriated the court's majority" and became "the blueprint for how liberals talk about the Supreme Court's decision."[78] Similarly, the frequent dissents of the late Justice Antonin Scalia have been distinguished for their colorfulness and vigor.[79]

Over time dissents can win the day, earning the character of prophecy, when their interpretations, ideas, and sentiments support changes in the law. Perhaps the most famous example is Justice John Marshall Harlan's lone dissent in *Plessy v. Ferguson* rejecting the majority's endorsement of the "separate but equal" standard in cases involving differential treatment of races by the states. As Daniel Mangis notes, Harlan's dissent has been "literally cited thousands of times in legal decisions and scholarship" and it has become "arguably . . . the first of the three most important texts in the civil rights movement, preceding *Brown v. Board of Education* and Martin Luther King's 'I Have a Dream Speech.'"[80]

Concurring opinions tend to be less fiery as they function to support an outcome. However, they can provide different or additional reasons for a decision. They have received less attention from rhetorical scholars than dissenting opinions, though their rhetorical goals may require greater subtlety than dissents.[81]

Litigants and Interested Parties

The "case or controversy" requirement for addressing legal issues ensures that judging is not a hypothetical exercise but one that involves real parties with real interests. Those interests lead litigants to the difficult and often expensive route of resolving an issue through the judicial system. But litigants often come on a quest for justice because, as William Lewis notes: "People are hurt; they are wronged, robbed, deserted, beaten, raped, exploited, abandoned, lied to, cheated, murdered, misled, misunderstood, mistreated, used, broken and forsaken. [And they seek] the intervention of the Law, for [we are told,] it is only in a Law-less world that the wrongs inflicted on us by (presumably stronger) others must be endured without communal compensation."[82] Judicial opinions must address these aggrieved parties, not because the parties can ignore the high court's verdict, but because it is the role of the court to ensure "communal compensation"; indeed, Lewis argues, judicial opinions tend to oversell the court's ability to set things right with their "romantic epics" of heroic Law saving the day.

On the other hand, such overselling is understandable when the court tells a litigant, "No, we will not save you from capital punishment," "Yes, you must end racial segregation in all your public schools 'with all deliberate speed,'" "No, you do not have a right to engage in homosexual sodomy, even if you are gay and believe that is your only means for sexual intimacy," or "No, Congress, you do not have the authority to limit the First Amendment rights of corporations in political elections."[83]

Obviously, interested parties include those beyond the actual litigants, such as other inmates on death row, southern whites appalled at the scuttling of their Jim Crow system, gays and lesbians facing a life without sexual intimacy, and political candidates endlessly attacked by corporations when they run for office. Such "interested parties" obviously are justified in expecting a rationale for decisions that so affect their lives.

Coordinate Branches of Government

Among those interested parties noted above are coordinate branches of government whose work is shaped by what the judiciary does. They need to clearly understand what is required based upon the court's rulings and, in some cases, to take action to alter what the court has decided. Congress has a keen interest in how the high court interprets the legislation it approves, as well as how it interprets the Constitution which determines congressional powers and impacts the states which members of Congress represent along with their citizens. For example, the first major decision of the United States Supreme Court led Congress to support the Eleventh Amendment to overturn the court's decision rejecting the sovereign immunity of states from lawsuits.[84] The executive branch is expected to adhere to rulings regarding executive authority, criminal law, constitutional rights it is obliged to enforce, the interpretations of statutes involving regulatory agencies, and the like. For example, the ruling in *United States v. Nixon* obliged the president to turn over audiotapes related to the Watergate scandal.[85]

State Governments

Chief Justice John Marshall established the supremacy of federal law over state law and the authority of the federal courts to hear appeals from state court decisions implicating federal law or the US Constitution.[86] Some of the most controversial decisions of the court have thwarted state governments, from those involving racial segregation to abortion rights to the rights of those accused of crimes. Recalcitrant governments have sometimes resisted to the point where federal troops were required to enforce decisions, making relationships with the White-House-as-enforcer crucial. In light of this sometimes-strained relationship, it has been important for high court decisions opposing state policies to be clear and compelling.

Generally, the court has gone out of its way to try to respect the authority and dignity of the states, though the attitude is not always reciprocal. For example, *NAACP v. Alabama* was a 1958 case involving an attempt by the State of Alabama to keep the NAACP from operating in Alabama.[87] A state court found that the NAACP had not complied with a statute requiring foreign corporations to file information with the state. Part of the requested information included membership lists, which could have put NAACP members at personal risk. When the NAACP refused to submit this information, the Alabama Supreme Court found them in contempt and fined them $100,000. On appeal the US Supreme Court found that the NAACP's right to freedom of association was threatened by the state's request and overturned the contempt order. A recalcitrant Alabama Supreme Court found the US Supreme Court's decision was mistaken and reinstated the contempt ruling. An incredibly patient US Supreme Court ruled again in 1959, attributing the most generous reading possible to the state court: "We take it from the record now before us that the Supreme Court of Alabama evidently was not acquainted with the detailed basis of the proceedings here and the consequent ground for our defined disposition."[88] The high court concluded by giving the state court clear directions: "We assume that the State Supreme Court, thus advised, will not fail to proceed promptly with the disposition of the matters left open under our mandate for further proceedings."[89]

Other Courts

Because decisions of the highest court in a jurisdiction are authoritative law for all lower courts in that same jurisdiction, decisions of the United States

Supreme Court must be followed by all courts in the United States and its territories. Indeed, even if the high court's rulings appear to be taking the law in a new direction, lower courts are forbidden from engaging in the "anticipatory overruling" of doubtful precedents. In the 1989 case of *Rodriguez de Quijas v. Shearson/American Express, Inc.*, the Supreme Court forbade such overrulings, warning: "If a precedent of this Court has direct application in a case, yet appears to rest on reasons rejected in some other line of decisions, the Court of Appeals should follow the case which directly controls, leaving to this Court the prerogative of overruling its own decisions."[90]

Obviously judicial rhetoric directed to lower courts must be concerned about clarity in the law if the high court wants them to follow what it has ruled. And the default style of judicial rhetoric seems to support greater clarity. That style is formalist, presenting decisions as driven by the law and its rules, standards, and principles. Scordato notes that "law is an active professional discipline that continues to be conducted in traditional formalist terms, despite the larger intellectual revolution produced by the realists," adding that "this is especially true in trial and appellate court practice."[91] Judge and legal scholar Richard Posner calls formalism "the official jurisprudence of lawyers and laypeople alike."[92] Hasian also notes "the popularity of romantic or formalistic views of law."[93]

Lawyers as Audience

Edward B. Whitney complained in 1904 that courts were ignoring the past in favor of the present, "tend[ing] more and more to decide each case according to their own ideas of fairness as between the parties to that case, and [passing] the previous authorities by in silence." The result was that "the law is thrown into doubt, and a lawyer thereafter cannot advise his client how to act in order to enjoy his rights and keep out of harassing litigation."[94] Rhetorical theorists have noted the importance of lawyers as an audience of judicial opinions: Warren E. Wright said half a century ago that when the high court hands down a case, "the bar must understand the decision in order to intelligently advise future clients."[95] When law is changing quickly, lawyers have the greatest trouble, as tax lawyer Hugh M. Bennett complained at a conference in 1940 (in the aftermath of the Revolution of 1937): "It is not enough for a lawyer today to keep abreast of court decisions when they first appear in a bound book, or even in the advance sheets, but a lawyer must know what the court says before the ink is dry."[96]

Furthermore, when lawyers bring cases to court, they rely heavily on citations of precedents and are required by professional codes to report them accurately.[97] As early as an 1841 New York case, one justice could report that "lawyers, to which fraternity [legal] reporters usually belong, are in the habit of adhering with much zeal to legal precedents."[98] In 1944, Justice Owen Roberts dissented from an overruling by the Supreme Court in *Mahnich v. Southern Steamship Co.*, warning: "The evil resulting from overruling earlier considered decisions must be evident. In the present case, the court below naturally felt bound to follow and apply the law as clearly announced by this court. If litigants and lower federal courts are not to do so, the law becomes not a chart to govern conduct but a game of chance; instead of settling rights and liabilities it unsettles them. Counsel and parties will bring and prosecute actions in the teeth of the decisions that such actions are not maintainable on the not improbable chance that the asserted rule will be thrown overboard. Defendants will not know whether to litigate or to settle for they will have no assurance that a declared rule will be followed."[99]

Thus, Roberts argues, the rhetorical goal of the high court's decisions should not simply be clearly apprising the bar of what the law is, but to ensure enough consistency to prevent them from flooding the courts with cases under the assumption that they might just convince judges to change the law in their favor.

Legal Scholars as Audience

Legal scholars form an audience that scrutinizes every word of Supreme Court opinions. In distinguishing the scrutiny the high court receives from journalists versus legal scholars, I noted: "Scholars . . . have two key advantages over journalists and editorialists [who report on court cases]: space and time. Books and scholarly journals provide space for arguments to be elaborated, evidence to be adduced, and sources to be enumerated. And, unlike journalists and editorialists, who normally face deadlines, scholars typically have considerable leisure to ponder, research, write, and revise their [analyses]. They also benefit from a better-educated audience, especially those knowledgeable in the law."[100] Legal scholars' interest in Supreme Court decisions is not merely intellectual; most legal scholars are engaged in teaching in law schools, so they must scrutinize decisions to help their students come to an understanding of what the law is.

There are almost two hundred American Bar Association–accredited law schools, which employ over seventeen thousand law professors.[101] They (and in some cases, their students) publish in almost one thousand law journals.[102] Thousands of books in law are published each year.[103] The US Supreme Court and its decisions are a popular topic of legal scholarship, given the impact their rulings have on the legal system. It is hard to imagine a comparably sized academic community that scrutinizes the ongoing writings of such a small group of writers so assiduously.[104]

Of course, the justices of the Supreme Court are well aware of the scrutiny of the legal academy. They cite scholarly articles in their own opinions where supportive. They regularly give lectures at law schools. From their own law school days, they understand that their opinions may be included in casebooks.

Indeed, Ella Govshtein notes of Justice Scalia: "Unable to persuade his colleagues, Scalia has confessed that he writes with 'verve and panache' to ensure that his opinions are quoted by the editors of legal textbooks, so they can influence future generations of lawyers and scholars."[105]

While legal scholars may constitute a secondary audience at best, one can imagine that the Supreme Court justices would want to avoid being called out for making weak arguments, building on questionable assumptions or inconsistently applying legal philosophies to which they profess their allegiance. The legal community is about as close to Perelman and Olbrecht-Tytica's ideal universal audience as one might hope to find.[106]

The Public as Audience

As with most public audiences of discourse from specialized fields, legal discourse such as Supreme Court decisions normally reach them, if at all, through intermediaries. As Wright notes: "The people themselves are part of the audience, but they are not so likely to read the judicial opinion as a political speech. Although segments of the more important opinions do appear in the pages of the larger newspapers, the populace's contact with judicial rhetoric usually is through their own attorneys or through citations introduced into political speeches."[107] Charles F. Stafford insists that "the average citizen is not interested in complicated legal explanations. He neither understands nor appreciates the legal gymnastics involved, nor should we expect him to. Nevertheless, he does react to situations that offend his sense of fairness and his sense of right and wrong."[108] The public reaction to the Supreme Court's overruling of abortion rights in 2022 is a vivid example. (See chapter 7.)

Public sensibilities are likely to be brought to bear on controversial and consequential cases, particularly since these are the most likely to be reported by the news media. Yet, the news media are not always good at translating court decisions because of the lack of their audience's legal knowledge, the brevity of their reports (especially in television news), and their interest in emphasizing drama, as I show in my analysis of the coverage of *Bush v. Gore.*[109]

Despite these limitations, the public represents a crucial audience in terms of maintaining the court's standing and legitimacy. In 1904, Whitney recognized this interest, noting: "One of the functions of the judicial opinion is to help preserve the confidence of the bar and the public in the ability, learning, fairness and open-mindedness of the judiciary as a whole, as well as the careful attention due to the particular case, by indicating the grounds upon which the decision is based whenever the case is one not entirely clear."[110] Michael Gerhardt adds to such explanatory discourse the prior leanings of the public, insisting that "the public is more likely to retain confidence in the impartiality and consistency of the Court's decisionmaking if the reasons for the Court's choices are persuasive and if the Court generally adheres to principles that will reliably safeguard popular precedent."[111]

Posner distinguishes the US Supreme Court's relationship to the public from that of lower federal courts, insisting that "the Court is more constrained by public opinion than the lower federal courts are because of its much greater visibility, which is due to the greater impact of its decisions."[112] He illustrates this with a First Amendment case, noting: "A court of appeals can get away with declaring the phrase 'under God' in the Pledge of Allegiance unconstitutional because its decision is binding in only one region of the country, and even then only until reversed by the Supreme Court, as the decision in that case was, on a technical ground (lack of standing to sue) that enabled the Court to avoid the wrath of both sides in the heated national debate over the role of religion in public life."[113]

Justice Oliver Wendell Holmes Jr. stresses the congruency of law with community attitudes and needs, insisting: "The first requirement of a sound body of law is, that it should correspond with the actual feelings and demands of the community, whether right or wrong."[114] Charles Curtis supports this view, insisting: "Though prejudices and private fancies do exist and do indeed lead judges to decisions, they soon spend their small strength in an institution whose decisions depend for their enforcement upon the simple fact that enough of us agree with them. We too often forget that the reason for the great power of the Supreme Court is not that it interprets the Constitution to us, but that it reads our immanent patterns of behavior into our Constitution, and as it reads them into it, the Court explains them to us, and so makes us the more aware of them. And if it stresses the patterns of our better behavior, this is no more than the normative element in any good description. When enough of us kick against the pricks, the Court must save its face as best it can."[115]

The formalist style, which is undoubtedly discounted by courts, lawyers, and legal scholars, finds a more receptive audience in the public. Scordato recently argued: "While it may not be quite the revelatory journey that it seemed fifteen or twenty years ago, many students still come into first-year law school courses harboring expectations about the determinacy and the mechanistic nature of legal rules. Much of the popular culture, especially in depictions of the operation of the criminal law, conveys at least an implicit message of objectivity and traditional formalism."[116] That view, he adds, also is propagated by politicians (who should know better), who "continue to espouse the most deterministic version of formalism . . . [especially] during the nomination and confirmation of federal judges, particularly United States Supreme Court justices." He quotes President George W. Bush on nominating Samuel Alito to the court, where he insists that Alito "has a deep understanding of the proper role of judges in our society. He understands that judges are to interpret the laws, not to impose their preferences or priorities on the people." Even judicial nominees get into the game—and they do know better—such as nominee for Chief Justice John Roberts, who opened his confirmation hearing by stating: "Judges and justices are servants of the law, not the other way around. Judges are like umpires. Umpires don't make rules; they apply them."[117]

Balancing the Needs of the High Court's Composite Audience

Effectively addressing a composite audience with different relationships to and knowledge of a case and of the law, for different rhetorical purposes, through the limited form of the judicial opinion is challenging. For example, attracting fellow justices to an opinion may require greater ambiguity than a writer would like. While that adapts to the court's members as audience, it undermines the goal of clarity for litigants, for other courts, for the bar, and for legal academics who must teach the law. Following the law strictly and allowing injustice for litigants may make those seeking clarity in law happy while conveying to the public a sense of unfairness. Setting a new course to adapt to a changing society is liable to lead unhappy politicians to label a court "activist." Ignoring the dictates of one's professed legal philosophy can lead to charges of inconsistency and hypocrisy.[118]

Of course, writing like a legal formalist today, as most judges do, may suggest that the judicial opinion already is shot through with hypocrisy. But it also is a form driven by the rhetorical need for clarity and for legitimacy.[119] The rhetorical need for legitimacy is particularly keen in the overruling discourse of the United States Supreme Court, as the next chapter explains.

CHAPTER 2

Stare Decisis and Overruling in the US Supreme Court

The previous chapter suggests the importance of the United States Supreme Court following its own earlier decisions. Beyond forcing the high court to admit mistakes and throwing the law into question, overruling flouts the legal principle of stare decisis. This chapter explains the origins of stare decisis and its role in the US system of law. It also explains the development of the high court's attitudes about stare decisis in its own overruling practices. It provides an overall picture of overruling rhetoric throughout the Supreme Court's history.

STARE DECISIS AND THE ANGLO-AMERICAN TRADITION

The principle that one should adhere to precedents and not unsettle legal issues that are settled seems a prudent and rhetorically savvy one in as much as it ensures consistency in the law and suggests that courts are chained to the law rather than free to pursue their own preferences. On the other hand, new circumstances require that law be more flexible than following such a principle strictly would permit. The need for both stability and change has shaped the principle of stare decisis and its application. In Anglo-American law it has assumed a notable place, though with some differences in its role in Great Britain and in the United States.[1]

C. Sumner Lobingier argues "the principle [of stare decisis] is inherent in every legal system, at least in its primitive stage."[2] He notes that many ancient legal systems relied on precedents, even if they were not obliged to follow them, including Chinese, Sumerian, Babylonian, Assyrian, Hebrew, Arabic, Greek, and Roman systems.[3] The Anglo-Saxon tradition was shaped by Celtic law, which gave weight to prior decisions; after the Norman Conquest, precedent was important in the law of conveyances.[4] The *Year Books*, which are reports of decisions in medieval England, show little reliance on precedents, though the early English jurist Bracton cited hundreds of them.[5] However, Clive M. Schmitthoff asserts that *non est simile*, an argument to distinguish a case from earlier cases on the facts, "has been an argument of English counsel long before precedents acquired binding force." He notes that this argument appears in the *Year Books* for cases heard during the early fourteenth-century reign of King Edward II.[6]

Courts later began to acknowledge the fairness of following precedent. In a 1464 case, Judge Croxton urged: "It is not honorable for us or for this court or any other court to vary our judgments, as to give judgment in a matter in one term, and later in another term in another matter, or even in the same matter, different judgment. Therefore we wish to give judgment now as we have given before in like matters. And that is what I believe reason and conscience to be."[7] The next year, Barbara A. Singer notes, another British court stated that "precedents in a court make a law"; but she adds that most courts recognized precedents "only when it suited their needs, even ignoring cases they themselves had decided, particularly those they thought clearly wrong."[8]

One of the difficulties of following precedent in these times was the absence of reliable and detailed reporters. The emergence of written pleadings and reports by the end of the fifteenth century made stare decisis workable. Plowden's reports (1550–1580), for example, were respected for their accuracy.[9] Lobingier notes that a 1557 case was the first to use the term *precedent*, though that might have simply meant "forms."[10] By the eighteenth century, the term and the idea of giving weight to precedents was firmly fixed in the British system, so much so that the respected jurist Lord Mansfield felt obliged to establish limits on their authority in the 1774 case of Jones v. Randall: "The law of England would be a strange science if indeed it were decided upon precedents only. Precedents serve to illustrate principles and to give them a fixed certainty. But the law of England, which is exclusive of positive law, enacted by statute, depends upon principles, and these principles run through all the cases as the particular circumstances of each have been found to fall within the one or the other of them."[11] Here we see the influence of the declaratory theory, with decided cases "illustrat[ing] principles" rather than creating law.

Five years after this decision, Blackstone's *History of the Common Law* could state it as "an authoritative rule to abide by former precedents where the same points come again in litigation."[12] As noted in the previous chapter, Blackstone held out an exception for precedents that were "flatly absurd or unjust."[13] In 1898 it was established that the House of Lords, the highest judicial body in England, was bound by its own precedents; by 1966 that rule was abandoned and the House of Lords announced that it would not be bound by previous decisions if it seemed best to depart from them.[14] In 2009 the House of Lords passed its judicial duties to the Supreme Court of the United Kingdom.[15]

The US Supreme Court has never held itself absolutely bound by its previous decisions, though from its earliest days it relied on precedents as persuasive authority in its opinions. In its first major case, *Chisholm v. Georgia*, the majority is reported to have noted: "It might be reasonable to require from those who object thus [to the remedy provided in our decision], that they should produce some precedents at least, of another remedy taken."[16] It would be several decades before the principle of stare decisis was invoked to defend arguments against overturning cases. The term *stare decisis* does not appear in any Supreme Court opinion until 1831, when a passionate dissent from Justice Baldwin invoked it.[17] The first time it appeared in a majority opinion was 1847 in *Cook v. Moffat* to reject a plaintiff's appeal to change the law: "So far, then, as respects the point now before us, this court appear to have always been unanimous; and in order to meet the views of the learned counsel for the plaintiff in error, we should be compelled to overrule every case heretofore decided on this most difficult and intricate subject. But as the questions involved in it have already received the amplest investigation by the most eminent and profound jurists, both of the bar and the bench, it may be well doubted whether further discussion will shed more light, or produce a more satisfactory or unanimous decision. So far, at least, as the present case is concerned, the court do not think it necessary or prudent to depart from the safe maxim of stare decisis."[18] Four years later, in an early overruling case, Chief Justice Taney would claim for the majority that at least in cases involving property, "stare decisis is the safe and established rule of judicial policy, and should always be adhered to."[19] Nineteen years after this pronouncement, the court would reverse a decision that would affect most of the contracts in the country by allowing them to be satisfied with paper money or "greenbacks" rather than gold and silver coins, making Taney's property rule not so inflexible.[20] Much more will be said about the court's attitude toward stare decisis below. At this point it should be clear that stare decisis had been embraced as an important principle of adjudication by the high court by the first half of the nineteenth century, and as later examples will show, the spirit of stare decisis worked from the earliest days, even if it was not specifically invoked.

As in the British tradition, following precedent in the United States required reliable reports of those precedents, yet the high court had no paid reporter until 1817.[21] Before then, unpaid reporters took on the job of recounting Supreme Court cases as private ventures. As the second such reporter, William Cranch, noted in the introduction to his first volume: "Much of that uncertainty of the law, which is so frequently, and perhaps so justly, the subject of complaint in this country, may be attributed to the want of American reports."[22] The justices were not satisfied with the work of these unpaid reporters, such as the first unofficial reporter, Alexander J. Dallas, who sometimes relied on notes from lawyers when he missed a court session and who once delayed publishing the court's decisions for eight years.[23]

Not only did the regularizing of reporting cases of the high court allow for easier reference to what was decided before, it provided a check on legal decision-making that the court had not faced previously, as Duffy notes: "By making the actions of the court visible and subject to constant analysis and criticism, reports domesticated adjudication. No longer a matter of lawyers and judges applying alien, abstract, rigid doctrines in courtrooms, reports made the common law part of an ongoing, communal discussion conducted in the light of day."[24] Lawyers coming before the court could quote the justices' words back to them, verbatim, pressing them to adhere to their prior judgments.

By the end of the century comprehensive legal libraries would become nearly unaffordable and unmanageable for lawyers, or even some law offices, given the proliferation of reporters and cases. On the other hand, that proliferation made it easier to find quotable language to support a given case. Whitney complained about the multiplication of reporters in 1904, noting:

> At the beginning of the nineteenth century there was but an armful of judicial reports printed in the English language outside of England itself. For a long time subsequent the cases of authority upon a given point were still so few that court and counsel could thoroughly familiarize themselves with every one of them, while a really considerable proportion of the law likely to come up in court was embodied in cases whose names were commonly known to all members of the profession with any pretentions to learning. About a hundred years ago each of the states of the Union then admitted had begun to produce a series of reports of at least the decisions of its highest court. During the nineteenth century the number of states of the American Union increased from sixteen to forty-five. Reports were also being issued in the territories and in a large number of the British Colonies. Some of the individual States of the Union moreover, as well as England and the United States, were producing reports of their inferior tribunals.[25]

The problem of shelf space and costs to law offices would persist until the development of online legal databases, not to mention the challenge of reviewing a burgeoning set of relevant precedents on a given issue.

The proliferation of reporting also led to an overreliance on the *words* of court opinions rather than on their *actions*. As Karl Llewellyn complained in 1951, those arguing from precedent too often drew "exclusively from *language* that is found in past decision, and . . . citing and working with that language wholly without reference to the facts of the case which called the language forth."[26] Llewellyn's concern indexes a key challenge in following a precedent: figuring out what the holding of the case is to be followed; that is, determining what was *decided*, not simply what was *said*. Max Radin notes that "the confusion of the opinion with the decision is an inveterate one, particularly with students. . . . The rule is stare decisis, not stare opinionibus or even stare responsis."[27] Or, as Roscoe Pound put it succinctly: "It is the result that passes into law."[28]

Even acknowledging the important distinction between words and action in decisions, there remains the problem of interpretation and application to a new case. And, as Edward H. Levi has shown, a precedent's holding is not static; it may change in light of subsequent decisions and from the light a present case throws on a precedent's rationale.[29] Consider the eminent domain case of *Kelo v. City of New London*. The decision allowed an agency working for New London, Connecticut, to use eminent domain to take the modest riverside homes of residents for new developments to help the city's sagging economy and tax base.[30] Writing for the majority, Justice Stevens cited two important precedents in which eminent domain was used to remove a blighted neighborhood from Washington, DC (*Berman*) and to overcome an oligopoly in the housing market in Hawaii (*Midkiff*). Stevens admitted that "those who govern the City were not confronted with the need to remove blight" but insisted that "their determination that the area was sufficiently distressed to justify a program of economic rejuvenation is entitled to our deference" (454).

Justice O'Connor, dissenting, read these precedents more narrowly than simple endorsements for takings for public economic purposes. The purpose in those precedents, she insisted, was not merely improving economic conditions but removing harms: "The Court's holdings in *Berman* and *Midkiff* were true to the principle underlying the Public Use Clause. In both those cases, the extraordinary, precondemnation use of the targeted property inflicted affirmative harm on society—in *Berman* through blight resulting from extreme poverty and in *Midkiff* through oligopoly resulting from extreme wealth. And in both cases, the relevant legislative body had found that eliminating the existing property use was necessary to remedy the harm" (464–65). Obviously, the well-kept modest homes of New London did not represent a harm to be removed. The removal-of-harm requirement was not obvious in these precedents' holdings until the *Kelo* case offered a different kind of economic taking to support O'Connor's distinction. As Levi describes it, "the kind of reasoning involved in the legal process is one in which the classification changes as the classification is made."[31] Thus, for Stevens, *Berman, Midkiff,* and *Kelo* are to be classified as similar because of their interest in public economic benefit; for O'Connor, they are to be distinguished because *Kelo* did not involve the removal of a public harm.

Strategic constructions of what the court was doing in a precedent case can allow the court in a present case to dodge the problem of appearing to flout stare decisis in overruling a case. For example, authorities disagree over whether the 1868 case of *The Belfast* overruled the ten-year-old case of *Allen v. Newberry*, because a unanimous majority claimed: "Remarks, it is conceded, are found in the opinion of the court in the case of Allen et al. v. Newberry, inconsistent with these views [in our current opinion]; but they were not necessary to that decision, as the contract in that case was for the transportation of goods on one of the Western lakes, where the jurisdiction in admiralty is restricted, by an act of Congress, to steamboats and other vessels . . . employed in the business of commerce and navigation, between ports and places in different States and Territories."[32] But, of course, constructing a precedent court's action as "not in point" or its words as "dicta"—statements irrelevant to a decision that lack authority—is a common strategy for changing the law without appearing to violate stare decisis.

Thus far I have suggested that stare decisis was implicit in common-law systems that gave weight to precedents, including the British legal system. Both British and American law began to recognize stare decisis as a formal principle, notably in the summary of common law from Blackstone, which was popular in England, the American colonies, and the United States.[33] I also noted the role of reporters in supporting stare decisis, while at the same time promoting an overreliance on the words of courts over their actions and flooding law offices with legal precedents from which to draw. I next consider what courts and commentators have said about the role of stare decisis in a legal system and when it should be followed and when it may be flouted.

THE ROLE OF STARE DECISIS

There are numerous reasons for adhering to the principle of stare decisis and these reasons address the past, present, and future concerns of courts, and are adapted to the multiple audiences of court opinions. To begin with a very practical consideration, following precedent eases the burden on judges. As Justice Cardozo noted: "The labor of judges would be increased almost to the breaking point if every past decision could be reopened in every case, and one could not lay one's own course of bricks on the secure foundation of the courses laid by others who had gone before him."[34] Justice Lewis Powell believes that such labor reduction is doubly important for the high court because "few cases that reach the Supreme Court are easy. Most involve hours of study and reflection; the conscientious judge must make many close calls. It cannot seriously be suggested that every case brought to the Court should require reexamination on the merits of every relevant precedent that has gone before."[35] Powell also notes that following precedent—and thereby respecting stare decisis—is central to everyday decision-making in the Supreme Court: "The Court, in the exercise of certiorari jurisdiction, considers thousands of cases a year. The vast majority involve nothing more than application of previously decided cases. This is stare decisis."[36]

Perhaps the most important practical consequence of following precedents to those outside the court is stability in the law, so that the public can arrange its affairs with assurance, lawyers can advise clients confidently, and lower courts can follow the law. Thomas M. Cooley describes this interest in stability in an 1868 legal essay: "That state of things, when judicial decisions conflict, so that a citizen is always at a loss with regard to his rights and his duties, is a very serious evil; and the alternative of accepting adjudged cases as precedents in future cases resting upon analogous facts, and brought within the same reasons, is obviously preferable. Precedents, therefore, become important, and counsel are allowed and expected to call the attention of the court to them, not as concluding controversies, but as guides to the judicial mind."[37] An anonymous writer in the *Albany Law Journal* in 1872 praises the doctrine of stare decisis, asserting: "Without it the law would be nothing but 'a codeless myriad of precedents,' every court would be a law unto itself, and every lawyer, like a priest of Apollo, only able to advise after the oracle had spoken."[38]

Supreme Court justices recognize this purpose for following precedent as well. For example, in a 1945 case, Justice Douglas's majority opinion rejected a request to revise the settled understanding of a statute, noting "the problem of stare decisis": "We add only to the instability and uncertainty of the law if we revise the meaning of Section 20 [of the Criminal Code] to meet the exigencies of each case coming before us."[39] In a case from 1944, Justice Owen Roberts was particularly concerned about the impact of inconsistency on lower courts, complaining that overruling precedents will "shake confidence in the consistency of decision and leave the courts below on an uncharted sea of doubt and difficulty without any confidence that what was said yesterday will hold good tomorrow."[40] And, in one of the most famous dissenting comments on the failure to follow stare decisis, Roberts complained in another case that year that overruling "tends to bring adjudications of this tribunal into the same class as a restricted railroad ticket, good for this day and train only."[41]

Consistency in the law has been particularly stressed in cases involving property rights, as I noted in Chief Justice Taney's opinion earlier. For example, an 1807 Massachusetts case defended the need for such consistency in a statutory case involving property: "Of these statutes a practical construction early and generally obtained that in the power to dispose of lands was included a power to sell and convey the common lands. Large and valuable estates are held in various parts of the commonwealth, the titles to which depend on this construction. Were the Court now to decide that this construction is not to be supported, very great mischief would follow."[42]

Legal scholar James Ram summarized the attitude of courts in his frequently reprinted book of 1835, *The Science of Legal Judgment*: "A point closed, it is to be adhered to. A ground of such adherence is, the inconvenience of uncertainty in the law; an inconvenience, which, with regard to property, may affect every man, by the circumstance, that the ablest conveyancers may not be able to direct him." Another reason to adhere to rule of real property is, that many estates stand or depend upon the rule; or the danger, that "the new determination should have retrospect, and shake many questions already settled."[43] An 1858 New York court decision noted the resistance to change in the law of property, so that even "where a rule of property is erroneously settled, courts will rarely, if ever, depart from the decision, because such a departure will disturb rights acquired under the sanction of the rule."[44]

The US Supreme Court long has endorsed this view of the importance of settled property law. As recently as 2015, in reviewing a case, Justice Kagan noted: "*Brulotte* lies at the intersection of two areas of law: property (patents) and contracts (licensing agreements). And we have often recognized that in just those contexts—'cases involving property and contract rights'—considerations favoring stare decisis are 'at their acme.' E.g., *Payne,* 501 U.S., at 828; *Khan,* 522 U.S., at 20. That is because parties are especially likely to rely on such precedents when ordering their affairs."[45] Kagan calls the principle of not unsettling property rights a "superpowered form of *stare decisis*."[46]

Although error in a precedent was mentioned by Blackstone as a justification for overturning it, many have argued that stability is more important than correctness in some cases. The anonymous legal commentator from 1872 cited earlier suggested "that a decision is founded upon erroneous principles is not always sufficient reason for departing from [stare decisis], as has been time and again held, for it is said to be sometimes better to have the law *settled* than to have it *right*. Especially is this so of decisions affecting titles to property."[47]

The most frequently cited source for this position in recent times is Justice Brandeis's famous 1932 dissenting opinion (known as the "Brandeis brief") in *Burnet v. Coronado Oil & Gas Co.*, where he claims that "in most matters it is more important that the applicable rule of law be settled than that it be settled right."[48] Justice Stone, similarly, urged in a dissent from 1944 that a court must weigh the costs in overruling, "to make certain that more harm will not be done in rejecting than in retaining a rule of even dubious validity."[49] Justice Kagan noted in the previously mentioned 2015 case that "*stare decisis* has consequence only to the extent it sustains incorrect decisions; correct judgments have no need for that principle to prop them up."[50]

Instability in the law also leads to more lawsuits, so adhering to stare decisis also can discourage lawyers from testing existing precedents. As Emmet H. Wilson warned in 1945 in the face of a recent Supreme Court overruling: "Other litigants will be encouraged to test the question again, entertaining the impression that there is no reasonable fixity, definiteness, nor predictability in the law because the Court may be divided in the next case as before, with the majority on the other side; and in that event the last decision on any subject may be overruled as readily and as summarily as it overruled the former."[51] With the chipping away at abortion rights in a series of cases, for example, we saw this invitation to litigate at work, as antiabortion groups and pro-life states worked together to push the boundaries of the law, hollow out *Roe v. Wade*, and finally overrule it.[52]

Stability in the law that comes from respecting stare decisis ensures consistency and that, in turn, ensures that those subject to the law over time will be treated fairly in the sense that they are treated like those who came before them. Thus, Bradford lists "fairness and uniformity of treatment" as one of four key policy concerns supporting stare decisis.[53] James J. Eisenhower III notes that "this concept [of stare decisis] is based upon the idea that judicial decisions, in order to be fair and predictable, must be consistent," and that following precedent will help "to keep the scale of justice even and steady."[54]

The certainty and fairness that comes from adhering to precedents also helps a court maintain its legitimacy, a nineteenth-century justice from Wisconsin claimed: "The binding force of judicial precedents tends to reduce to a minimum that element of uncertainty which has been the occasion for popular reproach of law in all times and climes," and that "this is the only positive gain from the rigid obedience to the rule of *Stare Decisis*."[55] While acknowledging that judges may choose to follow precedent or not, Justice Jackson warned that "moderation in change is all that makes judicial participation in the evolution of the law tolerable."[56] Justice Owen Roberts argued that "the more deplorable consequence [of frequent overruling] will inevitably be that the administration of justice will fall into disrepute."[57]

One of the most controversial overrulings of the court was in 1871 in the Legal Tender Cases, which reversed an earlier split decision after only sixteen months.[58] Chief Justice Hughes noted the threat to the court of that overruling: "From the standpoint of the effect on public opinion, there can be no doubt that the reopening of the case was a serious mistake and the overruling in such a short time, and by one vote, of the previous decision shook popular respect for the Court."[59] As I show in chapter 7, the overruling of the half-century-old decision in *Roe v. Wade* ended the right to abortion and also caused great damage to the standing of the high court.

Unsurprisingly, complaints about threats to the court's legitimacy are popular with dissenters who dislike the court's backtracking on its precedents. Thus, when the Supreme Court began limiting *Roe v. Wade*'s holding in subsequent cases, Justice Blackmun, author of the landmark 1973 abortion decision, complained that "by refusing to abide not only by our precedents, but also by our canons for reconsidering those precedents, the plurality invites charges of cowardice and illegitimacy to our door. I cannot say that these would be undeserved."[60] In a 1974 dissent, Justice Powell insisted that "unless we respect the . . . decisions of this Court, we can hardly expect that others will do so."[61]

Single overrulings threaten the legitimacy of the high court less than a series of overrulings, such as we find in the Burger, Stone, Warren, and Rehnquist courts.[62] Walter Murphy and his colleagues, commenting on the politics of the judiciary, warned that "a tribunal that frequently reversed itself could not expect others to respect its decisions."[63] During such periods one finds a spike in complaints from legal scholars and judges about the "death of stare decisis."[64] The majority in *Planned Parenthood v. Casey*, an abortion decision that extensively reviewed reasons for not overruling *Roe v. Wade*, explained why frequent overruling by a court undermines its legitimacy: "There is a limit to the amount of error that can plausibly be imputed to prior Courts. If that limit should be exceeded, disturbance of prior rulings would be taken as evidence that justifiable reexamination of principle had given way to drives for particular results in the short term. The legitimacy of the Court would fade with the frequency of its vacillation."[65]

George Sullivan warned in 1902 that failing to respect stare decisis would do more than undermine the court's legitimacy—it also would undermine the foundations of our republican government because "by abolishing jurisprudence and legal principles and surrendering our property, our liberties, our persons—aye, even our very lives, absolutely and unreservedly to the ever-changing opinions of ever-changing judges, we place ourselves completely at their mercy, make uncertain the administration of the law, convert the courts themselves into theaters of political strife, and destroy every vestige of republican institutions—setting up a judicial oligarchy in their stead."[66]

Beyond legitimacy and respect for the judicial system, courts must be concerned that individual decisions are respected. Judicial decisions are meant to end conflicts peaceably. This can be problematic in contentious cases involving public issues, as Chief Justice Johnson of the New York Court of Appeals warned in an 1858 case:

> [Courts of last resort] are frequently called upon to decide questions in which, not individuals merely, but the whole people, take an interest, and in regard to which prejudices have become excited and passions inflamed. There must be an arbiter somewhere, to decide such questions, which will command respect, or they will be brought to the arbitrament of force; and nothing will contribute so much to secure this respect as a steady uniformity of decision, especially in regard to questions which affect large classes of men, and which lead, therefore, more or less, to the formation of parties.

> The overthrow of a single decision in a case of that character, unless upon reasons so clear and conclusive as scarcely to admit of controversy, is seriously to be deprecated, as tending to perpetuate an existing conflict of opinion.[67]

Unsurprisingly, in the explosive school desegregation decision of *Brown v. Board of Education*, members of the high court worked hard to maintain unanimity in overruling the "separate but equal" holding of *Plessy v. Ferguson*.[68] Chief Justice Warren wrote an opinion in *Brown* that was intended to be "short, readable by the lay public, nonrhetorical, unemotional and, above all, nonaccusatory."[69] Yet, despite this unanimity and effort to explain the decision to the public, the court faced massive public resistance in the South.[70]

Finally, many commentators have noted that to follow a precedent—especially a line of precedents—allows a court to draw upon the collective wisdom of others. For example, George Sullivan asserted in 1902: "But, manifestly, we cannot accept as law, we cannot accept in our decisions, we cannot accept as the administration of justice the reason and preferences, ever changing as they are, of judges who from time to time make up our courts. What we must attain, and can only make practical use of, is the collective wisdom of them all."[71] This reflects the "wisdom of the ages" respect typically given the British common law, standing as it has since "time immemorial."

That sort of respect makes overruling an act of hubris, as Cincinnati attorney Edward F. Alexander suggested to a legal conference in 1940: "As has been said before, the court realizes that if a principle has been in effect for a hundred years, and that there have been other able judges who have considered the question and who have come to a certain conclusion, there seems a lack of modesty, perhaps, in saying: 'Well, our opinion is better than the opinion of those judges.'"[72]

It is not just that other judges might be wiser; rather, it is the testing of a view over time, as Roscoe Pound describes it: "The common-law technique is based on a conception of law as experience developed by reason and reason tested and developed by experience. It is a technique of finding the grounds of decision in recorded judicial experience, making for stability by requiring adherence to decisions of the same question in the past, allowing growth and change by the freedom of choice from among competing analogies of equal authority when new questions arise or old ones take new forms."[73] Pound's support for stare decisis recognizes that the law evolves through "growth and change," the competition among analogies, and the press of new questions in new circumstances. It is to those circumstances of change in conditions and in legal understanding that I turn next to consider the reasons relied upon to flout stare decisis and overturn precedents.

JUSTIFICATIONS FOR OVERTURNING PRECEDENTS

Despite the powerful reasons for adhering to stare decisis, the United States Supreme Court has explicitly reversed over 350 of its decisions through almost three hundred overruling cases from its beginnings through the 2021/2022 Supreme Court term.[74] How they and other legal authorities and scholars justify ignoring stare decisis is considered generally in this section, and in detail in case studies in the remainder of the book.

Early in the history of invoking the principle of stare decisis in American jurisprudence, jurists were aware of the need to ignore its call to follow precedent in certain circumstances. Chief Justice Black of Pennsylvania, writing in an 1853 case, called stare decisis "a principle of great magnitude and importance" but then noted when it might be ignored: "A palpable mistake, violating justice, reason, and law must be corrected, no matter by whom it may have been made. There are cases in our books which bear such marks of haste and inattention that they demand reconsideration. There are some which must be disregarded, because they cannot be reconciled with others. There are old doctrines of which the authority has become obsolete by a total alteration in the circumstances of the country and the progress of opinion. 'Tempora mutantur.' We change with the change of the times as necessarily as we move with the motion of the earth."[75] I will elaborate and extend Black's list in light of what legal scholars and jurists have said about justifiable overruling.

Blaustein and Field, whose 1958 review of Supreme Court overrulings predated several other studies, distinguish between *necessary* overrulings and *optional* overrulings. I will build upon and elaborate this distinction, beginning with *necessary* overrulings. The first necessary overruling they identify is where the Supreme Court must choose between conflicting precedents so that both may not stand.[76] Here, stare decisis may be said to operate, but for only one precedent and not the other, or as Justice Powell put it in a 1978 case, where "considerations of stare decisis cut in both directions."[77] In one of the earliest overrulings, Chief Justice Marshall admitted: "We should be much inclined to adhere to the decision in Wilson vs. Daniel, had not a contrary practice since prevailed."[78] Thus, because the court ignored its own precedents (perhaps because of a lack of good and timely reporters to ensure their consistency), he chose to follow the more recent practice. In a 1944 case, the Supreme Court noted that two lines of cases suggested opposite outcomes in a tort dispute. Supporting liability against the owner of a vessel on which a seaman was injured, the court admitted: "We cannot follow it [*Plamals v. Pinar Del Rio*] and also follow *The Osceola*, supra, the cases which it approved and *Carlisle Packing Co. v. Sandanger*, supra. We prefer to follow the latter as the more consonant with principle and authority."[79]

Sometimes the competition between precedents suggests the overruled case is an anomaly. An example is the 1941 case of *United States v. Darby* that overruled *Hammer v. Dagenhart,* a tragic decision that prevented the government from banning the use of child labor. The court said the case conflicted with rulings before and after it: "The conclusion is inescapable that *Hammer v. Dagenhart,* was a departure from the principles which have prevailed in the interpretation of the Commerce Clause both before and since the decision and that such vitality, as a precedent, as it then had has long since been exhausted."[80]

Sometimes such conflicting cases arise because the court implicitly overruled a previous case and is forced to recognize that it did not own up to that overruling in the original case. Such cases have been called virtual, sub silentio, and stealth overrulings.[81] They hide the actual number of overrulings by the high court by refusing to acknowledge them. However, in later cases the court may highlight the conflict between an implicit overruling case and the case it overruled, forcing it to choose between two conflicting precedents. Rhetorically, this approach avoids the awkwardness of acknowledging the flouting of stare decisis in the implicit overruling, while "forcing" the court to choose between conflicting precedents later. As a "necessary" overruling to resolve the conflict, the court again can sidestep the responsibility for ignoring stare decisis.

Barry Friedman identified a different judicial motive for such overrulings in the Rehnquist court, drawing on that court's implicit reversal of *Miranda v. Arizona.* He argues "that stealth overruling occurs when the Justices have reason to be concerned about a strong negative reaction to their decision yet are determined to change the law nonetheless."[82]

Frequently, an overruling is not so much the product of a strategic choice by the court to sidestep responsibility for overruling, but rather an evolution in the law to the point that the case from which its progeny evolved is at odds with a present case. Justice Douglas describes the process by noting that "the overruling itself is at times not the true measure of the change. Commonly the change extended over a long period; the erosion of a precedent was gradual. The overruling did not effect an abrupt change in the law; it rather recognized a *fait accompli.*"[83] Thus, in 1962's *Smith v. Evening News Association,* the court insisted: "subsequent decisions here have removed the underpinnings of *Westinghouse* and its holding is no longer authoritative as a precedent."[84] Since the process of erosion usually takes time, the court can put distance between itself and the court it would overrule.

Another type of erosion occurs through distinguishing precedents to the point where they fairly stand alone. For example, in the 1957 case of *Green v. United States,* the court was determining when someone convicted of a crime had been placed in "double jeopardy" by the justice system. [85] The court was urged to follow *Trono v. United States,* but the court rejected the case as having unusual circumstances that did not give it precedential value, insisting: "All that was before the Court in *Trono* was a statutory provision against double jeopardy pertaining to the Philippine Islands—a territory just recently conquered with long-established legal procedures that were alien to the common law. Even then it seems apparent that a majority of the Court was unable to agree on any common ground for the conclusion that an appeal of a lesser offense destroyed a defense of former jeopardy on a greater offense for which the defendant had already been acquitted" (197; citations omitted).[86]

A related approach to avoiding precedent is narrowing its holding to avoid its relevance to a present case. Richard M. Re claims that, especially in the Roberts court, "cases are narrowed far more frequently than they are overruled, as the Court routinely encounters scenarios in which a past decision is worth pruning but not abolishing."[87] He cites examples of the Roberts court's narrowing, including "abortion, campaign finance, standing, affirmative action, the Second Amendment, the exclusionary rule, and Miranda rights."[88]

An odd sort of necessary overruling follows from the complex federal-state relationship. It occurs in cases in which the Supreme Court relies on a state court's interpretation of a state statute or constitution, and then the state court changes that interpretation.[89] The high court then faces the problem of ignoring the effective change in state law or recognizing it and changing its own earlier decision. This occurred in one of the earliest overruling cases, *Green v. Lessee of Neal* (1832), in which the high court followed the Tennessee Supreme Court's interpretation of a 1797 statute through decisions handed down in 1816 and 1829, only to find in *Green* that the act "was never considered as finally settled until 1828" when Tennessee reinterpreted the statute.[90] The Supreme Court concluded: "As it appears to this court, that the construction of the statutes of limitations [in the Act of 1797] of Tennessee is now well settled, different from what was supposed to be the rule at the time this court decided the case of Patton's Lessee v. Easton, and the case of Powell's Lessee v. Green; and as the instructions of the circuit court of Tennessee were governed by these decisions, and not by the settled law of the state; the judgment must be reversed, and the cause remanded for further proceedings." The court explained the technical rationale for this willingness to reverse itself: "The decision of this question by the highest tribunal of a state, should be considered as final by this court; not because the state tribunal in such a case has any power to bind this court; but because, in the language of the court in the case of Shelby et al. v. Guy, 11 Wheat. 361, 'a fixed and received construction by a state in its own courts, makes a part of the statute law.'"[91]

There are exceptions to this necessary form of overruling. In 1863, the high court was irritated that the Supreme Court of Iowa reversed a long-standing series of decisions that allowed municipal corporations to issue bonds to support the construction of railroads extending beyond their city limits.[92] Because of what it viewed as a temporary change in the law, the high court refused to reverse itself to follow the state court, ruling: "Where a question was once definitely settled by a series of decisions in the state court, such decisions being sustained by reason and authority, and one or two later cases overrule them, against all law and reason, the Supreme Court will not feel itself bound to follow every oscillation of opinion."[93] Sixteen years later Chief Justice Waite added a second caveat, admitting: "We recognize fully, not only the right of a State Court, but its duty to change its decisions whenever, in its judgment, the necessity arises . . . for new reasons, or because of a change of opinion in respect to old ones and ordinarily we will follow them." But he carved out an exception where "they affect rights vested before the change was made."[94] Thus, when bonds were issued under a previous rule, a later interpretation could not invalidate that issuance.

Other necessary overrulings are based upon obvious error in prior decisions. Of course, one court's error is another court's good reasoning, so this potentially raises problems. However, the emphasis on *obvious* error, or on Blackstone's "flatly absurd or unjust" standard for erroneous decisions, should indicate something more than a difference of opinion.[95] Among those errors, W. M. Lile, writing in 1916, includes the reliance on a previously discredited authority, a gross misreading of an authority, or ignoring an obvious authority.[96]

In cases involving statutory interpretation, clear misunderstanding of a statute in a precedent supports overruling it, as Justice Frankfurter stated in 1941's *Helvering v. Hallock*: "Surely we are not bound by reason or by the considerations that underlie stare decisis to persevere in distinctions taken in the application of a statute which, on further examination, appear consonant neither with the purposes of the statute nor with this Court's own conception of it."[97] In another 1941 overruling the court indicated clear error in the prior court's judgment:

> In 1918 this Court in Toledo Newspaper Co. v. United States, 247 U.S. 402, 418, 419, stated that "there can be no doubt" that the first section of the Act of March 2, 1831 "conferred no power not already granted and imposed no limitations not already existing"; and that it was "intended to prevent the danger by reminiscence of what had gone before, of attempts to exercise a power not possessed which . . . had been sometimes done in the exercise of legislative power." The inaccuracy of that historic observation has been plainly demonstrated. Frankfurter & Landis, Power of Congress Over Procedure in Criminal Contempts in "Inferior" Federal Courts—A Study in Separation of Powers, 37 Harv. L. Rev. 1010.[98]

Statutory interpretation of federal legislation is a unique case for overruling, because if the court gets it wrong, Congress can revise a statute to clarify its meaning. That raises a question about whether congressional acquiescence in a particular interpretation should be read by the court as an endorsement of its interpretation. Justice Powell was skeptical about Congress's ability to fix misinterpretations, suggesting, contrary to the view of some of his colleagues: "It reflects an unrealistic view of the political process and Congress' ability to fine-tune statutes. Correction of erroneous statutory interpretations may in some cases be vital to the effective administration of justice and coherence of the law. But correction may have little political constituency in Congress. The Court therefore has a responsibility both to ensure that its statutory interpretations follow the intent of the drafting Congress, and to ensure that erroneous interpretations do not damage the fabric of the law."[99] In short, Powell supports overruling bad statutory interpretations.

Despite Powell's view, other justices have viewed overruling statutory interpretations differently. In a 2015 case, the majority urged:

> stare decisis carries enhanced force when a decision, like *Brulotte*, interprets a statute. Then, unlike in a constitutional case, critics of our ruling can take their objections across the street, and Congress can correct any mistake it sees. See, e.g., *Patterson v. McLean Credit Union*, 491 U.S. 164, 172–173 (1989). . . .
>
> Congress took the lead in changing the treatment of tying agreements and, in doing so, conspicuously left *Brulotte* in place. Indeed, Congress declined to enact bills that would have modified not only tying doctrine but also *Brulotte*. That choice suggests congressional acquiescence in *Brulotte*, and so further supports adhering to *stare decisis*.[100]

A dissenting Justice Alito reiterated Powell's position, arguing: "Even where Congress has considered, but not adopted, legislation that would abrogate a judicial ruling, it cannot be inferred that Congress' failure to act shows that it approves the ruling," adding, "Passing legislation is no easy task."[101]

Perceived errors in interpreting the United States Constitution are considered strong grounds for overruling prior opinions, not only because it is the court's responsibility to interpret the Constitution but also because of the great difficulty of changing bad interpretations through the constitutional amendment process. Thus, in an 1849 case, Chief Justice Taney disagreed with the majority's revision of its prior interpretation of the Constitution but stated: "I . . . am quite willing that it be regarded hereafter as the law of this court, that its opinion upon the construction of the Constitution is always open to discussion when it is supposed to have been founded in error, and that its judicial authority should hereafter depend altogether on the force of the reasoning by which it is supported."[102]

Despite Justice Brandeis's insistence in a dissenting opinion, noted earlier, that it is often best to have a rule of law settled than to have it settled rightly, he carved out an exception for constitutional cases, noting that "in cases involving the Federal Constitution, where correction through legislative action is practically impossible, this court has often overruled its prior decisions."[103] Indeed, Earl M. Maltz notes that since that famous "Brandeis brief," the high court has generally assumed that it owed less deference to precedents involving constitutional interpretation.[104] Thus, a year after Brandeis's influential dissent in *Burnet v. Coronado Oil & Gas Co.*, Justice Douglas dissented from a case, noting: "I mention the two regimes that filed the unanimous opinions in those cases to indicate the vintage of the authority which decided them. Their decisions, of course, do not bind us, for they dealt with matters of constitutional interpretation which are always open."[105]

Eleven years later in *Smith v. Allwright*, a landmark voting rights case from Texas, the majority insisted: "In constitutional questions, where correction depends upon amendment and not upon legislative action this Court throughout its history has freely exercised its power to reexamine the basis of its constitutional decisions."[106] Five years later, Justice Douglas wrote in a law review article on stare decisis explaining the unique situation in overruling decisions involving constitutional interpretation: "A judge looking at a constitutional decision may have compulsions to revere past history and accept what was once written. But he remembers above all else that it is the Constitution which he swore to support and defend, not the gloss which his predecessors may have put on it. So he comes to formulate his own views, rejecting some earlier ones as false and embracing others. He cannot do otherwise unless he lets men long dead and unaware of the problems of the age in which he lives do his thinking for him."[107] Douglas's final point, about changes in times as supporting a departure from stare decisis, gets into what may be considered "optional" overrulings, though obviously one justice's option is another's necessity.

A whole host of changes in circumstances can make old law either poorly adapted to the times or even irrelevant or illogical as applied to new situations. Even Ram recognized this in 1835, urging: "When a rule relates to the nature of things, as such nature existed at a former period, and the reason of the rule corresponds to that nature, then at an after time, if the nature of the things is altered, and by the alteration the rule is become too general, and the reason given for it fails, the rule in a case of this kind is no longer binding."[108] This sentiment has been frequently repeated. For example, in a 1970 case Justice Harlan II insisted that "no precedent is sacrosanct and one should not hesitate to vote to overturn this Court's previous holdings—old or recent—or reconsider settled dicta where the principles announce prove either practically . . . or jurisprudentially . . . unworkable, or no longer suited to contemporary life."[109]

Jerome Frank warned that "our society would be straight-jacketed were not the courts, with the able assistance of lawyers, constantly overhauling the law and adapting it to the realities of ever-changing social, industrial and political conditions."[110] As Moore and Oglebay note: "Certain rules of law enunciated for the horse and buggy era may excellently serve our machine age; but, just as surely, certain rules will not. In refusing to follow a precedent a court must not always assert that its predecessor erred [as Kent would have it]. Yesterday's wise decisions were commands for yesterday, but only instructions for today."[111] Technological changes provide an obvious case. For example, the common-law rule of paternity that presumes the father of a child is the mother's husband might rightly be changed in a day when genetic testing can establish paternity with near certainty.[112]

Perhaps most threatening to models of law as objective, universal, and timeless is the need for law to adapt to changes in values. Heimanson suggests:

> The need for re-thinking, for reappraisal of old values, for adjustment to changing conditions—so vital in all fields of human activities—applies to our case law, too. The natural way to meet this need is by *overruling*. . . .
>
> [For example,] in New York, the Schloendorff principle of 1914, which exempted charity hospitals from tort claims, was overruled in 1957 by *Bing v. Thunig* as "out of tune with life about us, at variance with modern-day needs." This is not a castigation of the 1914 view but a recognition of the subsequent change in attitude, for today we no longer feel that dependence on free aid takes away a man's dignity and right.[113]

Such a change in values was central in *Lawrence v. Texas*, which overruled *Bowers v. Hardwick*'s support for state bans on homosexual sodomy, as I will explain in chapter 6.

Roscoe Pound noted that even issues such as reasonableness in the law can be influenced by changing times, weakening the need to follow precedents: "What was unreasonable in a rural agricultural society is not necessarily unreasonable in an urban industrial society. What is unreasonable under the circumstances of yesterday may or may not be under circumstances of tomorrow. . . . If the difference between application of such a rule and application of a standard is seen and borne in mind, it will be apparent that decisions as to what was arbitrary and unreasonable under conditions of the past are not binding under the doctrine of stare decisis unless the conditions of the time and place and the surrounding circumstances are the same."[114]

Professor Jerold H. Israel notes a rhetorical advantage to stressing changed conditions as a justification for overruling a precedent, since "an opinion emphasizing the changed circumstances naturally will contain the counter suggestion that, in any event, the former Court might well have decided differently if confronted with today's conditions. Thus, with the change-in-circumstances rationale, the Court may obtain the best of both worlds. Not only is the prior decision overruled, but the adverse emphasis upon differences in the Court's personnel that normally attend such action is eliminated, or at least diluted, by relying upon grounds consistent with the concept of impersonal decision-making ordinarily supported by stare decisis."[115]

In general, there is a tension between existing law and law as it ideally would be, drawing on what Kenneth Burke recognizes as the perfecting impulses of human language itself.[116] As Vincent M. Barnett Jr. noted, eloquently, in 1942: "A colleague of Justice Brandeis once said of one of his dissenting opinions, 'I am afraid our brother Brandeis is stating the law as it should be, but unfortunately not as it is.' . . . From the very beginning, however, the law as it should be and the law as it is have both played a part in constitutional interpretation. To enforce the latter at the expense of the former is to forgo progress. To enforce the former at the expense of the latter is to jeopardize order. Here, as elsewhere, the reconciliation of order and progress is a task of the most difficult nature."[117]

A variety of other considerations are weighed in deciding whether to overrule a previous decision. Noland notes that courts consider unfavorable experiences with the rule endorsed in the old decision, the consequences of overturning that rule, and the logical consequences of adopting another rule in its stead.[118] For example, in the 1965 case of *Swift & Co. v. Wickham*, the court found that a jurisdictional rule they had set down three years earlier was too vague and was causing problems. Justice Harlan II insisted: "We believe that considerations of stare decisis should not deter us from this course. Unless inexorably commanded by statute, a procedural principle of this importance should not be kept on the books in the name of stare decisis once it is proved to be unworkable in practice; the mischievous consequences to litigants and courts alike from the perpetuation of an unworkable rule are too great."[119]

Who is involved in setting a precedent decision or overruling it is sometimes thought important. Justice Lewis Powell offered that "a new Justice is less bound by precedent in construing a provision of the Constitution than a Justice who was sitting when a precedent was decided."[120] Indeed, Richard Posner argues, "A newly appointed Supreme Court Justice may pay lip service to most of the Court's earlier decisions even if he dislikes the policies on which they rest. But he will construe those decisions narrowly in order to minimize their impact. And when he finds himself, as he often will, in the open area in which conventional sources of law, such as clearly applicable precedents, give out, he will not feel bound by those policies. So if he can command a majority the law will veer off in a new direction. Eventually the old precedents will be interpreted to death or, finally, overruled explicitly."[121]

On the other hand, Justice Sotomayor insisted in a 2013 overruling case: "No doubt, it would be illegitimate to overrule a precedent simply because the Court's current membership disagrees with it."[122] As I indicated in the opening to this book, Justice Stevens complained about the overruling of two precedents in *Citizens United v. Federal Election Commission* by noting, disdainfully, "The only relevant thing that has changed since *Austin* and *McConnell* is the composition of this Court."[123] Almost a century and a half earlier, a bitter Chief Justice Salmon Chase made a similar complaint when a pair of new justices reversed a decision he authored for the court less than two years earlier, stating:

> This reversal, unprecedented in the history of the court, has been produced by no change in the opinions of those who concurred in the former judgment. One closed an honorable judicial career by resignation after the case had been decided, after the opinion had been read and agreed to in conference, and after the day when it would have been delivered in court, had not the delivery been postponed for a week to give time for the preparation of the dissenting opinion. The court was then full, but the vacancy caused by the resignation of Mr. Justice Grier having been subsequently filled and an additional justice having been appointed under the act increasing the number of judges to nine, which took effect on the first Monday of December, 1869, the then majority find themselves in a minority of the court, as now constituted, upon the question.[124]

This case will be analyzed more fully in the next chapter.

Justice Scalia argued that justices who change their minds have good standing to overrule. In a case involving the regulation of casino gambling by Indian tribes, Scalia dissented from a position he had previously taken, noting that its "error has grown more glaringly obvious" over the years and that he should be able to "clean up a mess that I helped make" in establishing the problematic precedent.[125] In the 1874 case of *Union Pacific Railway v. McShane*, Justice Miller authored a unanimous decision overruling a unanimous precedent he himself had authored two years earlier, insisting that "a fuller argument and more mature consideration" led them to conclude that "the proposition [of the prior case] is not tenable."[126] Twelve years later in *Wabash, St. Louis & Pacific Railway Co. v. Illinois*, Justice Miller again admitted his culpability in an erroneous decision nine years earlier: "Of the members of the court who concurred in those [problematic precedent] opinions, there being two dissentients, but three remain, and the writer of this opinion is one of the three. He is prepared to take his share of the responsibility for the language used in those opinions, including the extracts above presented. He does not feel called upon to say whether those extracts justify the decision of the Illinois court in the present case. It will be seen, from the opinions themselves, and from the arguments of counsel presented in the reports, that the question did not receive any very elaborate consideration, either in the opinions of the court or in the arguments of counsel."[127]

In one overruling involving the change of position of two members who had supported the previous decision and now reversed their position, the court offered a general explanation for the switch. In the 1880 case of *Tilghman v. Proctor,* a unanimous court overruled a seven-year-old precedent, *Mitchell v. Tilghman,* involving the same patent holder who had been stiffed in the previous decision.[128] Justice Bradley authored the opinion, explaining the reasons for the change:

> The evidence in the present case, which is quite an unwieldy mass, is much the same as in that [precedent case], being supplemented, however, by the testimony of the patentee respecting the nature of his original experiments and the practicability of using profitably the coil apparatus described in the patent, together with certain exhibits relating to the novelty of the alleged invention. Upon *the renewed consideration which has been given to the subject,* the Court is unanimously of opinion, contrary to the decision in the Mitchell case, that the patent of Tilghman must be sustained as a patent for a process, and not merely for the particular mode of applying and using the process pointed out in the specification, and that the defendants have infringed it by the processes used by them. (708; emphasis added)

The unanimity of the decision was afforded by the unmentioned reversals of Justices Miller and Field, and the absence of Justices Clifford and Hunt, who had previously voted with the 4-3 majority.

The number of justices supporting a precedent decision is often invoked in overruling. Obviously, a decision by an evenly divided court (usually 4-4) creates no precedent and need not be followed.[129] However, decisions by closely divided courts are often highlighted to suggest there was not a strong consensus on what the law is. Thus, in a 1967 case about expatriation, the court used the split nature of the precedent decision to diminish its standing and support the overruling: "That case [*Perez v. Brownell*], decided by a 5-4 vote almost 10 years ago, has been a source of controversy and confusion ever since, as was emphatically recognized in the opinions of all the judges who participated in this case below."[130] A 1990 case interpreting the constitutional provision against ex post facto laws, supported overruling a nineteenth-century case by noting it had reversed a lower court "by a vote of 5 to 4."[131]

When precedents are decided by courts that are not fully staffed, those precedents are easier to attack. For example, Justice Strong's majority opinion in the Legal Tender Cases justified reversing *Hepburn v. Griswold* by noting: "That case was decided by a divided court, and by a court having a less number of judges than the law then in existence provided this court shall have."[132]

The age of a precedent decision is a consideration that may cut both ways. An older decision may deserve respect, at least to the extent that age "may foretell . . . the degree of reliance that has been placed upon it."[133] That reliance may be related to the property interests of individuals and companies that have been organized around prior decisions (as noted above), or even the interests of a state, the nation, the public, or legislators that have relied upon a precedent.[134] Ram cites authority suggesting that "mere length of time since the decision of an earlier case does not weaken the authority of it."[135] On the other hand, older cases may deserve less respect to the extent that they are outdated. Thus, Justice Holmes complained: "It is revolting to have no better reason for a rule than that so it was laid down in the time of Henry IV. . . . [Especially] if the grounds upon which it was laid have vanished long since, and the rule simply persists from blind imitation of the past."[136] Justice Brandeis authored the majority opinion in the landmark case of *Erie v. Tompkins,* which overturned almost a century of federal civil procedure case law, eliminating "federal common law" and creating a choice of state law about where to bring a suit. He argued: "Experience in applying the doctrine of Swift v. Tyson, had revealed its defects, political and social; and the benefits expected to flow from the rule did not accrue."[137] Justice Douglas, speaking for the majority in a 1974 case, illustrates the "changed circumstances" argument, noting: "*Liggett,* decided in 1928, belongs to that vintage of decisions which exalted substantive due process by striking down state legislation which a majority of the Court deemed unwise." Noting the change in legal understanding that made this precedent anachronistic, he says, with some surprise, "*Liggett* has to date not been expressly overruled."[138]

Newer decisions may deserve respect because they can rarely be justified by changes over shorter periods, as Justice Marshall argued in his vehement dissent in *Payne v. Tennessee,* which overruled a four-year-old case and a two-year-old case that followed it: "The majority does not suggest that the legal rationale of these [overruled] decisions has been undercut by changes or developments in doctrine during the last two years. Nor does the majority claim that experience over that period of time has discredited the principle that 'any decision to impose the death sentence be, and appear to be, based on reason rather than caprice or emotion,' Gardner v. Florida, 430 U.S. 349, 358, 51 L. Ed. 2d 393, 97 S. Ct. 1197 (1977) (plurality opinion), the larger postulate of political morality on which Booth and Gathers rest."[139] Indeed, Justice Harlan II thought a special justification was required to overrule a recent precedent involving the Commerce Clause, admitting: "The overruling of a six-to-two decision of such recent vintage, which was concurred in by two members of the majority in the present case, and the opinion in support of which was written by an acknowledged expert in the field of federal jurisdiction, demands full explication of our reasons."[140] Chief Justice Hughes thought the overruling in the Legal Tender Cases threatened the court's standing in part because of the short time of the reversal—just over a year.[141]

On the other hand, Justice Bradley's concurrence in the Legal Tender Cases used the newness of the overruled precedent (not yet two years old) as support for overruling, though he added other factors as well, insisting: "Where the decision is recent, and is only made by a bare majority of the court, and during a time of public excitement on the subject, when the question has largely entered into the political discussions of the day, I consider it our right and duty to subject it to a further examination, if a majority of the court are dissatisfied with the former decision."[142] More recently, Justice Scalia unsuccessfully called for overruling a two-year-old case while suggesting older cases deserved more respect: "The only distinctive feature here is that the overruling would follow not long after the original decision. But that is hardly unprecedented [citing three cases overruled after a short period]. Indeed, I had thought that the respect accorded prior decisions increases, rather than decreases, with their antiquity, as the society adjusts itself to their existence, and the surrounding law becomes premised upon their validity. The freshness of error not only deprives it of the respect to which long-established practice is entitled, but also counsels that the opportunity of correction be seized at once, before state and federal laws and practices have been adjusted to embody it."[143]

Another consideration for overruling involves assessments of the quality of the precedent decision in terms of how thoroughly the issues were briefed by counsel or discussed in the opinions, as well as whether able counsel pleaded the cause and respected justices rendered the opinions. For example, in one of Ram's revised volumes, he and his coauthor note: "A circumstance that strengthens the authoritative force of a decision is that it was decided 'after consideration,' 'on great consideration,' or by 'most learned judges'; that it underwent grave consideration by a court, which at the time was filled by very learned judges."[144]

In *Genesee Chief*, Chief Justice Taney had to decide an issue of admiralty previously settled by Justice Story, one of the most eminent jurists on maritime law. He combined arguments about technological change (notably, the commercialization of the steamship) to suggest an inadequacy of consideration by the court a quarter century earlier, "when the great importance of the question as it now presents itself could not be foreseen; and the subject did not therefore receive that deliberate consideration which at this time would have been given to it by the eminent men who presided here when that case was decided."[145]

Justice Field used the opposite argument in dissenting in the Legal Tender Cases, insisting the precedent case was well argued: "That [precedent] judgment was reached only after repeated arguments were heard from able and eminent counsel, and after every point raised on either side had been the subject of extended deliberation. The questions presented in that case were also involved in several other cases and had been elaborately argued in them. It is not extravagant to say that no case has ever been decided by this court since its organization, in which the questions presented were more fully argued or more maturely considered. It was hoped that a judgment thus reached would not be lightly disturbed."[146]

Noland emphasizes that strong precedents will have been fully argued and briefed.[147] In a 1978 case, Justice Powell insisted: "We owe somewhat less deference to a decision that was rendered without benefit of a full airing of all the relevant considerations."[148] Lile believes that certain cases do not lend themselves to sufficiently rigorous arguments, such as those involving "friendly litigation" (where parties are almost "invited" to engage in litigation to address a legal issue) and ex parte cases which are for the benefit of one side only and not adversarial.[149]

Although this review of justifications for overruling has listed numerous reasons the high court has provided for overruling, it is unusual for a court to overrule one of its precedents based solely upon the charge that the prior case erred in interpreting the law. There needs to be error plus something more. Chief Justice Roberts insisted in *June Medical Services, LLC v. Russo* (2020) that "for precedent to mean anything, [stare decisis] must give way only to a rationale that goes beyond whether the [prior] case was decided correctly."[150] Justice Kagan insisted in *Kimble v. Marvel Entertainment, LLC* (2015) that "an argument that [the court] got something wrong—even a good argument to that effect—cannot by itself justify scrapping settled precedent."[151] Justice Thurgood Marshall insisted in *Vasquez v. Hillery* (1986) that "every successful proponent of overruling precedent has *borne the heavy burden* of persuading the Court that changes in society or in the law dictate that the values served by stare decisis yield in favor of a greater objective"[152]

A widely cited standard reflecting this error-plus standard was offered in *Arizona v. Rumsey* (1984), where the court insisted: "Although adherence to precedent is not rigidly required in constitutional cases, any departure from the doctrine of *stare decisis* demands *special justification*."[153] Justice Powell referenced this "special justification" standard for overruling in *Garcia v. San Antonio Metropolitan Transit Authority* (1985), Justice O'Connor in *Welch v. Texas Department of Highways and Public Transportation* (1987) and in *Adarand Constructors, Inc. v. Peña* (1995), Justice Thurgood Marshall in *Payne v. Tennessee* (1991), Justice Souter in *United States v. Dixon* (1993), Justice Thomas in *United States v. International Business Machines Corp.* (1996), Chief Justice Rehnquist in *Dickerson v. United States* (2000), Chief Justice Roberts in *Citizens United v. Federal*

Election Commission (2010) and in *Halliburton Co. v. Erica P. John Fund, Inc.* (2014), Justice Sotomayor in *Alleyne v. United States* (2013), Justice Alito in *Gamble v. United States* (2019), and Justice Kagan in *Michigan v. Bay Mills Indian Community* (2014) and *Allen v. Cooper* (2020).[154] Thus, justices from the most conservative to the most liberal, and those in between, all insist that overruling requires "special justification," not run-of-the-mill arguments about error without more.

Now that I have reviewed the reasons for overruling, I turn in the next section to a general summary of overruling in the United States Supreme Court, indicating what kinds of cases have been overruled, by which courts, by which justices, and for what reasons.

AN OVERVIEW OF OVERRULING IN THE UNITED STATES SUPREME COURT

At this point I will commit to my specific estimate that as of the end of the 2021/2022 term 284 Supreme Court cases have overruled 358 of their own precedents; I offer this estimate because these numbers will be the basis of several quantitative assessments I make in this section.[155] While those numbers are specific, they remain tentative because it is impossible to objectively assess, in every instance, whether a case overruled a previous case, or simply distinguished it, qualified it, or otherwise diminished it. Many of the court's decisions have been unambiguous about their overrulings. For example, in the Legal Tender Cases of 1871, the court was clear: "But, without extending our remarks further, it will be seen that we hold the acts of Congress constitutional as applied to contracts made either before or after their passage. In so holding, we overrule so much of what was decided in *Hepburn v. Griswold*, as ruled the acts unwarranted by the Constitution so far as they apply to contracts made before their enactment."[156] In the 1923 case of *Lee v. Chesapeake & Ohio Railway*, the court stated: "We had occasion to criticise [ex parte *Wisner*] in General Investment Co. v. Lake Shore & Michigan Southern Ry. Co., supra, and now on further consideration we feel constrained to pronounce it essentially unsound and definitely to overrule it."[157] In 1968's *Peyton v. Rowe*, the court discussed habeas corpus law before noting: "we turn to consideration of the *McNally* holding and the reasons which compel us to overrule it."[158] In the 2000 case of *Mitchell v. Helms*, the court noted: "To the extent that *Meek* and *Wolman* conflict with this holding, we overrule them."[159]

Some overrulings employ different language that nonetheless is clear. For example, in a 1925 overruling the court said: "So far as the language of *Baltic Mining Co. v. Massachusetts*, 231 U.S. 68, 87, tends to support a different view it conflicts with conclusions reached in later opinions and is now definitely disapproved."[160] In *Craig v. Boren* (1976), the court added in a footnote: "Insofar as *Goesaert v. Cleary,* 335 U.S. 464 (1948), may be inconsistent, that decision is disapproved."[161] In *Escobedo v. Illinois,* the court announced: "In any event, to the extent that *Cicenia* or *Crooker* may be inconsistent with the principles announced today, they are not to be regarded as controlling."[162]

Other pronouncements are less direct. For example, in *Taylor v. Louisiana* (1975), the court stated: "We cannot follow the contrary implications of the prior cases, including *Hoyt v. Florida.*"[163] In the 1963 case of *Ferguson v. Skrupa,* the court did not overrule so much as announce that a prior case had been overruled, urging: "Not only has the philosophy of *Adams* been abandoned, but also this Court almost 15 years ago expressly pointed to another opinion of this Court as having 'clearly undermined' *Adams.*"[164] Instead of noting disapproval, the court in *Federal Power Commission v. Hope Natural Gas Co.* (1944) said: "We cannot approve the contrary holding of *United Railways Co. v. West,* 280 U.S. 234, 253–254."[165] In a 1996 First Amendment case, the majority said, drawing a distinction: "Without questioning the holding in *LaRue,* we now disavow its reasoning insofar as it relied on the Twenty-first Amendment."[166] In an 1858 case, the court did not explicitly overrule or disapprove, but refused to follow a precedent, admitting: "It is possible that some rights may be disturbed by refusing to follow the opinion expressed in that case [Brown's Lessee v. Clements]; but we are satisfied that far less inconvenience will result from this dissent, than by adhering to a principle which we think unsound, and which, in its practical operation, will unsettle the surveys and subdivisions of fractional sections of the public land, running through a period of some twenty-eight years."[167]

One of most indirect overrulings to escape the "implicit overruling" label is *Griffin v. Breckenridge,* where the court repeatedly attacked a precedent without coming out and announcing it was rejected. The majority said: "Whether or not Collins v. Hardyman was correctly decided on its own facts is a question with which we need not here be concerned. But it is clear, in the light of the evolution of decisional law in the years that have passed since that case was decided, that many of the constitutional problems there perceived simply do not exist."[168] They refer to Collins's "artificially restrictive construction" of 42 U.S.C. §1985 (3) (96), and note that "very similar language in closely related statutes has early and late received an interpretation quite inconsistent with that given to § 1985 (3) in Collins" (97). In short, they say that Collins is mistaken, but they do not say outright that it is no longer law. Nonetheless, this rejection of its reasoning is strong enough for five different sources to identify Griffin as overruling Collins.[169]

Because cases may reach more than one conclusion regarding the law in deciding a case, some cases are only overruled "in part." Dozens of overrulings involve such partial reversals. The 1963 case of *Construction Laborers v. Curry* provides an illustration.[170] The case involved an attempt by a construction company to keep union picketers away from its job site. Sympathetic union members sided with the picketers, making it hard for the company to get materials delivered for its work. The Supreme Court of Georgia agreed with the plaintiff that the picket was designed to force the company to hire only union workers and issued an injunction against the union. The US Supreme Court determined that the state court had no jurisdiction because the National Labor Relations Board had exclusive jurisdiction in the case. A second issue concerned the nature of the state court judgment. A precedent case suggested that the high court was limited in its ability to review state court decisions that were not "final judgments"; since the state court's injunction was temporary, the construction company argued, the high court had no jurisdiction. Justice White characterized the state court's decision as final:

> The Georgia Supreme Court not only finally asserted its power to deal with the subject matter of this suit, but it also resolved the merits of the issues raised in the course of the hearing upon the temporary injunction. Petitioner's conduct was adjudged to be in violation of the Georgia right-to-work law and an injunction was authorized. Petitioner conceded before this court that he had no further factual or legal issues to present to the Georgia trial court and respondent does not suggest that the matters adjudicated by the Georgia Supreme Court are not final and conclusive upon petitioner and the lower court. Since there was nothing more of substance to be decided in the trial court, the judgment below was final within the meaning of 28 U.S.C. § 1257 and within the scope of the *Pope* and *Richfield* cases. (551)

Even if the state court's judgment was not final, its assertion of jurisdiction was wrong. This judgment was stymied to some extent by an eleven-year-old precedent, *Building Union v. Ledbetter Co.*, which the court urged had been displaced by later decisions. It qualified its reversal in noting: "To the extent that *Ledbetter* may be said to prohibit our review of a final and erroneous assertion of jurisdiction by a state court to issue a temporary injunction in a labor dispute, when a substantial claim is made that the jurisdiction of the state court is preempted by federal law and by the exclusive power of the National Labor Relations Board, we decline to follow it" (552).

I include a complete list of cases overruling in whole or in part in appendix A. This list draws upon a great deal of prior work by legal and political scholars, government sources, statements from the court or its members, and my own analysis.[171] I include all overrulings identified by at least two of the eleven sources I draw upon. For those overrulings identified by a single source I have reviewed the cases myself to make an independent determination. I will refer to cases which reverse earlier decisions as "overruling cases," and those precedents that are overruled as "overruled," "reversed," or "overturned" cases.

A STATISTICAL PROFILE OF SUPREME COURT OVERRULINGS

As I noted, in my best estimate, 284 cases have overruled 358 precedents, for an average of just over one-and-a-quarter overruled precedent for each overruling decision. More than three-quarters of all overruling decisions reverse a single decision, though forty-eight reverse two earlier cases, ten reverse three, eight reverse four, and two reverse five. The case that reversed the most precedents is probably *Pennhurst State School & Hospital v. Halderman,* which a dissenting Justice Stevens, joined by three of his colleagues, accused of overruling more than two dozen precedents (though the majority rejected that claim).[172]

A few cases have been both overruling and overruled. These include the 1895 case of *Pollock v. Farmers' Loan & Trust Co.* that overruled the ninety-nine-year-old case of *Hylton v. United States* on the issue of direct taxation, but ninety-two years later was overruled itself in *South Carolina v. Baker.*[173] A habeas corpus case from 1950 was reversed in part by *Fay v. Noia,* in 1964, which was reversed in 1977—the court's greater procedural leniency for those accused of crimes in the 1964 case sandwiched by less forgiving courts.[174] However, the Warren court got the last word in another reversed reversal when a 1948 case allowed a Fourth Amendment search without a warrant because it was impractical to get one, a 1950 court rejected this practicality standard for a warrantless search in favor of a reasonableness standard, and, on Warren's final day on the bench in 1969, the court reversed again, requiring probable cause for a warrantless search rather than reasonableness.[175]

In a series of cases concerning whether the Fair Labor Standards Act (FLSA) could be applied to state employees, a 1968 case supported the federal government's authority to regulate some labor practices involving state workers. That was overturned by a 1976 ruling urging that such regulations stepped on state sovereignty, and this decision was overturned by a 1985 decision again recognizing federal authority.[176] *National League of Cities v. Usery* (1976) was the overruling and overruled case in the middle. *National League of Cities* was particularly concerned about minimum pay and maximum hour regulations under the FLSA. Justice Rehnquist argued for respecting state sovereignty, insisting:

> Congress may not exercise that [Commerce] power so as to force directly upon the States its choices as to how essential decisions regarding the conduct of integral governmental functions are to be made. We agree that such assertions of power, if unchecked, would indeed, as Mr. Justice Douglas cautioned in his dissent in *Wirtz,* allow "the National Government [to] devour the essentials of state sovereignty," 392 U.S., at 205, and would therefore

> transgress the bounds of the authority granted Congress under the Commerce Clause. While there are obvious differences between the schools and hospitals involved in *Wirtz,* and the fire and police departments affected here, each provides an integral portion of those governmental services which the States and their political subdivisions have traditionally afforded their citizens. We are therefore persuaded that *Wirtz* must be overruled. (855)

Nine years later Rehnquist, one year short of his promotion to chief justice, would be a dissenter when the court reconsidered this reversal in *Garcia v. San Antonio Metropolitan Transit Authority*. The majority cited difficulties in determining what state functions were "traditional," the changing political landscape that gave more power to the people to directly elect national representatives (and, thus, influence the such legislation without the intercession of the state legislature), and even the fact that mass transportation of the sort addressed in this case received considerable federal support to offset concerns over the costs of federal mandates.[177] In justifying the reversal, the court noted: "We do not lightly overrule recent precedent. We have not hesitated, however, when it has become apparent that a prior decision has departed from a proper understanding of congressional power under the Commerce Clause. See *United States v. Darby*, 312 U.S. 100, 116–17 (1941). Due respect for the reach of congressional power within the federal system mandates that we do so now."[178] Rehnquist warned in dissent: "I do not think it incumbent on those of us in dissent to spell out further the fine points of a principle that will, I am confident, in time again command the support of a majority of this Court."[179] Although he was not able to overturn *Garcia,* he did strike a blow against an expansive Commerce Clause power in *United States v. Lopez,* which invalidated the Gun-Free School Zones Act of 1990 as a congressional overreach not justified by its power under the Commerce Clause.[180] And a conservative Congress in 1985 amended FLSA to give states more flexibility in meeting its requirements.[181]

The distribution of overrulings has changed considerably over the history of the court. There were very few overrulings before mid-nineteenth century. Partly this can be explained by the lack of precedents to overturn. We can add the weak reporting of cases as well, that allowed the court to rely on its memory more than its words. Finally, the caseload of the court has fluctuated over the decades, and more cases decided obviously provide more opportunities for overruling. Partly this is a function of the number of cases changing with the growth of the nation and its law. Early courts had around one hundred cases seeking redress each year, but by the 1990s that number was more than six thousand. However, with a growing backlog of cases by the late nineteenth century, Congress began limiting the court's jurisdiction (such as by raising the amount of money required to be at stake in a civil suit) and later gave the high court more and more discretion in deciding which cases to hear.[182] Such variables led courts in the 1970s to 1980s to hear around one hundred and fifty cases a year; however, since 1998 the court has limited that number to less than eighty.[183] So, variations in overrulings also reflect how many bites at the apple the court was afforded. I provide more detail on caseloads and their relation to overruling below.

The first overruling was in *Hudson v. Guestier*, an 1810 case in Chief Justice Marshall's court, though in thirty-four years Marshall would see only three overruling decisions.[184] The Taney (1836–1864) and Chase (1864–1873) courts overruled four cases apiece. The Waite court (1874–1888), by contrast, would be much more active, with thirteen cases in fourteen years, before the Fuller court (1888–1910) returned to the nineteenth-century norm with four overruling decisions in twenty-two years. The White (1910–1921) and Taft (1921–1930) courts also were fairly restrained with seven and six overruling cases, respectively, with a smaller annual average than Waite, but much higher than earlier courts.

The big change in overruling came with the Hughes court (1930–1941), which included the Revolution of 1937. As I detail in chapter 5, the high court had been invalidating much of President Franklin D. Roosevelt's New Deal legislation as unconstitutional when the president threatened to pack the court in early 1937 by increasing the number of justices to fifteen. This is when the court appeared to make a "switch in time that saved nine."[185] The Revolution of 1937 led to an explosion in overrulings. Starting with *West Coast Hotel Co. v. Parrish*, which supported Washington State's minimum wage law in 1937 while overruling *Adkins v. Children's Hospital* and a 1936 decision that followed it, the court issued twenty-four overrulings by the end of Hughes's tenure in 1941.[186] Their annual overruling average was triple that of its predecessor. In its five years, the Stone court (1941–1946) would continue the upward trend, with seventeen overrulings and a 50 percent higher annual average than Hughes.

Frederick Vinson's court (1946–1953) dropped back just below the Hughes court average, but the Warren court (1953–1969) returned to near the Stone court average, overruling a hefty fifty-four cases, or just under 3.4 cases per year, during the former California governor's sixteen-year tenure. Although the Warren court's controversial rulings on school segregation, civil rights, and criminal law and procedure mark its public image as the kind of activist court that would overrule frequently, it stands third in the average number of overruling cases per year and second in the total number of such cases.[187] The most activist court in Supreme Court history in the frequency and total of overruling cases is the Burger court (1969–1986), which issued sixty-two overruling opinions in seventeen years, or over 3.6 overruling cases per year.

The Rehnquist court (1986–2005) began a downward trend, issuing forty-five overrulings at the lowest frequency since the Vinson court. The Roberts court

(2005–present), continued this trend in reducing overrulings, with twenty-six in the first seventeen years of the court (through the 2021/2022 term). That is about 1.5 per year—the lowest number of overrulings and frequency since the Taft court. However, as I noted above, the early Roberts court often sought to narrow precedents—to the point of gutting them—while avoiding explicit overruling.[188] Table 1 summarizes the overrulings by court.

When considering how often a court has overruled precedents it is useful to take account of their caseloads. Courts that hear fewer cases may be overruling more often than their counterparts in terms of the percentage of cases they overrule of all the cases they decide. As noted above, caseloads have varied wildly during the Supreme Court's history.[189] The first three courts heard only a handful of cases per year. In contrast, the three courts between 1874 and 1921 heard a huge number of cases at over 200 per year. The Fuller court (1888–1910) was by far the busiest, deciding an enormous 415.5 cases per year.

Table 1. Overruling Decisions by Court

Court	Years	Overruling Decisions	Yearly Average
John Jay	1789–1795	0	0.0
John Rutledge	1795–1795	0	0.0
Oliver Ellsworth	1796–1800	0	0.0
John Marshall	1801–1835	3	0.1
Roger Taney	1836–1864	4	0.1
Salmon Chase	1864–1874	4	0.4
Morrison Waite	1874–1888	13	0.9
Melville Fuller	1888–1910	4	0.2
Edward D. White	1910–1921	7	0.6
William Howard Taft	1921–1930	6	0.7
Charles Evan Hughes	1930–1941	24	2.2
Harlan Fiske Stone	1941–1946	17	3.4
Frederick Vinson	1946–1953	15	2.1
Earl Warren	1953–1969	54	3.4
Warren Burger	1969–1986	62	3.6
William Rehnquist	1986–2005	45	2.4
John Roberts	2005–2022*	26	1.5

*Through the 2021/2022 term.

The Roberts court (2005–present) has carried less than a fifth of that average at 80.5 decisions per year. That lower caseload brings their overruling record more in line with courts of the past eighty years, who have averaged overruling a little more or less than 2 percent of all the cases they decided. The explosion of overrulings in the Hughes court marked a significantly higher number of overrulings per case heard but is close to half of the average annual percentage of cases overruled since that court. Frequency pushes the Warren court to the top in terms of overruling percentages, with almost one out of forty cases they decided overruling a precedent. Table 2 lists this information, including a final line tallying averages for the entire history of the court, showing that about 1 percent of all the high court's decisions overruled its own precedents.

Table 2. Percentage of Cases that Overrule Precedents

Court	Years	Overruled Decisions	Total Decisions	Percentage of Decisions Overruling
John Jay	1789–1795	0	15	0%
John Rutledge	1795–1795	0	5	0%
Oliver Ellsworth	1796–1800	0	43	0%
John Marshall	1801–1835	3	1,280	0.23%
Roger Taney	1836–1864	4	1,670	0.24%
Salmon Chase	1864–1874	4	1,370	0.29%
Morrison Waite	1874–1888	13	3,650	0.36%
Melville Fuller	1888–1910	4	4,986	0.08%
Edward D. White	1910–1921	7	2,548	0.27%
William Howard Taft	1921–1930	6	1,598	0.38%
Charles Evan Hughes	1930–1941	24	1,915	1.25%
Harlan Fiske Stone	1941–1946	17	781	2.18%
Frederick Vinson	1946–1953	15	812	1.85%
Earl Warren	1953–1969	54	2,205	2.45%
Warren Burger	1969–1986	62	2,808	2.21%
William Rehnquist	1986–2005	45	2,044	2.20%
John Roberts	2005–2022*	26	1,369	1.90%
All Courts	*1789–2022*	284	*29,099*	*0.98%*

*Through the 2021/2022 term.

The most frequent authors of overruling opinions are Justice Douglas at twenty-two opinions, Justice/Chief Justice Rehnquist and Justice Brennan with seventeen apiece, followed by Justice White at fourteen. Three conservatives—Justices Thomas and Alito and Chief Justice Roberts—are tied for most frequent author of overruling decisions on the current court, at four apiece (through spring 2022). Chief Justice Warren, widely depicted by his critics as an activist, authored only six overruling opinions in his sixteen years on the bench. Nine overrulings in the high court's history have been per curiam, anonymous opinions "by the court." The overruling in *Planned Parenthood v. Casey* written jointly by Justices O'Connor, Kennedy, and Souter, is an unusual multiple-authored overruling opinion.[190]

All but one justice appointed from the turn of the twentieth century to the end of the 2021/2022 term have joined or authored an overruling opinion, down to and including 2020 appointee Justice Amy Coney Barrett.[191] With only a handful of overrulings in the nineteenth century (and none in the eighteenth), fifteen early justices never even voted in an overruling case.[192] But that means that the vast majority of justices—101 of 117—have signed onto an overruling.[193] The justices who have authored, joined in, concurred with, or agreed with the judgment in the most overruling decisions are Justices Brennan with 106, Douglas at 104, and Black at 93. All three men participated in about a third of all the overrulings in the Supreme Court's history. They were able to do this because all three of them enjoyed careers longer than thirty years and served in the decades after the Revolution of 1937 kicked off a sharp rise in overrulings. Among current members of the court, Justice Thomas, who also has been on the high court for over thirty years, holds the record for joining in the highest number of overrulings at twenty-eight. His meager total compared to earlier long-serving justices reflects the downward trend in overruling in the two most recent courts upon which he served.

The most frequent dissenters in overruling cases are Justice Stevens at thirty-seven, Justice Harlan II at thirty-five, and Justice/Chief Justice Rehnquist at thirty-two.[194] In this ranking, Harlan II is notable for being listed with these thirty-plus year veterans when he was on the court for only sixteen years; indeed, he has the same number of supports for overruling, giving him the smallest majority/dissent ratio (1-to-1) of any justice who has participated in at least ten overruling cases. Justice Douglas, at the other extreme, had a 104-to-12 (or roughly 9-to-1) ratio of majority-to-dissenting opinions in overruling cases. Unsurprisingly, aside from Harlan II, all other justices have more majority than dissenting votes in overruling cases (and usually a great many more), which would have to be the overall trend if overrulings were to take place with any frequency.

Almost a third of all overrulings are unanimous while just over a quarter are closely split at 5-4 (with a few at 4-3). Surprisingly, several unanimous overrulings overturn precedents that themselves were unanimous, demonstrating that a sea change in judicial attitude can occur with time.[195] Of the split decisions (5-4 and 4-3), there is a distinct trend. Very few overrulings before the Warren court were split decisions (though a single split decision among the Chase and Fuller courts' four overrulings each makes for a 25 percent split overruling rate). The Warren court had split decisions in just over a fifth of all its overrulings. The Burger court had less than a sixth of its overrulings that were split. The most recent courts are quite different. The Rehnquist court had split decisions in about 29 percent of its decisions. The Roberts court, shockingly, had split decisions in 92 percent of its overruling cases! Although there is an upward trend in split overrulings since the Burger court, the present court made an exponential jump. Table 3 contextualizes the anomaly of the Roberts court's overruling record.

Table 3. Percentage of Split Overruling Decisions by Court

Court	**Years**	**Overruling Decisions**	**Overruling Decisions Split**	**Percentage of Overruling Decisions Split**
John Jay	1789–1795	0	0	-
John Rutledge	1795–1795	0	0	-
Oliver Ellsworth	1796–1800	0	0	-
John Marshall	1801–1835	3	0	0%
Roger Taney	1836–1864	4	0	0%
Salmon Chase	1864–1874	4	1	25%
Morrison Waite	1874–1888	13	0	0%
Melville Fuller	1888–1910	4	1	25%
Edward D. White	1910–1921	7	0	0%
William Howard Taft	1921–1930	6	0	0%
Charles Evan Hughes	1930–1941	24	1	4%
Harlan Fiske Stone	1941–1946	17	3	18%
Frederick Vinson	1946–1953	15	2	13%
Earl Warren	1953–1969	54	12	22%
Warren Burger	1969–1986	62	11	18%
William Rehnquist	1986–2005	45	13	29%
John Roberts	2005–2022*	26	24	92%
All Courts	*1789–2022*	*258*	*68*	*26*

*Through the 2021/2022 term.

The greater percentage of split decisions in the most recent courts may reflect the politicization of the high court in recent years that has led to stark divisions.[196] But it also may reflect a changed attitude about stare decisis. Undoubtedly one of the most important factors in supporting an overruling is the number of justices who agree to ignore precedents. Unanimous overrulings suggests great consensus on problems with an overruled precedent. Split decisions, by contrast, suggest there is great disagreement over whether a precedent is erroneous, in conflict with other precedents, out-of-date, impractical in application, or otherwise problematic. A four-person dissent, aligned with existing precedent and the judges who set it, is a strong position to overcome; such overrulings often lead to questions about the legitimacy of the decision and its majority, as the Legal Tender Cases, a highly controversial 5-4 decision, illustrates.[197] (See chapter 3 for an analysis of this overruling.) The 2022 overruling of *Roe v. Wade,* discussed in chapter 7, is perhaps the most highly controversial split decision in the court's history.[198]

The earliest case to have been overruled is *Hylton v. United States,* decided in 1796 and reversed a century later over the issue of direct federal taxation.[199] The most recently decided case to be overruled (as of 2022) is *Sykes v. United States,* a 2011 case overruled in 2015 by *Johnson v. United States,* which found a federal criminal statute unconstitutionally vague.[200] Only the decades of the 1780s and the 2020s in the court's history has been spared from having its decisions overruled (through the 2021/2022 term), and only the Jay and Rutledge courts have escaped having their decisions overturned.[201] The courts who have had the greatest number of their decisions overruled are the Warren court (fifty-six), the Burger court (forty-three), and the Fuller court (thirty-eight). Many factors may explain these numbers; among the most important are: How many decisions did a particular court hand down? More decisions provide more targets for overruling. Longer-standing courts, such as the thirty-four-year-long Marshall court, have more time to develop a stable of cases for reconsideration. However, as I noted above respecting the number of overrulings, caseload influences the number of total decisions handed down for possible reconsideration. Second, how long have those cases been on the books; that is, how long have they been *available* for reconsideration? The age of precedents may embed them into law so that overturning them is difficult; on the other hand, the same age may make them anachronistic in light of changes in the country, including new needs and more enlightened ideas, such as those involving civil rights. Third, did a court regularly grapple with volatile areas of law where differences of opinion frequently arise, such as those involving the Commerce Clause, substantive due process, criminal procedure, affirmative action, and sex discrimination, among others?

Despite the age of the Marshall court and the length of the chief justice's rule, very few of its decisions were overruled—a mere nine. The Fuller court lasted about a third of the length of the Marshall court, yet thirty-eight of its decisions were overruled, particularly after courts gave more leeway to state and federal regulators to tax them and restrict their actions in the wake of the Great Depression. The Hughes court lasted about as long as the Fuller court, but its reversal of the laissez-faire positions of Fuller and others had fairly good staying power, with only twenty-nine of its decisions overruled.

The Warren court waded into some of the most contentious issues of the 1950s and 1960s, including racial desegregation and the protection of rights of criminal defendants, resulting in fifty-six of its decisions being overruled by the increasingly conservative courts that followed it. The Burger court waded into some of the same issues, reversing some and creating its own overruling targets, including *Roe v. Wade*, that legalized abortion nationwide, and *Bowers v. Hardwick*, that allowed states to criminalize homosexual sodomy.

The Rehnquist and Roberts courts have had less time for a reconsideration of their decisions, so their overruled numbers are small. However, the conservative Rehnquist court has given way to an even more conservative Roberts court, so reconsideration of conservative precedents might be expected to be less likely in any case.

When the total number of overruled decisions handed down by a court is assessed as a percentage of all its decisions, we find a different ranking. The Ellsworth court, with its forty-three cases at the end of the eighteenth century, had almost one-in-twenty of its decisions overruled by later courts. The Vinson court comes in second, with a little over one-in-twenty-five of its decisions overruled. The Warren court comes in third with about one-in-forty of its decisions overruled. The Burger court, which had the second highest raw number of cases overruled, falls into sixth place behind the Stone and Taft courts, with the Hughes court following it. The Roberts court, which has had very little time for its cases to be reconsidered, has the lowest percentage of cases overruled since the eighteenth century. The Rehnquist court, the second most recent, has the lowest percentage of its cases overruled since the highly productive Fuller court. Table 4 below summarizes these numbers, including the percentage of all cases decided in the Supreme court's history that have been overruled—1.2 percent.

One would expect courts dominated by particular ideological or jurisprudential philosophies to scrutinize and overrule decisions of courts with contrary philosophies. For example, the laissez-faire courts of the early twentieth century who gave a cramped reading to federal powers under the Commerce Clause would be reversed by courts, such as the later Hughes court, who saw the need for greater regulation and taxation during the Great Depression. The Warren court's decisions supporting minority rights and the rights of criminals would be tempered by more conservative courts that followed.

Table 4. Overruled Cases and Their Percentage of All Decisions

Court	Years	Overruled Decisions	Total Decisions	Percentage of Decisions Overruled
John Jay	1789–1795	0	15	0%
John Rutledge	1795–1795	0	5	0%
Oliver Ellsworth	1796–1800	2	43	4.7%
John Marshall	1801–1835	9	1,280	0.7%
Roger Taney	1836–1864	21	1,670	1.2%
Salmon Chase	1864–1874	15	1,370	1.1%
Morrison Waite	1874–1888	15	3,650	0.4%
Melville Fuller	1888–1910	38	4,986	0.7%
Edward D. White	1910–1921	30	2,548	1.1%
William Howard Taft	1921–1930	27	1,598	1.7%
Charles Evan Hughes	1930–1941	29	1,915	1.5%
Harlan Fiske Stone	1941–1946	17	781	2.1%
Frederick Vinson	1946–1953	33	812	4.1%
Earl Warren	1953–1969	56	2,205	2.5%
Warren Burger	1969–1986	43	2,808	1.5%
William Rehnquist	1986–2005	21	2,044	1.0%
John Roberts	2005–2022*	2	1,369†	0.1%
All Courts	*1789–2022*	*358*	*29,099*	*1.2%*

*Through the 2021/2022 term.

†This figure is an estimate of total decisions through the end of the 2021/2022 term. The Spaeth database has a list of all decisions through the end of the 2019/2020 term. Chief John Roberts reported in the *2021 Year-End Report on the Federal Judiciary*(Washington, DC: Government Printing Office, 2021) that his Court heard seventy-two cases during 2020/2021 term (7). I assumed the same number for 2021/2022 to get the total number of cases.

The greatest hostility between courts as evidenced by overrulings is the Burger court's overruling of nineteen decisions of its immediate predecessor, the Warren court. The Rehnquist court also reversed fourteen Warren court decisions. The Warren court itself had overruled a dozen cases handed down by its immediate predecessor, the Vinson court. It also overruled ten cases by the Hughes court, although all but two were from that court's pre–Revolution of 1937 decisions. The Rehnquist court overruled thirteen of the Burger court's decisions.

Among the most notable overrulings are those where a court overrules its own earlier decisions, since those overrulings will typically involve decisions that some justices still sitting on the court wrote. Overruling justices will have to face their colleagues and say, effectively, "You got this wrong." These overrulings may come because of a change of heart by some justices, as in the Flag Salute Cases (see chapter 6), where the overruling may include a mea culpa. Others may involve cases relying on state law that are reversed after the highest state court reverses its position on that law, as in the Marshall court's decision in *Green v. Lessee of Neal*.[202] Most controversially, they may be a result of a change of personnel that swings the court against its earlier positions, as happened seven years into the Hughes court after the Revolution of 1937, when opponents of New Deal legislation began retiring and were almost all replaced by President Roosevelt (see chapter 5).

The Warren court holds the record for reversing the greatest number of its own cases at twelve. All of these overruled cases were decided between 1955 and 1962. With the exception of two rehearing cases, all the other overruling cases were decided between 1962 and 1968. The two rehearing cases were odd overrulings. *Reid v. Covert* and its companion case concerned two military spouses who murdered their husbands on overseas military bases, were tried by military courts that dismissed their insanity pleas, and were sentenced to life in prison.[203] Following a 5-4 decision upholding the conviction in 1956, two replacements on the bench contributed to a change to a 6-2 verdict in favor of the women during a rehearing. Justice Brennan replaced Justice Minton and reversed the position his predecessor took. Justice Whittaker replaced Justice Reed, replacing the latter's vote to uphold the conviction with no vote by the by the new justice. Those switches would have freed the women with a 5-3 decision, but Justice Harlan II changed his previous vote to make it a solid 6-2 decision.

Justice Harlan II had silently joined the majority after the first hearing. In the rehearing he offered an explicit mea culpa, noting: "Since I am the only one among today's majority who joined in the court's opinions of June 11, 1956, which sustained the court-martial jurisdiction in these cases, 351 U.S. 470, 351 U.S. 487, I think it appropriate to state the reasons which led to my voting, first, to rehear these cases, 352 U.S. 901, and, now, to strike down that jurisdiction" (65). Those "reasons" emphasized first and foremost his lack of time to think through the issues after the first hearing: "The petitions for rehearing which were filed last summer afforded an opportunity for a greater degree of reflection upon the difficult issues involved in these cases than, at least for me, was possible in the short interval between the argument and decision of the cases in the closing days of last Term. As a result I became satisfied that this court-martial jurisdiction could, in any event, not be sustained upon the reasoning of our prior opinion" (65). In a footnote, he specifies that the court had just over a month to render a decision in June following oral argument in May (65n2). His new position stood "on the narrow ground that, where the offense is capital, Article 2(11) cannot constitutionally be applied to the trial of civilian dependents of members of the armed forces overseas in times of peace" (65).

The second overruling on rehearing, in *Ladner v. United States,* was a rare reversal of a tied decision—a 4-4 nonverdict that allowed the lower court's ruling to stand.[204] The case, involving whether the criminal conviction of Ladner for assaulting two federal officers with a deadly weapon could be counted as two separate crimes under a federal statute, ended as an 8-1 decision. However, since the previous vote was only recorded as tied, without indicating who took which side, it is impossible to see who switched to join the 8-1 decision.[205] Justice Brennan's majority opinion does not contain any clues. However, Justice Clark obviously did not switch his vote. In his dissent he complains bitterly about the majority's decision that one shotgun blast harming two officers should be counted as one assault, insisting that this means that "assaults on the lives of federal officers come just 'as cheap by the dozen'" (179–80).

One change in personnel that supported several overrulings of the Warren court's earlier decisions was the retirement of Justice Frankfurter, who practiced judicial restraint and often deferred to elected officials. For example, he was a staunch holdout when three of his colleagues switched their votes to favor the Jehovah's Witnesses in the Flag Salute Cases, following widespread violence against them following the court's original ruling (see chapter 6).[206] President Kennedy appointed Arthur Goldberg to the "Jewish seat" on the court in 1962, replacing Frankfurter.[207] He would have a short tenure—President Johnson maneuvered him off the bench to make way for Abe Fortas in 1965.[208] Both men were advocates for using the judiciary to protect the rights of minorities and those accused of crimes, so it is unsurprising that they reached conclusions different from Frankfurter.[209]

Justice Goldberg authored a majority opinion in *Escobedo v Illinois* to ensure those interrogated by the police had access to legal counsel, reversing *Crooker v. Illinois* and *Cicenia v. Lagay,* both of which Frankfurter had supported.[210] Two years later, with the support of Justice Fortas, *Miranda v. Arizona* expanded *Escobedo's* support for suspects and the right to counsel on a more substantial foundation in the right against self-incrimination. As if *Escobedo*'s overruling was not clear enough, Chief Justice Warren stated: "In accordance with our holdings today and in *Escobedo v. Illinois*, 378 U.S. 478, 492, *Crooker v. California*, 357 U.S. 433 (1958) and *Cicenia v. Lagay*, 357 U.S. 504 (1958), are not to be followed."[211]

Justice Fortas also provided a switch from Frankfurter's position in a 5-4 decision in *Brown v. United States* on federal rules of criminal procedures through a 5-4 overruling in *Harris v. United States*.[212] That case concerned the right against self-incrimination, as did *Spevack v. Klein* two years later, where Justice Fortas again reversed a position taken by Frankfurter in *Cohen v. Hurley* six years earlier.[213]

Other changes in personnel, as well as some changes of mind, supported the Warren court overruling its earlier configurations in several cases. In *Camara v. Municipal Court*, Justices Fortas and White both reversed the positions of their predecessors in *Frank v. Maryland*, to change a 5-4 precedent into a 6-3 overruling in a Fourth Amendment case.[214] Justices Fortas and White also voted differently from their predecessors in *Afroyim v. Rusk*, where an American was stripped of his citizenship after voting in an election in Israel.[215] However, these switches did not overrule *Perez v. Brownell*, because Justice Whittaker, White's predecessor, had dissented from *Perez* and White dissented in *Afroyim*. It would take Justice Brennan reversing his earlier position to overrule this 5-4 precedent with a 5-4 vote. Although Justice Brennan did not explain his change of heart in *Afroyim*, Justice Black's majority opinion quietly mentioned in a footnote that "in his concurring opinion in [*Kennedy v.*] *Mendoza-Martinez*, MR. JUSTICE BRENNAN expressed 'felt doubts of the correctness of *Perez*.'"[216]

In *Carafas v. LaVallee*, Justices Fortas and White were joined by Justice Thurgood Marshall in changing their predecessors' positions in *Parker v. Ellis*.[217] However, Justices Harlan II and Stewart had a change of heart in this federal habeas corpus case, turning a 5-4 precedent into an 8-0 overruling. Justice Fortas's unanimous opinion does not explain the change of heart of the two justices but cites the concerns of the chief justice's dissent in the overruled case, explaining how "the doctrine of *Parker* simply aggravates the hardships that may result from the 'intolerable delay[s] in affording justice.'"[218]

A huge shift in personnel and thinking moved the 1955 decision in *Westinghouse Employees v. Westinghouse Corporation* from a 6-2 holding to an 8-1 overruling in *Smith v. Evening News Association* seven years later.[219] The cases raised the question of whether certain suits charging a violation of a collective bargaining contract might be brought to other tribunals besides the National Labor Relations Board. *Westinghouse* said no and denied such an appeal to a federal court; *Smith* said yes and supported such an appeal to a state court.

Between the two cases, Justices Reed, Frankfurter, Burton, and Minton had left the court and Justices Brennan, Stewart, White, and Goldberg had joined it. All four changed the votes of their predecessors.[220] Justice Harlan II had sat out *Westinghouse* but joined the overruling majority in *Smith*. Justice White's majority opinion minimized the impact of personnel changes by insisting that three of the *Westinghouse* majority had had second thoughts:

> Three of the Justices in that case were driven to their conclusion because, in their view, § 301 was procedural only, not substantive, and therefore grave constitutional questions would be raised if § 301 was held to extend to the controversy there involved. However, the same three Justices observed that if, contrary to their belief, "Congress has itself defined the law or authorized the federal courts to fashion the judicial rules governing this question, it would be self-defeating to limit the scope of the power of the federal courts to less than is necessary to accomplish this congressional aim." [*Westinghouse*] at 348 U.S. 442. *Textile Workers v. Lincoln Mills*, 353 U.S. 448, of course, has long since settled that § 301 has substantive content, and that Congress has directed the courts to formulate and apply federal law to suits for violation of collective bargaining contracts. There is no constitutional difficulty, and § 301 is not to be given a narrow reading. Id. at 348 U.S. 456, 348 U.S. 457. (199)

Justice Black had joined a dissent in *Smith* and also dissented in *Westinghouse*, appearing to switch sides. However, his concerns in *Smith* were a bit different from those in *Westinghouse*.[221] Justice Black joined Justice Douglas's dissent in *Westinghouse* to complain about the majority's refusal to give the union standing to sue. In *Smith* he stood alone against his eight brethren, insisting that the state court had no jurisdiction and accusing the majority of conducting a "major statutory surgical operation" on the federal statute (§ 301) to support jurisdiction.[222]

Similar shifts in personnel and thinking were involved in *Swift & Co. v. Wickham*'s 1965 overruling of the three-year-old case of *Kesler v. Department of Public Safety*.[223] The controversy in *Swift* arose from a New York statute that required those selling stuffed poultry in the state to list the weights of the bird with and without stuffing, while a federal statute required only listing the stuffed weight. The company tried to comply with a new label, but the federal government denied them permission to make such a change (113). Before stepping in to resolve this issue, the district court was required to determine whether the issue should be addressed by a three-judge panel under a statute developed to streamline such decisions, 28 U.S.C. § 2281. The rules under that statute had been elaborated in the *Kesler* decision, but they were difficult to discern in some cases. As Justice Harlan II's majority opinion in *Swift* noted:

> [In *Kesler*] we decided that, in suits to restrain the enforcement of a state statute allegedly in conflict with or in a field preempted by a federal statute, § 2281 comes into play only when the Supremacy Clause of the Federal Constitution is immediately drawn in question, but not when issues of federal or state statutory construction must first be decided, even though the Supremacy Clause may ultimately be implicated. Finding itself unable to say with assurance whether its resolution of the merits of this case involved less statutory construction than had taken place in *Kesler,* the District Court was left with the puzzling question how much more statutory construction than occurred in *Kesler* is necessary to deprive three judges of their jurisdiction. (115)

Harlan II noted the inadequacy of *Kesler*'s directive and offered a mea culpa on behalf of the court, admitting "that candor compels us to say that we find the application of the *Kesler* rule as elusive as did the District Court, and that we would fall short in our responsibilities if we did not accept this opportunity to take a fresh look at the problem" (116).

Kesler had been a 5-3 decision, but lots of movement of people and minds switched that to a 6-3 vote the other way in *Swift*. Justice Clark and Chief Justice Warren were the only two who voted in favor of *Kesler* and against *Swift*. Justice Douglas provided a third negative vote for *Swift,* but he also had dissented in *Kesler*. Every other justice changed their or their predecessors' positions. Justice Fortas reversed Frankfurter's vote and Justice White voted in the *Swift* majority while his predecessor did not participate in the decision.[224] Justice Stewart concurred in *Kesler* and also supported *Swift*. Justices Brennan and Harlan II supported the majorities in both cases. And Justice Black dissented in both cases.

Rather than a series of explanations from each justice, Justice Harlan II explained for the majority the reasons for such a huge shift in opinion. He acknowledged that the court was "overruling a six-to-two decision of . . . recent vintage, which was concurred in by two members of the majority in the present case" (116). He even claimed the *Kesler* majority opinion "was written by an acknowledged expert in the field of federal jurisdiction [i.e., Justice Frankfurter]," insisting that this overruling "demands full explication of our reasons" (116).

Harlan II notes that the current rule had confused lower courts and drawn the contempt of legal commentators (124). He offers a close reading of the statute (126–27), a consideration of its purposes (127–28), and a review of the administrative problems associated with using *Kesler*'s more expansive reading of the statute (128), to support what he deems a "return" to a pre-*Kesler* understanding of the statute, "the *Buder-Branford-Case* rule" he drew out of his reading of three precedents. That rule held "that three-judge courts are not required in Supremacy Clause cases involving only federal-state statutory conflicts" (128).

Overall, Justice Harlan II pulled out all the stops to justify the flip-flopping of he and his colleagues, piling reasons on top of reasons: *Kesler* was a departure from a consistent, historical interpretation of § 2281 that fits the language and purposes of the statute, provides clear guidance, makes the courts run more efficiently, and will satisfy the states.

A final example has the Warren court reversing itself on a Sixth Amendment decision—a case where the chief justice finally changed his mind. Chief Justice Warren voted to change his position on a precedent set by his court only once, despite his participation in all overruling and overruled cases during his tenure. Justices Black and Douglas served during the entire court also, but they both had dissented in an overruling case and the case it overruled.[225] Of those who served a substantial part of the Warren court—Justices Clark, Harlan II, Brennan, and Stewart—only Clark never changed his position on one of the court's precedents.

The case in which Warren switched sides by voting to overrule a precedent he supported involved the defendant's Sixth Amendment right to confront witnesses against him or her, providing greater protection to the defendant. Statements made out of court against a defendant are violations of the Sixth Amendment because there is no opportunity for cross-examination. *Delli Paoli v. United States* had allowed a statement from a codefendant read in court to avoid the problem of confronting witnesses because the judge had instructed the jury to ignore portions of that statement inculpating the defendant. A decade later in *Bruton v. United States*, the court rejected that remedy for such evidence, requiring that it never be heard by a jury on the assumption that they would not be able to ignore it as instructed.[226]

Chief Justice Warren's reasons for shifting his position are unclear, since he simply joined the majorities in each case. Justice Brennan's overruling majority opinion had to address the concerns expressed in Justice White's dissenting opinion about the court's majority making joint trials rarer, foregoing several benefits: "Unquestionably, joint trials are more economical and minimize the burden on witnesses, prosecutors, and courts. They also avoid delays in bringing those accused of crime to trial. This much the Court concedes. It is also worth saying that separate trials are apt to have varying consequences for legally indistinguishable defendants" (143). Justice Brennan cites recent cases to support his claim that "since *Delli Paoli* was decided, this Court has effectively repudiated its basic premise." (126). He notes efforts to ensure that evidence that does not permit confrontation is excluded, notably an amendment to a procedural rule concerning requests to provide separate trials for codefendants that allows a court to "order the attorney for the government to deliver to the court for inspection in camera any statements or confessions made by the defendants which the government intends to introduce in evidence at the trial"

(132). He quotes cases where opinion writers evince skepticism that a jury can ignore such evidence, despite instructions to do so from a judge, such as Justice Jackson's claim that it is a "naive assumption that prejudicial effects can be overcome by instructions to the jury . . . [which] all practicing lawyers know to be unmitigated fiction."[227]

Justice Brennan's conclusion apparently was sufficient for the chief justice to finally reverse himself: "Here, the introduction of Evans' confession posed a substantial threat to petitioner's right to confront the witnesses against him, and this is a hazard we cannot ignore. Despite the concededly clear instructions to the jury to disregard Evans' inadmissible hearsay evidence inculpating petitioner, in the context of a joint trial we cannot accept limiting instructions as an adequate substitute for petitioner's constitutional right of cross-examination" (137).

The Burger court reversed itself ten times. The cases offer a broad assortment of reasons for overruling; less than half of the reversals were caused by changes in personnel. For example, when faced with the question of whether a federal grant of land to a state along the bank of a river or stream ("riparian land") is to be interpreted under federal or state law, three members of the court changed their minds on the issue between 1973 and 1977, contributing to the reversal of a 7-1 decision by 6-3 decision.[228] Perhaps Justice Rehnquist's majority opinion in the overruling case convinced Chief Justice Burger and Justices Powell and Blackmun to change their positions and join him, but there was no explanation about why these particular members of the court changed their minds. Instead, Justice Rehnquist, who was on the court but had not participated in the 1973 opinion, spoke for his silent colleagues, insisting in the corporate voice: "Our error, as we now see it, was to view the equal-footing doctrine enunciated in *Pollard's Lessee v. Hagan* as a basis upon which federal common law could supersede state law in the determination of land titles. Precisely the contrary is true; in *Pollard's Lessee* itself, the equal-footing doctrine resulted in the State's acquisition of title notwithstanding the efforts of the federal government to dispose of the lands in question in another way" (371). In concluding, he insisted that the court's "full reconsideration of our decision in *Bonelli*" led them to "conclude that it was wrong in treating the equal-footing doctrine as a source of federal common law after that doctrine had vested title to the riverbed in the State of Arizona as of the time of its admission to the Union" (381).

A year later in *United States v. Scott,* Justice Rehnquist again offered a mea culpa for the court in a case involving double jeopardy, except this time he spoke for himself and four other members of the court who had supported his majority opinion in the three-year-old precedent of *United States v. Jenkins.*[229] He insisted that the court had learned a lot about this constitutional issue in three years because "our vastly increased exposure to the various facets of the Double Jeopardy Clause has now convinced us that *Jenkins* was wrongly decided. It placed an unwarrantedly great emphasis on the defendant's right to have his guilt decided by the first jury empaneled to try him so as to include those cases where the defendant himself seeks to terminate the trial before verdict on grounds unrelated to factual guilt or innocence. We have therefore decided to overrule *Jenkins,* and thus to reverse the judgment of the Court of Appeals in this case" (86–87). Rehnquist reviews prior understandings of the constitutional requirements of avoiding double jeopardy, which were available to him when *Jenkins* was decided. He suggests that the *Jenkins* decision was not a gross misunderstanding but a misplacement of emphasis whereby, insisting, "we pressed too far in *Jenkins* the concept of the 'defendant's valued right to have his trial completed by a particular tribunal'" (100). Justice Rehnquist's reversal of his own majority opinion reflects his attitude in another case where he dissented and asserted that he ought to be able to "clean up a mess that I helped make" in creating an erroneous precedent.[230]

Justice Rehnquist would have several messes to clean up given his overruling record. In yet another case in which he wrote the majority opinion, *Parratt v. Taylor,* Rehnquist would follow up with a majority opinion in *Daniels v. Williams* reversing himself.[231] This time, however, he brought five other justices and the chief justice to switch sides as well! Only Justice Marshall stood by his former position, and Justice O'Connor was not on the court for the precedent decision.

The issue in *Parratt* was whether a prisoner deprived of his property could claim a Fourteenth Amendment "deprivation" without due process of law. *Parratt* ruled that "the alleged loss, even though negligently caused, amounted to a deprivation" (536–37). A prisoner in the *Daniels* case, who was injured when a correctional deputy left a pillow on the stairs that caused him to trip, sought to make a similar "deprivation" claim. Rehnquist relied on his former colleague, Justice Stewart, who insisted in a concurrence in the result in *Parratt* that "deprivation" required a state of mind not required by mere negligence (547–48). While Rehnquist and his colleagues had been unconvinced by this concern in the precedent case, he admitted: "Upon reflection, we agree, and overrule *Parratt* to the extent that it states that mere lack of due care by a state official may 'deprive' an individual of life, liberty, or property under the Fourteenth Amendment" (330–31).

Although Justice Rehnquist could worry about "the inconsistent approaches [following *Parratt*] taken by lower courts in determining when tortious conduct by state officials rises to the level of a constitutional tort" (329), his second reversal of an opinion he himself wrote makes him a candidate for the most wishy-washy justice in terms of overruling precedents.

Another Burger court decision reversed by the same court was occasioned by a change of heart, which turned a 5-4 precedent into a 5-4 overruling.[232] Justice Blackmun justified reversing a decision he had concurred in involving federal regulation of state government employees under the FLSA. *National League of Cities v. Usery* had forbidden such federal regulation in areas involving "traditional government functions" of the state.[233] Almost a decade after *Usery*, Blackmun noted that its rule had proven vague and unworkable, quoting a frustrated district court complaining: "Despite the abundance of adjectives [in *Usery* about what counts as 'traditional government functions'], identifying which particular state functions are immune remains difficult."[234]

In the volatile area of Fourth Amendment law, the Burger court reversed a 6-3 decision in *Robbins v. California* with another 6-3 decision in *United States v. Ross* in only a year.[235] This was afforded by the replacement of the author of the overruled opinion, Justice Stewart, with Justice O'Connor, who joined the overruling case, as well as a quick reconsideration by Chief Justice Burger and Justice Powell, whose tepid support for the earlier ruling evaporated. The chief justice did not explain his change of heart but simply joined Justice Stevens's majority opinion in *Ross*. Justice Powell felt it important to explain his new position, adding a nod to the silent chief justice: "It became evident last Term . . . from the five opinions written in *Robbins*—in none of which THE CHIEF JUSTICE joined—that it is essential to have a Court opinion in automobile search cases that provides 'specific guidance to police and courts in this recurring situation.' *Robbins v. California*, supra, at 453 U.S. 435 (POWELL, J., concurring in judgment). The Court's opinion today, written by JUSTICE STEVENS and now joined by THE CHIEF JUSTICE and four other Justices, will afford this needed guidance" (826). Justice Powell's quotation of himself is something of an exoneration, emphasizing his consistent support for clear rules.

The Rehnquist court overruled itself eight times. All its overruled decisions preceded the 1990 replacement of the progressive Justice Brennan with the more moderate Justice Souter by President George H. W. Bush.[236] The change was immediate with 1991's *Payne v. Tennessee* reversing *South Carolina v. Gathers*, decided only two years earlier, and the 1987 case it followed, *Booth v. Maryland*.[237] Justice Thurgood Marshall was livid:

> Power, not reason, is the new currency of this Court's decisionmaking. Four Terms ago, a five-Justice majority of this Court held that "victim impact" evidence of the type at issue in this case could not constitutionally be introduced during the penalty phase of a capital trial. *Booth v. Maryland*, 482 U.S. 496 (1987). By another 5-4 vote, a majority of this Court rebuffed an attack upon this ruling just two Terms ago. *South Carolina v. Gathers*, 490 U.S. 805 (1989). Nevertheless, having expressly invited respondent to

> renew the attack, 498 U.S. 1076 (1991), today's majority overrules *Booth* and *Gathers* and credits the dissenting views expressed in those cases. Neither the law nor the facts supporting *Booth* and *Gathers* underwent any change in the last four years. *Only the personnel of this Court did.* (844; emphasis added)

Justice Marshall warned: "The implications of this radical new exception to the doctrine of *stare decisis* are staggering. The majority today sends a clear signal that scores of established constitutional liberties are now ripe for reconsideration, thereby inviting the very type of open defiance of our precedents that the majority rewards in this case" (845).

Justice Marshall was prescient. In the next twenty years the court overruled itself in two cases involving double jeopardy, three on the death penalty, one on the sovereign immunity of states, and one on affirmative action.[238] Six of their self-overrulings were supported by the conservative turn in the court's personnel. However, Justice Kennedy, who would be an occasional swing vote, joined progressives in finding the capital punishment of minors to be unconstitutional and, in an odd Sixth Amendment case involving the procedural requirements for capital punishment, a majority of the conservative justices joined Justice Ginsburg's opinion for the court in *Ring v. Arizona*.[239]

The other courts trail behind these three frequent self-overrulers. The Hughes court overruled five of its decisions in four overrulings—all the former coming in 1937 or earlier, all the latter in 1938 or later (that is, post–Revolution of 1937); thus, changes of personnel were central.[240] The Waite court replaced five of its members from 1877 to 1882 through appointments by three presidents (two Republicans and a Democrat).[241] That sea change in personnel shaped its four post-1876 overrulings of four pre-1877 decisions.[242] The Vinson court reversed three of its own decisions: two cases from 1950 overruling two cases from 1948, and a rehearing case whose original decision was heard and reversed in 1947.[243] The Marshall and Taney courts overruled themselves in two cases each, though those cases overruled three and four precedents, respectively.[244] The White and Stone courts both used two overruling cases to overrule only one of their precedents.[245] The Chase and Taft courts reversed themselves once, the former in the infamous Legal Tender Cases, and the latter in a rehearing case.[246] Although the Ellsworth and Fuller courts overruled some cases, they never overruled themselves.

The authors of overruled decisions span the history of the court. Justice William Paterson, appointed to the high court in 1793, has the distinction of authoring the earliest decision to be overruled by a subsequent court. *Hylton v. United States*, handed down in 1796, was overruled in 1895 by *Pollock v. Farmers' Loan & Trust Co.*[247] However, Paterson was vindicated almost two centuries after he penned his decision when *Pollock* was overruled in 1988 by *South Carolina v. Baker*.[248] Justice Kennedy authored the most recent decision to be overruled (as of 2022), *Sykes v. United States*, decided in 2011 and overruled in 2015.[249]

Chief Justice Marshall authored seven decisions that were subsequently overruled, making him the most overruled majority opinion writer of the nineteenth century.[250] Justice Sutherland, one of the "Four Horsemen" who resisted New Deal legislation, holds the record as the most overruled opinion writer in the court's history at fourteen, even though he served only sixteen years to reach that record. Justice Frankfurter, who served on four different courts (Hughes, Stone, Vinson, and Warren), authored eleven decisions that were subsequently overruled. Justice Stewart, who overlapped with Frankfurter on the Warren court and completed his tenure on the Burger court, comes in third with ten overruled decisions. Justices Breyer and Alito were the only justices on the 2021/2022 court to have authored overruled decisions, with one apiece.

Justice Brandeis—who participated in deciding sixty-three cases that were subsequently overruled, agreeing thirty-six times and dissenting twenty-seven times—has the distinction of never authoring a majority opinion in an overruled case. No other member of the court comes close to this record. And he did not achieve this record by avoiding writing for the court. He was one of the most productive justices in history with 454 majority opinions in twenty-three years.[251] Perhaps that speaks to the care and authority with which he wrote his decisions, though most great jurists have had their opinions rejected. Justice David Davis, who joined the court during the Civil War, avoided leading any of the twenty-one overruled decisions he joined. Justice Whittaker, who served five years on the Warren court, participated in nineteen overruled cases without authoring one. Justice George Shiras Jr., who spent ten years on the Fuller court, managed to participate in sixteen overruled cases without authoring one. Many other members of the high court avoided writing a majority opinion in an overruled case, but none with so many opportunities to do so.

Justice Brandeis did side with the majority in thirty-four cases that were eventually overturned, though he dissented in twenty-three others. Justice Van Devanter, who served on the White, Taft, and Hughes courts, holds the record for joining the most decisions that were later overruled, with sixty-nine; he dissented from only three overruled cases. His participation as one of the Four Horsemen led to this record after Hughes and later courts renounced their hardline, probusiness, antiregulation positions. Justice Brennan, who served on the Warren, Burger, and Rehnquist courts over his long career, agreed with the majority sixty-five times versus twenty-eight dissents in overruled cases. Justice Holmes agreed with the majority in fifty-eight overruled cases and took the other side in twenty-two.

Justice William O. Douglas served on five courts—Hughes, Stone, Vinson, Warren, and Burger—over a thirty-six-year career and participated in more overruled decisions than anyone in the high court's history. In 111 cases that were subsequently overruled, he split his support fairly evenly, joining the majority fifty-eight times and joining the dissent fifty-three times. The only justice to actually dissent more than he agreed with decisions that were later overturned is Justice Hugo Black, the first justice appointed by Franklin D. Roosevelt, immediately following the Hughes court's Revolution of 1937. Black continued onto the Stone, Vinson, Warren, and Burger courts in his thirty-four year career on the high court, where he agreed with the majority forty-two times, while disagreeing with them fifty-two times, in cases later overruled. Undoubtedly, the long tenure of these record-setting justices is a key factor in their high level of participation in both overruled and overruling decisions (on the latter see the numbers above). Serving on the Warren and Burger courts, who set records both for overruling and for being overruled, contributed to these justices' records as well.

The average age of a case when it is overruled is thirty-two years.[252] The oldest case when overruled is *Minturn v. Maynard*, which was 136 years old when it was rejected by the Rehnquist court in *Exxon Corp. v. Central Gulf Lines, Inc.* on an issue of admiralty jurisdiction.[253] Many overrulings have taken a year or so, though these are typically rehearings that are more significant in reversing the court's position regarding particular litigants than in reversing law established by those short-lived precedents.[254] There are exceptions. Already mentioned above is the Legal Tender Cases, overturned in a little over a year. Four years after that landmark case, Justice Miller, surprisingly, authored a unanimous decision reversing a unanimous decision he authored two years before. *Union Pacific Railway v. McShane* involved a question about when a state could tax lands in the process of being transferred from the United States government to a corporation.[255] Miller reconsidered some tedious legal issues about whether title had passed with a patent, with a congressionally supported mortgage of the land, or with the completion of a required survey before determining that Nebraska could not tax the lands that had not been surveyed or patented (i.e., legally granted by the government to the railroad). Ultimately, he justified the overruling by noting: "We are now of opinion, on a fuller argument and more mature consideration, that the proposition [of the prior case] is not tenable" (461).

A 1982 decision, *United States v. Ross*, overruled a splintered plurality decision from the previous year in *Robbins v. California*.[256] At issue was whether police who have probable cause to search an automobile may search containers within that vehicle. Justice Stevens, who had dissented in the previous decision, now commanded a majority with the replacement of Justice Stewart by Justice O'Connor and supported the conviction of Ross upon the evidence (drugs and cash) seized from containers in his trunk. He dismissed stare decisis concerns, insisting that "the doctrine of *stare decisis* does not preclude this action. . . . Although we reject the precise holding in *Robbins*, there was no Court opinion supporting a single rationale for its judgment, and the reasoning we adopt today was not presented by the parties in that case. Moreover, it is clear that no legitimate reliance interest can be frustrated by our decision today. Of greatest importance, we are convinced that the rule we apply in this case is faithful to the interpretation of the Fourth Amendment that the Court has followed with substantial consistency throughout our history" (824).

The *Ross* decision reflects the court's more lenient attitude toward overruling constitutional cases, noted earlier, and explains why almost half of all the high court's overrulings are constitutional cases, though constitutional cases may not be a majority of the cases heard by the court.[257] A little less than a third of overruling cases concern the interpretation of federal statutes. Thirty do not identify a particular legal provision at issue. A dozen and a half concern state statutes. The remainder concern court rules or other issues.

The high court's overrulings have primarily grappled with four contentious areas of the law. The most prevalent are rulings involving economic activity (seventy-five cases), especially state and local taxation and regulation, patents and copyrights, and antitrust. Criminal procedure has led to seventy-three flip-flops by the court, especially on issues of search and seizure, double jeopardy, and habeas corpus. Civil rights have been involved in forty-one cases, including several involving racial desegregation, voting rights, sex discrimination, and abortion. Also prevalent in this general "rights" area are overrulings dealing with the First Amendment and due-process cases, with about a dozen cases each. Judicial power (thirty-four cases) and issues of federalism (twenty-one cases) constitute a final area involving changes of opinion about government power, with the largest number of cases involving national supremacy, federal taxation, and federal preemption of state court jurisdiction.

Of constitutional overruling cases, about one-fifth involve Article I issues, especially those implicating the Commerce Clause. An early example is an 1886 case holding that an Illinois statute regulating charges by a railway company engaged in interstate commerce violated the Commerce Clause of Article I of the Constitution, overturning a nine-year-old case.[258] A 1941 case overruled a century-old precedent and voided a California statute aimed at keeping "Okies" fleeing the Dust Bowl from moving to the state.[259] A 1996 case found a unanimous court overturning a 1912 precedent on whether states could levy an "intangibles tax" that taxed individuals who owned corporate stock more if the corporations were out of state, since that tax discriminated against interstate commerce.[260]

Another fifth of constitutional overruling cases concern Fourteenth Amendment issues, almost exactly halved between due process or equal protection issues. Those involving due process include a 1917 case supporting a state's fixing of rates for commuters on railroads, a 1949 case supporting city and state ad valorem taxes on ships operating in intrastate commerce, and a 1964 case overturning a murder conviction based on a confession taken while the defendant was suffering a considerable loss of blood and the effects of pain killers in the hospital; that confession was presented to the jury to determine whether it was "voluntary" and, if not, to disregard it in deciding the case.[261] A 1930 equal protection case rejected Minnesota's attempt to tax bonds it issued when a New York resident passed them to his heirs.[262] Others include a 1966 case invalidating a Virginia poll tax, a 1976 case invalidating an Oklahoma statute allowing females to buy beer at eighteen while requiring males to be twenty-one, and, in 2015, the overturning of state statutes discriminating against gay and lesbian couples seeking marriage licenses.[263]

The First, Fourth, Fifth, and Sixth Amendments are involved in a dozen or more overruling cases each, including free speech cases involving Jehovah's Witnesses, a Ku Klux Klan spokesman, liquor advertisers, and political campaign contributors; Fourth Amendment cases involving admissible evidence, searches and seizures, and warrant requirements; several double jeopardy and self-incrimination cases under the Fifth Amendment; and Sixth Amendment cases involving the right to a jury, the right to counsel, and the right to confront witnesses.[264] The Eighth and Eleventh Amendments are involved in a handful of cases, such as the execution of minors and the mentally disabled, and sovereign immunity.[265] The Second, Tenth, and Fifteenth Amendments have one overruling case apiece.[266]

Statutory overrulings most commonly deal with admiralty law, antitrust, habeas corpus, labor, patent law, revenue, and judicial processes.[267] Because statutory overrulings often deal with particular and less well-known legal issues, I will illustrate them with a couple of extended examples. The first involves only the second overruling in the history of the Supreme Court. The case turned on an interpretation of the Judiciary Act of 1789. In *Gordon v. Ogden* (1830) Chief Justice John Marshall considered whether the high court had jurisdiction to hear a dispute over a tort claim. The original case sought over $2,000 in damages, but the plaintiff won less than $2,000 in the lower court. The Judiciary Act limited the Supreme Court's jurisdiction to disputes of $2,000 or more and the question was whether that limit was based on what was sought or what was awarded. Marshall rejected the appeal for want of jurisdiction, though he had to overturn a precedent to do so: "The counsel for the plaintiff in error relies on the case of Wilson vs. Daniel, 3 Dall. 401. That case, it is admitted, is in point. It turns on the principle that the jurisdiction of this court depends on the sum which was in dispute before the judgment was rendered in the circuit court. Although that case was decided by a divided court, and although we think, that upon the true construction of the twenty-second section of the judicial act, the jurisdiction of the court depends upon the sum in dispute between the parties as the case stands upon the writ of error, we should be much inclined to adhere to the decision in Wilson vs. Daniel, had not a contrary practice since prevailed."[268] Marshall reviews a couple of cases after *Wilson* that enforced the judgment amount as the crucial one, and, after reviewing the second, admits: "Since this decision we do not recollect that the question has been ever made" (35). In addition to the reprieve provided by his reliance on memory rather than on reporters, Marshall appeals to the problem of having to choose between two precedents and diminishes the strength of the precedent by emphasizing the divided nature of the prior ruling.[269]

A 1984 case involved an interpretation of the Sherman Antitrust Act. In *Copperweld Corp. v. Independence Tube,* the court reconsidered its earlier determination that under §1 of that act a corporation could be guilty of conspiring with its wholly owned subsidiary.[270] The court suggests that prior cases were inadequate because "in no case has the Court considered the merits of the intra-enterprise conspiracy doctrine in depth" (760). It suggests "the problem began with *United States v. Yellow Cab Co.,*" a 1947 case that held that "an unreasonable restraint [of trade] '*may result as readily from a conspiracy among those who are affiliated or integrated under common ownership as from a conspiracy among those who are otherwise independent.*'"[271] This passage and others, the court urged, "later breathed life into the intra-enterprise conspiracy doctrine" (761).

The court acknowledged "that a pattern of acquisitions may itself create a combination illegal under §1, especially when an original anticompetitive purpose is evident from the affiliated corporations' subsequent conduct" (761). Indeed, the *Yellow Cab* decision could have turned on the initial acquisitions which "were *themselves* illegal" (761) and provided "a predicate for its holding that any postacquisition conduct violated the Act" (761n5). The court urged that *Yellow Cab*'s "ambiguous . . . holding" led later cases to cite it for the proposition that intra-enterprise conspiracies were recognized by the Sherman Act (763). Thus, in *Kiefer-Stewart Co. v. Joseph E. Seagram & Sons, Inc.,* "the Court *offhandedly* dismissed the defendants' argument that their status as 'mere instrumentalities of a single manufacturing-merchandising unit' makes it impossible for them to have conspired in a manner forbidden by the Sherman Act" (763–64; emphasis added).[272] Later decisions following this precedent were just as lax and "do little more than cite *Yellow Cab or Kiefer-Stewart*" (764).

The *Copperweld* court's own interpretation of the statute considers its purposes and concludes that "it is perfectly plain that an internal 'agreement' to implement a single, unitary firm's policies does not raise the antitrust dangers that §1 was designed to police" (769) and that "the coordinated activity of a parent and its wholly owned subsidiary must be viewed as that of a single enterprise for the purposes of §1 of the Sherman Act" (771). "Indeed," the court insists, "the very notion of an 'agreement' in Sherman Act terms between a parent and a wholly owned subsidiary lacks meaning" (771). The court concluded by rejecting what it described as problematic precedents, stating: "We hold that Copperweld and its wholly owned subsidiary Regal are incapable of conspiring with each other for purposes of § 1 of the Sherman Act. To the extent that prior decisions of this Court are to the contrary, they are disapproved and overruled" (777). Chapter 4 will provide extended analyses of three statutory interpretations cases.

The handful of overrulings in common-law cases involve admiralty, res judicata (determining limits on the relitigation of settled disputes by the same parties), or other issues. Such cases typically do not refer to "the common law" as a body of law so much as to practices that the court has followed. They are distinguished in making no reference to "positive" law, such as a statutory or constitutional text that would anchor their legal reasoning.[273] The very first overruling by the Supreme Court involved the common law respecting an admiralty issue. An American defendant named Guestier had purchased the cargo of the *Sea Flower*, a ship condemned by the French for trading with Hispaniola during a period of slave revolt.[274] The owners brought the case to recover the value of the property. Justice Livingstone cited no specific law of the United States to resolve the issue, but merely noted the determination of the French court regarding the condemnation and insisted: "The judge must have had a right to dispose of every question which was made on behalf of the owner of the property, whether it related to his own jurisdiction, or arose out of the law of nations, or out of the French decrees, or in any other way: and, even if the reasons of his judgment should not appear satisfactory, it would be no reason for a foreign court [i.e., the US Supreme Court] to review his proceedings, or not to consider his sentence as conclusive on the property" (284–85). The conclusion followed this deference to the French court: "Believing, therefore, that this property was changed by its condemnation at Guadaloupe [where the court presided], the original owner can have no right to pursue it in the hands of any vendee under that sentence, and the judgment below must, therefore, be affirmed" (285). Livingstone dismissed the precedent of *Rose v. Himely* by insisting that only three judges supported the contrary view of that case (285).[275] Chief Justice Marshall, the lone dissenter, said he thought that *Rose* had been concurred in by four judges, but the reporter noted: "But in this he was mistaken" (285).

Another example involves a 1947 North Carolina case where the plaintiff lost in state court but, instead of appealing the legal issues to a federal court, he instituted a new suit for trial in a federal district court on the same issue. That was a violation of res judicata, that a matter adjudged by a competent court is final and may not be pursued further by the same parties. An appeal would have been a continuation of the matter adjudged, but a new suit would not.[276] Writing for the overruling majority, Frankfurter rejected a 1912 precedent as "obsolete insofar as they are based on a view of diversity jurisdiction which came to an end with *Erie Railroad v. Tompkins*," a case that "drastically limited the power of federal district courts to entertain suits in diversity cases that could not be brought in the respective State courts or were barred by defenses controlling in the State courts."[277]

CONCLUSION

This chapter has explained the place of stare decisis in the United States legal system, with particular attention to its role in the Supreme Court. I have enumerated justifications for ignoring it and demonstrated that the court has done so on many occasions, particularly since the second third of the twentieth century. Overrulings have focused on four major areas: economic activity, criminal procedure, constitutional rights, and federal power. Constitutional cases have been balanced with federal and state statutory cases, cases involving court rules, and a few common-law cases.

Overall, there is a substantial body of discourse devoted to overruling in the court. I have provided a profile of cases, courts, justices, issues, and practices in this genre. In the remaining chapters I will examine extended cases of overruling discourse, divided by time period or topic to provide a fuller appreciation of what the court is doing when it acknowledges a need to change course.

CHAPTER 3

Overruling in the Nineteenth Century

Maritime and Money

INTRODUCTION

As I noted in the previous chapter, the nineteenth century was a unique period for overruling decisions. First, the Supreme Court lacked a paid (and reliable) reporter until 1817, which led the court to rely upon its memory rather than verbatim reports of its opinions for many early cases. Second, even if it had a reporter, there were a limited number of cases that might be overruled until the court's age and case load grew and it addressed more and more issues of first impression as the decades passed. Third, the doctrine of stare decisis had not formally been endorsed by the high court until about midcentury, though the cases discussed in this chapter acknowledge that it was an important principle from the beginning of the court. Finally, it was a century of evolving assumptions about legal reasoning and judicial decision-making, moving from an undertheorized version of natural law at the beginning of the century to some influence from Jeremy Bentham's legal positivism by midcentury and, finally, to Christopher Columbus Langdell's "scientific" approach to legal reasoning near the end of the century.

Because justices of the Supreme Court in the nineteenth century were born and studied law mostly in the eighteenth century and the first half of the nineteenth century, some version of natural law, if only as an inchoate theory, had the greatest influence over the nineteenth century, though Justice Swayne cited Bentham a few times.[1] Langdell's case law method sought to classify cases as scientists classified biological organisms to better assess what the law is, making categorization and deduction central to legal reasoning.[2] However, his case method was not used at Harvard Law School until 1870, and would not be used outside that institution until 1890, so his influence on early justices of the high court was extremely limited.[3]

Two cases illustrate nineteenth-century attitudes toward overruling. Both involve constitutional issues, though the first one turns on a rereading of common law. The first is a jurisdictional case decided at midcentury. The second case is a post–Civil War case that involves an explosive and hasty reversal on an important federal power. Both involve notable men who found themselves on both sides of the issue in question.

DEFINING ADMIRALTY JURISDICTION

In 1825 the United States Supreme Court heard an appeal from a sailor who was not paid for working on a boat that left Shippingport, Kentucky, sailed west on the Ohio River to the Mississippi, then north to and up the Missouri River and returned.[4] The eminent Justice Joseph Story delivered the bad news to the stiffed crewman in the *Thomas Jefferson* that the court had no jurisdiction to hear the case, as the district court below had concluded. Noting that Article III of the Constitution conferred onto the federal courts authority over "all Cases of admiralty and maritime jurisdiction," Story insisted that such work on interior rivers was beyond its jurisdiction, stating that "the Admiralty never pretended to claim, nor could it rightfully exercise any jurisdiction, except in cases where the service was substantially performed, or to be performed, upon the sea, or upon waters within the ebb and flow of the tide" (428).[5]

Twenty-six years after this decision, Chief Justice Roger Taney, writing in *The Propeller* Genesee Chief *v. Fitzhugh,* overruled *The* Thomas Jefferson, charging that Story's decision had erred in limiting the admiralty jurisdiction to the ebb and flow of the tide, providing for a more generous reading of that common-law jurisdiction to include "public navigable waters."[6] This decision constituted only the fifth time the high court had reversed an earlier decision in its sixty-two-year history, and only the second case in which the court explicitly announced that it was overruling a precedent.[7]

Chief Justice Taney recognizes the rhetorical problems he created for the court in this overruling, noting that "it is the decision in the case of the Thomas Jefferson which mainly embarrasses the court in the present inquiry" (456). To overcome this embarrassment and bolster his decision, Taney makes an extraordinary argument, claiming that his ruling actually was not changing a centuries-old rule on admiralty jurisdiction, but following it. He urges that the precedent court and Justice Story made an understandable mistake in its previous ruling. Thus, by ensuring that the law had not really changed, Taney bolstered his allegiance to past law, and by assuring that the prior court made an innocent and understandable error, he plumps up a court which his correction threatens to undermine. I will explain in detail how he constructed this argument in *The Propeller* Genesee Chief *v. Fitzhugh.*

The *Genesee Chief* was a steamship crossing Lake Ontario on the night of May 6, 1847, forty miles from Niagara Falls, when it ran into a schooner, the *Cuba,* damaging the sailing vessel so severely that she sank in less than half an hour. The owners of the *Cuba* brought a case in the federal district court in Auburn, New York, to recover the value of the vessel and its cargo of almost six thousand bushels of wheat, after showing that the collision "was occasioned by the carelessness and mismanagement of the officers and crew of the propeller, without any fault of the officers or crew of the Cuba" (450). Judge Alfred Conkling ruled in favor of the owners of the *Cuba,* awarding them $13,054.06 in damages.[8] The owners of the *Genesee Chief* appealed the verdict, challenging the *Cuba*'s able law firm (featuring William H. Seward, who would be elected to the US Senate later that year and thirteen years later serve as President Lincoln's secretary of state). The Second Circuit Court of Appeals in Northern New York affirmed the decision. The owners of the *Genesee Chief* appealed the ruling to the US Supreme Court, again claiming that the federal courts had no jurisdiction over the case because the collision did not occur on the high seas or within the ebb and flow of the tide and thus was beyond the "admiralty and maritime" jurisdiction given to the federal courts by Article III of the Constitution.

One might wonder why the lower courts held that the federal judiciary had jurisdiction over the case when a clear precedent, *The* Thomas Jefferson, held that such jurisdiction was limited to the ebb and flow of the tide. Their recognition of jurisdiction was based upon a new Judiciary Act, passed on February 26, 1845.[9] That act, known as the Great Lakes Act, indeed, seemed to take care of the jurisdictional question, giving federal district courts the power to hear cases "arising in, upon, or concerning, steamboats and other vessels of twenty tons burden and upwards, enrolled and licensed for the coastal trade, and at the time employed in [the] business of commerce and navigation between ports and places in different States and Territories upon the lakes and navigable waters connecting said lakes."[10]

Ironically, this statute was reportedly drafted by Justice Joseph Story in the same year he died.[11] Thus did the eminent justice provide a means for reversing the limitations on the federal courts' authority to hear such suits which he announced in *The* Thomas Jefferson. As the statute indicates through its emphasis on commerce, Story seems to rest Congress's power to confer such jurisdiction not on the admiralty clause of Article III but on the Commerce Clause.[12] But, for whatever reason, Chief Justice Taney and his majority were unwilling to draw upon the Commerce Clause, rejecting Story's new foundation for its jurisdiction.[13] Instead, Taney took a route seemingly more threatening to the high court's credibility, reversing *The* Thomas Jefferson and rejecting the interpretation of admiralty jurisdiction laid down by his late colleague twenty-six years earlier.

Taney admits that notable commentators had indeed stated that the new statute rested on the Commerce Clause, but he rejected that reading, insisting: "The law . . . contains no regulations of commerce; nor any provision in relation to shipping and navigation on the lakes. It merely confers a new jurisdiction on the district courts; and this is its only object and purpose" (451). Latching onto the title of the statute, which refers to jurisdiction, Taney insists that "if the constitutionality of this law is supported as a regulation of commerce, we shall impute to the legislature the exercise of a power which it has not claimed under that clause of the Constitution; and which we have no reason to suppose it deemed itself authorized to exercise" (452). He appeals to the language of the statute as well: "Indeed it would be inconsistent with the plain and ordinary meaning of words, to call a law defining the jurisdiction of certain courts of the United States a regulation of commerce" (453). That rather cramped reading dismisses the idea that providing for appropriate means of appeal in cases of conflict involving commerce is a kind of regulation of commerce.

On the other hand, the cramped reading Justice Story gave to the admiralty and maritime jurisdiction, in Taney's view, was yet more troubling. He worries that such a rule would leave without federal judicial remedies people living in the western states, "confin[ing] these rights to the States bordering on the Atlantic, and to the tide-water rivers connected with it, and . . . deny[ing] them to the citizens who border on the lakes, and the great navigable streams which flow through the western States" (454).

Having rejected the Commerce Clause as a way out of this problem of unfairness, Taney sets the bar very high, insisting that "if this [1845] law . . . is constitutional, it must be supported on the ground that the lakes and navigable waters connecting them are within the scope of admiralty and maritime jurisdiction, as known and understood in the United States when the Constitution was adopted" (453).

Taney urges that, indeed, the scope of admiralty at the time the Constitution was adopted was broad enough to include lakes and navigable waters—even those not connected to the sea. He supports this remarkable claim by insisting that the centuries-old standard for admiralty jurisdiction had been wrongly stated since roughly the fifteenth century. He reinterpreted the "original" meaning of the "ebb and flow" standard by contextualizing its use in light of England's geography.

As Kenneth Burke has famously noted, one common way of explaining motives for an action is with reference to the scene, suggesting that "the scene contains the act."[14] That is precisely Taney's strategy when he notes:

> In England, undoubtedly the writers upon the subject, and the decisions

> in its courts of admiralty, always speak of the jurisdiction as confined to tide-water. And this definition in England was a sound and reasonable one, because there was no navigable stream in the country beyond the ebb and flow of the tide; nor any place where a port could be established to carry on trade with a foreign nation, and where vessels could enter or depart with cargoes. In England, therefore tide-water and navigable water are synonymous terms, and tide-water, with a few small and unimportant exceptions, meant nothing more than public rivers, as contradistinguished from private ones; and they took the ebb and flow of the tide as the test, because it was a convenient one, and more easily determined the character of the river. Hence the established doctrine in England, that the admiralty jurisdiction is confined to the ebb and flow of the tide. In other words, it is confined to public navigable waters. (454–55)

Thus, because England is an island and all of its commercial rivers have tidewater, Taney urges, judges adopted the tidewater rule out of "convenien[ce]." Presumably, following Taney's reasoning, had England any rivers that were navigable, yet beyond the ebb and flow of the tide, these same jurists might have been pressed to find a different term, such as "public navigable water."

Taney draws upon an inventional opportunity afforded by prior judicial decisions: because such decisions are *acts,* in the full-blooded sense of that term, undertaken by judicial agents, using judicial agencies, for judicial purposes, in historical and spatial scenes, they may be scrutinized as acts and reconfigured in line with Burke's *grammar* of motives.[15] By changing the scene of action, you can change the motive of the act. Thus, Taney highlights a geographical island scene, filled with rivers influenced by the tides, to scrutinize an agency of judicial decision: the standard of "ebb and flow of the tide" as demarcating the extent of the historic admiralty jurisdiction.

Of course, Taney's construction is strategic and limited in its consideration of ancient judicial motives. He does not investigate the historic divisions of jurisdiction between "the civil law of maritime and international commerce" on the one hand, and "the common law of England ashore" on the other.[16] The original jurisdictional rule, notes Staring, was to prevent the territorial feuding between the Lord Admiral, who wielded enormous power over issues related to sea traffic, and the sheriffs of various counties who watched over river traffic, as well as over some maritime contracts made on lands within their jurisdictions.[17]

We should add that the analogy between British and American applications of this rule is made difficult by the American concern with federalism, whereby the division is not merely between the seas and the internal waterways jealously guarded by local authorities but among different state jurisdictions, whereby "interstate commerce" could leave a litigant wondering where to turn when actions involve work, contracts, or other issues that cross state lines. Early colonial governors were made vice admirals who oversaw more than their British counterparts, addressing issues on the seas near their colonies as well as on fresh waterways.[18]

Taney raises the interstate commerce issue indirectly when he uses scene once again to make the case for jurisdiction particularly in the *Genesee Chief* case. He insists that Lake Ontario, where the collision occurred, and its sister lakes "are in truth inland seas. Different States border on them on one side, and a foreign nation on the other. A great and growing commerce is carried on upon them between different States and a foreign nation, which is subject to all the incidents and hazards that attend commerce on the ocean. Hostile fleets have encountered on them, and prizes been made; and every reason which existed for the grant of admiralty jurisdiction to the general government on the Atlantic seas, applies with equal force to the lakes" (453). Taney's special pleading, indeed, points out the difficulty of drawing a distinction between these huge inland lakes and the salty seas. However, that analogy does not necessitate rereading the long-standing admiralty jurisdiction with respect to inland rivers and small states. This foot in the door does, however, allow him to return to the issue of fairness and equality for those outside of the Great Lakes and of the tide-influenced rivers. He insists that such fairness was "one of the great objects of the framers of the Constitution: that is, a perfect equality in the rights and the privileges of the citizens of the different States; not only in the laws of the general government, but in the mode of administering them" (454).

Taney does not bolster his argument about "public navigable water" as the effective standard with reference to particular British cases employing something like that standard. His goal is to generalize all of the common law on the issue, casting aside the "few small and unimportant exceptions" to his generalization without an explanation of why they are exceptional or why they are distinguishable from the others. Instead, he makes pragmatic arguments about the need for a federal admiralty jurisdiction across the various waters of the United States. He insists that the lack of such jurisdiction would cause a "great public inconvenience" because the advent of steamships, the settlement of the Mississippi Valley, and the growth of the commerce to support a growing country created problems. He notes that "Courts of admiralty have been found necessary in all commercial countries, not only for the safety and convenience of commerce, and the speedy decision of controversies, where delay would often be ruin, but also to administer the laws of nations in a season of war, and to determine the validity of captures and questions of prize or no prize in a judicial proceeding" (454). Taney does not consider the possibility that state courts could handle such issues, as indeed they had for decades, or whether jurisdictional conflicts among states might make their processes problematic—though an argument could certainly be made for them.[19]

The change in river commerce since Story's earlier decision was certainly dramatic. The flatboats and keelboats common to the Mississippi River were giving way to steam-powered vessels that could easily move upstream. Frank H. Dixon's *A Traffic History of the Mississippi River System* notes that in 1814 New Orleans reported twenty-one steamships using its port; by 1851, when *Genesee Chief* was decided, there were almost 3000.[20]

Of course, issues of inconvenience, of technological innovation challenging ancient legal frameworks, or of large inland lakes appearing like seas do not get to the question Taney himself poses about the meaning of admiralty and maritime jurisdiction "as known and understood in the United States when the Constitution was adopted" (453). Indeed, the original constitutional scene would appear to run against concerns that only subsequent history would make problematic for Taney. Unfortunately, there was no legal philosophy akin to legal realism, with its assumption that law is an organic thing that must grow and adapt to changing social needs, to which Taney could appeal.

However, Taney could appeal to a broader understanding of admiralty by Congress from the earliest days. The 1789 Judiciary Act stated that federal district courts "shall have exclusive cognizance of all civil causes of admiralty and maritime jurisdiction, including all seizures under the laws of impost, navigation, or trade of the United States, where the seizures are made *on waters which are navigable from the sea* by vessels of ten or more tons burden, within their respective districts, as well as upon the high seas" (quoted at 457; emphasis added). Taney implies that as early as 1789, Congress recognized that commerce that runs from the sea up rivers, perhaps even beyond the tides' influence, was within the admiralty jurisdiction. But, oddly, Taney cuts off this argument by insisting that, like England, the original United States had only rivers influenced by the tides. As he explains: "At the time the Constitution of the United States was adopted, and our courts of admiralty went into operation, the definition which had been adopted in England was equally proper here. In the old thirteen States the far greater part of the navigable waters are tide-waters. And in the States which were at that period in any degree commercial, and where courts of admiralty were called on to exercise their jurisdiction, every public river was tide-water to the head of navigation" (455).

This parallel between Mother England as an island with tidewater in its rivers and its offspring colony-turned-independent-country with its Atlantic Seaboard and rivers full of tides explains why the rule persisted, in a scene-agency logic. But it also seems to suggest a limited original constitutional meaning for "admiralty and maritime jurisdiction." For Taney, it simply explained the continuation of an unreasonable rule.

At this point, Taney at least has an excuse for Story's earlier error in *The* Thomas Jefferson, a way to explain and forgive the precedent court. Taney describes that case as yielding "an erroneous decision into which the court fell" (456). A passive "falling" is certainly more forgivable than an active flouting of "the law" as the court should have recognized it. To explain this failure, Taney again uses scene-act logic, paralleling his argument about the British courts that erroneously used "ebb and flow of the tide" when they meant "public navigable water." Taney notes first that "the decision was made in 1825, when the commerce on the rivers of the west and on the lakes was in its infancy, and of little importance, and but little regarded compared with that of the present day" (456). The original colonies that became the first states of the Union were on the Eastern Seaboard, with rivers that had tidewater. Unsurprisingly, no troubling cases arose in this geographical setting, as Taney notes: "It so happened that no seizure was made, and no case calling for the exercise of admiralty power arose for a long period of time, upon any navigable water where the tide did not ebb and flow. As we have before stated, there were no navigable waters in the United States upon which commerce in the usual acceptation of the word was carried on, except tide-water, until the valley of the Mississippi was settled and cultivated, and steamboats invented, and no case therefore came before the court during the early period of the government that required it to determine whether this jurisdiction could be extended above tide" (457).

If we are to concede that Taney met his own standard for upholding his broad interpretation of the admiralty jurisdiction—that "public navigable water" was the standard "known and understood in the United States when the Constitution was adopted"—we need a curious conception of "known and understood." Because neither the Founding Fathers nor the early courts were challenged by extensive commerce on waters above the ebb and flow of the tide, they did not have to think about that. Therefore, "meaning" in the Constitution's language is extended to consider *what they would have thought* about the meaning of admiralty under those "pressing" circumstances. It is not exactly "original intent" by a Scalia or Thomas standard. It is more like, "What would reasonable people like the Founding Fathers think?"

A final appeal by Taney noted the apparent belief of the legislative branch of government that, indeed, they had authority under the Constitution to extend admiralty jurisdiction beyond tidewaters. The 1789 Judiciary Act, coming right on the heels of the Constitution's passage, had extended the federal courts' jurisdiction beyond the seas to "waters which are navigable from the sea," which certainly could have included rivers beyond the reach of the tides. Adding that to the 1845 Act, which Taney insists did not rest on the Commerce Clause, meant that the court had "the opinion of the legislative department of the government, twice deliberately expressed, upon the subject" (458). And, Taney added, while "these opinions of course are not binding on the judicial department . . . they are always entitled to high respect. And in this instance we think they are founded in truth and reason; and that these laws are both constitutional, and ought therefore to be carried into execution" (458).

Taney's appeal to "truth and reason" as a standard for judging what is constitutional and, presumably, what the Constitution *meant* when its words were framed, provides an ultimate trump card for this constitutional adjudication. Indeed, his arguments about historical changes in the United States' size, its economic development, and its technological innovations were not foreseeable by the framers of the Constitution or Justice Story. Nevertheless, Taney implies, had they foreseen such changes, they would have understood the admiralty jurisdiction differently. They would have applied truth and reason to judge that the rule they inherited from the British was limited by the mother country's own geographical setting.

This is not a historical conception of "intent of the framers," but an appeal to what words should mean if we could conceive of different circumstances. Of course, this form of reasoning about what the Constitution means comes awfully close to a mere pragmatist's view of what is advantageous, a kind of "judge-made law" for the sake of convenience. No doubt it proved useful to ship owners, seamen, banks, and businesses using this new, much cheaper mode of transport. But it also must have chagrined states' rights advocates who worried about the encroachment of the federal courts upon local tribunals.

MAKING MONEY

The second nineteenth-century overruling I want to examine involves one of the most controversial decisions of that century, and certainly the most controversial overruling of that early period. The Legal Tender Cases of 1871 overruled *Hepburn v. Griswold,* a sixteen-month-old decision that denied congressional authority to make paper money a legal tender for obligations prior to passage of the Legal Tender Act of 1862.[21] *Hepburn* marked only the third time the US Supreme Court had declared an act of Congress unconstitutional (after *Marbury v. Madison* and *Dred Scott v. Sanford*). The Legal Tender Cases marked only the fifth time the court explicitly overruled an earlier decision. Chief Justice Salmon Chase, who wrote the majority opinion in *Hepburn,* declared unconstitutional an act he himself helped push through Congress when he was Lincoln's secretary of the treasury during the Civil War! His 5-3 majority became a 4-5 minority through a retirement and two judicial appointments made by President Grant. I will begin with the *Hepburn* decision, which itself was quite controversial.

The case begins in 1862 when the country was embroiled in the Civil War and Lincoln's new secretary of the treasury, Salmon Chase, needed to raise money fast. The Treasury was empty and the war effort required hundreds of millions of dollars every year and, eventually, three billion dollars overall.[22]

Minor tax increases and the sale of bonds proved inadequate. Soldiers were paid in demand notes, which they redeemed in banks, dissipating their coin reserves. A plan to organize a series of national banks was begun, but that would take too long to address the short-term money crunch. So, Congress and the Treasury turned to another solution: printing paper money, or "greenbacks," which the Legal Tender Act of 1862 made a legal tender.[23]

Since 1792, US currency had been based on gold and silver. Thus, Charles Fairman notes, "the proposal now for the first time to give the Government's paper notes the quality of a tender which in law would discharge a debt ran counter to deep convictions."[24] Indeed, the Treasury Secretary shared those deep convictions, as Spaulding's *History of the Legal Tender Paper* notes: "Chase was opposed in principle to legal tender paper: but so was everyone else. The question was, what to do to meet the exigency of January and February 1862."[25] When Congress asked him to review a bill to create legal tender paper, Chase "'regrett[ed] exceedingly' that this approach was necessary," "but heartily desir[ed] to co-operate with the Committee [framing the bill]."[26] Chase wrote to William Cullen Bryant, editor of the *New-York Evening Post*, explaining his position: "Your feelings of repugnance to the legal tender clause can hardly be greater than my own; but I am convinced that, as a temporary measure, it is indispensably necessary."[27]

Chase resigned as treasury secretary in 1864. Lincoln nominated him to be chief justice after Roger Taney died in October 1864. A number of state cases questioned the reach of the Legal Tender Act, but it was near the end of the 1860s that these cases reached the US Supreme Court. The two most important cases were *Hepburn v. Griswold* and two joined cases, *Knox v. Lee* and *Parker v. Davis*, better known as the Legal Tender Cases, which overturned *Hepburn* in sixteen months after it was handed down.

Hepburn addressed the issue of whether the federal government had the power to make paper money, or "greenbacks," a legal tender. "Legal tender" meant, by the terms of the Legal Tender Act of 1862, that greenbacks could be used to pay "all taxes, internal duties, excises, debts, and demands of every kind due to the United States, except duties on imports, and of all claims and demands against the United States of every kind whatsoever, except for interest upon bonds and notes, which shall be paid in coin; and shall also be lawful money and a legal tender in payment of all debts, public and private, within the United States, except duties on imports and interest as aforesaid."[28] Particularly important was the requirement that private debts were subject to payment in greenbacks.[29] That led "Mrs. Hepburn" to discharge her payment of $11,250 to Henry Griswold, two years late (with interest), in paper money. Had she paid the debt on time, she would have had to pay it in gold or silver coin, since the debt was due five days before the Legal Tender Act was passed. Since greenbacks often were worth less than their nominal value, Griswold sued to force Hepburn to discharge the debt in gold or silver coin, arguing that Congress exceeded its authority in making greenbacks a legal tender.[30]

Chief Justice Chase wrote the majority opinion and sided with Griswold, limiting the issue to the case of the act's retrospective effect on obligations. He insisted that if the law were read to cover debts made prior to the act's passage it would cause great harm, because "no one will question that the United States notes, which the act makes a legal tender in payment, are essentially unlike in nature, and, being irredeemable in coin, are necessarily unlike in value, to the lawful money *intended by parties to contracts for the payment of money made before its passage*" (607; emphasis added). This position reflects the court's attitudes toward the stability of laws affecting property rights, which I noted in the previous chapter was often cited as a reason for not overruling existing decisions and unsettling contracts and other property relations. In this case, to allow such a change in the term of contracts, Chase argued, "alters arbitrarily the terms of the contract and impairs its obligation, and . . . is contrary to justice and equity" (609).

Nonetheless, Chase concluded, the act did appear to have been intended to cover those prior debts, leading him to inquire "whether Congress has power to make notes issued under its authority a legal tender in payment of debts, which, when contracted, were payable by law in gold and silver coin" (610). Given that the court had only overturned two previous laws as unconstitutional, Chase took it for granted "that acts of Congress must be regarded as constitutional, unless clearly shown to be otherwise" (610). Yet, he insisted "that the government of the United States is one of limited powers, and that no department possesses any authority not granted by the Constitution" (613).

Since the Constitution includes no "express grant of legislative power to make any description of credit currency a legal tender in payment of debts" (614), Chase considered whether the power was implied, and whether the Legal Tender Act was "necessary and proper" under the Constitution (614–15). While the Constitution specifically empowers the government to "coin money" and set the value of it, Chase insists that is different from printing money and giving it a value that is not intrinsic to it (616). "Nor is the power to make notes a legal tender," he added, "the same as the power to issue notes to be used as currency" (616).

Counsel for Hepburn argued from a different power—no doubt hitting close to home with Chase—that making greenbacks a legal tender is "a means appropriate and plainly adapted to the execution of the power to carry on war" (617). Chase retorted that "the argument . . . seems to prove too much" (617), since money is required for all sorts of government actions. Reviewing the history of the government's issuing of greenbacks during the war, Chase admits that the government could make paper money a legal tender but insisted it could not change the expectations for the payment of preexisting debts (619). He admits that forcing debtors to accept the paper money might help prop up its value in support of the government's efforts, but doubts there is "any appreciable advantage" to applying that requirement to preexisting debts; on the other hand, there were plenty of evils associated with interfering in contracts this way (621). Ultimately, Chase finds that making greenbacks a legal tender applicable to past debts is neither necessary nor proper under the Constitution as a means adopted under any federal powers (621–22). Nor is such government action "consistent with the spirit of the Constitution" (622), particularly since it violates the Constitution's admonition that "no person shall be deprived of life, liberty, or property, without due process of law," which changing the terms of a contract after the fact effectively flouts (624). Indeed, he urges: "It is difficult to conceive what act would take private property without process of law if such an act would not" (625).

In addition to the practical orders to the lower court following this conclusion, Chase mounts a defense of those (including himself) who supported the Legal Tender Act of 1862, mimicking Taney's *Genessee Chief* opinion in relying on a changed scene to explain changed attitudes:

> It is not surprising that amid the tumult of the late civil war, and under the influence of apprehensions for the safety of the Republic almost universal, different views, never before entertained by American state[s]men or jurists, were adopted by many. The time was not favorable to considerate reflection upon the constitutional limits of legislative or executive authority. If power was assumed from patriotic motives, the assumption found ready justification in patriotic hearts. Many who doubted yielded their doubts; many who did not doubt were silent. Some who were strongly averse to making government notes a legal tender felt themselves constrained to acquiesce in the views of the advocates of the measure. Not a few who then insisted upon its necessity, or acquiesced in that view, have, since the return of peace, and under the influence of the calmer time, reconsidered their conclusions, and now concur in those which we have just announced. (625–26)

Chase's thorough assessment of the constitutional issue was marred by an irregularity in the final decision. Justice Grier heard the original case but had retired before the decision was handed down. Chase recorded his vote as supporting the majority nonetheless, as he explained: "It is proper to say that Mr. Justice Grier, who was a member of the court when this cause was decided in conference [on November 27, 1869], and when this opinion was directed to be read [on January 29, 1870] stated his judgment to be that the legal tender clause, properly construed, has no application to debts contracted prior to its enactment; but that upon the construction given to the act by the other judges he concurred in the opinion that the clause, so far as it makes United States notes a legal tender for such debts, is not warranted by the Constitution" (626). That was a generous attribution to Grier because when the justices discussed the case on November 27, 1869, Grier initially voted the other way, leaving a 4-4 split. A Kentucky court had declared the Legal Tender Act invalid, and Grier wanted to reverse the state court. A 4-4 split would have affirmed the lower court and established no principles. When the justices turned to discuss another case involving greenbacks and distributions by the executor of an estate from California, Grier took the opposite position from that he had just taken in *Hepburn*.[31] When a fellow justice noted the inconsistency, Grier switched his vote in *Hepburn*, giving Chase a majority of 5-3.[32] Garrow argues that "it was only the presence of a mentally incompetent justice that allowed Chase to manipulate the Court's consideration of Hepburn in the way that he did."[33]

The reason Grier was absent when the final decision was handed down in *Hepburn* is that the justices encouraged the seventy-six-year-old justice to take an attractive retirement package just approved by Congress.[34] With Grier's retirement and Congress's addition of a new, ninth seat withheld from Lincoln's unpopular successor, President Grant made two nominations to the High Court *on the day Hepburn was handed down*.[35] The change in the court was more than symbolic, as the new justices would provide a majority willing to overturn *Hepburn*, though not without a cost to the high court's reputation. As Fairman noted, the change of personnel that led to the 5-4 overruling decision in the Legal Tender Cases made the court appear political as "the Court's authority as expositor of the Constitution was seriously impaired by this unfortunate business."[36]

The daunting rhetorical task of justifying the quick overruling of such an important case on the heels of these two new appointments fell to one of the new justices, the abolitionist Democrat-turned-Republican, Justice William Strong. The briefs, majority, concurring, and dissenting opinions reported in the case run for more than two hundred pages, with Chief Justice Chase's dissent the largest at sixty-four pages. As I will show, Chase was more adamant about defending his former decision than in upholding the reputation of the court as an institution.

One of the two cases decided as the Legal Tender Cases, like *Hepburn*, involved a woman, a "Mrs. Lee," who was not a debtor but rather one whose property had been taken by the Confederacy.[37] Although she lived in Pennsylvania, she owned a flock of sheep in Texas that was seized and sold to Mr. Knox, and she sought to recover its value. She won a verdict of $7,368 after the trial judge instructed the jury to keep in mind that the damages "can be discharged by the payment of such an amount in legal tender notes of the United States" (458). Knox thought this charge urged the jury to increase the award, given the depreciation of greenbacks, and appealed.

In the second case, *Parker v. Davis,* the seller of land refused to accept payment in greenbacks and transfer title to a buyer. A contract for the sale was made before the passage of the Legal Tender Act so that, under *Hepburn,* the seller presumably could demand payment in coin (461–63). The court heard lengthy arguments from the US Attorney General Amos T. Akerman and New York Democratic Congressman Clarkson Nott Potter. They addressed the very issue decided in *Hepburn* regarding the application of the Legal Tender Act to contracts made before its passage, as well as whether the law covered transactions since its passage (463).

Potter warned the court about the risks to its reputation in overruling *Hepburn,* urging:

> To now, for the first time in its history, so gratuitously and needlessly review an abstract constitutional question so solemnly decided; to review it, not because of changes or doubts on the part of those who shared in the decision, but *through a change in the composition of the court, is to divert the regard of the people from the court itself to the personnel of those who compose it*; and would, as it seems to me, be in effect to abdicate the highest function with which your honors are intrusted. For men cannot be expected to submit their views of the powers of government to the construction of this tribunal when they once learn that, after a construction has been most solemnly established, they can change that construction by changing the persons who compose the tribunal. (517; emphasis added)

Potter's concerns cut to the heart of the problem of overruling under these circumstances.

Akerman countered that "the absence of a court as large as now, lessened the force of that decision, and induced a great portion of the legal profession to desire a reconsideration of the question" (528). Besides, this case brought a new question: Whether the government could require obligations made after the act was passed to be met with greenbacks (528).[38]

Strong's central argument was that the Legal Tender Act was "necessary and proper" given the extraordinary scene of war facing Congress, rather than some abstract sense of necessity and propriety. Thus, just like Taney's opinion in *Genesee Chief,* Strong drew on an argument from scene to justify the act, noting: "Plainly to this inquiry, a consideration of the time when they were enacted, and of the circumstances in which the government then stood, is important. It is not to be denied that acts may be adapted to the exercise of lawful power, and appropriate to it, *in seasons of exigency*, which would be inappropriate at other times" (540; emphasis added). That exigency included a war raging "which seriously threatened the overthrow of the government and the destruction of the Constitution itself" and required the raising "of money to an extent beyond the capacity of all ordinary sources of supply" to fund the large armies and navies (540).

This argument might have painted Strong into a corner to the extent that this extraordinary power was good for "seasons of exigency" and perhaps not for other times. How could the court recognize that power outside of an ongoing war? Strong insisted that they must because war could return again and a negative ruling would leave "the government . . . without those [financial] means of self-preservation," which, he insists, are "possessed by every independent sovereignty other than the United States" (529).

Strong contrasted the 1862 Congress's decision to pass the Legal Tender Act in a time of emergency with the court's judgment in the current, peaceful scene, complaining: "It is urged now, after the lapse of nine years, and when the emergency has passed, that treasury notes without the legal tender clause might have been issued, and that the necessitates of the government might thus have been supplied. Hence it is inferred there was no necessity for giving to the notes issued the capability of paying private debts. At best this is mere conjecture" (541). But if the change in scene did not warrant a critical judgment of congressional action, neither did the institution doing the judging. Strong asserts that "Congress had the choice of means for a legitimate end, each appropriate, and adapted to that end, though, perhaps, in different degrees" (542). For the court to second-guess that choice "would be to assume legislative power, and to disregard the accepted rules for construing the Constitution" (542).

In answer to concerns that property relations would be upset by an overruling, Strong argued that debt incurred prior to the act was small in the larger scheme of things, whereas changing the rules for post-Act contracts would upset the expectations of those engaged in a huge number of contracts and lead to runs on gold, "general distress," and widespread bankruptcy (529–30). But, setting these practical concerns aside, the question was whether "Congress [can] constitutionally give to treasury notes the character and qualities of money" (530).

Strong suggested that there were many powers of the federal government beyond those "definitely intrusted to Congress and mentioned in detail" (533) and these certainly included "the power of self-preservation" (533) which, he had argued, Congress had deemed the making of a legal tender central to ensuring. One could deduce such powers "from more than one of the substantive powers expressly defined, or from them all combined" (534). Indeed, he urges, the Founding Fathers recognized the expansiveness of federal power and, therefore, passed the Bill of Rights to restrict some of those powers that were "neither expressly specified nor deducible from any one specific power, or ancillary to it alone, but which grew out of the aggregate powers conferred upon the government, or out of the sovereignty instituted" (535).

Strong invokes Justice Story's volume on the Constitution for examples whereby the government exercised unenumerated powers (535) and notes that an 1825 federal criminal code "defined and provided for the punishment of a large class of crimes other than those mentioned in the Constitution" (536). He adds examples including incidental postal regulations and the establishment of a national bank that were approved (537). He quotes Chief Justice Marshall's admonition that "it would be incorrect and would produce endless difficulties if the opinion should be maintained that no law was authorized which was not indispensably necessary to give effect to a specified power" (quoting *Fisher v. Blight* at 538). He also quotes Marshall warning in *McCulloch v. Maryland* that the judiciary ought not "to tread on legislative ground" where a law is not prohibited and "is really calculated to effect any of the objects intrusted to the government" (quoted at 539).

Ultimately, of course, Chase would deny that making greenbacks a legal tender concerned one of "the objects intrusted to the government." Chase would inquire into "the degree of its necessity," not in ignorance of Marshall's admonition but as a means to figure out what power was at stake and if, indeed, it was one that Congress could exercise. Strong thought the survival of the union hung in the balance (and all countries have the power of self-preservation), while Chase urged that this means was not adapted to that end and, therefore, that this was not the unenumerated power at stake here.

Even Strong admitted that "Congress is not authorized to enact laws in furtherance even of a legitimate end, merely because they are useful, or because they make the government stronger. There must be some relation between the means and the end; some adaptedness or appropriateness of the laws to carry into execution the powers created by the Constitution" (543).

Strong draws an analogy to a case where Marshall found constitutional a heavy tax on state bank notes that prevented them from competing with federal bank notes.[39] He summarizes: "It was said there can be no question of the power of this government to emit bills of credit; to make them receivable in payment of debts to itself; to fit them for use by those who see fit to use them in all the transactions of commerce; to make them a currency uniform in value and description, and convenient and useful for circulation" (544). Suggesting an a fortiori conclusion, he says that "it is not easy to see why, if State bank notes can be taxed out of existence for purposes of making United States notes more convenient and useful for commercial purposes, the same end may not be secured directly by making them a legal tender" (544).

Strong turns next to the argument that in referencing the power to "coin money" the Constitution "contains an implication that nothing but that which is the subject of coinage, nothing but the precious metals can ever be declared by law to be money, or to have the uses of money" (544). He cites a criminal case precedent to urge that "it has been ruled that power over a particular subject may be exercised as auxiliary to an express power, though there is another express power relating to the same subject, less comprehensive" (544–45).

In another analogy, he notes that the circulation of paper money in the states under the Articles of Confederation was halted with the Constitution's exclusive granting of the power to regulate money to the federal government. If Congress also was to be denied this power, he asks, "why . . . was such denial not expressly extended to the new government, as it was to the states?" (546). Indeed, he insists, even those who read the coinage clause strictly "are compelled to concede to Congress large discretion" (547). That must include "what metals may be coined," "the legal value of metals," the correspondence between nominal value and "their intrinsic value in the market" (547). Given that discretion, and the denial of state authority over money, he wonders if one can find "an implied prohibition to Congress against declaring treasury notes a legal tender, if such declaration is appropriate, and adapted to carrying into execution the admitted powers of the government" (547).

Strong turns to what he considers "the main reliance of those who assert the unconstitutionality of the legal tender acts. It is that they are prohibited by the spirit of the Constitution because they indirectly impair the obligation of contracts" (547). This is *Hepburn*'s particular concern relating to contracts made before the Act of 1862. He denies that the obligation of contracts is weakened because "the *obligation* of a contract to pay money is to pay that which the law shall recognize as money when the payment is to be made" (548; emphasis in original). Contracts involving money, obviously, are "necessarily subject to the constitutional power of the government over the currency." (549). He reviews the various ways in which the government can, even directly, interfere in past and future contracts such as through bankruptcy laws and embargoes (549–50). He insists that "contracts must be understood as made in reference to the possible exercise of the rightful authority of the government, and no obligation of a contract can extend to the defeat of legitimate government authority" (551).

Hepburn had argued that the Legal Tender Act resulted in a taking of property without due process of law, forbidden by the Fifth Amendment. Strong objects that this provision involved "only . . . a direct appropriation, and not . . . consequential injuries resulting from the exercise of lawful power" (551). An example in point, he notes, is Congress's provision to reduce the value of gold in coins by about six percent, making "all creditors . . . [subject] to a corresponding loss," though that was never found to violate due process (551).

Strong also rejected the idea that any authorized money had to have intrinsic value. Strong responds with prescience given that it would be more than sixty years before the United States abandoned the gold standard, urging that "value is an ideal thing" rather than something that inheres to an object like gold (553). So, even though "the coinage acts fix its unit as a dollar . . . the gold or silver thing we call a dollar is, in no sense, a standard of a dollar. It is representative of it" (553). Ultimately, he notes, the value comes from the state, and "the government's promises to pay money . . . [is] equivalent in value to the representative value determined by the coinage acts, or to multiples thereof" (553).

Strong was explicit about the court's departure from *Hepburn*: "But, without extending our remarks further, it will be seen that we hold the acts of Congress constitutional as applied to contracts made either before or after their passage. In so holding, we overrule so much of what was decided in Hepburn v. Griswold, as ruled the acts unwarranted by the Constitution so far as they apply to contracts made before their enactment" (553). Ironically, in a move that would be reproduced by later courts, he urged that there were *precedents* for overruling such precedents, though, with few other overruling cases by the Supreme Court, he referenced overrulings "in courts of last resort, both *in this country and in England*" (554; emphasis added).

Strong also picked up on the attorney general's argument suggesting that the court was less robust than such a momentous decision required, noting that *Hepburn* "was decided by a divided court, and by a court having a less number of judges than the law then in existence provided this court shall have" (553–54). Strong had enough of a sense of decorum not to get into Grier's lack of mental acuity or of the *Hepburn* majority's influence over their muddled brethren. But he did contrast the "less than full" and divided *Hepburn* court with the current court, noting such important constitutional cases were normally heard by a full court exercising its most "careful consideration" (553–54).

Chief Justice Chase, in his dissent, directly refuted the suggestion that the *Hepburn* court was inadequate to the task: "A majority of the court, five to four, in the opinion which has just been read [by Strong], reverses the judgment rendered by the former majority of five to three, in pursuance of an opinion formed after repeated arguments, at successive terms, and careful consideration; and declares the legal tender clause to be constitutional. . . . And this reversal, unprecedented in the history of the court, has been produced by no change in the opinions of those who concurred in the former judgment" (572). So, Chase was not going to go along with Strong's attempt to construct the *Hepburn* court as understaffed and giving less consideration than the issues required. On the other hand, Chase's 5-3 construction of *Hepburn* did gloss over the vacillations of Grier, doubling down on his position by insisting that the *Hepburn* decision "closed an honorable judicial career by resignation after the case had been decided, after the opinion had been read and agreed to in conference, and after the day when it would have been delivered in court, had not the delivery been postponed for a week to give time for the preparation of the dissenting opinion" (572). Chase focused on Grier's larger career, rather than his sad last days, and on what might have been a decision handed down closer to his retirement, making him closer to the ultimate "5-3" decision. Chase repeatedly calls the Legal Tender Cases majority "the then minority [of *Hepburn*]" (573, 575, 580) and the Legal Tender Cases' minority "the then majority [of *Hepburn*]" (572, 573, 575), reminding them of the unfortunately change of positions wrought by changes in personnel.

Rejecting Strong's emphasis on the context of war, Chase insisted: "We perceive no connection between the express power to coin money and the inference that the government may, in any contingency, make its securities perform the functions of coined money, as a legal tender in payment of debts" (574). Chase invoked an originalist reading of the Constitution, arguing: "But the terms of the only express grant in the Constitution of power to establish such a standard leave little room for presumptions. The power conferred is the power to coin money, and these words must be understood as they were used *at the time the Constitution was adopted*. And we have been referred to no authority which at that time defined coining otherwise than as minting or stamping metals for money; or money otherwise than as metal coined for the purposes of commerce" (583–84).

Finally, Chase played his trump card: his role as treasury secretary when the Legal Tender Act was passed to support the war. He had not even mentioned his role as secretary of the treasury in the *Hepburn* decision, but in dissent he invoked his insider's knowledge, though in an odd third person form, saying of himself as secretary:

> He was extremely and avowedly averse to this [legal tender] clause, but was very solicitous for the passage of the bill to authorize the issue of United States notes then pending. He thought it indispensably necessary that the authority to issue these notes, should be granted by Congress. The passage of the bill was delayed, if not jeoparded, by the difference of opinion which prevailed on the question of making them a legal tender. It was under these circumstances that he expressed the opinion, when called upon by the Committee of Ways and Means, that it was necessary; and he was not sorry to find it sustained by the decisions of respected courts, not unanimous indeed, nor without contrary decisions of State courts equally respectable. Examination and reflection under more propitious circumstances have satisfied him that this opinion was erroneous, and he does not hesitate to declare it. He would

> do so, just as unhesitatingly, if his favor to the legal tender clause had been at that time decided, and his opinion as to the constitutionality of the measure clear. (576)

So, ironically, Chase would now—in these more propitious circumstances—reverse what he had done before. This is something of a mea culpa—an admission that he had erred, perhaps lending credence to the stance he now took. It is also ironic that Strong acknowledges the stresses of war time and would use those to justify the extreme actions the government took. But, as I noted, Strong also would recognize those actions now, in more propitious circumstances, as constitutional as well.

The Legal Tender Cases threatened the high court's authority to a greater extent because Chase's personal stake in the decision led him to break decorum by drawing attention to the politics of the decision, rather than taking his licks and sustaining the court's standing as a disinterested legal panel. But he also was disingenuous in overstating the intensity of Grier's allegiance to the *Hepburn* court's verdict.

Both sides took liberties in constructing the robustness of the *Hepburn* court—Justice Strong in suggesting that the technical deficit of personnel in the court reflected a deficit in reflection and analysis by the majority on the constitutional questions; Chief Justice Chase, again, in overstating the fullness of the court despite Grier's vacillations.

Chase's personal testimony, as former treasury secretary scrambling to raise money, would have been more powerful if he had used the first-person pronoun instead of referring to himself in third person. But, perhaps as spokesperson for himself and three colleagues, he felt it necessary to speak in a corporate voice—drawing the line of decorum here. Nonetheless, for Strong—a judge who had been on Pennsylvania's supreme court during the Civil War—to write about the challenges faced by the federal government was hard when the very man in charge of raising money for the war was writing in a dissent against him.

A review in *American Law Review*, probably written by the editor Oliver Wendell Holmes Jr. noted that *Hepburn* "presented the curious spectacle of the Supreme Court reversing the determination of Congress on a point of political economy."[40] The Legal Tender Cases, overruling *Hepburn* on the basis of personnel changes, offer a different kind of spectacle, which highlighted judicial politics and challenged the high court's unique position as an impartial bulwark of constitutional democracy.

CONCLUSION

The Supreme Court would issue about nineteen more overruling opinions during the remainder of the nineteenth century, in cases involving the

Commerce Clause, statutory law, and federal taxation, among other matters. None would be as controversial as the Legal Tender Cases or as rhetorically audacious as Chief Justice Taney's rewriting of four centuries of common law. However, they would make overruling more common and, thereby, less "unprecedented." They also would become easier to spot, thanks to the growth of reliable legal reporters.

Eventually, overruling courts would include justices who were trained to view the law more systematically, such as a command from a sovereign that could be tied to positive laws (though the generality of the Constitution would continue to require "gap-filling"), or as a collection of precedents subject to scientific study that allowed categorization and deductive reasoning or, eventually, as a tool of social betterment.

Before we leave the nineteenth century, the next chapter will consider overruling decisions that overlay most of the history of the court's overruling. Statutory overrulings, as the previous chapter explained, were very different from the constitutional overrulings of this chapter. Thus, the next chapter separates out this smaller group of overrulings for special attention.

CHAPTER 4

Overruling Statutory Interpretations

Jurisdiction, Patents, and Civil Rights

THIS CHAPTER WILL ANALYZE THREE cases spread over the history of the court that involve three distinct issues: an 1844 jurisdiction case, a 1917 patent case, and a 1978 civil rights case. As this analysis makes clear, although such cases turn on statutory interpretation, they often implicate constitutional law and common law as well.

FEDERAL JURISDICTION AND CORPORATE LITIGANTS

In 1806, Chief Justice Marshall wrote a 162-word opinion addressing the question of diversity jurisdiction for the federal courts. Article III, Section 2 of the US Constitution gives the federal courts jurisdiction over cases "between citizens of different states." The Judiciary Act of 1789, building on that grant of jurisdiction, specified that this jurisdiction covers cases "between a citizen of the State where the suit is brought, and a citizen of another State."[1] The purpose of giving federal jurisdiction over disputes between citizens of different states is to ensure a "neutral" forum for those decisions, avoiding elected judges or local juries who may favor litigants from their states and giving decisions to life-tenure judges and broader jury pools.

The 1806 case of *Strawbridge v. Curtiss* required the court to clarify the meaning of the Judiciary Act of 1789.[2] The case involved multiple plaintiffs and defendants, who were all from Massachusetts with the exception of Curtiss, who was from Vermont. The question was whether having a single litigant from a second state satisfied the diversity requirement for federal jurisdiction. Marshall, in a unanimous (6-0) decision, held that it was not, giving rise to the "complete diversity" standard. He explained: "Where the interest [in the litigation] is joint, each of the persons concerned in that interest must be competent to sue, or liable to be sued, in those courts" (267).

Three years after *Strawbridge*, a related diversity-jurisdiction issue was raised in a case involving a corporation. *Bank of the United States v. Deveaux* involved a suit by a bank corporation against two officials of the State of Georgia who seized money from its Savannah branch for nonpayment of taxes.[3] Despite the fact that the bank was in Georgia, Chief Justice Marshall found diversity jurisdiction because the bank's officials were residents of Pennsylvania. He rested that decision on an English common-law case involving jurisdiction that relied on looking beyond the corporation to its members. Ignoring the corporation itself as irrelevant to jurisdiction, because it is "a mere creature of the law, invisible, intangible, and incorporeal" (88), was not unusual at this early period when corporations played a more limited role in the economic life of the country.[4]

Commercial and Railroad Bank v. Slocomb, in 1840, would combine the foregoing precedents to unanimously find that a corporation with some members from the same state as those of the opposing party defeated complete diversity jurisdiction, even though the companies were incorporated in different states.[5] As Justice Barbour noted after reviewing the doctrines of *Strawbridge* and *Deveaux*: "The application of these doctrines to this case, would seem to be decisive of its fate; unless there is something in other points which were argued at the bar to obviate their force. For it has already been stated that the plaintiffs in the Court below were citizens of the state of Louisiana, and two of the members of the corporation sued were also citizens of Louisiana; so that some of the defendants being citizens of the same state with the plaintiffs, it follows, that although each of the plaintiffs was capable of suing, yet each of the defendants was not capable of being sued in the Circuit Court of Mississippi" (64). Although a revision to the Judiciary Act in 1839 specifically provided for federal jurisdiction in cases involving multiple parties where there was incomplete diversity, Justice Barbour urged that this did not apply to corporate litigants (65–66). These three precedents would confront the court in *Louisville, Cincinnati & Charleston Railroad v. Letson* four years later.[6]

Thomas W. Letson was suing the railroad over a contract. The Louisville, Cincinnati & Charleston Railroad Company was formed with John C. Calhoun as a board member and the company's presidency assumed by the staunch southern states-rights politician Robert Y. Hayne. Hayne had been the mayor of Charleston, governor of South Carolina, and a US senator before seeking to challenge north–south trade with his southern, east–west railroad.[7] Unfortunately, a year after he assumed the presidency of the corporation, the Panic of 1837 hit and caused financial problems for the company; then in 1839, Hayne died. Letson was seeking $18,000 from the troubled company.[8]

The railroad relied on the foregoing precedents to argue that the federal court lacked jurisdiction to hear the case because some members of its corporation were citizens of the same state as the plaintiff Letson. Letson's attorney, James L. Petigru was "a distinguished Whig and an opponent of the political leadership of Hayne and Calhoun."[9] The US attorney general, Hugh S. Legaré, "another distinguished Whig from South Carolina," filed a brief supporting Letson's side and urging the overruling of the diversity precedents that were limiting federal jurisdiction over corporations.[10] The court sided with Letson, rebuffing the railroad and reversing its former decisions.

Justice Wayne was able to deliver a unanimous (5-0) decision overruling the unanimous decisions of two of the previous cases while qualifying the holding in *Deveaux*.[11] He raises a quandary based upon the language of the Judicial Act of 1789, which gives federal courts jurisdiction in suits where "the United States are plaintiffs or petitioners, or an alien is a party, or the suit is *between a citizen of the state where the suit is brought and a citizen of another state*."[12] That particular language is troubling for two reasons: First, it ignores suits involving more than two competing litigants (in using the singular, "citizen"). Second, it implies that only those who are a citizen of the state where the suit is brought may be litigants on one side of the controversy, while the other litigants must be from another state. Wayne notes that cases obviously "need not be between citizen and citizen, but may be between citizens" (553). Furthermore, while the statutory language seems to "limit the jurisdiction to a case in which all the defendants are citizens of the same state" (553), the constitutional language is broader,

> extend[ing] to controversies "between citizens of different states." The words in the legislative grant of jurisdiction, "of the state where the suit is brought and a citizen of another state," are obviously no more than equivalent terms to confine suits in the Circuit Courts to those which are "between citizens of different states." The words in the Constitution then are just as operative to ascertain and limit jurisdiction as the words in the statute. It is true, that under these words "between citizens of different states," Congress may give the courts jurisdiction between citizens in many other forms than that in which it has been conferred. But in the way it is given, the object of the legislature seems exclusively to have been to confer jurisdiction upon the court, strictly in conformity to the limitation as it is expressed in the Constitution, "between citizens of different states." (553–54)

This rather awkward explanation seems to suggest that despite the constitutional grant of jurisdiction, the legislature could limit that jurisdiction ("giv[ing] . . . in many other forms than that in which it has been conferred"). However, he reads the legislative act as an inartful expression of "between citizens of different states," ignoring the "citizen versus citizen" language.

Of course, this becomes more complicated when addressing a corporation as litigant, and Wayne is not much clearer here except in his support of jurisdiction. Initially, he appears ready to call the corporation itself equivalent to a citizen for the purposes of jurisdiction, insisting: "A suit then brought by a citizen of one state against a corporation by its corporate name in the state of its locality, by which it was created and where its business is done by any of the corporators who are chosen to manage its affairs, is a suit, so far as jurisdiction is concerned, between citizens of the state where the suit is brought and a citizen of another state" (554). His emphasis on the "corporate name" shifts the suit from the "corporators" (owners) to the corporation itself. Indeed, he suggests: "It may be said that the suit is against the corporation, and that nothing must be looked at but the legal entity, and then that we cannot view the members except as an artificial aggregate. This is so, in respect to the subject-matter of the suit and the judgment which may be rendered" (554). His qualification of what "may be said" of the suit reflects an ambiguity between the owners and the corporation, where he recognizes that "the corporators as individuals are not defendants in the suit" while adding that "they are parties having an interest in the result, and some of them being citizens of the state where the suit is brought, jurisdiction attaches over the corporation" (554). So, he excludes the corporators but emphasizes their citizenship nonetheless. Despite this muddle, he insists that "we [cannot] see how [jurisdiction] can be defeated by some of the members, who cannot be sued, residing in a different state" (554). Finally, he emphatically states that "if it be right to look to the members to ascertain whether there be jurisdiction or not, the want of appropriate citizenship in some of them to sustain jurisdiction, cannot take it away, when there are other members who are citizens, with the necessary residence to maintain it" (554).

Wayne does not get to the heart of the problem, perhaps because early corporations were generally closely held and managed directly by locals who owned them.[13] It would be six more years before a more cogent argument would be offered by Justice Grier in *Marshall v. Baltimore & Ohio Railroad Co.* Grier notes the hypocrisy of those who take advantage of the corporate form to do business, but then fall back on its intangibility to avoid lawsuits: "The necessities and conveniences of trade and business require that such numerous associates and stockholders should act by representation, and have the faculty of contracting, suing, and being sued in a factitious or collective name. But these important faculties, conferred on them by State legislation, for their own convenience, cannot be wielded to deprive others of acknowledged rights [such as suing in federal court]. It is not reasonable that those who deal with such persons should be deprived of a valuable privilege by a syllogism, or rather sophism, which deals subtly with words and names, without regard to the things or persons they are used to represent."[14]

Wayne obviously is troubled by Chief Justice Marshall's requirement of complete diversity for federal jurisdiction from *Strawbridge* and a requirement that all corporators reside in states different from opposing litigants, though at this point he seems unready to hold the owners' citizenship as irrelevant. He acknowledges the corporation's argument "that the cases of Strawbridge and Curtis, 3 Cranch, 267, and that of the Bank of the United States and Deveaux, 5 Cranch, 84—hold a different doctrine" (554). He dismisses the first case by suggesting the court inadequately considered the case, urging that it "was decided without argument" (555). On the other hand, he admits that "the [case involving] Bank and Deveaux [was decided] after argument of great ability." But, he insists, the argument in the present case was just as well argued, "with the really distinguished ability of the arguments of the counsel in this—[which] in no way was surpassed by those in the former [case of *Deveaux*]" (555).

To tip the balance of decision in favor of his own assessment, Wayne stresses the circumstances of the case, wherein "we are called upon in the most imposing way to give our best judgments to the subject, yielding to decided cases every thing that can be claimed for them on the score of authority except the surrender of conscience" (555). He does not explain why this case imposed more on the court than *Deveaux*. For example, he does not reference the growth of railroads—the first large and often not closely held corporations, which created all sorts of new legal problems for society and for the courts.[15] Nor does he reiterate Attorney General Legaré's argument that "if a citizen of New York could not thus be protected in his dealing with a corporation whose place of business and whose officers were located in South Carolina, 'everybody will admit that there is somewhere a great chasm in our laws, and a serious grievance in our practice.'"[16] He simply insists that the court has engaged in "mature deliberation" making them "feel free to say that the cases of Strawbridge and Curtis and that of the Bank and Deveaux were carried too far, and that consequences and inferences have been argumentatively drawn from the reasoning employed in the latter which ought not to be followed" (555). He rejects the *Slocomb* case as "most reluctantly decided upon the mere authority of [*Strawbridge* and *Deveaux*]" (555). He adds that another case already might have implicitly overruled these precedents, insisting that "it is difficult not to feel that the case of the Bank of the United States and the Planters' Bank of Georgia is founded upon principles irreconcileable [*sic*] with some of those on which the cases already adverted to were founded" (555).[17]

Wayne also offers a list of those who dislike these precedents, including the esteemed author of the original two:

> The cases of Strawbridge and Curtis and the Bank and Deveaux have never been satisfactory to the bar, and that they were not, especially the last, entirely satisfactory to the court that made them. They have been followed always most reluctantly and with dissatisfaction. By no one was the correctness of them more questioned than by the late chief justice [John Marshall] who gave them. It is within the knowledge of several of us, that he repeatedly expressed regret that those decisions had been made, adding, whenever the subject was mentioned, that if the point of jurisdiction was an original one, the conclusion would be different. We think we may safely assert, that a majority of the members of this court have at all times partaken of the same regret, and that whenever a case has occurred on the circuit, involving the application of the case of the Bank and Deveaux, it was yielded to, because the decision had been made, and not because it was thought to be right. We have already said that the case of the Bank of Vicksburg and Slocomb, 14 Peters, was most reluctantly given, upon mere authority. (555–56)

This argument in favor of overturning precedents relies on the widespread dislike of the decision to suggest that others believe the precedents are erroneous or at least problematic. Those are standard justifications for overruling, as I explained in chapter 2. Wayne's subjective assessment about the legal community's attitudes includes his "insider's" view of Chief Justice Marshall, the originator of the complete diversity doctrine and of the *Deveaux* ruling who is said to have had a change of mind on the issue. Suggesting that even the originator of the legal doctrine would no longer embrace it provides powerful support for overruling.

The revised Judiciary Act of 1839, which Barbour dismissed as irrelevant in application to corporation, was taken by Wayne to add Congress to the list of those unhappy with *Strawbridge* and *Deveaux* (and, by implication, *Slocomb*), since "it was passed exclusively with an intent to rid the courts of the decision in the case of Strawbridge and Curtis" (556). Not only does congressional sentiment coincide with that of the bar, the courts, and Chief Justice Marshall, as Wayne constructs them, but the 1839 revision to the Judiciary Act, he urges, "enlarges the jurisdiction of the courts, comprehends the case before us, and embraces the entire result of the opinion which we shall now give" (556). To support this contention, he grapples directly with the statutory language.

Wayne quotes the revised act's description of federal jurisdiction, which provides "that wherein any suit at law or in equity, commenced in any court of the United States, there shall be several defendants, any one or more of whom shall not be inhabitants of, or found within the district where the suit is brought, or shall not voluntarily appear thereto, it shall be lawful for the court to entertain jurisdiction, and proceed to the trial and adjudication of such suit between the parties who may be properly before it; but the judgment or decree rendered therein, shall not conclude or prejudice other parties, not regularly served with process, or not voluntarily appearing to answer" (quoted at 556). Wayne reads Congress's intention in this revision is to fix the problem in the Judiciary Act of 1789 that led to Marshall's complete diversity principle and create "difficulties which occurred in practice, in cases both in law and equity, under that clause in the 11th section of the Judiciary act, which declares, 'that no civil suit shall be brought before either of said courts against an inhabitant of the United States, by any original process, in any other district than that whereof he is an inhabitant, or in which he shall be found at the time of serving the writ.'" (556–57).

In remaining consistent with the Constitution's diversity requirement ("between citizens of different states"), Wayne reads the 1789 act as concerned with procedure: those outside of a district may not be served notice of a lawsuit, since they are remote from the district's boundaries. The 1839 revision fixes this problem by exempting those outside the district, whereby the court's judgment "shall not conclude or prejudice [these] other parties, not regularly served with process, or not voluntarily appearing to answer." If they are exempted, then the suit can proceed ahead without them, sidestepping the problem of complete diversity by leaving them out of the case.

Although *Slocomb* reached this conclusion about the purposes of the 1839 revision, Wayne insisted that *Slocomb* mistakenly assumed "that the act did not contemplate a change in the jurisdiction of the courts as it regards the character of the parties" (557). He explains:

> The clause, that the judgment or decree rendered shall not conclude or prejudice other parties, who have not been regularly served with process, or who have not voluntarily appeared to answer, is an exception, exempting parties so situated from the enactment and must be so strictly applied. It is definite as to the persons of whom it speaks, and contains no particular words, as a subsequent clause, by which the general words of the statute can be restrained. The general words embrace every suit at law or in equity, in which there shall be several defendants, "any one or more of whom shall not be inhabitants of, or found within the district where the suit is brought, or who shall not voluntarily appear thereto." The words, "shall not be inhabitants of," applies as well to corporators as to persons who are not so; and if, as corporators, they are not suable individually and cannot be served with process, or voluntarily appear in an action against the corporation of which they are members, the conclusion should be that they are not included in the exception, but are within the general terms of the statute. Or, if they are viewed as defendants in the suit, then, as corporator, they are regularly served with process in the only way the law permits them to be, when the corporation is sued by its name. (557)

This technical analysis draws a distinction, which *Slocomb* did not, between the general jurisdiction granted ("every suit at law and equity"—implicitly limited, of course, to those between citizens of different states), on the one hand, and those exempted from that jurisdiction (those "not regularly served with process, or who have not voluntarily appeared"). In the case of corporators (owners), those who cannot be served with process are exempted, and that exemption yields complete diversity. That is, leaving out the troubled corporators who might live in the same state as litigants on the other side avoids the problem of a lack of diversity.

But Wayne's final point about suing a corporation by name ("the only way the law permits" a corporation to be sued), lays a foundation for a new position regarding corporate liability. He rejects the requirement of the earlier cases that the court must look to the corporators to see where they live to determine diversity and makes the case for corporations themselves as the ultimate "individuals" addressed by such lawsuits. For "although an artificial person," a corporation is "capable of being treated as a citizen of that state, as much as a natural person"; and it should so be treated since it makes contracts and can sue and be sued (in its name, anyway) (558).

As I have explained elsewhere, corporations would slowly be transformed by appellate courts from intangible creatures of limited "chartered" action (initially, only capable of failures of action) to agents capable of malicious actions, as the nineteenth century progressed and sprawling corporations were accused of injuring others and of violating a flurry of criminal statutes states passed to constrain them.[18] This 1844 case comes in the midst of this transformation and Wayne is latching onto the most obvious means of corporate action recognized by the courts—legal action. For the purposes of identifying those who were litigants in cases to determine diversity, that was sufficient. In retrospect, we may see this as a fateful step that eventually would lead to the attributing of First Amendment rights to corporations involving political contributions and even religious freedoms.[19]

Wayne cites precedents—notably *Dartmouth College v. Woodward*—to establish that incorporation "is chiefly for the purpose of clothing bodies of men in succession with these qualities and capacities, that corporations were invented and are in use. By these means a perpetual succession of individuals are capable of action for the promotion of the particular object like one immortal being."[20] Additionally, as even early English cases show, corporations have been considered inhabitants for purposes such as taxation; and, Wayne reasons, "if it be so for purposes of taxation, why is it not so for the purposes of a suit in the Circuit Court of the United States, when the plaintiff has the proper residence?" (559). Thus, he concludes: "We confess our inability to reconcile these qualities of a corporation—residence, habitancy, and individuality, with the doctrine that a corporation aggregate cannot be a citizen for the purposes of a suit in the courts of the United States, unless in consequence of a residence of all the corporators being of the state in which the suit is brought. When the corporation exercises its powers in the state which chartered it, that is its residence, and such an averment is sufficient to give the Circuit Courts jurisdiction" (559).[21]

The *Letson* decision justifies overruling most or part of three precedents by arguing that the bar, the courts, and Chief Justice Marshall were not happy with the principle of complete diversity as it was applied to corporations; that Congress had changed the court's jurisdiction in any case and broadened it more than *Slocomb* recognized; and that the nature of corporations made them sufficiently like citizens to stand as the primary litigants for purposes of diversity jurisdiction.[22] Although the case featured close technical analysis of statutory language, it also appealed to judicial and congressional motives and an almost philosophical analysis of the concept of the corporation to see how and whether that was captured by the statutes.

Wayne did not appeal as much to changes in economic conditions, such as the rise of corporations that were not closely held who exercised great economic power which might give rise to suits such as Letson's. He does allude, vaguely, to "difficulties which occurred in practice, in cases both in law and equity, under that clause in the 11th section of the Judiciary act" (556), but that is a weak appeal to changed conditions that undergirds many overrulings. The appeal is more to the unworkability of the rule.

We next jump ahead seventy-three years to a case involving a corporation when the form had evolved sufficiently to move Congress to act against trusts. In this instance the trust was joined by one of the United States' most beloved inventors, Thomas Edison, whose disputes over his patents almost throttled the movie industry in its infancy.

HOLLYWOOD'S CHALLENGE TO EDISON'S TRUST

A 1917 patent case pitted a trust joined by Thomas Edison against independent filmmakers and exhibitors while all litigating parties were developing the burgeoning movie industry. It is a story of inventors and patent infringers, monopolists and independent artists, the East Coast and the West Coast. At stake were millions of dollars and the future economics and aesthetics of the film industry.

The story begins in the late 1880s when Thomas Edison directed one his key engineers, W. L. K. Dickson, to lead a team to develop a machine to record and play back moving images. Their work succeeded and in 1891 Edison patented the first movie camera, the Kinetograph, and a device for playing the recorded film back, the Kinetoscope.[23] The Kinetoscope played back films that were about twenty-seconds long and viewed by one person at a time through a peephole. Edison hosted exhibitions of the new technology over the next few years, with the first commercial exhibition of motion pictures coming in April 1894 in the Holland Brothers' Kinetoscope Parlor in New York City.[24] Sales of the machines, and a coin-fed version, did very well for the first few years.[25]

Edison made three key mistakes that prevented him from completely cornering the early movie market: First, he failed to apply for international patents on these inventions. As Matthew Josephson's biography of Edison notes: "By his blunder in failing to apply for European patents for his motion picture apparatus in 1891, Edison had lost the monopoly of the process of film making; his various competitors in the industry had purchased American patent rights to English and French machines that were obvious imitations or improved models of his invention."[26]

The second mistake was his failure initially to create a projection system for showing films to larger audiences. That decision was connected to a third mistake, his assumption that audiences would prefer extremely short films, from twenty seconds to a few minutes. These early "shorts" featured a strong man flexing his muscles, someone sneezing, a kiss, a rushing Niagara Falls, or other quick subjects, which Edison created for his Kinetoscope. As Barak Y. Orbach explains, "Edison perceived motion pictures as a short form of entertainment, publicly declined proposals to develop a projecting machine, and dedicated only limited resources to such a project in a secret laboratory."[27] Other inventors saw the potential for mass exhibitions of moving pictures and invented early projectors in 1895 and 1896.[28] Edison played catch-up by buying a patent from another inventor which he adapted as his own Vitascope.[29] To keep up with French filmmakers who were experimenting with longer narrative forms and to overcome waning interest in the novelty of the Kinetoscope, Edison's company produced the ten-minute-long film *The Great Train Robbery* in 1903, which became a blockbuster.[30]

Competition was growing fierce in the industry as vaudeville shows began including short films prior to the live acts and, eventually, permanent movie theaters were opened. By 1912 there were almost 13,000 movie theaters in the United States.[31] One of Edison's competitors was the man Edison put in charge of developing the Kinetograph, W. K. L. Dickson, who left Edison to found a competing company, American Mutoscope Company (later renamed American Mutoscope and Biograph Company).[32] Biograph used a 70mm film that produced an image four times the size of Edison's 35mm.[33] Biograph also began to produce "story films" as early as 1900, featuring both moral tales and burlesque shorts.[34]

It took ten years of litigation for Edison to finally win a lawsuit in 1907 against those who built upon his original motion picture patents.[35] By this point, Edison and his chief competitors were ready to make a deal to stop their infighting and secure their positions in the growing industry. Edison's financial manager, Frank

L. Dyer, worked with their chief rival, Biograph, to bring together ten companies to form the Motion Picture Patents Company (MPPC) in December 1908, including Edison, Biograph, Vitagraph, Essanay, Kalem, Selig Polyscope, Lubin, Stare Film, Pathé Frères, and Kleine Optical.[36] Jon Lewis explains the goals of the trust: "The MPPC effectively exploited key industry patents on motion picture technology to fix prices, restrict the distribution and exhibition of foreign-made pictures, regulate domestic production and control film licensing and distribution. The trust was supported by an exclusive contract with the Eastman Kodak Company (then the principal and only dependable provider of raw film stocks), which was signed the same day the MPPC trust agreement was signed."[37]

To support its stranglehold on the industry, in 1910 the trust created its own film distribution company, the General Film Company. The company required its ten thousand exhibitors to pay a two-dollar-per-week license fee. As Collins notes, because "it was generally acknowledged that motion pictures shot on Kodak stock with trust-protected cameras were far superior to any others available, most exhibitors, though outraged by the fee, had little choice but to go along with the agreement."[38] Edison already had successfully sued to protect his movie camera, which employed two significant innovations: the Latham loop (which took tension off the film and prevented breakage) and the "maltese cross" shutter mechanism to reduce flicker.[39] (These innovations also were used in his movie projectors.) So, the trust was attempting to control the entire industry, from production to distribution to exhibition. They enforced their regulations with exhibitors they had licensed by threatening to revoke those licenses, effectively ending their businesses. As one contemporary film magazine described the situation, "the sword is always suspended over the head of the [exhibitor]. Not a reassuring state of affairs to an ordinary business man."[40]

Independent filmmakers, who were not licensed to use the equipment of the MPPC, faced different threats. As Conot explains, "the MPPC tried to drive all the independent producers and nickelodeon operators out of business. [A private detective who worked for Edison, Joseph] Gumshoe McCoy hired goons, who signed up as extras in unlicensed productions, then broke up the sets and smashed the cameras."[41] Such independents "were sometimes called 'blanket companies,' after the blanket used to hide their illegal cameras."[42] To escape the scrutiny of the MPPC, as well as enjoy more clear days for filming and cheaper operating costs, many independents moved to California; thus did Edison and his group contribute to the establishment of Hollywood.[43]

Despite its efforts, the MPPC could not snuff out the independent film industry. Kodak was lured away from an exclusive agreement with the trust by an agent who wanted a huge, ongoing order of raw film stock for independent filmmakers; in 1911 Kodak amended its agreement with the MPPC to take advantage of the deal.[44] Large exhibitors who would become titans in the movie industry challenged the MPPC's attempt at monopoly in this age of trust-busting.[45] Carl Laemmle, whose company became Universal Studios, won a suit over the use of the Latham loop in 1912.[46] However, the death blow would come from an antitrust suit launched by William Fox, who created Fox Film Corporation (which became 20th Century Fox and, recently, 20th Century Studios).[47] In 1915 the courts found the MPPC in violation of the Sherman Antitrust Act, making the group liable for triple damages from injured parties.[48]

The overruling case I want to examine here involves one creative attempt by the MPPC to use its patents to squeeze out the competition. *Motion Picture Patents Co. v. Universal Film* overruled a five-year-old case, *Henry v. Dick*.[49] I will begin with a review of the overruled case.

The *Henry* majority decision was written by the short-serving Justice Horace Lurton. The case involved the A. B. Dick Company's sales of its mimeograph machines. The company required that purchasers of its machines use supplies that it sold for use with the machine, including its stencil paper and ink (11). The company brought suit against the Henry Company for selling ink to a Miss Skou for use in Dick's patented machine. Although Lurton asserts that "the license agreement constitutes a contract not to use the machine in a prohibited manner," Dick was not suing for a broken contract but rather a patent infringement that the Henry Company was said to have aided and abetted (14).

Lurton takes it for granted that Dick could use its patents in such a manner, insisting: "That a patentee may effectually restrict the time, place or manner of using a patented machine, so that a prohibited use will constitute an infringement of the patent, is fully conceded" (17). In support of this claim he notes: "The books abound in cases upholding the right of a patentee owner of a machine to license another to use it subject to any qualification in respect of time, place, manner or purpose of use which the licensee agrees to accept. Any use in excess of the license would obviously be an infringing use and the license would be no defense. Robinson on Patents, §§ 915, 916 and notes. This is so elementary we shall not stop to cite cases" (18).

Lurton suggests that attaching such requirements preserves the "identity" of the invention. Thus, "any transfer of the patentee's property right in a patented machine carries with it the right to use the entire invention so long as the identity of the machine is preserved, irrespective of any restrictions placed by the patentee upon the use of the article and accepted by the buyer" (18).

Lurton spends most of the opinion trying to discern "the kind of limitation which may be lawful[ly] imposed upon a purchaser" by a patentee, and whether Henry and Miss Skou stayed within such limitations (26). Determining what kind of limitations on use might be imposed and what may not, he states, "is a question of statutory construction," that is, of discerning what the patent statute allows and prohibits (26).

One obvious limitation he acknowledges is that the purchaser must have notice that there are limitations on a patented product's uses (26). Beyond that, he insists, we must recognize that the patent statute "is a statute creating and protecting a monopoly. It is a true monopoly, one having its origin in the ultimate authority, the Constitution" (27). He admits that contrary interpretations of the purposes for allowing a monopoly might be inferred, asking: "Shall we deal with the statute creating and guaranteeing the exclusive right which is granted to the inventor with the narrow scrutiny proper when a statutory right is asserted to uphold a claim which is lacking in those moral elements which appeal to the normal man? Or shall we approach it as a monopoly granted to subserve a broad public policy, by which large ends are to be attained, and, therefore, to be construed so as to give effect to a wise and beneficial purpose?" (27).

Notice that, despite the fact that he is grappling with a statute's meaning, he does not quote it but considers in a larger sense what its purpose *must be*.[50] He genuflects to the need to be balanced, insisting "that we must neither transcend the statute, nor cut down its clear meaning, is plain" (27). Yet, instead of looking at the statute's words, he looks at the words of a case in which Chief Justice Marshall expresses the "favorable view which the law takes as to the protection extended to the exclusive right [of patent]." Such protection, Marshall says, "is the reward stipulated for the advantages derived by the public for the exertions of the individual, and is intended as a stimulus to those exertions"; furthermore, he insists, "the public yields nothing which it has not agreed to yield; it receives all which it had contracted to receive."[51]

What the public has yielded in granting a patent monopoly is significant, in Lurton's reading, "extend[ing] to the right of making, selling and using, and these are separable and substantial rights" (28). He quotes at length a sixteen-year-old case, *Bloomer v. McQuewan*, for the proposition that machine patent holders have "the right to exclude every one from making, using or vending the thing without the permission of the owner."[52] He draws upon an 1896 Sixth Circuit Court of Appeals case, commonly known as the *Button-Fastener* cases, to insist that a patent holder held so much authority over his property that he could hold a patent and neither use it nor let anyone else use it.[53] And, if he did let another use it, he could exercise his property rights, according to another case, with "absolute freedom in the use or sale of rights under the patent laws of the United States . . . [because] the very object of these laws is monopoly, and the rule is, with few exceptions, that any conditions which are not in their very nature illegal with regard to this kind of property, imposed by the patentee and agreed to by the licensee for the right to manufacture or use or sell the article, will be upheld by the courts. The fact that the conditions in the contracts keep up the monopoly or fix prices does not render them illegal."[54] Indeed, Lurton infers, in addition to fixing prices for patented articles, "any other reasonable stipulation, not inherently violative of some substantive law, imposed by a patentee as part of a sale of a patented machine, would be equally valid and enforceable" (31).

Given the patentee's considerable authority to impose conditions on one using its patented machine, Lurton finds the requirement that those using Dick's mimeograph machine buy its unpatented ink and paper perfectly appropriate (31–32). The patentee created the market with her new invention and without it "no ink could have been sold" for use in it (32).

Lurton rejects a slippery slope argument offered through "many fanciful suggestions of conditions which might be imposed by a patentee [that] have been pressed upon us," not because those suggestions are fanciful but because, ultimately, "the public is always free to take or refuse the patented article on the terms imposed. If they be too onerous or not in keeping with the benefits, the patented article will not find a market" (34).

Ultimately, Lurton endorses a strong patentee right to dictate terms as central to the idea of a monopoly afforded by a patent. He perhaps overstates the case in insisting that "an attack upon the rights under a patent because it secures a monopoly to make, to sell and to use, is an attack upon the whole patent system" (35). He sidesteps the question of whether this was the intent of those who created US patent law by insisting: "We are not at liberty to say that the Constitution has unwisely provided for granting a monopolistic right to inventors, or that Congress has unwisely failed to impose limitations upon the inventor's exclusive right of use" (35). Once again, without quoting any statute, he insists that "Congress alone has the power to determine what restraints shall be imposed. As the law now stands it contains none, and the duty which rests upon this and upon every other court is to expound the law as it is written" (35). Lurton continues on, citing many cases supporting a strong patent right, though he admits that "the precise question here involved has never been decided by this court" (43).

Lurton was joined by three justices, Justices McKenna, Holmes, and Van Devanter. Justice Harlan had recently died and Justice Day did not hear the argument. Chief Justice White wrote a dissent that was joined by Justices Hughes and Lamar, leaving a 4-3 split. White thought the decision was unfounded and would lead to great evil. He encourages Congress to amend the patent law to reverse the court's reading (49–50). He stresses that "the ink was not covered by the patent," though Lurton treated it though it effectively was (51). The decision, he says, held "that a patentee in selling the machine covered by his patent has power by contract to extend the patent so as to cause it to embrace things which it does not include" (50). White draws a distinction between the patented machine and the materials employed in using it; the former is covered by the patent, but the latter are not (52–53). Furthermore, he urges, Lurton failed to distinguish between third parties selling ordinary commodities (ink in this case) and the purchasers of the patented machine who entered a contract with the patentee. The result was that the ruling would "extend to every human being in society without reference to their privity to any contract existing between the patentee and the one to whom he has sold the patented machine" (54). By relying on federal patent law as thus extended in its coverage, White also worried that cases that traditionally fell under state jurisdiction would be snatched from the hands of local courts (53–54).

White offers a parade of examples (no doubt Lurton's "fanciful suggestions") to show how a patentee could abuse property rights recognized in this ruling:

> Take a patentee selling a patented engine. He will now have the right by contract to bring under the patent laws all contracts for coal or electrical energy used to afford power to work the machine or even the lubricants employed in its operation. Take a patented carpenter's plane. The power now exists in the patentee by contract to validly confine a carpenter purchasing one of the planes to the use of lumber sawed from trees grown on the land of a particular person or sawed by a particular mill. Take a patented cooking utensil. The power is now recognized in the patentee to bind by contract one who buys the utensil to use in connection with it no other food supply but that sold or made by the patentee. Take the invention of a patented window frame. It is now the law that the seller of the frame may stipulate that no other material shall be used in a house in which the window frames are placed except such as may be bought from the patentee and seller of the frame. (55)

Of course, Lurton's point was, Yes, a patentee could do that, but no one would buy her product.

White goes on to cite "many adjudications of this court [that] directly refute the existence of a supposed right of extension by contract of the patent laws, and are therefore, as I understand them, in conflict with the ruling now made" (56). He notes that the *Button-Fastener* case had led companies to regularly "increase the scope of the monopoly granted by a patent . . . by resorting to the device of license restrictions manifested in various forms," causing a "burden [to] the public in the exercise of their common rights," and, with this decision, to likely pursue contractual stipulations that are "unconscionable and oppressive" (70–72).

White would not have to wait long to reverse Lurton's decision. Five years after the *Henry* case the court found an opportunity in *Motion Picture Patents Co. v. Universal Film*. No one changed his position, but personnel changed significantly: Lurton died and was replaced by Justice McReynolds. Justice Day was not absent this time. Justice Harlan, who died before the *Henry* case was decided, was replaced by Justice Pitney. Two of White's fellow dissenters also were replaced: Justice Lamar died and was replaced by Justice Brandeis; Justice Hughes resigned to run as the Republican nominee for president in 1916 and was replaced by Justice Clarke. (Hughes would lose to Woodrow Wilson but return to the court as its chief justice fourteen years later.) The former majority of four, with Lurton gone, became a minority of three, with Justice Holmes leading the dissent. The other six justices—four of them new to the court—lined up behind Justice Clarke's majority opinion to overrule *Henry*.

Holmes's dissent was very short, reiterating the point that if one can deny an invention completely, she also could put stipulations on it which a wary buyer could avoid by refusing to purchase it (519). He denied that there was an overriding public interest in preventing such stipulations and defended them as "an ordinary incident of ownership" (520). Finally, he warned about upsetting settled law (without mentioning stare decisis), particularly in a case such as this which involved property rights. He said:

> Not only do I believe that the rule that I advocate is right under the Paper Bag Case, but I think that it has become a rule of property that law and justice require to be retained. For fifteen years, at least since Bement v. National Harrow Co., 186 U.S. 70, 88–93, if not considerably earlier, the public has been encouraged by this court to believe that the law is as it was laid down in [the *Button-Fastener* case] and numerous other decisions of the lower courts. I believe that many and important transactions have taken place on the faith of those decisions, and that for that reason as well as for the first that I have given, the rule last announced in Henry v. Dick Co., 224 U.S. 1, should be maintained. (520)

By extending the age of the rule past *Henry* and to a fifteen-year-old case, Holmes attempts to establish reliance by property owners, so that abandoning that would unsettle property rights—the most sacred law due protection under stare decisis. This lays the stress a bit differently than Lurton had in noting that *Henry* was a case of first impression. In any case, Justice Clarke had his hands full in justifying this overruling.

The MPPC brought suit against corporate defendants for infringing its Latham loop patent on its movie projector (505). The "infringement" did not involve a competing projector using the technology, but simply playing a non-MPPC film on a projector using the patented device in violation of an accompanying licensing agreement. A warning against such infringements was attached to a plate on the projector with a "Licensing Notice" telling users that they must comply with the company's terms of use or suffer a termination of the right to use the machine (507). Despite this warning, the Seventy-second Street Amusement Company (through its lessee, the Prague Amusement Company) played two films from the Universal Film Manufacturing Company (later Universal Studios), prompting the MPPC suit (507). The district and circuit courts dismissed the suit and the MPPC appealed (508).

Unlike Justice Lurton's precedent decision, Justice Clarke's opinion cited specific statutes at issue in resolving the questions. First he noted that "Rev. Stat. § 4900, Comp. Stat. 1913, § 9446 requir[es] that patented articles shall be marked with the word 'Patented'" and covers damages for infringement of such items; the following section, § 9447, protects the inventor (509). However, he notes, "neither one [of these provisions] contemplates the use of such a 'License Notice' as we have here, and whatever validity it has must be derived from the general, and not from the patent, law" (509).

The larger question was whether the MPPC could demand such compliance from purchasers of its projectors. That required the court to "determine the meaning of Congress when in Rev. Stats., § 4884, it provided that 'Every patent shall contain . . . a grant to the patentee, his heirs or assigns, for the term of seventeen years, of the exclusive right to make, use, and vend the invention or discovery throughout the United States, and the Territories thereof.' We are concerned only with the right to 'use,' authorized to be granted by this statute, for it is under warrant of this right only that the plaintiff can and does claim validity for its warning notice" (509–10).

Clarke framed his analysis of the issue in light of three principles that challenged the sweeping monopoly rights Lurton had found:

> 1st. The scope of every patent is limited to the invention described in the claims contained in it, read in the light of the specification. These so mark where the progress claimed by the patent begins and where it ends that they have been aptly likened to the description in a deed, which sets the bounds to the grant which it contains. . . .
>
> 2nd. It has long been settled that the patentee receives nothing from the law which he did not have before, and that the only effect of his patent is to restrain others from manufacturing, using or selling that which he has invented. . . .
>
> 3rd. Since Pennock v. Dialogue, 2 Pet. 1, was decided in 1829 this court has consistently held that the primary purpose of our patent laws is not the creation of private fortunes for the owners of patents but is "to promote the progress of science and useful arts" (Constitution, Art. I, § 8). (510–11)

The first point would stress what the patent covered, using an effective spatial metaphor to mark out boundaries. The second would note its effect, to prevent others from stealing one's ideas or the products of those ideas. And the last would indicate the purpose of the law.

On the purpose of patent law, which Lurton insisted must be to give a monopoly with few restrictions, Clarke quoted Justice Story's alternative view that "while one great object [of our patent laws] was, by holding out a *reasonable reward* to inventors, and giving them an exclusive right to their inventions for a limited period, to stimulate the efforts of genius; the main object was 'to promote the progress of science and useful arts'" (511; emphasis added). So, where Lurton would give an inventor carte blanche to tell the purchaser how she must use his patented work and exact whatever money the market would bear, Clarke suggests Story's "reasonable reward" to the inventor, which itself was subsidiary to promoting science and useful arts. Lurton might counter that *only* unlimited control is sufficient incentive for inventors to contribute to such progress, but Clarke obviously believes a more limited concession will suffice.

Redirecting the purpose of patent law to a public good over a large private reward undergirds Clarke's narrower reading of what the patent holder can demand. He insists that the statute's language "of the exclusive right to . . . use . . . the invention or discovery," along with "established rules to which we have referred" are concerned "plainly" with "the mechanism described in the patent as necessary to produce the desired results" (such as projecting a film) and "has nothing to do with the materials with which or on which the machine operates" (512). Yet, he notes, "both in form and in substance the [projector's License] notice attempts a restriction upon the use of the supplies only and it cannot with any regard to propriety in the use of language be termed a restriction upon the use of the machine itself" (512–13).

Clarke's argument implies that Lurton's decision erred in reading the statute as tipping the balance in favor of the patentee over the public good. He hangs a lot of argument on "use" as a term in the statute but relies even more on an understanding of the overall purpose of patent law. He goes on to suggest how some bad precedents led others astray (including the *Henry* court) and revealed the bad consequences of giving patent holders such power while denying bad consequences for innovation from the more limited power he would give patentees. Clarke describes a causal chain that begins with the original rule of limited patentee power (which he defends) and its good outcomes, to a change in law that led to bad outcomes, to an assurance that a return to the original rule will be best.

He notes that giving the inventor "the right to an exclusive use of the new and useful discovery which has been made . . . and nothing more" was a sufficient reward. Indeed, he insists, "for more than a century this plain meaning of the statute was accepted as its technical meaning, and that it afforded ample incentive to exertion by inventive genius is proved by the fact that under it the greatest inventions of our time, teeming with inventions, were made" (513). The idea of pushing patent rights beyond these limits came with the development of modern corporations "in which the full possibilities seem first to have been appreciated of uniting, in one, many branches of business through corporate organization and of gathering great profits in small payments, which are not realized or resented, from many, rather than smaller or even equal profits in larger payments, which are felt and may be refused, from a few, that it came to be thought that the "'right to use . . . the invention' of a patent gave to the patentee or his assigns the right to restrict the use of it to materials or supplies not described in the patent and not by its terms made a part of the thing patented" (513–14). The innovation in the law was made, Clarke explains, in the *Button-Fastener* case decided by the Sixth Circuit Court in 1896 (514). But while that court "recogniz[ed] the pioneer character of the decision it was rendering" and the "novel restrictions" set by the patentee in the case, it refused to "'mark the boundary line around the patentee's monopoly which will *debar him from engrossing the market for an article not the subject of a patent*'" (514; quoting 77 Fed. 288 with emphasis). It reached an erroneous decision by "proceed[ing] upon the argument that, since the patentee may withhold his patent altogether from public use, he must logically and necessarily be permitted to impose any conditions which he chooses upon any use which he may allow of it" (515). The error came from "the substituting of inference and argument for the language of the statute, and from failure to distinguish between the rights which are given to the inventor by the patent law and which he may assert against all the world through an infringement proceeding, and rights which he may create for himself by private contract, which, however, are subject to the rule of general, as distinguished from those of patent, law" (514).

Not only was the decision wrong in failing to draw this distinction, it also "led to an immediate and widespread adoption of the system, in which these restrictions expanded into more and more comprehensive forms" for which the case at bar serves as an extreme example (515). The MPPC would make "a machine sold and paid for . . . subject not only to restriction as to supplies to be used, but also subject to any restrictions or conditions as to use or royalty which the company which authorized its sale may see fit, after the sale, from time to time to impose" (515). Clarke calls this "the perfect instrument of favoritism and oppression" allowing the MPPC to, "for its own profit or that of its favorites, by the obviously simple expedient of varying its royalty charge, ruin anyone unfortunate enough to be dependent upon its confessedly important improvements for the doing of business" (515).

In addition to error and bad consequences, Clarke emphasizes the prevalence of dissenters from the Button-Fastener rule and "the division of this court when the question involved first came before it in Henry v. A. B. Dick Co. . . . and in the disposition not to extend the doctrine in Bauer v. O'Donnell" (515). *Bauer*, decided in 1913, rejected the idea that a patentee could "fix a price at which the patented article might be sold and resold under penalty of patent infringement" citing "the language of the statute from which all patent right is derived" (516). Drawing an analogy to the case, Clarke insisted "the statutory authority to grant the exclusive right to 'use' a patented machine is not greater, indeed, it is precisely the same, as the authority to grant the exclusive right to 'vend'" (516).

Finally, Clarke draws upon a source unique to statutory overruling—Congress—to support his interpretation of patent law. Congress had passed a statute (38 Stat. 730) disallowing persons engaged in interstate commerce from selling patented or unpatented goods conditioned on an agreement that the purchaser not use their competitors' products with those goods (517). Clarke says that legislation was passed "as if in response to" the *Henry* decision (517). If Congress outlawed such stipulations, "as if" responding to *Henry*'s endorsement of the use of them, then the court has reason to believe that the patent statutes should follow the legislature's lead in this regard.

Clarke is explicit about the overruling, noting: "It is obvious that the conclusions arrived at in this opinion are such that the decision in Henry v. A. B. Dick Co. supra, must be regarded as overruled" (518). In disposing of the MPPC case, he is direct: The Company may not restrict whose films are played on the patented projector since "such a restriction is invalid because such a film is obviously not any part of the invention of the patent in suit" (518). The opinion also rejected an attempt to continue the monopoly after the patent had expired and to impose an ongoing royalty on the use of the machines "after its machines have been sold and paid for."[55] It warns that allowing such practices would "give to the plaintiff such a potential power for evil over an industry which must be recognized as an important element in the amusement life of the nation," ignoring patent law's public interest, "which we have seen is more a favorite of the law than is the promotion of private fortunes" (519).

Clarke misses a chance to criticize Lurton's opinion for failing to quote the statute directly to support his reading of the statute's purposes, which the former justice admitted was supreme. But he does show that cases from the 1896 *Button-Fastener* cases to *Henry* were an aberration from what had come before, so that his opinion was returning to the original understanding of the law. This explains the dissension over the years he notes, particularly in the wake of the bad consequences reflected in corporate exploitation of the rule. Generally, Clarke has a strong argument for overruling, despite the decision's unsettling of property law.

DEFENDING PREGNANT WORKERS BY REVISITING CIVIL LIABILITY FOR MUNICIPALITIES

Jane Monell was a social worker at a shelter for girls in Brooklyn, New York, in the fall of 1970. The United States had just celebrated the fiftieth anniversary of the passage of the Nineteenth Amendment's grant of suffrage to women and second wave feminists were in the streets advocating for women's equality. Although Presidents Kennedy and Johnson had shepherded policies to address discrimination against women in the workplace, plenty of obstacles remained.[56] When Monell's district director stopped by the shelter he found that she was visibly pregnant and told her she would have to go on unpaid leave for the remainder of her pregnancy to comply with the city's policy. Monell's husband, Oscar G. Chase, was a young law professor who channeled her anger at the policy into a legal case that would be joined with teachers in the city and eventually reach the US Supreme Court.[57] Monell's challenge to the policy was complicated by the fact that it was a municipality that was discriminating against female employees and it was unclear that the applicable civil rights statute, or the principles of federalism, allowed damages against a municipality. The case would turn on the interpretation of that statute, with a constitutional weighing of federal powers tipping the balance.

While the city admitted that it had a policy of requiring pregnant women to take unpaid leave after the fifth month of pregnancy (unless a two-month extension was approved by a city physician and an agency head), it quickly changed the policy after the suit was commenced (661n2). The plaintiffs sued several city administrators in their official capacities, seeking injunctive relief from the policy and back pay for periods of unlawful forced leave (661).

The statute under which their claim was made is 42 U.S.C. § 1983, which holds: "Every *person* who, under color of any statute, ordinance, regulation, custom, or usage, of any State or Territory or the District of Columbia, subjects, or causes to be subjected, any citizen of the United States or other person within the jurisdiction thereof to the deprivation of any rights, privileges, or immunities secured by the Constitution and laws, shall be liable to the party injured in an action at law, suit in equity, or other proper proceeding for redress, except that in any action brought against a judicial officer for an act or omission taken in such officer's judicial capacity, injunctive relief shall not be granted unless a declaratory decree was violated or declaratory relief was unavailable" (emphasis added). The entire case turned on whether "person" in this statute included municipalities and school boards. In a case the previous year, a unanimous court had rejected an appeal to make this determination because the issue was "not before us" and should be left "for another day."[58] That day had arrived.

The language of § 1983 is exactly the same as its predecessor, § 1 of the Civil Rights Act of 1871. Also known as the Ku Klux Klan Act and the Third

Enforcement Act, the law provided teeth for enforcing the Fourteenth Amendment's equal protection of the laws for recently freed slaves and others. It clearly provided a means to recover damages from members of groups such as the KKK that oppressed African Americans. However, it was less clear whether it might be used against states or local government institutions within states, such as municipalities and school boards, when they engaged in discriminatory actions based on suspect or quasi-suspect categories, or allowed or failed to stop such actions by private citizens.[59]

In the *Monell* case, the District Court for the Southern District of New York found that the city's actions were unconstitutional but held that the case was moot because the city had changed its policy. It also rejected the request for back pay because municipalities were immune from such suits under the US Supreme Court's interpretation of § 1983 in its decision in the 1961 case of *Monroe v. Pape.*[60] On appeal to the Second Circuit, the plaintiff teachers tried to distinguish their Board of Education as a "person" rather than a "municipality" who was subject to a lawsuit under § 1983. The appellate court rejected that argument, also citing *Monroe* for the immunity of the city from the suit (662). And though officials were "persons" under the statute, they could not be sued either because damages would have to be paid by the city in any case (662). The Supreme Court granted certiorari to consider "whether local governmental officials and/or local independent school boards are 'persons' within the meaning of 42 U.S.C. § 1983 when equitable relief in the nature of back pay is sought against them in their official capacities" (662). They resolved the issue by overruling *Monroe* in its holding "that local governments are wholly immune from suit under § 1983" (662).

The *Monroe* precedent involved an appeal for damages from the City of Chicago after members of its police department violated the civil rights of an African American family, which the complaint described in horrific detail:

> The complaint alleges that 13 Chicago police officers broke into petitioners' home in the early morning, routed them from bed, made them stand naked in the living room, and ransacked every room, emptying drawers and ripping mattress covers. It further alleges that Mr. Monroe was then taken to the police station and detained on "open" charges for 10 hours, while he was interrogated about a two-day-old murder, that he was not taken before a magistrate, though one was accessible, that he was not permitted to call his family or attorney, that he was subsequently released without criminal charges being preferred against him. It is alleged that the officers had no search warrant and no arrest warrant and that they acted "under color of the statutes, ordinances, regulations, customs and usages" of Illinois and of the City of Chicago. (169)

The *Monroe* court found that the police officers could be sued under R.S. § 1979, 42 U.S.C. § 1983; however, the liability of the City of Chicago turned on the question of whether the city was a "person" under the statute.[61]

The court's opinion traced Revised Statute § 1979 back to the 1871 act and noted that Congress clearly had the power to enforce the Fourteenth Amendment, though it insisted that this case dealt with "narrower [question] of whether Congress, in enacting § 1979, meant to give a remedy to parties deprived of constitutional rights, privileges and immunities by an official's abuse of his position" (171–72). The court agreed that this was the intent of the statute, with one rather large caveat: that municipalities were exempt from suits seeking damages. The court quoted extensive arguments over the legislation, particularly those involving the rejection of the "Sherman amendment," which specifically made municipalities liable to damages, concluding: "The response of the Congress to the proposal to make municipalities liable for certain actions being brought within federal purview by the Act of April 20, 1871, was so antagonistic that we cannot believe that the word 'person' was used in this particular Act to include them. Accordingly we hold that the motion to dismiss the complaint against the City of Chicago was properly granted" (191–92).

Justice Brennan, writing for the *Monell* majority, directly challenged *Monroe*'s assumption that the rejection of this amendment to include municipalities in what was proposed as § 7 of the statute meant that the entire statute (especially § 1) purposefully excluded them from liability under the statute. He insisted that "the sole basis for this conclusion [that municipalities lack civil liability under § 1983] was an inference drawn from Congress' rejection of the 'Sherman amendment' to the bill which became the Civil Rights Act of 1871, 17 Stat. 13, the precursor of § 1983" (664). Brennan urged that concerns over the Sherman amendment were narrower than the *Monroe* court implied and, therefore, that its ruling of immunity for municipalities was broader than necessary to resolve the case. He also insisted that *Monroe* was at odds with other precedents finding school boards liable to similar actions, so that a new ruling was needed to resolve inconsistencies in the high court's decisions. Thus did the court invoke two standard reasons for overruling a precedent: that it was wrongly decided and that it conflicted with other decisions so that stare decisis cut two ways.

The Sherman amendment, which was voted down in the debate over the Ku Klux Klan Act, provided a cause of action against "any persons riotously and tumultuously assembled together . . . with intent to deprive any person of any right conferred upon him by the Constitution and laws of the United States, or to deter him or punish him for exercising such right, or by reason of his race, color, or previous condition of servitude" (quoted at 666). Most controversially, a version of the amendment that came out of the first conference over the Senate and the House versions "provided that the action would be against the county, city, or parish in which the riot had occurred and that it could be maintained by either the person injured or his legal representative" (667) and, if the municipality were found liable, damages could be collected "by execution, attachment, mandamus, garnishment, or any other proceeding in aid of execution or applicable to the enforcement of judgments against municipal corporations; and such judgment [would become] a lien as well upon all moneys in the treasury of such county, city, or parish, as upon the other property thereof" (quoting the draft at 667). The conference committee probably added this provision to get around the problem of suing unknown attackers and of securing a source of compensation for victims (667).

The *Monroe* court had relied heavily on a broad statement about municipal immunity made in the debate over the amendment by Representative Luke Potter Poland (R-VT), who spoke for the House conferees on the final draft of the bill. He warned that the Sherman amendment's municipal liability was a nonstarter for House members, because "the House [in voting against the Sherman amendment] had solemnly decided that in their judgment Congress had no constitutional power to impose any *obligation* upon county and town organizations, the mere instrumentality for the administration of state law" (*Monell* at 664, quoting *Monroe* at 190, with emphasis added to Poland's words). Brennan explained that the *Monroe* court had relied on Poland's statement to suggest "that Congress doubted its 'constitutional power . . . to impose *civil liability* on municipalities' and that such doubt would have extended to any type of civil liability" (664, quoting *Monroe* at 190 with emphasis). That interpretation, Brennan argued, "incorrectly equated the 'obligation' of which Representative Poland spoke with 'civil liability,'" and he offered a "fresh analysis" to support an alternative reading (665).

Brennan suggested that the House's objections were reasonable when the original provision was compared with similar laws. It was not unusual to hold a government financially accountable for the actions of private individuals—England and several US states had statutes that sought "to enlist the aid of persons of property in the enforcement of the civil rights laws by making their property 'responsible' [e.g., in this case,] for Ku Klux Klan damage" (667). However, the debated provision was harsher than statutes in other places, Brennan argued, because "the conference substitute, unlike most state riot statutes, lacked a short statute of limitations and imposed liability on the government defendant whether or not it had notice of the impending riot, whether or not the municipality was authorized to exercise a police power, whether or not it exerted all reasonable efforts to stop the riot, and whether or not the rioters were caught and punished" (668). While the Senate supported this version, the House rejected it as unconstitutional in requiring municipalities "to keep the peace if those corporations were neither so obligated nor so authorized by their state charters" and, furthermore, to suffer damages if they did not keep the peace (668).

When this version failed to pass the House, a second conference watered down the amendment, removing municipal liability while making "'any person or persons having knowledge [that a conspiracy to violate civil rights was afoot], and having power to prevent or aid in preventing the same,' who did not attempt to stop the same, liable to any person injured by the conspiracy" (quoted at 668–69). This version passed both houses, though it seemed to undermine Brennan's argument that Congress might hold municipalities liable elsewhere. To make that case, Brennan scrutinized the legislative history of the act to show that "the constitutional objections raised against the Sherman amendment—on which our holding in *Monroe* was based, see *supra*, at 664—would not have prohibited congressional creation of a civil remedy against state municipal corporations that infringed federal rights" (669). This is an exceedingly weak argument since there is a wide gulf between not prohibiting something and positively supporting it, as Brennan would urge; however, he makes a fair case for early recognition of the federal government's authority over states in protecting individual citizens.

In the absence of a detailed argument by proponents of the Sherman amendment, Brennan sought "to piece together [a constitutional] argument from the debates on the first conference report and those on § 2 of the civil rights bill, which, because it allowed the Federal Government to prosecute crimes 'in the States,' had also raised questions of federal power" (669). He relied heavily upon the comments of Representative Samuel Shellabarger (R-OH), who sponsored the House version of the bill. Shellabarger had drawn upon a now classic statement on the Constitution's "privileges and immunities" clause from Article IV of the Constitution to shed light on similar language in the Fourteenth Amendment. This came from Justice Bushrod Washington, nephew of the first US president, who was an early member of the US Supreme Court. In a circuit court case (which early Supreme Court justices sat upon by "riding the circuit"), Washington admitted that it would be "more tedious than difficult to enumerate" a list of "fundamental privileges" covered by Article IV, but nevertheless began a short list of "general heads" of such privileges with "protection by the Government."[62]

Even in 1825, Shellabarger had noted, the court recognized that the federal government protected citizens against the states, enforcing "every one of the provisions of the Constitution," including extraditing criminal defendants to states that request their return, ensuring that "citizens of each State" are afforded "all the privileges and immunities of citizens in the several States," and ensuring that slave owners retain their property rights when their slaves travel to free states (670–71).[63]

It is this last example of privileges and immunities, involving slave owners' rights, that Brennan notes "ironically" provides the best analogy to the Sherman amendment. The federal authority in such cases had been asserted in a statute (the act of Feb. 12, 1793) and found constitutional in an 1842 case, *Prigg v. Pennsylvania.*[64] Brennan notes: "There, Mr. Justice Story, writing for the Court, held that Art. IV gave slaveowners a federal right to the unhindered possession of their slaves in whatever State such slaves might be found. 16 Pet., at 612. Because state process for recovering runaway slaves might be inadequate or even hostile to the rights of the slaveowner, the right intended to be conferred could be negated if left to state implementation. *Id.*, at 614. Thus, since the Constitution guaranteed the right and this in turn required a remedy, Story held it to be a "natural inference" that Congress had the power itself to ensure an appropriate (in the Necessary and Proper Clause sense) remedy for the right. Id., at 615" (672). Upon this precedent, Shellabarger argued, the federal government clearly had the authority to meet its duty to protect citizens from the states (672).

Shellabarger also took on the question of whether a county or municipality—a "part" of the state—was subject to such federal intervention, as Brennan documents. Shellabarger noted that as early as 1861 the US Supreme Court had upheld the power of the courts to enforce the Contract Clause against a municipality (673).[65] Brennan added a list of cases since that time that reached the same conclusion (673n28). Shellabarger's opponents noted that some municipalities might not have been vested with police powers by the state and, therefore, making them liable for not exercising a power they did not have was unreasonable. Representative Blair, for example, warned that states "create these municipalities, they say what their powers shall be and what their obligations shall be. If the Government of the United States can step in and add to those obligations, may it not utterly destroy the municipality?" (quoted at 675).

Opponents of the amendment also relied on a recent (1871) US Supreme Court decision that barred the federal government from taxing the income of a Massachusetts state judge "because the independence of the States within their legitimate spheres would be imperiled if the instrumentalities through which States executed their powers were 'subject to the control of another and distinct government.'"[66] Another case ten years earlier, *Kentucky v. Dennison*, seemed to deny the federal government the power to compel positive actions from state officers.[67] There the court would not enforce an order for a governor to return a criminal defendant to another state, since "if it [the federal government] possessed this power, it might overload the officer with duties which would fill up all his time, and disable him from performing his obligations to the State, and might impose on him duties of a character incompatible with the rank and dignity to which he was elevated by the State" (quoting 107–8 at 678). Brennan admitted that, although this precedent was not cited in the debates over the amendment, "the principles upon which it stands were well known to Members of Congress" (678–79). "Thus," he concludes, "there was ample support for [Representative] Blair's view that the Sherman amendment, by putting municipalities to the Hobson's choice of keeping the peace or paying civil damages, attempted to impose obligations on municipalities by indirection that could not be imposed directly, thereby threatening to 'destroy the government of the States'" (679). But, Brennan argued, the federal government was not imposing an obligation on the municipalities, but rather enforcing an existing obligation imposed by the states themselves. Where municipalities were already "obligated by the state law to keep the peace," the federal government could impose civil liability for the failure to do so when that failure violated the Fourteenth Amendment's equal protection requirement (679). Representative Poland had offered a similar distinction in urging that "the enforcing [of] a liability, existing by their own contract, or by a State law, in the courts, is a very widely different thing from devolving a new duty or liability upon them by the national Government, which has no power either to create or destroy them, and no power or control over them whatever" (quoted at 680).

Against concerns that such liability violated our system of dual sovereignty, Brennan noted that the court already had allowed such federal intervention to enforce the Contract Clause: "Since § 1 of the Civil Rights Act simply conferred jurisdiction on the federal courts to enforce § 1 of the Fourteenth Amendment—a situation precisely analogous to the grant of diversity jurisdiction under which the Contract Clause was enforced against municipalities—there is no reason to suppose that opponents of the Sherman amendment would have found any constitutional barrier to § 1 suits against municipalities" (681–82).

Brennan's final argument sought to blur the difference between the liability of state officials to civil suits under § 1 and the liability of municipalities. He insists: "Section 1 without question could be used to obtain a damages judgment against state or municipal officials who violated federal constitutional rights while acting under color of law," citing several participants in the debate over § 1 (682). Furthermore, a series of cases involving suits against state officials, "as Blair and others recognized . . . [made] no distinction of constitutional magnitude between officers and agents—including corporate agents—of the State: Both were state instrumentalities and the State could be impeded no matter over which sort of instrumentality the Federal Government sought to assert its power" (682).[68] Indeed, Brennan quotes Representative Blair in urging that he "was quite conscious that he was extending these cases by applying them to municipal corporations" (682, 682n43).

Brennan boldly asserts that his review of legislative history "compels the conclusion that Congress *did* intend municipalities and other local government units to be included among those persons to whom § 1983 applies" and that no constitutional provisions disallow liability for violating equal protection rights (690). He further argues that *Monroe* was a departure from prior cases and that numerous post-*Monroe* § 1983 cases included school boards as defendants.[69] While he admits that stare decisis normally has more force in statutory cases (since Congress can correct errors), he notes that "we have never applied *stare decisis* mechanically to prohibit overruling our earlier decisions determining the meaning of statutes" (695). In any case, as Justice Powell made explicit in his concurring opinion, the inconsistencies before and after *Monroe* that were noted by Brennan meant that "considerations of *stare decisis* cut in both directions" (Powell, J., concurring, at 708). And, although Congress could correct the court's error with a statutory provision, some of their actions appeared to endorse municipal liability, as Brennan notes in their rejection of efforts remove jurisdiction over school boards from the federal courts in the wake of resistance to school busing (696–97n62). Finally, Brennan added, states should not be allowed to plead that they had "arranged their affairs" in reliance on the *Monroe* decision, thereby giving them leave to "violate constitutional rights indefinitely" (699).

While Justice Powell's concurring opinion builds on Brennan's forty-plus-page majority opinion, in a quarter of the space he makes a more pointed argument. He summarizes the implications of Brennan's argument more clearly than its author in noting: "The Court correctly rejects a view of the legislative history that would produce the anomalous result of immunizing local government units from monetary liability for action directly causing a constitutional deprivation, even though such actions may be fully consistent with, and thus not remediable under, state law. No conduct of government comes more clearly within the "under color of" state law language of § 1983. It is most unlikely that Congress intended public officials acting under the command or the specific authorization of the government employer to be *exclusively* liable for resulting constitutional injury" (707). This last point about the liability of officials was particularly damning of the *Monroe* decision, which "exempted local governments from liability at the same time it opened wide the courthouse door to suits against officers and employees of those entities even when they act pursuant to express authorization"—an "[odd] . . . result" (705).

Powell characterizes the legislative rejection of the Sherman amendment more simply than Brennan in suggesting that Congress sought to avoid applying a *respondeat superior* standard of liability, common in tort law, whereby the states would be vicariously liable for the wrongs of its officers against its citizens or, in the case of the Sherman amendment's most radical version, of its riotous citizens against their victims (707).[70] Such master-servant models, built upon an employer-employee relationship, were distinguishable from the more acceptable municipal liability for "the consequences of activities actually undertaken [by officials] within the scope of the powers conferred by state law" (707n2).

Powell's final, devastating rejection of *Monroe*, complained that the court erred procedurally, as well as on the law: "In *Monroe* and its progeny, we have answered a question that was never actually briefed or argued in this Court—whether a municipality is liable in damages for injuries that are the direct result of its official policies" (708). The Chicago police who harassed a Black family and its patriarch were not following official policies but rather breaking them; hence, *Monroe*'s conclusion that municipalities are not liable under § 1983 overreached in not considering liability when those policies were being followed.[71] Because of that overreach, the specific issues of municipal liability where an official policy is implemented were not at issue and, therefore, the decision "was rendered without benefit of a full airing of all the relevant considerations," calling for less deference to the precedent (709n5).

Justice Rehnquist dissented. He called the claim that *Monroe* departed from earlier cases "patently erroneous," insisting that neither in earlier nor in later cases was the question currently before the court even raised (715–16). He implied that Brennan showed only that the legislative history of the Ku Klux Klan Act might not have concluded that municipal liability was unconstitutional, but it did not demonstrate that the legislature *intended* to impose such liability (719). Given the high bar he would set for overruling ("the highest degree of deference"), he thought Brennan's case fell short (719). He endorsed *Monroe*'s reliance on the Sherman amendment debate as "the only occasion in which the question [of municipal liability] was explicitly presented" (723).

Only Chief Justice Burger would join Rehnquist in dissent; all the other justices joined the majority opinion or concurred in whole or in part. Thus did the high court reverse itself and recognize municipalities and school boards as persons liable to civil damage suits under § 1983. But the largest impact has been its use in combating police brutality by holding municipalities liable to damages in cases where citizens' civil rights have been violated.[72]

The story of this case might be viewed as a victory for progressivism in defense of civil liberties. Ironically, though, *Monroe* itself was a landmark case for holding police officers (though not the municipality) liable to damages for violating civil rights. But Chase and Chase argue that "*Monell* was even more significant because it 'opened the "deep pockets" of government treasuries to civil rights plaintiffs who could demonstrate that they had been hurt by employees whose wrongful acts were the results of such egregious customs, practices, and policies, including poor supervision and training.'"[73] They note that verdicts in police brutality cases skyrocketed, forcing cities to take greater care in selecting, training, and overseeing the work of their officers in blue. Obviously, such monetary liability has not ended the kind of race-based civil rights violations by police that motivated the Black Lives Matter movement.[74]

CONCLUSION

Just because Congress can fix legislation it believes the Supreme Court has misinterpreted does not mean that the high court will avoid rethinking its interpretations of statutes. As this chapter shows, such overrulings start with the concern that a prior interpretation was erroneous. The court may suggest that the prior case did not receive sufficient consideration, as the *Monell* majority implies by insisting that the court ruled on a matter not raised in the pleadings. Or, in the MPCC case, that the prior court misunderstood the purposes of the patent laws. Or the court's concern for error might turn on indications of legislative discontent, such as the new legislation on diversity jurisdiction cited by the *Letson* court, the MPCC court's suggestion that new patent legislation seemed to be a response to the verdict in *Henry v. Dick* case, or even a lack of action such as Congress's decision not to remove federal jurisdiction from suits involving school boards and busing in the *Monell* case.

In addition to error, experience with a precedent's ruling often demonstrates that a rule is unworkable—for example, the diversity-jurisdiction matter, whereby courts grappled with whether to include corporations as persons for diversity or whether all litigants on one side had to be from different states. And changing conceptions in the law, such as the further development of corporate personhood by the time of the *Letson* case, bolstered a new view of who could be counted in identifying diversity for jurisdictional purposes. Reliance on former rulings, in these cases, proved no barrier to reconsideration. Even widely recognized nineteenth-century concerns over the sanctity and certainty of property rights implicated in *Letson* case did not prevent the court from reconsidering this thirty-eight-year-old precedent which had been endorsed several times by the high court. In the other property case involving patents, the court might have been less concerned in overruling its five-year-old ruling in *Henry v. Dick*. But Justice Clarke was obviously concerned with a very practical problem: that more and more powerful corporations were taking unfair advantage of Justice Lurton's reading of patent law to support monopolistic practices.

Although changes in personnel clearly influenced these cases, neither the overruling majorities nor the dissenters said much about that. *Letson* did offer the unique argument that the writer of the 1806 precedent, Chief Justice

Marshall, himself had come to regret his ruling on diversity jurisdiction; however, only references to the personal knowledge of long-serving justices, rather than Marshall's written acknowledgment of a change of heart, was offered for this claim.

Finally, despite the statutory concerns of these cases, all implicate constitutional issues and were informed by reflections on what the Constitution meant about diversity jurisdiction, or giving patents, or protecting civil rights under the Fourteenth Amendment.

CHAPTER 5

Justifying the "Switch in Time That Saved Nine"

The Supreme Court's About-Face Following FDR's Court-Packing Threat

On February 5, 1937, President Franklin Roosevelt announced a plan to reorganize the federal judiciary, ostensibly to help federal courts more efficiently handle the caseloads confronting them. But a key provision of this proposal served a different purpose: to enlarge the Supreme Court by up to six new members in order to arrest the court's tendency to invalidate New Deal legislation.[1] While the plan was never passed by Congress, the high court made an apparent about-face on the New Deal seven weeks later, on March 29, 1937, in *West Coast Hotel v. Parrish*. Although this decision involved a state's efforts to address the fallout from the Great Depression, it represented a change of direction for a court that often reflected a laissez-faire ideology skeptical of government regulation at the state or federal level. This decision allowed Washington State to set a minimum wage, overturning a fourteen-year-old precedent, *Adkins v. Children's Hospital*, and distinguishing another case relying on *Adkins* decided a year earlier. Two weeks later the high court supported the National Labor Relations Act and, after that, the Social Security Act.[2] Never again would the Supreme Court invalidate a New Deal law.[3]

Scores of books and articles have tried to explain what commentators at the time dubbed "the switch in time that saved nine."[4] That change of direction in *Parrish* and subsequent cases raised three rhetorical challenges for the court in justifying its decisions: First was the perception that the high court changed its position on the New Deal because of FDR's threat to pack the court. The Supreme Court is supposed to be above the political fray, making decisions in light of law and justice, so the timing of the change was problematic. Second, *Parrish* and the many other overruling cases which followed it in the next few years had to grapple with the deference the court is supposed to give to its prior rulings, respecting the principle of stare decisis. Finally, since several members of the Hughes court retired in the next few years, starting two months after *Parrish* was handed down, the court also faced the perception that personnel changes were the primary reason for the increasingly progressive positions it took. This challenged the notion that judges and their approaches to interpreting the law were somewhat objective and consistent rather than a function of the age, personality, or ideology of those sitting on the bench. As chapter 3 above demonstrates, the coincidence of new justices and the court's change of position in the Legal Tender Cases threatened to undermine the court's standing.

Although the simplistic story of Roosevelt's court-packing plan leading to a "switch in time that saved nine" was widespread at the time and has persisted for decades, scholars and commentators writing in the past seventy years have provided a much richer account of the complex factors that likely shaped the decisions in *Parrish* and subsequent cases by the Hughes court. Among these are the president's ongoing efforts to push his reform bill and manage public perceptions, the efforts of allies and opponents of the measure in Congress, the media, and the legal community; the actions of the court and its members in its decisions, public comments, and retirements (and Roosevelt's replacements); the swings in public opinion regarding the reform plan, President Roosevelt, and the Supreme Court; and the untimely death of a key senator. In any case, as I will show, perceptions of the high court, the president, and judicial reform efforts in this complex and shifting situation created an awkward setting for the court to justify an overruling. Nevertheless, after the initial shock of March 1937 receded, a court radically altered by Roosevelt's appointments proceeded to overrule nineteen more cases in the next five years, seven of them in 1941 alone. Indeed, after a slow start in 1930, the Hughes court would rack up more overrulings than any court up to that time and would not be surpassed until the Warren court.[5]

This chapter's analysis of overruling rhetoric is different from the analyses in other chapters because it looks at multiple overrulings by the same court (i.e., the Hughes court) in an evolving situation that challenged the Supreme Court's ability to justify its reversals. It provides a rich account of the rhetorical situation of the court at different points in its string of overrulings. Unlike other chapters, it shows how overrulings themselves become part of the context in which other overrulings are made, how the changing membership of the court shaped the standing of the court during this period, and how complex economic, social, and especially political factors influenced how the court's motives might be viewed.

I begin with a brief history of the Supreme Court's rulings regarding the Congress's power to regulate interstate commerce, because that power was central to justifying much of the legislation Roosevelt championed to address the country's economic disaster. Next, I turn to the overruling cases, beginning with the challenging early overrulings that featured Justice Roberts's apparent change of heart, then turning to later overrulings that relied on a Roosevelt's appointees with their new vision of the court as an agent of social progress.

THE SUPREME COURT AND THE COMMERCE CLAUSE

In 1916 Congress sought to remedy the widespread exploitation of child workers across the country through the Keating-Owen Child Labor Act. That act prohibited factories from employing children under fourteen, mines from employing children under sixteen, and any company from working children after 7:00 p.m. or before 6:00 a.m. or more than eight hours a day. The law was invalidated two years later in one of the most notorious decisions in the Supreme Court's history, *Hammer v. Dagenhart*.[6] The issue was whether the federal government could regulate how goods were manufactured—in this case with the use of child labor—simply because those goods were sold and shipped across state lines. Drawing on a Sherman Antitrust case from 1895, the court reiterated its recently articulated principle of *dual federalism* whereby states enjoyed police power over some aspects of business production within their borders, while the federal government could regulate the shipment of those goods in interstate commerce with no overlap between their respective jurisdictions. *United States v. E. C. Knight Co.* had ruled that if the impact of that production on interstate commerce was indirect, the federal government had no jurisdiction to regulate it.[7]

The 5-4 *Knight* majority claimed that if the federal government could control production in this way, "all freedom of commerce will be at an end . . . and thus our system of government be practically destroyed."[8] Although Congress had previously used its Commerce Clause powers to prevent obscene literature, diseased cattle, women transported for illicit purposes, and liquor from entering interstate commerce, the child labor restriction was deemed different because these shipped goods were "of themselves, harmless" (272). Furthermore, "the act, in its effect, does not regulate transportation among the States, but aims to standardize the ages at which children may be employed in mining and manufacturing within the States" (271–72). Reiterating the production/commerce distinction, the court insisted that "the making of goods and the mining of coal are not commerce, nor does the fact that these things are to be afterwards shipped or used in interstate commerce make their production a part thereof" (272). The court even invoked the seldom-referenced Tenth Amendment, insisting: "The grant of authority over a purely federal matter was not intended to destroy the local power always existing and carefully reserved to the States in the Tenth Amendment to the Constitution" (274).

Justice Holmes filed a strident dissent, noting that the Constitution gives Congress the power to regulate interstate commerce "in unqualified terms," regardless of whether "it might interfere with the carrying out of the domestic policy of any State" (277–78). As to the "harmless[ness]" of the goods themselves, Holmes insisted that "it does not matter whether the supposed evil precedes or follows the transportation. It is enough that, in the opinion of Congress, the transportation encourages the evil" (279–80). Finally, Holmes noted the national nature of the problem and its solution: "The national welfare, as understood by Congress, may require a different attitude within its sphere from that of some self-seeking State" (281).

The closeness of the *Dagenhart* decision and its strong advocacy by majority and dissenting justices in this Commerce Clause case presaged the coming battles in the court, particularly those following a devastating economic depression that led President Franklin Roosevelt and his Democrat-dominated Congress to test the limits of their authority to address the crisis. As to the child labor problem, Congress passed the Child Labor Amendment to the Constitution in 1924, though its ratification was rejected by enough states to kill it by 1925.[9] The problem would remain unaddressed by the federal government until the Supreme Court reversed *Dagenhart* in its 1941 spree of overrulings.

In addition to *Dagenhart*'s reiteration of the distinction between direct and indirect influences on interstate commerce, two other cases provided innovations that would shape later decisions. The 1877 case of *Munn v. Illinois* would grapple with when a state could deploy its police powers to regulate businesses within its borders. The court noted that government-granted monopolies, such as for toll roads and ferries, traditionally had been regulated because they were free from market pressures that otherwise might control their prices. The court identified a "public interest" that made such businesses susceptible to regulation. The majority opined that when an owner devoted his or her property to "a use in which the public has an interest, he [or she], in effect, grants to the public an interest in that use, and must submit to be controlled by the public for the common good, to the extent of the interest he [or she] has created."[10] The court concluded that grain elevator operators in Illinois, who enjoyed great latitude in fixing rates for storing grain produced by local farmers, could be regulated by the state in the interest of the public.

Justice Field dissented, complaining that the court granted too much power to the states and put "all property and all business in the State . . . at the mercy of the Legislature" (140). Field notes that the recently passed Fourteenth Amendment holds that no state "shall deprive any person of life, liberty, or property without due process of law." He insisted: "By the term 'liberty,' as used in the provision, something more is meant than mere freedom from physical restraint or the bounds of a prison. It means freedom to go where one may choose, and to act in such manner, not inconsistent with the equal rights of others, as his judgment may dictate for the promotion of his happiness—that is, to pursue such callings and avocations as may be most suitable to develop his capacities and give to them their highest enjoyment" (142). Notably, he added, "the same liberal construction which is required for the protection of life and liberty, in all particulars in which life and liberty are of any value, should be applied to the protection of private property" (142). Field inaugurates here what would become known as *substantive due process*, opening the door to an examination of the extent of private rights to stand against encroachment by the government.

In 1905 Justice Holmes would deploy a fertile metaphor to win a unanimous decision to enforce the Sherman Antitrust Act against the monopolizing efforts of the beef industry. In *Swift & Co. v. United States*, he urged that "commerce among the States is not a technical legal conception, but a practical one, drawn from the course of business. When cattle are sent for sale from a place in one State, with the expectation that they will end their transit, after purchase, in another, and when, in effect, they do so, with only the interruption necessary to find a purchaser at the stockyards, and when this is a typical, constantly recurring course, the current thus existing is a *current of commerce* among the States, and the purchase of the cattle is a part and incident of such commerce."[11] Holmes's "current of commerce" evoked a continuous flow which linked multiple acts, where problems with any of them might stymie that interstate "flow." It eventually helped to undermine claims by businesses that they were "intrastate" because the individual acts they were engaged in were done within a state and severable from the "flow" that they might affect.

Barry Cushman notes that Holmes's opinion was viewed as a compromise by his conservative colleagues because it still required that a public interest be involved in the regulation, therefore: "An intrastate business affected with a public interest could not be reached by the federal commerce power unless it could be located within a current of interstate commerce, and an intrastate business activity did not constitute part of a federally regulable current of commerce unless it was also a business affected with a public interest."[12] However, he notes, while the category of businesses affected with a public interest was initially small, it would grow significantly in later decisions because "the current of commerce doctrine had the capacity to transform the local into the national."[13]

The tug-of-war between direct and indirect impacts on interstate commerce, public interests and private interests, goods in the current of commerce and those wholly intrastate would provide dividing lines for arguments among the justices that led to less consistency than a president facing the greatest economic crisis in the history of the country might prefer. The next section considers the situation of the court in the early 1930s and their back-and-forth rulings that led up to Roosevelt's fateful decision to try to enlarge the US Supreme Court.

THE SUPREME COURT CONFRONTS THE NEW DEAL

The economic downturn central to the Great Depression created the greatest trauma for Americans since the Civil War.[14] Drastic declines in consumer spending, a stock market crash, widespread bank failures, a devastating rise in unemployment, a huge reduction in the money supply, and plummeting production in the United States marked an economic decline that hit Americans in 1929 and continued for virtually a decade. Farmers who did well during World War I had expanded their operations only to be saddled with huge debts when the economic crisis dragged agricultural prices down by 60 percent. The stock market lost a third of its value, one-fifth of US banks failed, industrial production fell by almost half, US gross domestic product (GDP) went down 30 percent, and unemployment exceeded 20 percent. Although the economy began improving by the time President Roosevelt was inaugurated in 1933, with GDP rising by an average 9 percent a year from 1933 to 1937, a short-lived recession began in May 1937. By the middle of 1938, growth was even higher than before the recession, though the country would not make up the economic ground lost in terms of national output until 1942.

In his inaugural address, President Roosevelt made clear that he would use all the power of his office to address the crisis, insisting: "This nation asks for action, and action now. Our greatest primary task is to put people to work. I am prepared under my constitutional duty to recommend the measures that a stricken nation in the midst of a stricken world may require."[15] He immediately called Congress into a special session that would last three months and pushed them to pass fifteen major bills to address the crisis.[16] He created the Federal Emergency Relief Administration to provide money to states and localities to support the jobless. He created government jobs for millions of Americans to build dams, water systems, hospitals, and national parks, and to support regional projects such as the rural electrification program of the Tennessee Valley Authority. The newly created Federal Deposit Insurance Corporation protected bank deposits and other legislation reformed bank practices. Farmers were given a new source of badly needed loans with the Farm Credit Act. The National Industrial Recovery Act allowed the president to regulate wages and prices, and to craft industrial codes to encourage fair competition.[17]

In the following years legislation and administrative rules were crafted to protect farmers and others from bankruptcy and foreclosure, to secure retirement benefits for workers, to support collective bargaining by workers, to regulate the stock market, and to control production to keep markets in agricultural products, oil, and other commodities from collapsing, among many other things. Businesses and interest groups flooded the courts with legal challenges to these programs and required the US Supreme Court to decide how much power federal and state governments could wield to address the economic crisis and how much they could infringe on the rights of property owners.

Those weighty decisions would be heard by a court that was fairly evenly divided in terms of ideology from 1932 to 1937. On the conservative side were four laissez-faire justices, known as the "Four Horsemen" for their stalwart opposition to the New Deal: Justices Van Devanter, McReynolds, Sutherland, and Butler. On the liberal side were Justices Brandeis, Stone, and Cardozo. And among the moderates were Chief Justice Hughes and Justice Owen Roberts. Both Hughes and Roberts would shift between the conservatives and liberals on particular cases, though Roberts was more likely than Hughes to side against New Deal legislation.

In early 1934 it appeared that the Supreme Court was willing to give great latitude to states to address the economic crisis. On January 8, 1934, the high court handed down a decision upholding a Minnesota law that authorized a state court to respond to requests from farmers (and others) facing foreclosures for a reprieve "during the continuance of the emergency and in no event beyond May 1, 1935." Both the chief justice and Justice Roberts joined the liberals in a 5-4 decision in *Home Building & Loan Association v. Blaisdell.*[18] Writing for the majority, Chief Justice Hughes acknowledged the serious economic crisis the state and country were experiencing and insisted that "while emergency does not create power, emergency may furnish the occasion for the exercise of power" (426). He acknowledged earlier economic decisions in which "it was thought that only the concerns of individuals or of classes were involved, and that those of the State itself were touched only remotely"; but he insisted that the increasing complexity of modern economies affected the states more directly so that "the question is no longer merely that of one party to a contract as against another, but of the use of reasonable means to safeguard the economic structure upon which the good of all depends" (442). In dissent, Justice Sutherland wrote for the Four Horseman that emergencies did not affect state powers and, as a Michigan jurist proclaimed, "Constitutions cannot be changed by events alone."[19]

In *Nebbia v. New York,* handed down two months later, Justice Roberts authored the majority opinion supporting the state's authority to regulate the price of milk.[20] He did not rely on the economic emergency to support the decision, but rather a virtual abandonment of the public/private distinction in government regulation of business. Cushman notes that from 1877 to 1923 the court handed down one decision after another that enlarged the category of businesses affected with a public interest, thus making them subject to state regulation.[21] But in considering the public/private demarcation, Roberts insisted:

"The phrase 'affected with a public interest' can, in the nature of things, mean no more than that an industry, for adequate reason, is subject to control for the public good" (536). Given this broad interpretation of public interest, he could conclude: "So far as the requirement of due process is concerned, and in the absence of other constitutional restriction, a state is free to adopt whatever economic policy may reasonably be deemed to promote the public welfare, and to enforce that policy by legislation adapted to its purpose. [Furthermore,] the courts are without authority either to declare such policy, or, when it is declared by the legislature, to override it. If the laws passed are seen to have a reasonable relation to a proper legislative purpose, and are neither arbitrary nor discriminatory, the requirements of due process are satisfied." (537). This "reasonable relation" test raised the bar incredibly high for invalidating state regulations that were not patently absurd.

Barry Cushman, Laura Kalman, and other scholars mark the "revolution" from the laissez-faire court as beginning with these 1934 cases; however, 1935 saw the court majority backtrack on this change of direction.[22] On January 7, 1935, the court confronted a New Deal initiative for the first time in *Panama Refining Co. v. Ryan*.[23] President Roosevelt had used a provision of the National Industrial Recovery Act, passed in 1933, to help staunch a collapse in the oil markets caused by a stalled economy and overproduction. The administration's "hot oil" program prohibited the shipment of oil in interstate commerce over quotas set by the oil-producing states, decreasing supply to support sustainable prices. Oil had dropped to as low as four cents a barrel before intervention helped it return to ten cents a barrel.[24] The court ruled narrowly that Congress had delegated too much authority to the executive through its vague legislation, violating the separation of powers: "[The legislation] establishes no criteria to govern the President's course. It does not require any finding by the President as a condition of his action. The Congress in § 9(c) thus declares no policy as to the transportation of the excess production. So far as this section is concerned, it gives to the president an unlimited authority to determine the policy and to lay down the prohibition, or not to lay it down, as he may see fit. And disobedience to his order is made a crime punishable by fine and imprisonment."[25] This decision could not be laid at the feet of Roberts or Hughes—only Justice Cardozo dissented from this nearly unanimous decision. This legislative loss might better be blamed on an executive and Congress that rushed through so many major bills so quickly, though their radical new interventions in the economy had them navigating new constitutional waters undoubtedly unsure about what would pass muster.[26]

A month later President Roosevelt was bracing for a negative decision in three companion cases involving efforts to protect federal gold reserves during the economic emergency.[27] Echoing issues raised in the Legal Tender Cases (see chapter 3), legislation provided that private and public contracts which required payments in gold could now be discharged with currency instead. Bondholders complained that the legislation led to breaches of contract and violated the Fifth Amendment's protection against the deprivation of property without due process of law. Chief Justice Hughes wrote the opinion of the court, which Justice Roberts and the three liberal justices joined; the Four Horsemen filed a scathing dissent. Hughes argued that Congress had the authority to regulate the monetary system and, thus, did not unconstitutionally impinge on rights in private contracts whose "gold clauses" merely involved provisions for how those debts were to be paid. In two of the cases the legislation *did* impair the government's obligations in public contracts, but the court ruled that the damage to bondholders was nominal, involving only a breach of contract; seeking the small payouts available for such breaches did not even qualify those creditors for an appeal to the Court of Claims.

Justice McReynolds, speaking for the Four Horsemen in dissent, was apoplectic about this "repudiation and spoliation of citizens by their sovereign" and insisted the Founders would not have allowed the government "to annihilate its own obligations and destroy the very rights [the Founders] were endeavoring to protect."[28]

After the court flipped from resisting the government's efforts in the "hot oil" case to supporting them in the Gold Clause Cases, it flopped back again with a vengeance in a series of devastating New Deal setbacks. On May 6, 1935, the court struck down the Railroad Retirement Act, which sought to set up a pension program for railway workers after 760,000 of them lost their jobs. In *Railroad Retirement Board v. Alton Railroad Co.*, Justice Roberts wrote the majority opinion holding that the act violated the Due Process Clause of the Fifth Amendment and that Congress lacked the authority under the Commerce Clause for the regulation.[29] He systematically challenged the rationales for the act as means to increase safety, economy, and efficiency in the railroads. In particular, he questioned how the "social benefits" required by the act would serve such purposes, calling out a requirement for a pension for those who work for any railroad as an illogical means to create a kind of gratitude and loyalty toward a particular railroad company and, thereby, spurring greater effort (and, hence, efficiency).[30] Ultimately, he insisted, "The act is not in purpose or effect a regulation of interstate commerce within the meaning of the Constitution" (362).

Chief Justice Hughes dissented. He was particularly appalled by the breadth of the decision, which "denies to Congress the power to pass any compulsory pension act for railroad employees," no matter how carefully tailored (374–75). Citing four precedents, he insisted that "nothing which has a real or substantial relation to the suitable maintenance of that [railroad] service, or to the discharge of the responsibilities which inhere in it, can be regarded as beyond the power of regulation."[31]

The decision worried New Deal advocates. Legal scholars widely criticized the decision, noting that it could undermine a wide array of economic reform statutes for failing to meet the majority's standard for regulating interstate commerce.[32] Justice Stone worried privately that this holding on "constitutional power put us back at least thirty years."[33] The decision "galvanized organized labor, liberal Congressmen, and the Roosevelt administration to take the first serious efforts [to curb the power of the Supreme Court]."[34] But the train of blows against the New Deal had scarcely begun.

Three weeks later the court handed down three unanimous decisions undermining the New Deal on what was dubbed "Black Monday." They held unconstitutional the Frazier-Lemke Act, which provided federal mortgage relief to bankrupt farmers (*Louisville Joint Stock Land Bank v. Radford*); denied the president authority to replace at-will members of independent regulatory boards who were slow in implementing his policies (*Humphrey's Executor v. United States*), and, most famously, declared the National Industrial Recovery Act (NIRA) unconstitutional for delegating sweeping powers to the executive that belonged to Congress (*Schechter Poultry Corp. v. United States*).[35]

The *Radford* decision was written by Justice Brandeis, who systematically detailed how several provisions of the Frazier-Lemke Act were unprecedented in helping bankrupt farmers who would not only be given a five-year reprieve from foreclosure (while paying "rents"), but allowed to reduce their mortgages by paying only the current appraised value of the property, instead of the amount originally borrowed. In short, the act "has taken from the bank without compensation, and given to Radford, rights in specific property which are of substantial value" in violation of the Fifth Amendment.[36]

The *Schechter* case was not one the Roosevelt administration would have chosen for a test of the NIRA. Schechter Poultry Corporation operated a slaughterhouse in Brooklyn that processed chickens in New York State exclusively for sale within the state, although chickens were bought from other states. Chief Justice Hughes recognized the "current of commerce" that brought chickens to the slaughterhouse but insisted that Schechter operated at the terminus of that current, so that "so far as the poultry here in question is concerned, the flow in interstate commerce had ceased."[37] That made the authority of the federal government over Schechter's operation questionable. Hughes resurrected the amorphous direct/indirect effect on interstate commerce, which he insisted nonetheless could be determined "as individual cases arise," concluding that this Schechter's relation to interstate commerce was indirect (546).

But another constitutional issue was more pressing still. Under the NIRA, Congress had authorized the president to work with industries to develop their own "codes of fair competition," and within two years over 750 such codes had been promulgated.[38] These involved regulations relating to working conditions (such as maximum hours and minimum hourly pay), reporting, industrial practices, safety, and so forth. The problem was that Congress was so vague in directing the executive to develop these codes as to create an unconstitutional delegation of its authority apparently even more problematic than it had done in the "hot oil" case (530).

Justice Cardozo concurred, agreeing colorfully that "the delegated power of legislation which has found expression in this code is not canalized within banks that keep it from overflowing" (551). The legislation had allowed the president to create a "roving commission to inquire into evils and, upon discovery, correct them" (551). Yet, Cardozo noted, "delegation in such circumstances is born of the necessities of the occasion. The industries of the country are too many and diverse to make it possible for Congress, in respect of matters such as these, to legislate directly with adequate appreciation of varying conditions" (552). But the larger problem for Cardozo was that Schechter's business was essentially intrastate. He endorsed the direct/indirect distinction of the impact on interstate commerce made by Hughes and insisted that the impact was indirect, for "to find immediacy or directness here is to find it almost everywhere" and that would lead to "an end to our federal system" (554).

Roosevelt responded to the *Schechter* decision a few days later in a press conference, where he condemned the court's "horse-and-buggy definition of interstate commerce."[39] Interstate commerce in recent times had changed significantly, he explained:

> The prosperity of the farmer does have an effect today on the manufacturer in Pittsburgh. The prosperity of the clothing worker in the city of New York has an effect on the prosperity of the farmer in Wisconsin, and so it goes. We are interdependent—we are tied in together. And the hope has been that we could, through a period of years, interpret the interstate commerce clause of the Constitution in the light of these new things that have come to the country. It has been our hope that under the interstate commerce clause we could recognize by legislation and by judicial decision that a harmful practice in one section of the country could be prevented on the theory that it was doing harm to another section of the country. That was why the Congress for a good many years, and most lawyers, have had the thought that in drafting legislation we could depend on an interpretation that would enlarge the Constitutional meaning of interstate commerce to include not only those matters of direct interstate commerce, but also those matters which indirectly affect interstate commerce.[40]

Roosevelt spent a great deal of time parsing the decision and wondered aloud: "Does this decision mean that the United States Government has no control over any national economic problem?" He warned that leaving such issues to the states would "unavoidably develop sectionalism," as lax regulation in some states would attract businesses from those with more regulation. He claimed that "the implications of the [*Schechter*] decision are much more important than almost certainly any decision of my lifetime or yours, more important than any decision probably since the Dred Scott case."[41]

Roosevelt's public complaints did not sway the majority, and 1936 was as detrimental to the New Deal as 1935 had been. But cracks began to appear in the court as unanimity gave way to differences of opinion on the power of Congress to regulate the economy. On January 6, 1936, Justice Roberts led the Four Horsemen, plus Chief Justice Hughes, in invalidating the Agricultural Adjustment Act in *United States v. Butler*. The act sought to raise agricultural prices by limiting production with cash incentives to farmers, paid for with a tax on the first processors of the products. Roberts urged that the taxing of local processors invaded the sovereignty of state governments, violating the Tenth Amendment reservation of powers to the states; he ignored the subsequent entry of such processed food into interstate commerce.[42] He offered a simplistic metaphor to defend the court's actions by insisting: "When an act of Congress is appropriately challenged in the courts as not conforming to the constitutional mandate, the judicial branch of the Government has only one duty—to lay the article of the Constitution which is invoked beside the statute which is challenged and to decide whether the latter squares with the former. All the court does, or can do, is to announce its considered judgment upon the question."[43]

Justice Stone was livid, calling Roberts's purportedly objective reading "a tortured construction of the Constitution" and urging that "the only check upon our [the court's] exercise of power is our own sense of self-restraint." He insisted that in assessing the constitutionality of statutes "courts are concerned only with the power to enact statutes, not with their wisdom."[44]

In May 1936, the high court struck down the Bituminous Coal Conservation Act—the Guffey Act—in *Carter v. Carter Coal Co.* in a 5-4 ruling that found Hughes joining the Four Horsemen.[45] Congress sought to regulate the mining of coal to address the collapse of the coal market and better the working conditions and pay of the miners. Justice Sutherland insisted that Congress could not regulate mining simply because what was extracted flowed across state lines, because "the local character of mining, of manufacturing and of crop growing is a fact, and remains a fact, whatever may be done with the products" (304). Addressing Justice Holmes's "current of commerce" from *Swift & Co.*, Sutherland noted that the cattle in stockyards in that case were at something of a way station in the middle of that flow, while this case involved "the growth or production of the things which, after production, [enter] the flow" (305).

Congress had been so concerned about the constitutionality of its labor provisions in the Guffey Act that it specified that they were severable from the rest of the Act; yet Sutherland rejected that means to salvage the rest of the legislation. Sutherland insisted that "Congress must have been conscious of the fact that elimination of the labor provisions from the act would seriously impair, if not destroy, the force and usefulness of the price provisions" (314–15). Moore and Adelson noted, wryly, that "in its omniscience the Court knew that Congress had not intended what it clearly said."[46]

Justice Cardozo dissented. He noted that the price-fixing provision at the heart of the case certainly impacts interstate commerce sufficiently to warrant government intervention: it literally regulates the prices to be paid by buyers in various states (326). While Sutherland had found the act violated the Due Process Clause of the Fifth Amendment in taking property from coal operators, Cardozo balanced the harms that the statute sought to address in the coal industry as a consideration in the government's calculation: "Overproduction was at a point where free competition had been degraded into anarchy. Prices had been cut so low that profit had become impossible for all except the lucky handful. Wages came down along with prices and with profits. There were strikes, at times nationwide in extent, at other times spreading over broad areas and many mines, with the accompaniment of violence and bloodshed and misery and bitter feeling" (330–31). He concluded: "An evil existing, and also the power to correct it, the lawmakers were at liberty to use their own discretion in the selection of the means" (332). Justices Brandeis and Stone joined his dissent. Two days after this decision, Senator Guffey introduced a revised bill that removed the offending labor regulations, which was passed the next year.[47]

A week after the *Carter Coal* case came down, the court overturned the Municipal Banking Act in *Ashton v. Cameron County Water Improvement District No. 1*.[48] The act sought to rescue the growing number of municipalities unable to pay their debts by forcing minority shareholders to act with the majority and the debtor municipality to reach a settlement on adjusting their debts. This federal remedy was sought because state laws impairing such contracts would likely be found to violate the federal constitution.[49] The Four Horsemen, led by Justice McReynolds and joined by Roberts, effectively rejected this federal solution, against the dissents of the chief justice and the court's liberals. McReynolds's majority opinion, like Roberts's in *Butler*, accused the federal government of invading the province of the states, "despite the fact that the law required the consent of the states and that consent had been given."[50] McReynolds cited Roberts's opinion in *Butler*, insisting: "Neither consent nor submission by the states can enlarge the powers of Congress; none can exist except those which are granted."[51]

A week later, on June 1, 1936, the court handed down a decision so unpopular that even the Republican Party presidential platform repudiated it.[52]

Morehead v. New York ex rel. Tipaldo struck down a New York state minimum wage law for women and children, maintaining that the right to contract for wages in return for work is part of the liberty protected by the due process clause of the Fourteenth Amendment.[53] The opinion, which Roberts joined, seemed to deny any state authority to interfere with contracts for labor. In dissent, Justice Stone complained that "there is a grim irony is speaking of the freedom of contract of those who, because of their economic necessities, give their services for less than is needful to keep body and soul together."[54] He cited numerous cases where the court had supported the legislative power to restrict contracts for a public purpose, including the recently decided *Nebbia* case.[55]

Newspaper editorials savaged the decision, with 334 of 344 criticizing it.[56] Following the ruling, the wages of laundresses fell by half.[57] William E. Leuchtenburg argues that "of all the wounds the Court inflicted on itself, the *Tipaldo* decision cut deepest. It appeared to create a 'no-man's land,' in which neither the federal government nor any state government could act to protect the worker."[58] Even conservatives lambasted *Tipaldo*, with Herbert Hoover calling for an amendment to restore to the states "the power they thought they already had."[59] President Roosevelt would begin to ponder how to claw back the power to regulate the economy from this recalcitrant court.

FDR STRIKES BACK

By 1936 when Roosevelt faced reelection, the economy had improved somewhat. Unemployment was down, with six million more Americans gaining employment since the worst of the crisis; yet eight million remained unemployed. Industrial production was nearing pre-1929 levels. Farmers were doing better and banks were more secure.[60] But there was much more to be done and Roosevelt resented a court that tied his hands. And his overwhelming reelection victory gave him a mandate he believed would support a radical effort to remake the court in his image.

The Republicans suspected that Roosevelt might have designs on the Supreme Court and they wanted to make that issue part of the 1936 presidential election. The Republican platform pledged to defend the court and called on the president to announce his intentions. Former President Herbert Hoover and the Republican nominee for president, Alf Landon, raised the issue; but Roosevelt steered clear of it. The Democratic convention platform offered only vague language about needing "clarifying amendments" to support its intervention into the troubled economy.[61]

As Roosevelt entered the final weeks of the campaign, Roosevelt's attorney general, Homer Cummings, began working with a young Justice Department lawyer, Warner W. Gardner, investigating options for altering the court's composition. Years later Gardner recounted his charge: "Cummings said that if

Roosevelt were reelected, as was expected, he was determined to move against the five or six Justices who were so stubbornly opposed to any government regulation that nothing could be done to strengthen the still devastated economy of the nation. I was to survey every suggestion short of constitutional amendment that had been made, and to report back as soon as feasible after the election."[62]

Roosevelt was reelected in a landslide, winning forty-six of forty-eight states and 523 electoral votes against Landon's eight.[63] The Democrats also picked up six seats in the Senate and twelve seats in the House, for a roughly four-to-one advantage over the Republicans in each chamber. With this mandate, Roosevelt began meeting daily with the attorney general to discuss the judicial reform proposal. The work was done in secret so that even Solicitor General Stanley Reed was ignorant of their efforts.[64] By December Roosevelt and Cummings had Gardner's sixty-five-page memorandum, entitled "Congressional Control of Judicial Power to Invalidate Legislation," to help their planning.[65]

In the meantime the high court continued its inconsistent record in ruling on government regulation. Six days after the election, *Valentine v. Great Atlantic & Pacific Tea Co.* invalidated an Iowa statute creating a so-called chain-store tax, following a decision a year earlier in *Stewart Dry Goods Co. v. Lewis*.[66] The lineup of the 6-2 decision was the same as it had been in *Stewart*, with Hughes and Roberts siding with the Four Horsemen and Justice Stone out for illness.[67] However, two weeks later in a 4-4 stalemate they left in place a New York unemployment statute in *Chamberlin v. Andrews*, which the New York Court of Appeals had distinguished from the federal railroad retirement statute invalidated in *Alton*.[68] William G. Ross called this "a major stride toward approving the federal Social Security Act" since the Social Security Act and the New York statute shared many similarities.[69] Furthermore, Roberts, who apparently joined the liberal's side in *Chamberlin*, had written the opinion for the court in *Alton*.[70] But Harvard Law professor Thomas Reed Powell was less sanguine about Robert's switch here, noting in January 1937 that if "Roberts found a lesson in the results of the election, such a fact is yet to be established. His supposed acceptance of the New York Compensation Act proffers hope rather than assurance."[71] In a more mixed view of the decision, Ross notes: "Writing a few days after the *Chamberlin* decision, the syndicated columnist Arthur Krock acknowledged that *Chamberlin* had caused the Court-curbing movement to recede, but that it 'has not ended with the passive result in the unemployment insurance case. Rather has watchful waiting been substituted for demands for legislative action and Presidential recommendation.'"[72] The editor of *United States Law Week* took note of the speculation about the court possibly changing its stripes after the election, but seems to have sided with Wiley Rutledge, dean of the University of Iowa College of Law, who "told the journalist Irving Brant in the wake of *Chamberlin* that he failed to 'see the occasion for all the press talk about this case as evidencing an effect of the election on the Court. Roberts and Hughes may have squinted sideways at the returns, but the Four Horsemen do not know that we had an election.'"[73]

Before 1936 ended the high court offered one final ambiguous ruling in *Duke Power Co. v. Greenwood County*, where a per curiam opinion dismissed, on technical grounds, a review of the merits of Duke Power Company's claim that Public Works Administration loans to municipal power companies (Duke's competitors) were unconstitutional.[74] The fallout was significant, as Ross explains: "Secretary of the Interior Harold L. Ickes, the PWA [Public Works Administration] administrator, publicly complained that the Court's 'technical decision' would cause 'further delay in construction of some half a hundred PWA projects in the event that private power interests persist in dilatory tactics.' Similarly, Attorney General Homer Cummings expressed 'regret that a decision on the merits was deemed impossible. It is highly important that the constitutional questions involved should be settled as soon as possible.'"[75] Syndicated columnist Drew Pearson reported that "the administration is beginning to wonder if the Supreme Court is playing a sly game of ring-around-a-rosy."[76]

Roosevelt and Cummings continued their stealth work on the plan, though the idea of possible reform of the Supreme Court was in the air. For example, in December 1936 investigative journalist George Creel wrote an essay on "Roosevelt's Plans and Purposes" that mused about a constitutional amendment to change the court, adding that if that failed, then "Congress *can enlarge the Supreme Court*, increasing the number of justices from nine to twelve or fifteen."[77] That latter approach would prove similar to the proposal Roosevelt revealed in early February.

Roosevelt began laying the groundwork for reforming the court in occasional remarks; his opponents, expecting the worst, attempted to defend the court and preempt any reform proposals. Shortly after his reelection was certified by Congress on January 6, 1937, Roosevelt gave his State of the Union address. He said that the legislative and executive branches needed to step up to help the nation recover. But, he added: "The Judicial branch also is asked by the people to do its part in making democracy successful. We do not ask the Courts to call nonexistent powers into being, but we have a right to expect that conceded powers or those legitimately implied shall be made effective instruments for the common good."[78] He even managed a dig at the court in his annual budget report of the next day, complaining: "As a result of Supreme Court decisions, the Government lost about $457,000,000 in revenue from taxes levied under the Agricultural Adjustment Act and the Bituminous Coal Act. Had it not been for the invalidation of these taxes, the total revenues received during the fiscal year 1936 would have exceeded the revenue estimates of a year ago by $162,000,000."[79] At his press conference on January 22, 1937, a reporter asked

Roosevelt directly: "Can you tell us whether you will join or support any legislation seeking a change of practice of the Supreme Court with respect to legislation?" The president dodged him by calling that "a sort of 'iffy' question," though he acknowledged that Senator Sherman Minton, a critic of the court's recent decisions, would be meeting him to discuss the court situation.[80]

On February 1, 1937, Republican Senator William E. Borah of Idaho defended the court in a widely publicized radio address, praising their decisions in two recent civil rights cases: The 1935 Scottsboro Boys case that overturned the racist prosecution of African Americans for rape in Alabama and a January 4, 1937, case overturning the conviction of Communists protesting police shootings and raids on workers' homes in *De Jonge v. Oregon*.[81] Borah insisted that the court that the Democrats were excoriating had "interposed [itself] to avert great wrongs to personal freedom."[82]

Borah's efforts were not helped by the court, which on the same day handed down a decision in *Great Northern Railway Co. v. Washington* overturning the Washington Supreme Court's support for a state law that placed a small tax on utilities to finance its Public Service Commission.[83] The court sent the case back to the lower court to reconsider whether the state met its burden in proving that it did not violate the utilities' due process rights. Roberts again sided with the Four Horsemen. Cardozo dissented, rejecting the placement of the burden of proof on the state and was joined by the chief justice and the two other liberals sitting for the case.

On February 2, 1937, in a prelude to Roosevelt's judicial reform plan's announcement, Attorney General Cummings sent the president a letter of concern on the judiciary, declaring that "delay in the administration of justice is the outstanding defect of our federal judicial system."[84] He hyperbolized that "in some jurisdictions, the delays in the administration of justice are so interminable that to institute suit is to embark on a life-long adventure." He noted that "the average case load borne by each judge has grown nearly fifty percent since 1913, when the District Courts were first organized on their present basis" causing a backlog of fifty thousand cases.[85] With this inefficiency as a pretext, he called for new legislation to reform the courts.[86] That night Roosevelt hosted a gala dinner in the East Room of the White House, where most of the Supreme Court justices joined around ninety guests.[87]

Before announcing his plan, or even revealing it to many close advisers, Roosevelt discussed it with labor leaders—one of his most important constituencies. Membership in unions had skyrocketed in Roosevelt's first term, as his administration eased the way for organizing, despite the conservative court's resistance to those efforts.[88] John Lewis of the Congress of Industrial Organizations and Charlton Ogburn, legal counsel for the American Federation of Labor, pledged to support the proposal.[89] They sent letters to members of

Congress to urge support.[90] After the *Alton* decision blocked Roosevelt's railroad retirement plan, this large constituency also stood behind the president's reforms, with a resolution by the Railroad Employees National Pension Association claiming that the poor "are denied the right to enjoy life, liberty and happiness because of the viciousness of the justices of the Supreme Court in declaring acts of Congress unconstitutional."[91]

Ironically, the proposal Roosevelt would announce on February 5, 1937, built upon an idea first raised by one of the Four Horsemen years earlier. When Justice McReynolds was President Wilson's attorney general, he authored a 1913 report suggesting that "Judges of the United States Courts, at the age of 70, after have served 10 years, may retire upon full pay." He insisted that those who stayed on the bench after that age "have remained upon the bench long beyond the time that they are able to adequately discharge their duties, and in consequence the administration of justice has suffered."[92] To address this problem, McReynolds had suggested "an act providing that when any judge of a Federal court below the Supreme Court fails to avail himself of the privilege of retiring now granted by law, that the President be required, with the advice and consent of the Senate, to appoint another judge, who would preside over the affairs of the court and have precedence over the older one. This will insure at all times the presence of a judge sufficiently active to discharge promptly and adequately the duties of the court."[93] Justice McReynolds turned seventy-five two days before Roosevelt announced his plan to enlarge the court, following closely the policy McReynolds had pushed twenty-four years earlier for lower federal court judges. Roosevelt wanted to announce the plan before the high court began hearings on a case involving the National Labor Relations Act to avoid the appearance he was directly threatening the court.[94]

The morning of February 5, Roosevelt sent one of his advisers to the Supreme Court with a note to Justice Brandeis informing him of what was coming. In a prescient response, Brandeis told the messenger: "Tell your president he has made a grave mistake. All he had to do was wait a little while. I'm sorry for him."[95] A half hour before he publicly announced his plan, he informed his cabinet and met with key congressional leaders, engendering bad feelings by simply reporting his finished plan rather than requesting their input on this controversial legislation.[96]

At his press conference, Roosevelt noted, vaguely, that "for a long time the subject of constitutionality of laws has been discussed."[97] He said that a small group had been studying "the fundamentals of the subject rather than those particular details which make the headlines," concluding that "there is required the same kind of reorganization of the Judiciary as has been recommended to this Congress for the Executive branch of the Government." He read excerpts from the attorney general's letter concerning the inefficiency of the judiciary. It was this inefficiency that Roosevelt stressed in justifying his plan, rather than a concern over their troublesome overrulings of his New Deal legislation.

Roosevelt sent the details of the plan with a justification to Congress the same day. The most controversial provision would allow the president to nominate a new justice to the Supreme Court for every sitting justice who had not retired within six months of his or her seventieth birthday. Because six of the justices on the court were already over seventy, if they chose not to retire then Roosevelt could grow the court to as many as fifteen justices.

As Trevor Parry-Giles and Marouf Hasian Jr. explain, Roosevelt's proposal tangled with two ultimate national values, *necessity* and *liberty*, with these competing values setting the political battle lines over the court reorganization plan: "The exigencies of the Depression provided Roosevelt, Democrats, and legal realists with the material justification to invoke 'necessity' as an ideological touchstone for public policy and behavior. Simultaneously, the Supreme Court enshrined and expressed the powerful commitment to 'liberty' that Americans were taught was part of their birthright, the very essence of their community. This was the ideological environment facing FDR in the wake of his landslide victory at the polls in 1936 as he pondered how to solve his problems with the Supreme Court. And this was the symbolic context of those who sought to stop FDR from 'reorganizing' the judiciary in the name of New Deal progressivism."[98]

THE NATIONAL DEBATE OVER COURT REFORM

Reaction to the proposal was intense, sustained, and widespread. Leuchtenburg claims that the response to the court reorganization plan was "unmatched by any legislative controversy of this century, save perhaps for the League of Nations episode."[99] Republicans obviously opposed it; but so did many Democrats. The American Bar Association would deploy its legal expertise to warn against the dangers of the bill. Only two days after Roosevelt announced the plan, one of the members of his "brain trust," General Hugh S. Johnson, was already playing defense on a CBS radio broadcast, complaining that "opponents of the President have presented his proposals, melodramatically, as the death of the Constitution."[100] Johnson admitted that Roosevelt was seeking to change the direction of the court on his New Deal policies, but asked, "What is the matter with that?"[101] He noted "that Congress has absolute power to prescribe the number of Judges on the Supreme Court and that when Congress names the number, the President makes appointments."[102] In our government's system of checks and balances, he asked, what was the check on the Supreme Court's veto of what Congress and the Executive passed? He answered: "It is the power to fix the number of Judges, to name them, and to regulate their appellate jurisdiction."[103]

At his February 12 press conference Roosevelt was asked about the reaction of senators to his proposal and joked, "You don't want to be here all day, do you?"[104] He admitted that his proposal "took most people by surprise" but explained how it was developed carefully over one and a half years in response to the NIRA decision on Black Monday. He said that he rejected a constitutional amendment as too slow to pass and too uncertain. Legislative suggestions, such as requiring a unanimous or 8-1 decision threshold for invalidating federal laws were of dubious constitutionality. He concluded: "So, by a process of elimination, we came down to an action which was of undoubted constitutionality."

Less than a week later, the American Bar Association authorized a referendum on the president's plan; of more than fifty thousand responses, 77 percent opposed the plan's provisions for the high court.[105] The *ABA Journal* would feature numerous essays raising grave concerns about the plan over the spring.[106] Yale Law School professor and special assistant to the attorney general Thurman Arnold responded to several of the president's critics in the May issue of *ABAJ*, but noted he was arguing in "a hostile forum, with the satisfaction which comes from making a convert virtually denied me in advance."[107]

A number of senators defended the president's proposal, as Parry-Giles and Hasian have documented. For example, Indiana Senator Sherman Minton (D), who would be appointed to the high court by President Truman, warned that the "absolute veto power" of a majority of the court was thwarting Congress's efforts to address the crisis.[108] Senator Hugo Black of Alabama (D), who would shortly be appointed to the Supreme Court by Roosevelt, urged that "the time has arrived when those who favor fitting laws to modern needs in order to correct and cure social and industrial injustice must face their problems squarely and fairly," which requires overcoming "impassable barriers" thrown up by "a bare majority" of the Supreme Court.[109] In the midst of the rise of fascism in Europe, Senator Theodore Green of Rhode Island (D), rejected claims that the president was trying to set himself up as a tyrant, noting: "President Roosevelt has abided by adverse judicial decisions. He has not defied them. He has never ignored a summons, as did Jefferson; or challenged the Court to enforce its decisions once they were made, as did Jackson; or flouted a writ of habeas corpus, as did Lincoln; or campaigned for the popular recall of judicial decisions, as did Theodore Roosevelt."[110]

As the nation debated the fate of the Supreme Court, the high court offered a favorable ruling in *Holyoke Water Power Co. v. American Writing Paper Co.*, reiterating its prior holding in the Gold Clause Cases that Congress could repudiate the gold standard.[111] Although the same 5-4 division continued, Justice Cardozo's opinion offered a fresh way to analyze economic regulations such as this one. When the litigant insisted that their exceptional case would not interfere with national monetary policy, Cardozo stressed the cumulative effect of such minor cases, insisting that a "particular covenant, if viewed in isolation, may have a slight, perhaps a trivial, influence upon the effectiveness and symmetry of a new monetary policy. The aggregate of many covenants, each contributing its mite, may bring the system to destruction. Rivulets in combination make up a stream of tendency that may attain engulfing power."[112]

Roosevelt tried to keep Democrats unified at a victory dinner on March 4 at the Mayflower Hotel. Richard D. Friedman reports: "He gave a speech to the crowd. He called for party loyalty, emphasized the dire problems facing the country, and noted that a favorable Court was required for them to push forward. 'It will take courage,' he concluded, adapting a line from Brandeis' dissent in *New York State Ice Co. v. Liebman*, 'to let our minds be bold.'"[113]

Roosevelt sought to bolster public support with a full frontal assault on the sitting court in a Fireside Chat on March 9—the eve of Senate hearings on his proposal. He turned the positive decision of the Supreme Court in the Gold Clause Cases into a cause for concern, noting that the decision was 5-4: "In effect, four Justices ruled that the right under a private contract to exact a pound of flesh was more sacred than the main objectives of the Constitution to establish an enduring Nation." He warned that "the Courts . . . have cast doubts on the ability of the elected Congress to protect us against catastrophe by meeting squarely our modern social and economic conditions." While Congress and the Executive were responding to the crisis, the Supreme Court was not, he insisted with a farm metaphor: "Last Thursday I described the American form of Government as a three horse team provided by the Constitution to the American people so that their field might be plowed. The three horses are, of course, the three branches of government—the Congress, the executive and the Courts. Two of the horses are pulling in unison today; the third is not." In particular, the court was offering a cramped reading of the Constitution to invalidate New Deal programs. Roosevelt noted that the court had historically presumed legislation was constitutionally valid; however, "since the rise of the modern movement for social and economic progress through legislation, the Court has more and more often and more and more boldly asserted a power to veto laws passed by the Congress and State Legislatures in complete disregard of this original limitation." He accused the court of "acting not as a judicial body, but as a policy-making body." He quoted justices who reflected the same concerns, such as Justice Stone's dissent in the Agricultural Adjustment Act case, which said the majority relied upon a "tortured construction of the Constitution."[114]

He warned his listeners: "We have . . . reached the point as a Nation where we must take action to save the Constitution from the Court and the Court from itself." He explained that he considered all options, eliminated the untenable ones, and decided that "the only method which was clearly constitutional, and would at the same time carry out other much needed reforms, was to infuse new blood into all our Courts." He explained his proposal to appoint replacements for judges seventy and older if they did not retire. While he said little about the inefficiency in the courts he had highlighted when he first made his proposal, he noted that improving efficiency was one purpose, while another was "to bring to the decision of social and economic problems younger men who have had personal experience and contact with modern facts and circumstances under which average men have to live and work."[115]

Roosevelt's speech was followed by a bump in polling numbers favoring his approach.[116] Donovan Bisbee notes that "the volume of mail to the White House regarding the Court plan also increased after the speech (with a steady growth in favorable correspondence), with one day amassing 895 favorable letters and telegrams with 308 unfavorable, as compared to 150 favorable and 50 unfavorable before the speech."[117] However, as the debate raged through March polling numbers dipped again.[118] Ross believes that Roosevelt's switch from emphasizing the efficiency problem of the court to its emphasizing its anti–New Deal bias showed his "original disingenuousness" and caused damage to his proposal that "may have been irrevocable."[119]

This disingenuousness was highlighted in the Senate hearings on the bill that began the next day. The first witness, Attorney General Cummings, emphasized the problem of backlogged cases in the federal courts that his memo had documented. William Borah (R-Idaho), who was a fixture in the Senate, quickly asked Cummings a hypothetical question to tease out the real reason for the proposal: "'Suppose after six additional members of the Supreme Court are appointed, the Court should divide seven to eight, this entire plan would fall, would it not?' The attorney general replied that 'it would depend upon which side the seven were on and which side the eight were on.'"[120] Other witnesses included a labor leader, a representative from the National Lawyers' Guild, and a judge and former law school dean who offered a compelling graph showing that "as the average age of Supreme Court justices increased, so, too, did their propensity for declaring legislation unconstitutional."[121] Princeton University 's Edwin Corwin, a professor of politics, warned of the unchecked power of the Supreme Court, and quoted Chief Justice Charles Evans Hughes's notable statement that the "Constitution is what the judges say it is." Sitting in front of Borah, Corwin quoted the senator's own complaints when Hughes was being confirmed in 1930 that the court was the "economic dictator of the United States."[122]

The hearings went on for weeks and relied heavily on law school professors. As Kyle Graham notes: "Of the approximately eighty witnesses called, almost one-fifth were law teachers. Out of these, only two (three if you include William Draper Lewis of the American Law Institute) spoke in favor of the plan. A dozen others, including Columbia dean Young B. Smith, Harvard's Erwin Griswold, Michigan's Henry Bates, and Yale's Edwin Borchard, were opposed."[123] For example, Professor Erwin Griswold of Harvard Law School warned that Roosevelt was using concerns over the economic crisis to bully the court. He argued that increasing the size of the court would actually increase inefficiency.[124] Edwin Borchard of Yale Law School claimed that there was no longer an economic emergency and blamed the court's striking down of statutes on "poor legislation."[125] Justin R. Braga argues that "the opposition was able to convert the debate into a topic less favorable to the administration's position because lawyers, most of whom opposed the plan, were perceived as having greater credibility on matters of constitutional law and the judiciary."[126]

Among the other opposition witnesses was Dorothy Thompson, a popular syndicated columnist who had been kicked out of Germany in 1934 for her negative public comments about Hitler.[127] She warned the committee that "the nation was on the brink of tyranny" because of FDR's plan, despite her prior support for him.[128] But the most dramatic witness was Senator Burton Wheeler, a New Deal Democrat from Montana who broke with the president and attacked the judicial reform plan. He brought a letter written by Chief Justice Hughes that denied the administration's charge of inefficiency in the federal courts, which was signed not only by Justice Van Devanter, but also the liberal Justice Brandeis.[129] The letter pointed out that an enlarged court itself would lead to inefficiency (as Griswold had argued).[130] Opposition from other Democrats would doom Roosevelt's proposal.

DISSENT FROM WITHIN KILLS JUDICIAL REFORM

Given Roosevelt's huge congressional majorities, he could have succeeded on reform if he did not have so much opposition within his own party. In addition to Senator Wheeler's dramatic stand against the president, Senator Edward R. Burke (D-Nebraska) warned ominously that "this is not a battle between the President and the Court. Rather it is the President against the people."[131] He asserted that "what the President proposes is to make all judges dependent upon the will of the Executive."[132] Burke encouraged the American Bar Association (ABA) to create a "permanent research staff for Congress," consisting of "senior partners and some of the brightest young men from the country's largest law firms," to provide ammunition against the plan for the Senate hearings.[133] The ABA financed radio ads featuring prominent Democratic senators opposed to the plan.[134]

Many state Democrats began rallying against the plan immediately after it was announced. Stephen Early, the White House press secretary, warned Roosevelt on February 8, 1937, that the Texas state senate was passing a resolution against the proposal. The governor reported that the situation "is bad." It did not help that all but three members of the Texas legislature were lawyers.[135] Texas would be a harbinger for the South: Josiah M. Daniel III notes that "in 1937 most Southerners in Congress fought the court-packing plan, despite their deal with the President, because they feared that the increase in executive power the plan represented might be marshaled against Jim Crow."[136]

Numerous Democrats encouraged Roosevelt to consider less drastic alternatives to his plan. For example, three days after the plan was announced, Senator Key Pittman of Nevada wrote the attorney general to tout his more modest proposal for an eleven-member court.[137] On February 20, 1937, a delegation that included the vice president, Senate majority leader, and Senate Judiciary Committee chair suggested that the president compromise by simply adding two or three justices to the court; Roosevelt responded by "laugh[ing] in their faces."[138]

Only recently has the important role of House Judiciary Committee Chair Hatton Sumners of Dallas in defeating the plan been highlighted as central to this saga, by Josiah M. Daniel III.[139] He examines a widely reported incident after Roosevelt met with key Democrats prior to announcing his plan. Sumners was riding in a car back to the Capitol with Vice President John Nance Garner and House Majority Leader Sam Rayburn when he told them: "Boys, here's where I cash in."[140] Daniel says that Sumners's remark "was the first announcement of opposition to the plan."[141] Sumners held an off-the-record meeting the same day with members of the press, calling the proposal "infamous." The White House press secretary got wind of the press conference and told Roosevelt that Sumners was "savage in [his] attack upon your proposal."[142] The reporter told Early that Sumners had given the proposal "Hell, specifically and generally"[143]

Despite his presumed stealth moves against the proposal, Sumners thought he was doing the president a favor. In a letter to a constituent who asked about his reported remarks, Sumners explained: "You ask for an explanation, and briefly this is it. . . . My reaction was that the President must have been imposed on. I determined to go in and to do what I could to help straighten things out and not to count the cost to myself. . . . As I saw the situation somebody had to go in and try to be helpful about it. As I further saw it, the person who did go in would probably not come out politically alive."[144]

Daniel notes Sumners's explanation for his secret work against the bill in a letter to a Dallas businessman, where Sumners wrote on March 8: "Insofar as my political fortunes are concerned, I am perfectly willing to cash in if I can be useful to my country in this great emergency. That is confidential, because people would misunderstand it. They would think I am trying to put myself on parade."[145]

Sumners did more than oppose the plan. He introduced and pushed through two bills that would prove valuable in solving the court problem. The first bill addressed an appalling situation, which Daniel describes:

> In early 1932, Justice Oliver Wendell Holmes resigned at age ninety after thirty years' service. Rather quickly Holmes's pension was cut in half due to President Hoover's Economy Act that was enacted later that year. Sumners was appalled. By resigning, Holmes had lost his constitutional protection against reduction of compensation. The penny-pinching reduction of all judicial pensions also upset several of the justices. One of the Four Horsemen, Justice Van Devanter, had been planning to step down in 1933, but the severe reduction of Holmes' pension caused him to stay in office so he could continue to receive his full salary. Justice Sutherland felt the same way. Resignation would also have subjected these justices to income tax on their pensions which they had not been paying on their judicial salaries. Sumners was in touch with those justices and knew their inclinations.[146]

Although Sumners's initial bill was killed by penny-pinchers in Congress in 1935, the proposal became more popular as momentum grew to deal with the court problem. He reintroduced the bill in January 1937. The *Dallas Morning News* thought Sumners's Retirement Bill "might easily be the means of solving the Supreme Court issue entirely."[147] It was quickly passed by both houses and signed by the president on March 1, 1937, though it did not lead Roosevelt to abandon his judicial reform proposal.[148]

The second bill, sometimes called the Intervention Bill, addressed the problem that litigation over the constitutionality of New Deal programs was often conducted in private suits, without the participation of the Justice Department to defend the statutes under scrutiny. Several major cases from 1935 to 1936 invalidated legislation without hearing from government lawyers, including the *Railroad Retirement* case, the *Carter Coal* case, the Municipal Bankruptcy Act case, and the farmers' bankruptcy relief act.[149] Sumners's proposal, introduced in January 1937, required courts to notify the Justice Department when constitutional issues involving federal statutes were under scrutiny in court cases so that the government would have an opportunity to defend them.[150] The bill was signed into law in August 1937 after Roosevelt's plan failed.[151]

Sumners managed to delay consideration of Roosevelt's court reform bill by helping to ensure that it would initially be considered by the Senate Judiciary Committee, rather than in his own House Judiciary Committee where Roosevelt wanted it taken up.[152] This did not bode well for the bill; while opposition in the House was intense, "the Senate was more conservative and senatorial opinion was sharply divided."[153] William G. Ross notes that the chair of the Senate Judiciary Committee, Senator Henry F. Ashurst, was "lukewarm in his support of the Court-curbing bill," and maintained a "leisurely" pace for the measure's consideration, "provid[ing] time for supporters of the Court to rally their forces against it." Although he introduced the bill in the Senate on February 8,

1937, he would not hold hearings on it for another month.[154] Roosevelt was so mad at Ashurst that he "retaliated against the Arizona senator by helping to ensure his defeat for reelection three years later."[155]

Roosevelt did have a strong ally in Senate Majority Leader Joe Robinson of Arkansas, who was promised a seat on the Supreme Court at the next vacancy and pledged to push through the court reform bill. However, Roosevelt would find it inconvenient to nominate the conservative southerner when one of the Four Horsemen retired in June 1937.[156] Nevertheless, Robinson kept shepherding the bill, but suffered a fatal heart attack while alone at his Capitol apartment on July 13 during the final push for a revised version of Roosevelt's plan. His death stopped all momentum for the troubled bill, which died in committee on July 22.[157]

THE SUPREME COURT TURNS AROUND

The Supreme Court continued its regular business against the backdrop of the president's announcement of his court reform proposal, the reaction from Republicans, Democrats, the ABA, Labor, and others; the president's broadside against the court in the Fireside Chat of March 9, the Senate hearings over the next several weeks, the chief justice's letter rejecting calls for reform, and the floor debates over the proposal. As noted above, on March 1 it handed down a progovernment decision in another challenge to the Gold Clause. Two weeks later it denied a hearing over a challenge to the National Labor Relations Act but also invalidated the federal taxation of the income of a New York State employee who worked in essential government services.[158] While this continued bouncing back and forth on the constitutionality of government action did not mark a significant change from what had come before, three decisions handed down two weeks later would lead to charges that the court had blinked in the face of Roosevelt's threat to reshape it.

March 29, 1937, was dubbed "White Monday," in direct contrast with "Black Monday" two years earlier. White Monday featured a whole slew of proregulation decisions, including one that overruled a recent decision by the court. The court supported a state statute regulating milk as they had in the *Nebbia* case, with the Four Horsemen dissenting.[159] They unanimously supported a provision of the Railway Labor Act that required management to engage with union representatives of interstate railroad workers, a federal tax that regulated firearms dealers, and a revised Frazier-Lemke Act to stem farm bankruptcies.[160] Although the sheer quantity of proregulation decisions might be seen as a response to the president's threat, these decisions might simply be explained as following a prior decision (*Nebbia*), making original rulings, or approving revised legislation responsive to a prior negative decision. Harder to explain was a decision in *West Coast Hotel v. Parrish* to overrule a fourteen-year-old precedent that had been cited and followed by the Hughes court nine months earlier in *Morehead v. New York ex rel. Tipaldo.*[161] Justice Roberts switched sides from *Tipaldo* to *Parrish,* leading to decades of speculation about his motives and, in particular, whether Roosevelt's plan had pushed him toward a "switch in time."

The 1923 precedent on point in *Parrish* was *Adkins v. Children's Hospital.*[162] The case concerned a minimum-wage law that Congress had passed to help women and children workers in Washington, DC. Illustrating his long-term consistency as a protector of laissez-faire economics, Justice Sutherland would write the majority opinion invalidating the law. Although he insisted that he was following the Supreme Court's tradition of holding "every possible presumption . . . in favor of the validity of an act of Congress until overcome beyond rational doubt" (544), he found this statute provided "an unconstitutional interference with the freedom of contract included within the guaranties of the due process clause of the Fifth Amendment" (545). Ignoring the vicissitudes of economic conditions that shape the bargaining power of individuals—not to mention historic sexism in worker pay—Sutherland insisted that "the parties have an equal right to obtain from each other the best terms they can as the result of private bargaining" without interference from the government (545). Sutherland rejected analogies to legislation governing working conditions, such as maximum hours, which the high court had previously allowed, insisting that the DC statute "differs from them in every material respect" (554).

Sutherland showed great empathy for businesses required to pay a minimum wage to women such as hotel elevator operator Adkins. He complained:

> The law takes account of the necessities of only one party to the contract. It ignores the necessities of the employer by compelling him to pay not less than a certain sum not only whether the employee is capable of earning it, but irrespective of the ability of his business to sustain the burden, generously leaving him, of course, the privilege of abandoning his business as an alternative for going on at a loss. Within the limits of the minimum sum, he is precluded, under penalty of fine and imprisonment, from adjusting compensation to the differing merits of his employees. It compels him to pay at least the sum fixed in any event, because the employee needs it, but requires no service of equivalent value from the employee. (557)

Sutherland showed particular concern for smaller businesses "whose bargaining power may be as weak as that of the employee" (557). While he ignored economic downturns that might limit employees' bargaining power, he was concerned that the law "takes no account of periods of stress and business depression, of crippling losses, which may leave the employer himself without adequate means of livelihood" (557). If the minimum wage costs more than "the fair value of the services rendered," as Sutherland seems to think it might, "it amounts to a compulsory exaction from the employer for the support of a partially indigent person, for whose condition there rests upon him no peculiar responsibility, and therefore, in effect, arbitrarily shifts to his shoulders a burden which, if it belongs to anybody, belongs to society as a whole" (557–58). Even if the employer pays "poverty wages," he or she is not responsible for the inevitable outcome, Sutherland insists: "Certainly the employer, by paying a fair equivalent for the service rendered, though not sufficient to support the employee, has neither caused nor contributed to her poverty. On the contrary, to the extent of what he pays, he has relieved it" (558). Sutherland recognized that this was a contest between the liberty interests of business and the common good, but insisted: "To sustain the individual freedom of action contemplated by the Constitution is not to strike down the common good, but to exalt it, for surely the good of society as a whole cannot be better served than by the preservation against arbitrary restraint of the liberties of its constituent members" (561). Sutherland was joined by the other three Horsemen and Justice McKenna.

Chief Justice Taft dissented, describing a more realistic function of a minimum wage: "Legislatures, in limiting freedom of contract between employee and employer by a minimum wage, proceed on the assumption that employees, in the class receiving least pay, are not upon a full level of equality of choice with their employer, and, in their necessitous circumstances, are prone to accept pretty much anything that is offered. They are peculiarly subject to the overreaching of the harsh and greedy employer. The evils of the sweating system and of the long hours and low wages which are characteristic of it are well known" (562). Taft thought the majority was overstepping its bounds in invalidating the law, because "it is not the function of this Court to hold congressional acts invalid simply because they are passed to carry out economic views which the Court believes to be unwise or unsound" (562).

Justice Holmes, in his own dissent, challenged Sutherland's argument of the government forcing the paying of above-market wages and ruining businesses. He insisted: "This statute does not compel anybody to pay anything. It simply forbids employment at rates below those fixed as the minimum requirement of health and right living. It is safe to assume that women will not be employed at even the lowest wages allowed unless they earn them, or unless the employer's business can sustain the burden" (570). Justice Sanford joined Taft's dissent and Justice Brandeis did not take part, leaving a 5-3 decision striking down the minimum wage statute.

In 1936 the high court faced a similar case in *Tipaldo*. Instead of a federal minimum wage statute, this case involved a state statute. New York's lawyers apparently did not want to carry the burden of justifying an overruling of *Adkins* and tried to distinguish the two cases. Writing for the majority, Justice Butler rejected that argument by examining the definitions of "minimum wage" used by the legislatively mandated boards setting them: "Thus, it appears: the minimum wage provided for in the District Act [in *Adkins*] was one not less than adequate 'to supply the necessary cost of living to any such women workers to maintain them in good health and to protect their morals.' § 9. The New York Act [in the present case] defines an oppressive and unreasonable wage as containing two elements. The one first mentioned is: 'less than the fair and reasonable value of the services rendered.' The other is: 'less than sufficient to meet the minimum cost of living necessary for health.' § 551(7). The basis last mentioned is not to be distinguished from the living wage defined in the District Act" (606–7). Butler invoked the due process clause of the Fourteenth Amendment in *Tipaldo* as Sutherland had invoked the Fifth Amendment (which applies to the federal government) in *Adkins*. Similarly, he defended the individual's "right to make contracts about one's affairs" (610). He argued, as the *Adkins* majority had, that employees and employers "have equal right to obtain from each other the best terms they can by private bargaining" and insisted that "legislative abridgement of that freedom can only be justified by the existence of exceptional circumstances" (610). Justice Roberts joined the Four Horsemen silently in this decision, with Hughes and the three liberals in dissent. Cushman notes that "contemporary scholars . . . expressed considerable surprise when the *Tipaldo* decision came down,"[163] as did politicians (as I noted above).[164]

West Coast Hotel v. Parrish involved a Washington State minimum wage statute that was "virtually identical" to the federal one that was rejected for violating due process in *Atkins*, and likewise was grounded in the police power of the government.[165] Elsie Parrish, a chambermaid, complained that she was paid less than the $14.50 for a forty-eight-hour work week required by the statute and sought back pay for the shortfall (529). Like the employee's lawyers in *Tipaldo*, her lawyers tried to distinguish *Adkins*, urging that as a hotel employee she worked in an industry for which the state had a public interest (and therefore greater latitude in regulation). Chief Justice Hughes, writing for the majority, rejected that distinction, noting that the *Adkins* case also included a hotel employee as a litigant (530). However, he said that he and the minority in the *Tipaldo* case did find a distinction between the New York statute at issue and the federal statute in *Adkins*. In an apparent attempt to explain away *Tipaldo*, he insisted: "But the Court of Appeals of New York [ruling below] had said that it found no material difference between the two statutes, and this Court held that the 'meaning of the statute' as fixed by the decision of the state court 'must be accepted here as if the meaning had been specifically expressed in the enactment.' Id., p. 609. That view led to the affirmance by this Court of the judgment in the Morehead [v. Tipaldo] case, as *the Court considered that the only question before it was whether the Adkins case was distinguishable and that reconsideration of that decision had not been sought*" (530; emphasis added). In other words, Hughes made clear, *Tipaldo* never considered whether *Adkins* was still good law because lawyers for the petitioner never asked them to do so; they only requested that the statutes be distinguished so a different legal result might prevail. Because the state court had construed its own law and the federal courts were required to accept that construction, there was nothing more to be argued about but the one nail upon which the petitioners had hung their case.

That Hughes would stress the state court's finding as a determining factor in the case is ironic, since his dissent in *Tipaldo* argued that the state court's announcement that there was no difference in the statutes was not, in the chief justice's view, a construction of state law requiring the high court to follow it. Rather, he noted in that case: "When the opinion of the state court . . . says that the setting up of such a standard [for determining a minimum wage] does not create a material distinction when compared with the Act of Congress in the *Adkins* case, the state court is not construing the state statute. It is passing upon the effect of the difference between the two acts from the standpoint of the Federal Constitution. It is putting aside an admitted difference as not controlling. It is holding, as the state court says, that '[f]orcing the payment of wages at a reasonable value does not make inapplicable the principle and ruling of the *Adkins* case.' That, it seems to me, is clearly a federal and not a state question." (622). In *Parrish,* he is giving an account of the *Tipaldo* precedent that is the majority's justification, however weak he believed it to be. The benefit of that construction for Hughes was that he could discount *Tipaldo* as turning on a narrow technical issue that did not allow the court to raise larger constitutional questions, such as the continued vitality of *Adkins.*

Many years after this decision, that same narrow issue Hughes stressed to explain the *Tipaldo* result would be used to give cover to Justice Roberts, who switched sides from *Tipaldo* to *Parrish* in terms of his support for minimum wage legislation.[166] But that could not help the credibility of Justice Roberts or the court in the meantime, as they faced the appearance of an about-face just over seven weeks after Roosevelt's proposal to remake the court. Justice Roberts kept his head down on this change of direction, silently joining the majority in *Parrish* as he had silently joined the majority in *Tipaldo.*

As a dissenter in *Tipaldo,* Chief Justice Hughes did not have Roberts's credibility problem, and offered a full-throated argument against the due process underpinnings of both cases. He dismissed the claim that "freedom of contract" was in the Constitution, since the document does not mention it. He argued that liberty required protection "against the evils which menace the health, safety, morals and welfare of the people," and insisted such regulation only be "reasonable in relation to its subject and . . . adopted in the interests of the community" to meet due process requirements is due process (391). He cited numerous cases where freedom of contract had been restrained by federal and state governments in the public interest (392–94).

Hughes announced that *Adkins* was overruled (400). He justified ignoring stare decisis—which he never mentions as a concern—by arguing that the *Adkins* court was wrong about the constitutionality of such minimum wage laws, as noted above. He also sought to characterize the case as an outlier, claiming it "was a departure from the true application of the principles governing the regulation by the State of the relation of employer and employed . . . principles [that] have been reenforced by our subsequent decisions, including cases 're-strict[ing] the employment of women in restaurants at night' and 'regulating the commissions of insurance agents'" (397). As to the wisdom of such policies, he reiterated Roberts's *Nebbia* claim that "the courts are both incompetent and unauthorized to deal [with such questions]," though he listed good reasons for those policies (398–99).

A final way Hughes diminished the *Adkins* case is by highlighting the split in the court's decision. He pointed to "the dissenting Justices in the Adkins case [who] demand[ed] that the minimum wage statute be sustained," relying on an "array of precedents and the principles" to support their argument (395). He quoted two dissenters: the redoubtable Justice Holmes (396) and the eminent former president and chief justice William Howard Taft (397). Thus, not only was there strong dissent, but it came from respected jurists.

Although not pointed out by Hughes, the Supreme Court is less concerned about overruling prior decisions involving interpretations of the Constitution, as I noted in chapter 2. As Justice Brandeis had stated five years earlier in his famous dissent in *Burnet v. Coronado Oil & Gas Co.*, "in cases involving the Federal Constitution, where correction through legislative action is practically impossible, this court has often overruled its prior decisions."[167] Brandeis included a lengthy list of prior overrulings to support his claim.

Hughes did not say that *Tipaldo* should be overruled. As noted above, he offered a procedural dodge to explain that decision and render it less relevant to the present case because it never grappled with the constitutional issues raised by *Parrish*. That had the added benefit of not saddling Justice Roberts with supporting a decision explicitly reversed by the majority he now joined.

That subtle distinction was easily lost on the public at large, who saw a defiant court knock down a minimum-wage statute in 1936 and reverse its position the next year, just weeks after the president threatened to pack the court. The public could be forgiven for not knowing that *Parrish* had been decided two months before the president's proposal was announced or that "once the Court-packing plan was announced, Chief Justice Hughes waited to release his opinion [written in February] until late March, for he did not want to convey the impression that the Court was reacting to the plan."[168] It was not until a 1945 interview that

Roberts would tell a Pulitzer Prize–winning reporter that he joined the court majority in *Tipaldo* "because counsel challenging the New York law did not address the 'real issue' of whether Adkins should be overruled."[169] Over a decade later he would acknowledge to the Senate Judiciary Committee "the tremendous strain [in 1937] and the threat to the existing Court, of which I was fully conscious."[170] It is unsurprising that his reasons for the switch in this and subsequent cases are contested to this day. Because Roberts remained silent in the *Parrish* decision and the immediate aftermath, he was not in a position to explain his change of heart.

Justice Roberts would be the poster child for the court's "revolution" in 1937. His change of sides was a threat to the Supreme Court's standing as a body that operates above politics, applying impartial judgment while protected by lifetime appointments and its status as a coequal branch of government. The court's apparent reversal of its position from nine months earlier would cast suspicion on its justification for the *Parrish* decision.

The Four Horsemen maintained their consistency, with Justice Sutherland leading a dissent. With an assurance that the dissenters were fulfilling their oaths and following their convictions, he repeated their well-established positions from both *Adkins* and *Tipaldo*.

The news media saw *Parrish* as a clear change of direction for the court. As Parry-Giles and Hasian report: "As one columnist wrote in the *Literary Digest*, the 'Nine Old Men' had turned their conservative robes inside out and were looking with a more friendly eye upon New Deal social legislation.' *Time* [magazine] concluded that the majority opinion from Chief Justice Hughes made him seem 'amazingly like a New Dealer.' *Business Week* lamented that the 'due process' clause 'took a real beating at the hands of Chief Justice Hughes.'"[171] Although this notable change of direction provided fodder for those who opposed Roosevelt's court reform plan—rendering it unnecessary to get the court onboard with the New Deal—others saw this as another ping-ponging by a court that had shifted many times between supporting and opposing legislation aimed at addressing the economic problems of the nation. For example, Senator Sherman Minton (D-Indiana), who would later join the high court, thought the case reinforced the fluidity of the court's positions and held firm in support of the president's measure.[172] An April 2 labor editorial called the case the court's "latest flip-flop" made possible by "the whims and caprices of one man [i.e., Justice Roberts, whose actions] may affect the destiny of millions adversely."[173]

If the Four Horsemen's arguments were predictable, Justice Roberts's silent joining of the majority was not. However, it was explicable through what would become the most popular account of the change of heart: the court was frightened by Roosevelt's proposal into reversing itself. This idea was cemented into the public psyche after a newspaper columnist inaugurated a catchy phrase to concisely characterize the court's actions. John Q. Barrett only recently discovered the original source of the famous quotation and methodically traced its usage. He notes that a couple of weeks after *Parrish* was handed down and a second pro–New Deal landmark was decided, Cal Tinney wrote in his *New York Post* column: "I've been thinking for a[n] explanation of why Justice Roberts switched from the conservatives to the liberals. Is this it?—Maybe he figures that a switch in time'll save nine."[174] Although the quip appeared on page 21 of the newspaper, it quickly was bantered around among political insiders. Within a week, New York's City College campus newspaper included a slightly amended version of the statement, saying: "A switch in time saves nine."[175] The student newspaper credited Tinney as the source, but that would be the last reference to the creator of what was to become a pre-internet "meme" for 1937. In May, Professor Edward Corwin would ask Attorney General Cummings if he had heard "a switch in time saves nine" (he had not); by June a Washington journalist reported hearing it from four different people.[176] During a dinner speech on June 14, Yale Law School professor and future Supreme Court justice Abe Fortas offered: "Mr. Justice Roberts's theory must be a switch in time serves nine." He drew applause and was quoted in the *New York Times* the next day.[177] When Joseph Alsop and Turner Catledge's book on the failed court reform bill, *The 168 Days,* was published the next year, they would entitle one of their chapters "A Switch in Time Saves Nine."[178]

Two weeks after the *Parrish* decision, the court provided another data point to mark its change of direction. In *National Labor Relations Board v. Jones & Laughlin Steel Corp.,* the court upheld the Wagner Act, which supported labor unions and outlawed "company" unions (which were dominated or influenced by employers).[179] A contemporary commentator thought the case "furnished the most plausible reason for abandoning the old landmarks."[180] Jones & Laughlin Steel Corporation was involved in a mighty "current of commerce" involving interstate commerce from raw materials to finished products, as the Labor Board explained: The company's operations "might be likened to the heart of a self-contained, highly integrated body. They draw in the raw materials from Michigan, Minnesota, West Virginia, Pennsylvania, in part through arteries and by means controlled by the respondent; they transform the materials and then pump them out to all parts of the nation through the vast mechanism which the respondent has elaborated."[181] The company argued that, although it may have engaged in outlawed labor practices to thwart union activity, it was not covered by the Wagner Act because the activity was in a manufacturing facility within a single state. Hughes rejected the claim, noting: "The fact remains that the stoppage of those [manufacturing] operations by industrial strife would have a most serious effect upon interstate commerce. In view of respondent's far-flung activities, it is idle to say that the effect would be indirect or remote. It is obvious that it would be immediate, and might be catastrophic. We are asked to shut our eyes to the plainest facts of our national life, and to deal with the question of direct and indirect effects in an intellectual vacuum" (41). So, Hughes was not ready to abandon the direct/indirect distinction that determined whether an activity was intrastate or interstate in nature, but he was more open to finding direct effects.

The chief justice was joined by Justice Roberts and the three liberals, with the Four Horsemen dissenting. Kalman notes that this case represented another about-face for Roberts, because it "is more difficult to reconcile with his previous 'very right-wing opinion' in *Alton* striking down the Railroad Retirement Act."[182]

Following these decisions, the popular notion that the court was ready to play ball with Roosevelt bolstered the position that the court reform bill was no longer needed. At a press conference the day after the *Jones* decision was handed down, Roosevelt was asked if this decision changed his mind about his court reform proposal. He was still skeptical, opining: "As to how far the decision will be extended to other phases of interstate commerce, they say, 'The Lord only knows.'"[183] The attorney general noted that in such cases the administration "must face a court of nine, with four votes lost to it in advance. The margin is too narrow and the risk is too great."[184]

After the *Jones* decision, members of the Senate were more sanguine about the court and less supportive of the president's bill. Senate Majority Leader Joe Robinson ran into strong resistance, telling Assistant Attorney General Joe Keenan that "this bill's raising hell in the Senate. Now it's going to be worse than ever, but if the President wants to compromise I can get him a couple of extra justices tomorrow."[185] But Roosevelt was still unwilling to water down his plan. Despite pleas from senators, advisers, and his son James to compromise, upon returning from a fishing trip in the Gulf of Mexico on May 14, the president told cabinet and congressional leaders he would continue to fight for his plan.[186]

On May 18, Roosevelt got good news for his New Deal programs, but bad news for his court reform bill. One of the Four Horsemen, Justice Van Devanter, announced he would retire on June 2. The president also learned that Justice Sutherland planned to follow soon.[187] When queried by the press about whether Van Devanter's retirement would affect his court reform plans, he said obstinately, "I don't think there is any news in that."[188] The Senate Judiciary Committee apparently disagreed, voting on the same day to reject Roosevelt's reform bill by a ten-to-eight margin, along with six compromise proposals.[189]

Van Devanter's letter of resignation noted he intended to take advantage of the judicial retirement bill that House Judiciary Chair Hatton Sumners had won passage for on March 1. Senator William Borah had coaxed Van Devanter to step down, "[thinking] that a quick retirement would help the anti-Court-packing cause."[190] Van Devanter sent a copy of his letter of resignation to Sumners, who wrote back: "You have done a most courageous thing under the circumstances, a patriotic thing." Alabama Senator Hugo Black would take Van Devanter's place, tilting the court in Roosevelt's favor.[191]

On May 24, 1937, the Supreme Court upheld the Social Security Act and the Alabama Unemployment Compensation Act.[192] At his press conference the next day, Roosevelt admitted he was "very, very happy over the decisions of yesterday," but still cautious. He warned that their attempt to sustain a child labor law "would involve a direct reversal of a Supreme Court decision." Furthermore, there was still legislation at risk involving minimum wages, maximum working hours, regulations of employment conditions, and collective bargaining.[193] But Roosevelt's position had grown untenable and a little over a week later he relented and allowed the Senate Majority Leader to seek the best compromise he could get; however, "many were already saying that the time for compromise had come and gone."[194]

On July 13, Hatton Sumners took a victory lap on the success of his retirement bill and denied the necessity of even a compromise bill on judicial reform. He claimed his bill "created a condition with regard to that Court which makes it possible to change the relationship as much as adding two new judges would. There was no controversy, no noise." And with a final swipe at the president's proposal, he added that his bill had accomplished the feat "with a surgical instrument, not a meat ax."[195]

Roosevelt's now compromised bill would die that summer with Joe Robinson. Fortunately for Roosevelt, he did not need the reform bill. As Justice Brandeis had warned him, all he needed to do was wait. And with Hatton Sumners's help, time did its job.

Licking his wounds after the Senate defeated his compromise court reform bill on July 22, in a press conference the next day the president acknowledged the change of direction in the court and even suggested that his February 5 proposal had wrought this change:

> Before the 5th of February, the Supreme Court held the Triple A unconstitutional, limiting the Federal spending power. After the 5th of February, through the Social Security case, they, in effect, overruled the Triple A case. It was a new interpretation of Federal spending and taxing power.
>
> Before the 5th of February they held the Guffey Act unconstitutional, limiting the Federal commerce power, and after the 5th of February they held the Wagner Act constitutional, reversing the Guffey case. It was a new interpretation of the Federal commerce power.
>
> Before the 5th of February they held the New York Minimum Wage Law unconstitutional, limiting the states through the due process clause. They

> reversed that in the Washington Minimum Wage case, overruling the New York Minimum Wage case, which was a new interpretation of the due process clause applied to the states.
>
> The net result is that we have obtained certain objectives, talking in the large.[196]

Despite Roosevelt's positive spin, he came out of this lengthy fight much weakened, as many have noted. Cushman, for example, argues that "the President's Court-packing proposal helped to precipitate the formation of an opposition bloc in Congress that would frustrate much of his second-term legislative agenda. From the vantage of history, therefore, it appears that the Court-packing plan was an entirely unnecessary misadventure through which Roosevelt ultimately lost far more than he gained."[197] In terms of the court's change, by contrast, further retirements and additional appointments would cement its new direction and make the Hughes court into a New Deal court.

THE HUGHES COURT BECOMES A NEW DEAL COURT

Justice Sutherland was the next to follow Justice Van Devanter into retirement, leaving in January 1938. Justice Cardozo died the following summer. Justice Brandeis retired in early 1939. Justice Butler tried to hold on, but he was ill during the 1939 term and died in November that year. As a result of these deaths and retirements, Roosevelt was able to appoint a majority of the high court by early 1940. Justice McReynolds was the last of the Four Horsemen to go, retiring on February 1, 1941, with Chief Justice Hughes following him that summer.[198] Roosevelt elevated Justice Stone to replace Hughes as chief justice and appointed two more associates that summer to replace Stone's associate position and McReynolds's vacancy. Roosevelt made his final appointment in 1943. Justice Roberts, who had been the youngest on the court when Roosevelt announced his reform proposal, was never replaced by Roosevelt and retired in 1945, the summer following Roosevelt's death.

With these appointments the voices of the conservatives on the court were gradually silenced, from three in fall 1937, to two in spring 1938, to one in early 1940, to none in early 1941. The moderates, Chief Justice Hughes and Justice Roberts, would be reduced to one by fall 1941. Roosevelt's appointees brought a new judicial philosophy, no doubt shaped by the legal realist movement that gained prominence in the 1920s. It featured a skepticism about the shackles legal reasoning or logic places upon judicial decisions and a belief that law does and should serve social ends.[199] It was a philosophy well adapted to support a government passing laws to address pressing problems such as the Great Depression. It lessened respect for precedent and the principle of stare decisis, since earlier decisions did not deserve respect for following objective reasoning or adhering to timeless principles but instead were the product of human jurists with their own prejudices grappling with real-world cases that happened to come before them. Furthermore, since the laissez-faire philosophy of the Four Horsemen and their predecessors had made them activists in resisting efforts to address social ills, they stood against the progressive bent of Roosevelt's New Deal justices. It is unsurprising that a virtual replacement of the old court in four years would lead to a reaction against their conservative views and precedents. Thus, we find the late Hughes court overturned nineteen more precedents after the *Adkins* reversal.

As I noted above, reversals that come in the wake of court replacements challenge the public perception that judges engage in some mysterious art that ensures they are all "following the Law" and justifies the enormous power they wield in expounding the Constitution and invalidating laws that they believe run afoul of it. If a change of personnel alone is seen as the primary driver of judicial outcomes, then the high court loses some of its luster.[200]

If all judges do not read from the same jurisprudential bible in reaching their judgments, they still give *legal* justifications for what they do, even if some of them reference social ends as relevant factors. Thus, in the overruling cases that followed the Revolution of 1937 the justices worked mightily to reassure the public that the changes they wrought respected the Constitution and reflected good judicial reasoning. The remainder of this chapter will summarize their efforts to justify overruling precedents, though I will start with the efforts of those who resisted them.

The last of the Four Horsemen, Justices McReynolds and Butler, kept up their opposition until the bitter end. In all but one case where the court overruled itself, Butler authored five dissents and McReynolds joined all but one (when he was absent).[201] In a sixth case Butler concurred in the result, joined by McReynolds, but opposed overruling the case invalidated by the majority.[202] Butler's complaints were typical for those resisting overrulings:

> There is no occasion to review earlier decisions dealing with affirmative and negative administrative orders, and obviously none to overrule any of them or to repudiate or impair the doctrine they establish. (*Rochester Telephone Corp. v. United States*)[203]

> The opinion brings forward no real reason for so sweeping a change of construction of the Constitution. (*Helvering v. Mountain Producers Corp.*)[204]

> Appraisal of lurking or apparent implications of the Court's opinion can serve no useful end for, should occasion arise, they may be ignored or given direction differing from that at first seemingly intended. But safely it may be

> said that presently marked for destruction is the doctrine of reciprocal immunity that by recent decisions here has been so much impaired. (*Graves v. New York ex rel. O'Keefe*)[205]

> Our decisions ought to be sufficiently definite and permanent to enable counsel usefully to advise clients. Generally speaking, at least, our decisions of yesterday ought to be the law of today. (*Railroad Commission v. Pacific Gas Co.* [Rehearing])[206]

> For one convinced that the judgment now given is wrong, it is impossible to acquiesce or merely to note dissent. And so this opinion is written to indicate the grounds of opposition and to evidence regret that another landmark has been removed. (*O'Malley v. Woodrough*)[207]

Butler says the majority has no good reasons for considering a change or making a change. He insists changes have harmed the law and made it less easy for lawyers to counsel their clients. And he warns that not mere changes are being wrought, but "landmark[s]" are being removed.

After Butler retired, McReynolds joined Justice Roberts's dissents in two more overruling cases.[208] Although he appears to have lost his voice in not writing his own dissents in these seven overruling cases, he was happy to lend his support to his fellow Horseman and to Roberts's conservative swings.

Unsurprisingly, a large majority of the overrulings over the final four years of the Hughes court involved taxing and government regulation. The laissez-faire tradition taken up and enforced by the Four Horsemen often left a no-man's-land between state and federal regulators, keeping both out of the hair of businesses and taxpayers. For example, in the case of taxation, Frankfurter noted in his concurrence in *Graves v. New York ex rel. O'Keefe*, an "unfortunate remark" by Chief Justice John Marshall in the landmark case of *McCulloch v. Maryland* had turned a "dictum" into "a constitutional mandate." Marshall had warned that "the power to tax involves the power to destroy."[209] This influential attitude underlay the immunity typically given to state employees from federal taxation and federal employees from state taxation.[210] Writing for the majority, Justice Stone noted that several prior cases had taken the idea of government immunity too far: "In no case is there basis for the assumption that any such tangible or certain economic burden is imposed on the government concerned as would justify a court's declaring that *the taxpayer* is clothed with the implied constitutional tax immunity of the government by which he is employed" (486; emphasis added).

In *Helvering v. Mountain Producers Corp.*, Chief Justice Hughes considered whether a federal tax on money made by a company from a state lease was constitutional, again confronting "the power to tax is the power to destroy" attitude that limited such taxation.[211] He noted "grave doubt as to whether [such immunities from taxation] should longer be supported," particularly, he said, sounding like a legal realist, "in the light of the expanding needs of state and nation" (384). Indeed, "numerous decisions" had created the "occasion to declare the competing principle, buttressed by the most cogent considerations, that the power to tax should not be crippled" (385). He announced that cases from 1922 and 1932 were "out of harmony with correct principle" and were overruled.[212]

Hitting closer to home on taxation, Justice Reed wrote for the court in *O'Malley v. Woodrough* that the salaries of federal judges could be taxed without violating Article III, Section 1, of the Constitution, which provides that the compensation of "Judges . . . shall not be diminished during their Continuance in Office." Congress had already passed an act trying to get around a 1920 Supreme Court decision (reiterated in a 1925 decision), and Reed pointed out that the tax was "merely part of a taxing measure of general, nondiscriminatory application to all earners of incomes," rather than something aimed at judges.[213]

In *Madden v Commissioner,* the court said that Kentucky could tax interest on bank deposits within the state less than for those outside the state.[214] They dismissed a precedent decided in 1935, *Colgate v. Harvey,* "as repugnant to the line of reasoning adopted here," and noted that it "must be, and is, overruled" (93).[215]

While few of these cases led the court to reflect on when a case ought to be overruled, another case overturning two more 1935 precedents drew an extended discourse from former Harvard Law School professor, Justice Frankfurter. *Helvering v. Hallock* scrutinized some clever lawyer's attempt to avoid taxation of an estate by having a husband put his estate in a trust for his wife, whose income would be paid to her, but which he would recover if she died first.[216] Frankfurter stressed that, despite this inter vivos transfer of this estate, ultimately the husband's "own death should establish such final and complete dominion," as the trust was designed to effect (114). Under federal law, such a transfer at death was subject to taxation for whatever was in the estate at that time.

Frankfurter was following a unanimous decision, *Klein v. United States,* authored by none other than the Horseman Justice Sutherland, who rejected the efforts of other clever lawyers in 1931 by insisting: "Nothing is to be gained by multiplying words in respect of the various niceties of the art of conveyancing of the law of contingent and vested remainders. It is perfectly plain that the death of the grantor was the indispensable and intended event which brought the larger estate into being for the grantee and effected its transmission from the dead to the living, thus satisfying the terms of the taxing act and justifying the tax imposed."[217] But Justice Sutherland took the opposite position four years later when another clever lawyer devised a new inter vivos transfer, this one having a father put a trustee in charge of the trust and its set of securities, whose income his daughter could enjoy during her life and whose assets would be distributed after the father died. If the daughter died first, the trust would revert to the father. Sutherland thought that because "the grant was final and absolute in terms, and beyond the power of the grantor to revoke or alter," the trust was not taxable at the father's death.[218] Sutherland explained why *Klein* was not controlling: "Unlike the Klein case, where the death was the generating source of the title, here, as the court below said, the trust instrument and the death was [*sic*] the generating source. The death did not transmit the possibility, but destroyed it" (45–46). Sutherland had been joined by the other Horsemen and Justice Roberts, with the chief justice and the three liberals dissenting. The same result and division of the court prevailed in a companion case.[219]

Justice Stone could not see how this transfer was not the kind of "nicet[y] of the art of conveyancing" that Sutherland and the rest of the court had dismissed nine years earlier. He noted: "It seems plain that the gift here was not complete until decedent's death. He did not desire to make a complete gift. He wished to keep the property for himself in case he survived his daughter. He kept this hold upon it by reversing from his gift an interest, terminable only at his death, by which full ownership would be restored to him if he survived his daughter" (85). The father was simply "using a different form of words" to attain the same end and escape the estate tax (85).

When Justice Frankfurter wrote the majority opinion overruling these companion cases from 1935, he apparently thought he needed to justify the court's return to a position in line with the 1931 case. His primary argument was that the 1935 cases were erroneous and a departure from the correct rule regarding the taxation of estates. He pondered: "Surely the Klein decision was not intended to encourage the belief that a change merely in the phrasing of a grant would serve to create a judicially cognizable difference in the scope of § 302(c), although the grantor retained in himself the possibility of regaining the transferred property upon precisely the same contingency" (112). Sounding much like Sutherland did in the *Klein* case in warning against lawyers "multiplying words in respect of the various niceties of the art of conveyancing," Frankfurter pointed to "a mere difference in phrasing" in the case before the court "by which identic interests in property were brought into being—varying forms of words in the creation of the same worldly interest," which Sutherland's opinion in 1935 "found sufficient to exclude the St. Louis Trust settlements from the application of the Klein doctrine" (114).

In addition to deploying an argument that Sutherland himself had used in 1931, Frankfurter noted that the 1935 decisions did not garner unanimity as

Klein had; instead, "four members of the Court saw no difference [between the 1931 and 1935 cases]" (114). It was Sutherland's 1935 opinion itself that recognized troublesome "niceties of the art of conveyancing," creating a problem for the present court: "Our real problem, therefore, is to determine whether we are to adhere to a harmonizing principle in the construction of § 302(c) or whether we are to multiply gossamer distinctions between the present cases and the three earlier ones. Freed from the distinctions introduced by the St. Louis Trust cases, the Klein case furnishes such a harmonizing principle. Does, then, the doctrine of stare decisis compel us to accept the distinctions made in the St. Louis Trust cases as starting points for still finer distinctions spun out of the tenuosities of surviving feudal law? We think not. We think the Klein case rejected the presupposition of such distinctions for the fiscal judgments which § 302(c) demands" (118–19).

In typical form for overrulings, Frankfurter proclaimed the importance of stare decisis even as he rejected it, admitting that it "embodies an important social policy . . . , represents an element of continuity in law, and is rooted in the psychologic need to satisfy reasonable expectations" (119). But, he insisted, the application of stare decisis as a principle is more complex than "a mechanical formula of adherence to the latest decision, however recent and questionable, when such adherence involves collision with a prior doctrine more embracing in its scope, intrinsically sounder, and verified by experience" (119). This last sentence manages to highlight the recentness of the decision (implying it deserves less respect), its shaky standing (as a "questionable" decision), and its departure from a good policy ("a prior doctrine" which is "sounder," "more embracing in its scope," and "verified by experience").

Frankfurter recognized the peculiar problem of overruling a case that impinges on property rights, where there is reliance by those organizing their affairs. As a New York judge summarized the matter eighty-two years earlier: "Where a rule of property is erroneously settled, courts will rarely, if ever, depart from the decision, because such a departure will disturb rights acquired under the sanction of the rule."[220] So instead of ignoring this practice, Frankfurter argued that no reliance was at stake: "Nor have we, in the [1935] St. Louis Trust cases, rules of decision around which, by the accretion of time and the response of affairs, substantial interests have established themselves. No such conjunction of circumstances requires perpetuation of what we must regard as the deviations of the St. Louis Trust decisions from the Klein doctrine. We have not before us interests created or maintained in reliance on those cases. We do not mean to imply that the inevitably empiric process of construing tax legislation should give rise to an estoppel against the responsible exercise of the judicial process. But it is a fact that, in all the cases before us, the settlements were made, and the settlors died, before the St. Louis Trust decisions" (119).

Although Frankfurter makes a good case that Mr. Hallock had not relied on the 1935 precedent, since he died before that decision was handed down, his assertion that no "substantial interests have established themselves" is clearly speculative. It would not be surprising if estate lawyers took the successful tax-dodging strategy from the *Klein* decision and recommended it to their clients, creating irrevocable trusts which would be beyond alteration after the *Hallock* decision changed the tax consequences of that form.

Several other overrulings permitted the state or federal government to do what prior courts said they could not do. The court supported the Federal Communication Commission's requirement that a telephone company submit information on its business, rejecting a prior distinction "between 'negative' and 'affirmative' orders, as a touchstone of jurisdiction to review the Commission's orders . . . [as] serv[ing] no useful purpose," and insisting that prior cases relying on that distinction "can no longer be guiding" (143).[221] In a rehearing of a case that originally tied four to four (effectively leaving the district court's verdict unreversed), the court allowed utility rates set by a public commission to stand, insisting that due process rights had been met in light of the procedures followed in deciding those rates, while ignoring some substantive concerns the gas company had.[222] California was allowed to regulate "transportation agents" (such as taxi companies) without stepping on the toes of federal regulators of interstate commerce. A precedent case was dismissed as a "departure" from a principle "which has been recognized since [the 1851 case of] Cooley v. Board of Port Wardens," and followed in "later decisions of this Court which have likewise recognized and applied the principle" (116). Nebraska was allowed to set the maximum amount an employment agency may charge, despite *Ribnik v. McBride,* because "the drift away from [that 1928 case] has been so great that it can no longer be deemed a controlling authority."[223] Texas was allowed to use a criminal statute to punish the price-fixing of beer, rejecting an overturned precedent as "hav[ing] been worn away by the erosion of time, and . . . no longer controlling."[224] Here the conceit of a natural process—erosion—is offered as the engine of change, removing the Supreme Court as an active agent in that change.

There is a bootstrapping quality to the argument that precedents are out of line with other cases because of "drift" or "erosion" which the court itself created. I have referred to this strategy as *prospective argument,* which involves some person or group's words or actions changing symbolic or material conditions, followed by that person or group citing those changed conditions to justify further actions.[225] Because judicial rhetoric addresses particular cases as they come before the court, it becomes easy to ignore how justices divide the rhetorical labor over time, diminishing their role in changing the law over time, progressively extending their own ideas which have become "the Law." A blatant example of this is the companion abortion cases of *Roe v. Wade* and *Doe v. Bolton*, decided on the same day and appearing sequentially (*Roe* followed by *Doe*) in *United States Reports*.[226] *Doe* cites the just-decided *Roe* decision numerous times as precedent, making the court's immediate action grounds for authoritative argument about *Doe*. In the overruling cases analyzed here, the court's work that created the "drift" and "erosion" that become reasons for abandoning a precedent are more remote in time, as well as in the "space" of pages than the *Roe-Doe* example. Indeed, this "remoteness" makes them more potent, as the court's actions are reduced to directions ("drift") and processes ("erosion") that hide their agency and make it appear that they are taking "the Law" as they find it (rather than *as they made it*).

Two landmark overruling cases deserve mention, even though they did not discuss stare decisis at length. The 1941 case of *United States v. Classic* addressed the southern practice of excluding African Americans from primary elections, which almost always determined who held office given the overwhelming dominance of Democrats in the South at the time.[227] The 1921 case of *Newberry v. United States* had interpreted Article I, Section 4, of the Constitution as allowing the federal government to regulate "elections" but excluded primary elections from this coverage because the Founding Fathers had no experience with them and so could not have intended to cover them.[228] The 1935 case of *Grovey v. Townsend* had rejected an equal protection claim by African Americans at being excluded from white primaries because the State of Texas had privatized the primaries, leaving it to the parties to run them; thus, the "government" was not discriminating against Black voters and such "private" discrimination was not unconstitutional. Justice Stone, writing for the majority, noted that *Newberry* was a 5-4 decision (317), insisted that the Founders were not so myopic as to believe election procedures would never change (318), and insisted the right to vote must be protected "where the primary is by law made an integral part of the election machinery" (318) and especially where the primary vote virtually determines the outcome of the election (319).

Another landmark, *United States v. Darby*, finally overruled *Hammer v. Dagenhart*, the notorious antiregulation decision that allowed child labor to continue in the states.[229] It upheld the 1938 Fair Labor Standards Act, which set minimum wages and maximum hours for industries whose goods were shipped in interstate commerce. Justice Stone again wrote for the majority, emphasizing the "bare majority" supporting *Hammer* (115) and that case's powerful dissent from Justice Holmes (115). He insisted the case had not been followed (116). The Tenth Amendment's reservation of powers to the states was no obstacle to this legislation (123). The statute did not suffer from the vagueness which plagued earlier regulatory missives for the executive to follow (125–26).

One final overruling decision was so momentous as to merit extended consideration. It overturned a decision nearly a century old which had been followed hundreds if not thousands of times. It did not declare a federal law unconstitutional, but rather the court's own interpretation of a law unconstitutional in taking away power reserved to the states. And yet it was an overruling long sought by progressives because of the way businesses had abused the options it created.

ERIE RAILROAD CO. V. TOMPKINS

In the 1920s the Brown & Yellow Taxicab Company of Kentucky was trying to close a deal with the Louisville & Nashville Railroad to give it a monopoly on soliciting passengers and baggage at the Bowling Green railroad station, to the chagrin of its competitor, the Black & White Taxicab Company. Unfortunately for the Brown & Yellow, the common law of Kentucky made such a contract void. So the enterprising owners reincorporated in Tennessee and made the deal with the railroad. When it was challenged in federal court, the company relied on the 1842 decision in *Swift v. Tyson* to save its agreement.

In the *Swift* case Justice Story was grappling with a diversity-jurisdiction question—deciding what law would be used to resolve a dispute between citizens of different states. He turned to Section 34 of the Judiciary Act of 1789, which states: "The laws of the several States, except where the Constitution, treaties, or statutes of the United States otherwise require or provide, shall be regarded as rules of decision in trials at common law, in the courts of the United States, in cases where they apply." Story interpreted "laws of the several states" to include "positive statutes of the state" as constructed by "local tribunals" and "to rights and titles to things having a permanent locality, such as the rights and titles to real estate, and other matters immovable and intraterritorial in their nature and character."[230] However, there was a notable caveat in this understanding of "laws of the several states"; Story asserted that the phrase "does not extend to contracts and other instruments of a commercial nature, the true interpretation and effect whereof are to be sought not in the decisions of the local tribunals, but in the general principles and doctrines of commercial jurisprudence" (19). With this unanimous decision, the federal common law was born. Federal judges could ignore what state courts said about such issues and apply "general principles and doctrines of commercial jurisprudence" to resolve cases.

By reincorporating in Tennessee and creating a diversity-jurisdiction issue, the Brown & Yellow Taxicab Company could ignore Kentucky's antimonopoly common law and appeal to the federal common law, which it did so successfully, thanks to the growth of *Swift*'s doctrine. After the Civil War that doctrine "underwent a seemingly limitless expansion beyond the commercial law ambit of *Swift*, extending to municipal bonds, civil procedure, corporations, torts, real property, and workers' compensation," to the delight of the business community, as William M. Wiecek notes: "Conservatives extolled these substantive developments and the concomitant expansion of federal courts' diversity jurisdiction as vital to the protection of eastern investors' interests in the southern and western states, while progressives denounced the resort to federal courts by large corporations seeking to avoid state regulatory policies."[231]

Roosevelt's New Deal Court Took Aim at Swift in 1938

Erie Railroad Co. v. Tompkins involved a man walking along a path next to railroad tracks in Pennsylvania who was struck by an object protruding from the train which he did not see in the dark.[232] He sued the railroad in the US District Court in New York, where the railroad was incorporated, and was awarded $30,000 for his injuries. Under Pennsylvania law he would have been deemed a trespasser for walking next to the railroad tracks and denied compensation. Under the federal common law that prevailed in this diversity case, he could seek compensation. Justice Brandeis wrote the majority opinion overturning *Swift v. Tyson,* Justices Butler and McReynolds concurred separately, and Justice Cardozo did not participate in the decision.

Justice Brandeis opens the opinion with *Swift* in his sights, insisting: "The question for decision is whether the oft-challenged doctrine of *Swift v. Tyson* shall now be disapproved" (69). He notes that the lower courts rejected the railroad's claim that Pennsylvania's common law ought to apply, with the circuit court insisting that the question was one of general law, and, following *Swift,* stating that "upon questions of general law, the federal courts are free, in the absence of a local statute, to exercise their independent judgment as to what the law is, and it is well settled that the question of the responsibility of a railroad for injuries caused by its servants is one of general law" (quoting 90 F.2d 603, 604 at 70).

Following *Swift,* Brandeis noted, "the federal courts assumed, in the broad field of 'general law,' the power to declare rules of decision which Congress was confessedly without power to enact as statutes" (72); thus, he emphasized, the federal courts were going beyond what even Congress could do. He noted that the courts evinced concern over the exercise of this judicially declared authority, insisting: "Doubt was repeatedly expressed as to the correctness of the construction given § 34, and as to the soundness of the rule which it introduced," citing not judicial decisions, but ten scholarly articles published between 1873 and 1917 that scrutinized the doctrine (72). More criticism followed the decision in *Black & White Taxicab Co. v. Brown & Yellow Taxicab Co.* (73). But the most important source he highlighted was a 1923 article that argued that Justice Story's 1842 interpretation of Section 34 of the Judiciary Act of 1789 was wrong. This author, a "competent scholar,"[233] had reviewed the "original document" and concluded "that the purpose of the section was merely to make certain that, in all matters except those in which some federal law is controlling, the federal courts exercising jurisdiction in diversity of citizenship cases would apply as their rules of decision the law of the State, unwritten as well as written" (72–73).

Brandeis argued that the *Swift* doctrine had been troublesome. He blamed "the impossibility of discovering a satisfactory line of demarcation between the province of general law and that of local law [developing] a new well of uncertainties" (74). And, while the doctrine sought "to prevent apprehended discrimination in state courts against those not citizens of the State," the precedent "introduced grave discrimination by noncitizens against citizens" (74). This led to forum shopping by "[making] rights enjoyed under the unwritten 'general law' vary according to whether enforcement was sought in the state or in the federal court, and the privilege of selecting the court in which the right should be determined was conferred upon the noncitizen," leading to nonuniform results (74–75). These problems were exacerbated by the growth of what fell under the "general law" (75–76), mentioned above. Corporations took advantage of diversity jurisdiction by reincorporating, as the Taxicab company had done, "without even change of residence" (76–77). The error of *Swift*'s reading of Section 34 and its troublesome application might have been enough to justify overruling, but Brandeis insisted that there was no other remedy besides overruling, since the court itself had created the doctrine (80).

If the deified Justice Story had established the doctrine, the respected Justices Field and Holmes had criticized it. Half a century after *Swift*, Justice Field had warned in *Baltimore & Ohio Railroad Co. v. Baugh* that federal judges were using the doctrine to "[brush] aside the law of a State in conflict with their views" and threatening "the autonomy and independence of the States" (quoted at 78–79).[234] Holmes had attacked the decision in *Black & White Taxicab Co. v. Brown & Yellow Taxicab Co.* for "assum[ing] there is a '*transcendental body of law* outside of any particular State but obligatory within it unless and until changed by statute,' and that ''the parties are entitled to an independent judgment [from federal judges] on matters of general law."[235]

Erie can be seen as a "progressive" decision in the mold of other pro–New Deal decisions insofar as it called for limits on the power of the federal courts to second-guess state and federal governments. On the other hand, it probably proved attractive to Butler and McReynolds in its defense of states' rights. Although Justice Brandeis did not mention the Tenth Amendment specifically as placing limits on the federal courts' power as Justice Roberts had in fending off Congress's alleged overreach in the Agricultural Adjustment Act in *United States v. Butler*, the spirit was similar.[236] Of course, in the present case, the ruling also was procorporate, undermining the railroad's liability for injuring Tompkins.

Indirectly addressing the nearly century-old standing of the *Swift* precedent,

Brandeis drew on Holmes's insistence that the "unconstitutional assumption of [these] powers by courts of the United States" meant that "no lapse of time or respectable array of opinion should make us hesitate to correct [this erroneous precedent]" (79).

Ultimately, Brandeis urged, the problem was not a faulty statute, but the Supreme Court's unconstitutional declaration of its authority to ignore state law in favor of a federal common law which, he insisted, does not exist (78–80). He remanded the case back to the lower court so it could apply Pennsylvania's common law to a determination of the case (80).

We can draw from Brandeis's decision several lessons about overruling precedents: First, long-standing precedents are not immune from overruling. Second, precedents based upon erroneous judgments, which suffer from inconsistent and troublesome applications, and that yield unfair results may be overturned.

A LEGACY OF OVERRULINGS FROM THE REVOLUTION OF 1937

Although a small percentage of Americans in the 1930s were likely to consider themselves "Court watchers," it would be hard for even a casual follower of the news to fail to notice the about-face the Supreme Court made on President Roosevelt's New Deal legislation and in its attitude toward government regulation. Certainly the catchy phrase "a switch in time that saved nine" effectively painted the Supreme Court as the federal branch of government that blinked first in the showdown with the president. And the uproar over the *Tipaldo* decision from both liberals and conservatives in 1936 made the apparent reversal in *Parrish* even more noteworthy to the public at large. The drama of a showdown followed by a capitulation from one side was simple and understandable to onlookers in this clash of government titans, even if it was misleading in accounting for *Parrish*. Justice Van Devanter's retirement two months later could be cast in this drama as a defeated soldier leaving the field.

The drama did not end there of course, as Van Devanter's exit helped drive the final nail in the coffin of Roosevelt's audacious court reform bill. Despite Roosevelt's spin of the loss as a victory in scaring the court into changing its opposition to his policies, his long, unbending, and massive political investment in the reform had to make the loss appear sharp. It is ironic that as he reshaped the court in his image through eight appointments over the next eight years, he would have more trouble getting legislation passed for the now New Deal–friendly court to endorse.

The situation facing the post-*Parrish* court was more problematic, however. If the public saw a frightened court reverse its course initially, it would soon see a court reconfigured by new appointments not bending to Roosevelt's will, but rather aligning with his views. This was an extended version of the Legal Tender

Cases all over again, where President Grant's two appointments ensured a reversal. Chief Justice Chase's dissent excoriated the majority, for reversing a 5-3 decision through no changes in opinion from the former majority, but rather through a retirement and two new appointments.

No such lack of the usual judicial decorum came from the remaining Horsemen in the overrulings that followed Justice Van Devanter's retirement. Justice Butler, who authored six dissenting opinions in six overruling cases, said nothing about the change in personnel as relevant to the reversals he opposed; instead, he insisted that the majority's decisions misinterpreted the law. Justice Sutherland seems to have captured the sense of judicial etiquette shared by the Horsemen—and, indeed, most Supreme Court justices in the court's history—in his *Parrish* dissent, noting: "But it is the right of those in the minority to disagree, and sometimes, in matters of grave importance, their imperative duty to voice their disagreement at such length as the occasion demands—always, of course, *in terms which, however forceful, do not offend the proprieties or impugn the good faith of those who think otherwise*" (402; emphasis added). In raising the issue of *not* impugning the good faith of his colleagues, Sutherland indirectly suggests that perhaps that would be warranted *if not for the judicial etiquette he respects*. In any case, in the midst of Roosevelt's frequent personnel replacements and the court's continued backtracking on its prior interpretations of law, it was especially helpful to the court's standing that the Horsemen tempered their criticism of the new personnel of the emerging New Deal court.

It also helped the court's standing and hurt Roosevelt's reform plan that the American public maintained an enviable reserve of respect for the court and its place in our democratic system. The "New Deal" court that emerged in 1937 would need all the mythological awe they could muster to allay skepticism over its record overrulings during the remainder of Chief Justice Hughes's tenure at the helm.

If the number of overrulings made the court appear activist and radical, its arguments for reversing earlier decisions did not. Portraying many of the overruled laissez-faire decisions, made in the era when members of the Four Horsemen held the majority, as inconsistent with earlier and later decisions of the high court is pretty standard fare for overruling, as is the simple insistence that they misinterpreted the law. Although there was more emphasis on the bad outcomes of decisions—that they undermined attempts to address pressing social issues or were problematic in their application—such legal realist–leaning arguments were not predominant (except perhaps in *Erie Railroad*). Indeed, despite a demonstrable ideological shift, which Roosevelt sought, these overrulings fit quite comfortably within the genre of overrulings described in chapter 2 and illustrated in the other chapters.

More innovative in the overruling rhetoric of the post-*Parrish* Hughes court was their deployment of prospective argument. Because they were overruling lots of cases involving government taxing and regulation, their decisions could change the legal landscape to the point where the overruled cases were out of sync not merely with individual decisions, but with a train of decisions, a "drift" or an "erosion" of the old order. Although the analysis of this chapter highlights this prospective function, we should look for it in the practices of any long-serving courts or justices.

CHAPTER 6

Expanding Civil Rights and Challenging States' Authority

Fourteenth Amendment Overruling Cases

CHIEF JUSTICE HUGHES'S NEW DEAL court reduced judicial constraints on state and federal action to address the Great Depression. It recognized broad powers of the federal government under the Commerce Clause and opened the way for states to use regulation and taxation to address economic challenges. It was supported by a new judicial philosophy that considered not simply what the Founding Fathers intended, but also the social good that lawmaking could accomplish and the harm that judicial obstruction could cause.

Subsequent courts also would be concerned about the social good, though they increasingly turned their attention from issues of government economic regulation to the rights of individuals. Where the New Deal court had given a green light to government regulation, many of these courts put the brakes on government action—particularly by the states—that harmed religious minorities, racial minorities, criminal defendants, public speakers, women, and homosexuals. A revolution in constitutional rights would expand the freedom of individuals by preventing government from trampling on their religious beliefs, treating them differently because of their religion, race, sex, or sexual orientation; restricting their speech, trying them without legal representation, and controlling their reproductive choices, among many other things.

Richard Danzig notes that the turn from deference to the government to scrutiny of such legislation was anticipated in Justice Stone's majority opinion in *United States v. Carolene Products*, where the court employed what Danzig calls a "self-effacing rationality test," insisting: "regulatory legislation affecting ordinary commercial transactions is not to be pronounced unconstitutional unless, in the light of the facts made known or generally assumed, it is of such a character as to preclude the assumption that it rests upon some rational basis within the knowledge and experience of the legislators."[1] Justice Stone added a caveat in a famous footnote to that proclamation, which opened the door to "more searching judicial inquiry" when the court was faced with "statutes directed at particular religions, national or racial minorities," in which "the operation of those political processes ordinarily to be relied on to protect minorities" may be "curtail[ed]."[2] Danzig notes that this footnote held "the germ of a full-blown jurisprudence, [though it] lay dormant for some time after it was handed down."[3]

In overruling precedents that had given government more leeway in constraining individuals (especially minorities), the post–New Deal courts often appealed to changing attitudes, issues of fairness and justice, and a vision of a free society. Such appeals would draw the ire of constitutional originalists and textualists who were reluctant to endorse rights that the Founders and the authors of the Fourteenth Amendment did not appear to have recognized, creating a new contested ground where a tug of war would find the Warren court pulling hard toward greater protection of individuals and minorities and more conservative later courts increasingly pulling in the opposite direction, culminating dramatically in the later Roberts court's elimination of the long-recognized right to abortion.[4]

This chapter will analyze the overruling discourse of several landmark cases, including the Flag Salute Cases, *Brown v. Board of Education,* and a case involving gay rights. It considers decisions that bring us up to 2003 providing a historical bookend to chapter 3's consideration of nineteenth-century cases, chapter 5's coverage of cases after the turn of the century and up to the 1940s, and chapter 4's coverage of statutory rulings from three different periods. Chapter 7 will consider the overruling practices of the Roberts court, which has become the most conservative court in almost a century.

PROTECTING RELIGIOUS MINORITIES IN THE FLAG SALUTE CASES

West Virginia State Board of Education v. Barnette was an early overruling case protecting the rights of a religious minority. It is an unusual overruling case because it reversed *Minersville School District v. Gobitis,* decided three years earlier by an eight-to-one margin, after three justices in the *Gobitis* majority changed their positions and a new justice joined them.[5] The *Gobitis* decision reinforced the animosity many had toward Jehovah's Witnesses, leading to a wave of violence against the religious minority. Few decisions have inspired such judicial guilt about what the court had wrought through its actions or yielded such an eloquent statement about the importance of the freedom of Americans from government coercion.

Jehovah's Witnesses, who emerged from a late nineteenth-century religious group known as "Russellites" (after their founder, Charles Taze Russell) in 1931, were a tiny religious minority in the 1940s, with about sixty thousand members worldwide.[6] J. A. Weems explains why Jehovah's Witnesses often found themselves in conflict with federal and state governments in the first half of the twentieth century: "They believe that the present world is wholly under the dominion and control of an evil spirit, Satan. His rule will soon end after a fierce struggle, called the Battle of Armageddon, between the forces of good and evil with Christ in visible presence leading the former. Rejecting allegiance to any earthly government, they consider themselves citizens of Heaven. They neither vote nor hold public office, and they steadfastly refuse military service. Their 'witnessing' consists primarily of house-to-house canvassing, soliciting subscriptions to their religious pamphlets, distributing literature and playing phonograph records which denounce orthodox Christianity as a fraudulent racket."[7] The federal government tried to stop their anti-war messages during both world wars and local governments tried to stymie their door-to-door "witnessing" and sales of religious literature. They won many cases by appealing to the First Amendment to protect their free speech and religious liberty.[8] Indeed, their first serious legal setback was *Gobitis*.[9]

Justice Frankfurter recited the facts of that case in the opening of his majority opinion against the Witnesses: The Minersville School District in Pennsylvania required teachers and students to participate in a morning flag salute ceremony, involving a recitation of the Pledge of Allegiance while extending the right hand toward the flag (591). Two students, Lillian Gobitis and her brother William, refused to participate in the ceremony on religious grounds (591). They believed that such pledges were forbidden by God in *Exodus* 20:3–5, which states:

> Thou shalt have no other gods before me.
> Though shalt not make unto thee any graven image, or any likeness of anything that is in heaven above, or that is in the earth beneath or that is in the water under the earth.
> Thou shalt not bow down thyself to them nor serve them.[10]

The school district expelled the students who, because of their ages (ten and twelve), were still required to attend school. The Gobitis family complained that the cost of private school to meet this obligation was a financial burden (591–92).

Even though the US Supreme Court had refused to consider challenges to such flag salute-related requirements by schools in several prior per curiam opinions, the US District Court ruled against the school district and the court of appeals supported that position (592).[11] Faced with these contrary rulings, the high court took the case to reconsider the issue, which Frankfurter frames as determining "whether the requirement of participation in such a ceremony, exacted from a child who refuses upon sincere religious grounds, infringes without due process of law the liberty guaranteed by the Fourteenth Amendment" (592–93).

After acknowledging the historic significance of freedom of religion among the Founding Fathers that led them to enshrine protections in the US Constitution, Frankfurter insists it must be balanced against state interests, posing: "When does the constitutional guarantee compel exemption from doing what society thinks necessary for the promotion of some great common end, or from a penalty for conduct which appears dangerous to the general good?" (593). After insisting that "every possible leeway should be given to the claims of religious faith" (594), Frankfurter notes that "the religious liberty which the Constitution protects has never excluded legislation of general scope not directed against doctrinal loyalties of particular sects" (594). He cites several cases where the court had favored state legislation over religious liberty, where states deployed "specific powers of government . . . to secure and maintain that orderly, tranquil, and free society without which religious toleration itself is unattainable" (595).

He rejects a claim that freedom of speech was abridged in forcing the recitation of the pledge and salute (595). With war raging in Europe, Frankfurter praises the patriotic goals of the flag salute requirement and insists that "national unity is the basis of national security" (595). He invokes Lincoln's framing of a national dilemma: "Must a government of necessity be too strong for the liberties of its people, or too weak to maintain its own existence?" (596). In deferring to the state's judgment on this balance, he insists that "it is not the personal notion of judges of what wise adjustment requires which must prevail" (596). After deferring to the state, he nonetheless endorsed the state's attempt to instill patriotism (596).

Frankfurter never acknowledges that Jehovah's Witnesses are a religious minority. Indeed, he seems to suggest that they can appeal their concerns to legislative authorities, assuming that "the remedial channels of the democratic process remain open and unobstructed" to them (599). He notes that parents can offset the lessons of the schools through their "unmolested . . . right to counteract by their own persuasiveness the wisdom and rightness of those loyalties which the state's educational system is seeking to promote" (599). He never acknowledges that the act of pledging allegiance *itself* is a problem for Jehovah's Witnesses, not simply the lessons it teaches.

The majority opinion rejects a remedy that might allow the Gobitis children to opt out of the ceremony, such as by standing silently. Frankfurter insists that such an exemption "might introduce elements of difficulty into the school discipline, might cast doubts in the minds of the other children which would themselves weaken the effect of the [flag salute] exercise" (600).

Justice Stone wrote an impassioned dissent. He stresses the significance of the district's punishment of the Gobitis children for following their sincere religious convictions: making them "liable to expulsion from the public schools and to denial of all publicly supported educational privileges" (601). He finds the flag salute statute was unusual—"unique in the history of Anglo-American legislation"—and onerous in "suppress[ing] freedom of speech and . . . prohibit[ing] the free exercise of religion, which concededly are forbidden by the First Amendment and are violations of the liberty guaranteed by the Fourteenth" (601). The law seeks "to coerce these children to express a sentiment which, as they interpret it, they do not entertain, and which violates their deepest religious convictions" (601).

Although he admits that the court had recognized the state's power to pass legislation that infringes on free speech and religious liberties in support of important state purposes—particularly in an educational setting—he thought compelling speech such as a flag salute was too directly violative of specific constitutional restriction on government and that other means for promoting national unity were available (603–5). He doubts the Founding Fathers would so side against religious convictions (605).

Unlike Frankfurter, he acknowledges that such "small minorities" were often subject to "the popular will," invoking *Carolene Products* in its warning to protect minorities through "searching judicial inquiry" in such cases (606). And he thought the school could make "some sensible adjustment of school discipline" to accommodate the Gobitis children (607).

In June 1942, two years after *Gobitis* was handed down, the court took up another Jehovah's Witnesses case involving Opelika, Alabama's regulation of the distribution of books and pamphlets.[12] The court upheld the city's requirement that such distributors procure a license and pay taxes on the literature sold. Justice Reed's majority opinion stresses that the court needs to balance religious and free speech interests against reasonable regulation by government. He notes that the Witnesses raised money through their canvassing activities, making them similar to commercial agents, and concludes: "When proponents of religious or social theories use the ordinary commercial methods of sales of articles to raise propaganda funds, it is a natural and proper exercise of the power of the state to charge reasonable fees for the privilege of canvassing" (597). He specifically distinguishes the *Gobitis* case as concerned with religious symbolism involved in the flag salute (598).

Stone, now chief justice, dissented on First Amendment grounds, joined by Justices Black, Douglas, and Murphy. Justice Murphy filed a separate dissent, joined by the three other dissenters, which insisted that "ordinances that may operate to restrict the circulation or dissemination of ideas on religious or other subjects should be framed with fastidious care and precise language to avoid undue encroachment on these fundamental liberties" (611). He found the ordinances in the cases before the court were not carefully framed. For example, the license fees (ranging from twenty-five dollars a quarter to five dollars for one-time sales) would be hard to recoup in a small town (in one case, 1,545 people); indeed, "with so few potential purchasers, it would take a gifted evangelist indeed, in view of the antagonism generally encountered by Jehovah's Witnesses, to sell enough tracts at prices ranging from five to twenty-five cents to gross enough to pay the [twenty-five-dollar] tax" (616).

Justices Black, Douglas, and Murphy add a final note at the end of the case report, calling the decision "another step in the direction which Minersville School District v. Gobitis, 310 U.S. 586, took against the same religious minority, and is a logical extension of the principles upon which that decision rested" (623). They noted that they had joined the majority in *Gobitis* and admitted: "we now believe that it was also wrongly decided" given the need to accommodate the rights of religious minorities (623–24). This announcement of a reversal by three justices of the Supreme Court is rare; more common is a single justice admitting error and changing position (see chapter 2). Justices rarely reverse themselves and almost never en masse.[13]

What happened in the intervening two years between *Gobitis* and *Opelika* may explain this unusual turnaround. The widely publicized *Gobitis* case made Americans question the patriotism of the Witnesses, particularly members of the American Legion, who, Heller notes, did not "[hesitate] to resort to strong arm methods" such as force feeding castor oil to a Witness.[14] Local governments sought to prosecute Witnesses for "sedition, disrespect to the flag, riot, breach of the peace, disorderly conduct, conspiracy against the government, trespassing, vagrancy, blasphemy, violation of Sabbath laws, distribution of obscene material, etc."[15]

Hostilities against Witnesses rose as the United States became entangled in World War II. Witnesses resisted the Selective Service, leading to the conviction of almost four thousand of them by the end of the War.[16] Courts rejected their appeals for religious exemptions.[17] Witnesses' pacifist position led to accusations that they were siding with Germany, even acting as a fifth column against the government. A mob in Del Rio, Texas, attacked three Witnesses on May 23, 1940, accusing them of being Nazi agents. The American Legion commander at Meridian, Mississippi, stated in the *New Orleans Times-Picayune* on June 30, 1940, that his organization was working with the police to "round up these 'Witnesses'" and called on citizens to report them to authorities. He insisted that the literature they distributed was "printed chiefly in Germany by German printers and on German paper."[18] The ACLU reported that from May to October 1940 there were 335 mob attacks on witnesses in forty-four states involving 1,448 persons.[19] In Texas almost one hundred witnesses, including children and an old woman, were "lashed like cattle for ten miles down a railroad track in the blazing heat of midday and left . . . to fend for themselves."[20] One hundred emergency pipeline workers stormed a Witness meeting in Little Rock, Arkansas, beating witnesses with sticks, blackjacks, and pipes.[21]

The June 29, 1940, issue of *Time* magazine remarked on the rise in violence against Witnesses: "Witnesses have recently been mobbed from Maine to California. . . . Last week they suffered 1) at Columbus, Ohio, where Governor Bricker refused to reinstate a cancelled contract that would have permitted them to hold their national convention at the State Fair Grounds; 2) at Clarksburg, W.Va., where they were struck from relief roles for refusal to salute the flag; 3) at Ocean City, N.J., where Mrs. Ethel R. Winkler was jailed as a public nuisance for passing out Witness tracts."[22] In Kennebunk, Maine, Witnesses defended their headquarters from a group of rock throwers and the next night a mob of two thousand burned their headquarters to the ground. The Witnesses who defended the headquarters with buckshot were arrested for assault with intent to kill, while two arson suspects were arrested and freed after a court "hearing."[23]

The nationwide violence against Witnesses elicited remarks from US Solicitor General Francis Biddle, who noted in a Pennsylvania Bar Association meeting on June 19, 1940: "Self-constituted bands of mob patrioteers are roaming about the country, setting upon these [Witnesses], beating them, driving them out of their homes. In at least one instance, I am told a sheriff, pretending to lead them out of harm from the barn where they had taken shelter, terrified and powerless, brought them straight back to where the mob was waiting. The attorney general of the United States has ordered an immediate investigation by the FBI to see if any civil rights of these persons have been interfered with which we can protect. We shall not tolerate such nazi methods."[24]

The *Gobitis* decision inspired states and local governments to institute new flag salute statutes and rules across the country, leading to more confrontations with the Witnesses.[25] Some of these statutes carried criminal sanctions against the parents of students who refused the flag salute and even provisions to force such students into reform schools.[26] West Virginia hounded Witness children sent to private schools through a statute that seemed to require flag salutes in those institutions as well.[27] Some "patrioteers" thought *Gobitis* allowed local governments to require adults to salute the flag as well.[28]

While local governments were doubling down on flag salute requirements, legal experts and news commentators were condemning the *Gobitis* decision. Among prominent critics were constitutional scholars Edward S. Corwin, Robert E. Cushman, and Dean Ignatius M. Wilkinson of Fordham University School of Law; First Amendment scholar Zechariah Chafee; and many others.[29] Indeed, Francis H. Heller noted in 1943 that "Law Review comments were virtually unanimous in rejecting the majority view."[30]

Heller also listed dozens of newspapers that criticized the *Gobitis* decision on an "equally unanimous" basis.[31] For example, the *New York Times* insisted that "the principles for which the flag stands are by far more important than any gesture" and the *Post-Dispatch* of St. Louis called the decision "dead wrong."[32] The *New Republic* warned that "when the Supreme Court says in effect that we must imperil religious liberty in the interest of the American state, which is worth preserving because it guarantees religious liberty, it comes dangerous [sic] close to being a victim of [war] hysteria."[33]

The US Congress responded to the flag salute problem on June 22, 1942, passing a law codifying rules and customs for using and displaying the flag. Section 7 of Public Law No. 623 described how to properly salute the flag but added: "However, civilians will always show full respect to the flag when the pledge is given by merely standing at attention, men removing their headdress."[34]

It would be another year before the US Supreme Court reconsidered its controversial decision.

The *Barnette* case involved a West Virginia statute passed after the *Gobitis* decision that required the teaching of civics, history, and government "for the purpose of teaching, fostering and perpetuating the ideals, principles and spirit of Americanism, and increasing the knowledge of the organization and machinery of the government" (625). To meet these goals, in 1942 the Board of Education for the state required a flag salute ceremony in all public schools (626). Students refusing to participate were guilty of insubordination and subject to expulsion. Since school attendance is required for those of school age, unenrolled students could be sent to reform schools and their parents fined and jailed (629).

The district court heard an appeal from Jehovah's Witnesses and restrained enforcement of the flag salute requirement, despite the *Gobitis* precedent, noting: "Of the seven justices now members of the Supreme Court who participated in that decision, four have given public expression to the view that it is unsound, the present Chief Justice in his dissenting opinion rendered therein and three other justices in a special dissenting opinion in *Jones v. City of Opelika*."[35] The Board of Education appealed to the US Supreme Court.

Justice Jackson, writing for the majority, insists: "This case calls upon us to reconsider a precedent decision," which, he notes, "the Court, throughout its history, often has been required to do" (630). He adds a footnote referencing a prior case that listed a number of overrulings, particularly during Hughes's New Deal court years, as well as citing Justice Brandeis's famous list of overrulings in his dissent in *Burnet v. Coronado.*[36]

Jackson begins by noting that the peaceable refusal of Witnesses to participate in the flag salute ceremony "does not interfere with or deny rights of others to do so," making the issue simply one of the state's authority to coerce students into "making a prescribed sign and profession" (630), or what Chief Justice Stone had called in his *Gobitis* dissent "a compulsion of students to declare a belief" (631). Jackson draws an analogy to recent understanding of free speech under the First Amendment, noting: "It is now a commonplace that censorship or suppression of expression of opinion is tolerated by our Constitution only when the expression presents a clear and present danger of action of a kind the State is empowered to prevent and punish. It would seem that involuntary affirmation could be commanded only on even more immediate and urgent grounds than silence" (633). This argument follows a line of argument that Aristotle called a *correlative*, so that what applies to state authority regarding the prevention of speech is said to also apply to the compulsion of speech.[37]

Jackson notes Frankfurter's invocation of President Lincoln in his majority opinion in *Gobitis*, where he asked: "Must a government of necessity be too strong for the liberties of its people, or too weak to maintain its own existence?" (*Gobitis*, 596). Jackson follows that reasoning to the end of the line, invoking Lincoln for his side: "It may be doubted whether Mr. Lincoln would have thought that the strength of government to maintain itself would be impressively vindicated by our confirming power of the State to expel a handful of children from school. Such oversimplification, so handy in political debate, often lacks the precision necessary to postulates of judicial reasoning. If validly applied to this problem, the utterance cited would resolve every issue of power in favor of those in authority and would require us to override every liberty thought to weaken or delay execution of their policies" (636). Emphasizing the centrality of the Bill of Rights, Jackson assures his audience that "observance of the limitations of the Constitution will not weaken government in the field appropriate for its exercise" (637).

To Frankfurter's worry that ruling against the flag salute requirement would turn the court into the "school board for the country" (*Gobitis*, 598), Jackson notes that "there are village tyrants, as well as village Hampdens, but none who acts under color of law is beyond reach of the Constitution" (638). To Frankfurter's insistence that such decision be left to the political process, Jackson retorts: "The very purpose of a Bill of Rights was to withdraw certain subjects from the vicissitudes of political controversy, to place them beyond the reach of majorities and officials, and to establish them as legal principles to be applied by the courts" (638).

Jackson points to changed conditions in law and in society that require the justices to ignore precedents when assessing where the state has gone too far in trampling on constitutional rights, even if they do not have expertise in, say, educational policy. He insists, using a farm metaphor: "We must transplant these [eighteenth-century] rights to a soil in which the laissez-faire concept or principle of noninterference has withered, at least as to economic affairs, and social advancements are increasingly sought through closer integration of society and through expanded and strengthened governmental controls. These changed conditions often deprive precedents of reliability, and cast us more than we would choose upon our own judgment" (640). The metaphor of transplanting itself animates the idea of a living constitution that must be adjusted to the times.

Against Frankfurter's insistence that states may determine the means to reach the important end of national unity, Jackson admits that "national unity, as an end which officials may foster by persuasion and example, is not in question." But he adds that "the problem is whether, under our Constitution, compulsion as here employed is a permissible means for its achievement," warning that authoritarian governments throughout history often used compulsion to enforce unity. To those still concerned about unity in times of war, Jackson eloquently argues: "To believe that patriotism will not flourish if patriotic ceremonies are voluntary and spontaneous, instead of a compulsory routine, is to make an unflattering estimate of the appeal of our institutions to free minds" (641). Jackson notes the concurrence of Congress in this opinion regarding saluting the flag, where they passed a resolution making the flag salute voluntary (638).

Returning to the issue of state control, Jackson ends with a now famous, sweeping statement about state power and constitutional rights: "If there is any fixed star in our constitutional constellation, it is that no official, high or petty, can prescribe what shall be orthodox in politics, nationalism, religion, or other matters of opinion, or force citizens to confess by word or act their faith therein. If there are any circumstances which permit an exception, they do not now occur to us" (642). Jackson announces that *Gobitis* and the per curiam decisions that preceded it are overruled, affirming the district court decision against the West Virginia policy.

Justice Black and Douglas filed a concurring opinion that was "substantially in agreement" with Jackson's majority opinion. However, they narrowed their understanding of the limitations on state power to the particulars of the *Barnette* case. This prevented them from appearing as complete flip-floppers in changing their position from *Gobitis*. They explained their earlier motives, insisting: "Reluctance to make the Federal Constitution a rigid bar against state regulation of conduct thought inimical to the public welfare was the controlling influence which moved us to consent to the *Gobitis* decision" (643). They changed their minds after "long reflection [that] convinced us that, although the principle is sound, its application in the particular case was wrong" (643). More specifically, they note, "We believe that the statute before us fails to accord full scope to the freedom of religion secured to the appellees by the First and Fourteenth Amendments" (643).

Although Jackson had not referenced the horrific violence against Witnesses that no doubt gave the majority justices pause over their previous position, Black and Douglas managed to work in a vague reference in this recanting. Insisting that Witnesses lacked "any desire to show disrespect for either the flag or the country," they pointed to their sincere religious convictions arising from the interpretation of God's will and insisted that "the devoutness of their belief is evidenced by their willingness to suffer persecution and punishment, rather than make the pledge" (643).

They admitted, rather obviously, that "no well ordered society can leave to the individuals an absolute right to make final decisions, unassailable by the State, as to everything they will or will not do" (643). But there was a particular problem with the West Virginia requirement, and they criticized coerced speech as a means to inspire national unity, insisting: "Words uttered under coercion are proof of loyalty to nothing but self-interest. Love of country must spring from willing hearts and free minds, inspired by a fair administration of wise laws enacted by the people's elected representatives within the bounds of express constitutional prohibitions" (644). Hinting at the undetailed violence against Witnesses, they warned that the state's law was "a handy implement for disguised religious persecution" (644).

In his concurring opinion, Justice Murphy listed motives for his original support of *Gobitis,* including: "a reluctance to interfere with considered state action, the fact that the end sought is a desirable one, the emotion aroused by the flag as a symbol for which we have fought and are now fighting again," which are "all . . . understandable" (645). But, he countered, the right to believe and worship as one chooses must be weighed against such state efforts. Although he overlooked that in the *Gobitis* case, he reports that "reflection has convinced me that, as a judge, I have no loftier duty or responsibility than to uphold that spiritual freedom to its farthest reaches" (645).

Justices Roberts and Reed announced their continued support for *Gobitis.* Justice Frankfurter dissented, reiterating his previous claims about the importance of national unity and the need to leave decisions about how to achieve it to those more competent in the field of education and more responsive to political pressure. This position, Richard Danzig argues, "appeared to use . . . the same rationality test that had been endorsed in the text of *Carolene Products* in the context of legislation affecting economic interests," giving a wide berth to states on a huge range of issues.[38]

This overruling reinstated the Witnesses' strong record in challenging state encroachments and getting the courts to endorse broader rights for their minority religious group. It featured a rare change of position by three justices as a group who offered a mea culpa after "reflection" and found greater First Amendment freedoms than they had recognized earlier. It is somewhat curious that none of the justices' various opinions in support of the Witnesses detailed any of the horrendous violence against the religious minority the *Gobitis* decision had likely inspired across the country, for such details would have provided a strong reminder of the implications of the court's rulings and the importance of reversing this one. But perhaps it also would have injected an emotional weight to the decision that would detract from the ideal of rational judicial decision-making.

The most eloquent payoff was Justice Stone's paean to American freedom under our Constitution. It described a philosophy of law and government that would inform much of the subsequent revolution in individual and minority rights in the Warren court and even some of the more conservative courts to follow.

BROWN V. BOARD OF EDUCATION

The facts of *Brown v. Board of Education*—probably the most famous Supreme Court case in modern history—are well known.[39] The case ruled that state-mandated racial segregation in public schools was unconstitutional. It overruled the 1896 precedent, *Plessy v. Ferguson*, which allowed Louisiana to segregate Black and white passengers on trains so long as the accommodations were "equal," under the infamous "separate but equal" doctrine.[40] The *Brown* court ruled that "separate educational facilities are inherently unequal" and that such inequality constituted a deprivation of equal protection of the laws under the Fourteenth Amendment (483). After "massive resistance" from southern states fighting desegregation, the court's ruling ended legal segregation, though de facto segregation following "white flight" from large cities would stymie efforts to remedy this legacy of Jim Crow.[41]

What is less generally known about this case is how the high court specifically justified overruling *Plessy*, beyond the assertion that the case was wrongly decided. As I have explained at length elsewhere, the overruling relied heavily on rulings the Supreme Court made over a forty-year period leading up to the *Brown* case, so that the labor of overruling was divided; cumulative minor inroads paved the way for the widespread desegregation of public education.[42] Additionally, the court relied on the insights of social scientists to suggest that the *Plessy* court was uninformed (rather than racist). I will explain how these two factors justified the unanimous overruling decision that Chief Justice Warren authored.

The series of rulings that set the stage for *Brown* did not arise randomly. The NAACP, established in 1909 to fight for the rights of African Americans, developed a legal committee to handle its legal efforts, particularly in the fight against disenfranchisement and racial segregation in housing, public transportation, and public education.[43] Later formed as the Legal Defense Fund (LDF), its leaders, Charles Hamilton Houston and his successor, Thurgood Marshall, developed the first long-term litigation campaign in American history to challenge Jim Crow laws. They carefully nurtured a cadre of Black civil rights lawyers, identified ideal candidates on whose behalf they would bring lawsuits, carefully chipped away at precedents by selecting the time and place to bring suits, and eventually built a bridge to *Brown*.

Although their strategy would be persistent and thoughtful, the NAACP lawyers failed to support an early case that would prove invaluable to their cause.[44] Oklahoma responded to railroads who complained that it was not economically feasible to haul separate first-class sleeping and dining cars for African Americans because too few of them sought those accommodations. The state said that the railroads could drop such extra cars if it proved economically infeasible, leaving Black passengers with no "separate but equal" facilities. The US Supreme Court ruled on the case in 1914 in *McCabe v. Atchison, Topeka & Santa Fe Railway Co.*, holding the Oklahoma statute unconstitutional, because "it makes the constitutional right depend upon the number of persons who may be discriminated against, whereas the essence of the constitutional right is that it is a personal one"; in other words, "it is the individual who is entitled to equal protection of the laws."[45]

Given the specific strategy the LDF developed, this would become a critical precedent to build upon. They would focus their efforts on states' denial of admission of African Americans to white graduate schools. This strategy was brilliant because there were almost no graduate schools for Black students in segregating states, so that a denial of admission of qualified candidates to white graduate schools would be a denial of a "separate" and "equal" education. Without *McCabe*, the states could claim that the economic inefficiency of such schools—given the dearth of qualified Black students—allowed them to forgo meeting such "separate but equal" obligations.

The first response by states was to try to shuffle Black students to out-of-state graduate schools with scholarships. Maryland's attempt to do this with Donald Murray to keep him out of the University of Maryland School of Law was deemed inadequate by the state court, because the last-minute effort was not yet funded, it did not cover Murray's living expenses (which he would save if he lived at home in Baltimore while going to UM), and, importantly, it would not provide him an education in Maryland law.[46] The court cited *McCabe* to note that the small number of Black applicants could not support the state's denial of an equal education.[47] A US Supreme Court case two years later would face a better-financed effort to export Black students from Missouri, with a promise to add a law school to an existing Black university; the effort was rejected with a pronouncement that "the obligation of the state to give the protection of equal laws can be performed only where its laws operate, that is, *within the state*. It is there that the equality of legal right must be maintained."[48]

So segregating states were required to cough up money for a slew of new graduate schools upon request from Black applicants. How long could they take to build those schools? After some state and lower federal court setbacks, the US Supreme Court determined in 1948 that "the State must provide [an education] for [a Black applicant] in conformity with the equal protection clause of the Fourteenth Amendment and provide it as soon as it does for applicants of any other group."[49]

When a qualified Black student applied for doctoral study at the University of Oklahoma, the state legislature that had criminalized integrated education quickly passed a law requiring that education of Black students at white institutions be provided on a segregated basis. This was operationalized by have the student sit in an anteroom next to the classroom, sit at a separate table in the library, and eat at a different time than white students in the cafeteria. When the district court supported the state's efforts and Thurgood Marshall appealed to the US Supreme Court, the state roped off an area in the classroom "Reserved for Colored," and later gave him his own row.[50] The US Supreme Court found that Oklahoma's temporary isolationist accommodation while it developed a Black graduate program in education had "impair[ed] and inhibit[ed] [the student's] ability to study, to engage in discussions and exchange views with other students, and, in general, to learn his profession."[51]

When Texas quickly threw up a law school overnight for a Black applicant by renting a few rooms in Houston, attaching the "school" to a Black vocational college and hiring a couple of faculty, the keen lawyers on the US Supreme Court did not have any trouble finding that the facility was not equal to the sixty-seven-year-old law school at the University of Texas. Chief Justice Vinson, writing the majority opinion, noted:

> In terms of the number of faculty, variety of courses and opportunity for specialization, size of the student body, scope of the library, availability of law review and similar activities, the University of Texas Law School is superior. What is more important, the University of Texas Law School possesses to a far greater degree those qualities which are incapable of objective measurement but which make for greatness in a law school. Such qualities, to name but a few, include reputation of the faculty, experience of the administration, position and influence of the alumni, standing in the community, traditions

> and prestige. It is difficult to believe that one who had a free choice between these law schools would consider the question close.[52]

And in one of the early appeals to racial diversity, he notes that the student needed experience interacting with white students, because he would face a predominantly white population of "lawyers, witnesses, jurors, judges and other officials" as a member of the Texas bar (634). The LDF had found the right audience to make this judgment and to recognize that "intangible" qualities were relevant to the question of equality.

The court refused to uphold the *Plessy* decision, as Texas requested, but it also refused to overrule it (635–36). That left commentators wondering how a state could ensure Black students would immediately receive the benefits of the varied white graduate school programs and still maintain a segregation that undermined the "equality" side of the equation.[53]

Chief Justice Warren's opinion in *Brown* dismisses the historical arguments about what those who passed the Fourteenth Amendment meant by equal protection regarding racial segregation in public schools, insisting the evidence is "inconclusive" (489). Part of the problem was that "in the South, the movement toward free common schools, supported by general taxation, had not yet taken hold" (489–90). Indeed, education was not seen as a state responsibility in most places. Furthermore, education in many states was limited to small, ungraded schools; school was often only three months out of the year and not compulsory (490). Although some Northern states were more advanced in developing public schools, and there was racial segregation in Northern schools, "the effect of the Amendment on Northern States was generally ignored in the congressional debates" (490).

But the issue was much different by the time of *Brown*. Warren notes that "education is perhaps the most important function of state and local governments," and it was compulsory, preparing students to become good citizens who could be successful in the professions (493). This contrast meant that the issue of racial segregation was more pressing and that the new situation required different kind of thinking than the *Plessy* court might have imagined. In any case, as even the *Plessy* court would have acknowledged, such an important state function must be provided on an equal basis (493).

In canvassing early decisions interpreting the Fourteenth Amendment's application to racial discrimination, Warren stresses that "the Court interpreted it as proscribing all state-imposed discriminations against the Negro race" (490). He constructs *Plessy* as something of an anomaly, where the "separate but equal" doctrine made its first appearance, and required the court to "labor[] with the doctrine for over half a century" (491). After referencing two early decisions, Warren turns to the cases championed by the LDF.[54] He cites the Missouri,

Texas, and two Oklahoma cases (*Gaines, Sweatt, Sipuel,* and *McLauren*), noting that in each case "inequality was found in that specific benefits enjoyed by white students were denied to Negro students of the same educational qualifications" (492). He admits that "in none of these cases was it necessary to re-examine the doctrine to grant relief to the Negro plaintiff" but notes that in the Texas law school case of *Sweatt v. Painter* "the Court expressly reserved decision on the question whether *Plessy v. Ferguson* should be held inapplicable to public education" (492). Thus, Warren establishes that this series of cases brought the court to the threshold of an overruling, which *Brown* might cross.

Those graduate school cases differed from the *Brown* case in that the four states involved had equalized Black and white schools in their districts or were in the process of doing so; thus, the question of the constitutionality of segregated education was directly before the court (492). Warren clarifies the issue: "Our decision, therefore, cannot turn on merely a comparison of these tangible factors in the Negro and white schools involved in each of the cases. We must look instead to the effect of segregation itself on public education" (492).

Warren poses the central question: "Does segregation of children in public schools solely on the basis of race, even though the physical facilities and other 'tangible' factors may be equal, deprive the children of the minority group of equal educational opportunities?" He answered: "We believe that it does" (493). He mined the graduate school cases to show that the court had recognized that "intangible" factors are relevant to equality as well. In *Sweatt* the court had identified "those qualities which are incapable of objective measurement but which make for greatness in a law school"; in *McLauren,* the graduate student needed to be treated like white students for "intangible considerations," which affected "his ability to study, to engage in discussions and exchange views with other students, and, in general, to learn his profession" (493).

For K–12 students, the intangible factor was the emotional cost of segregation: "To separate [Black students] from others of similar age and qualifications solely because of their race generates a feeling of inferiority as to their status in the community that may affect their hearts and minds in a way unlikely ever to be undone" (494).

None of this should have been a revelation that the 1896 court did not have. But the *Plessy* court had rejected such claims as subjective and irrelevant. Ignoring social realities—perhaps too "intangible" for the court to consider—the *Plessy* majority stated: "We consider the underlying fallacy of the plaintiff's argument to consist in the assumption that the enforced separation of the two races stamps the colored race with a badge of inferiority. If this be so, it is not by reason of anything found in the act, but solely because the colored race chooses to put that construction upon it" (551). Warren tersely suggests that the nineteenth-century court lived in an uninformed age and that modern social science provided proof of the reality of the problem: "Whatever may have been the extent of psychological knowledge at the time of *Plessy v. Ferguson*, this finding [that segregation harms Black students] is amply supported by modern authority" (494). Warren cites seven social-scientific sources, including the famous "dolls" study by Kenneth Clark and Gunnar Myrdal's influential book, *An American Dilemma*. Leaving out any specific reference to overruling, Warren states that "any language in *Plessy v. Ferguson* contrary to this finding is rejected" (494–95).

Warren was more explicit in his direction to state schools regarding the present and similar cases, proclaiming: "We conclude that in the field of public education the doctrine of 'separate but equal' has no place. Separate educational facilities are inherently unequal. Therefore, we hold that the plaintiffs and others similarly situated for whom the actions have been brought are, by reason of the segregation complained of, deprived of the equal protection of the laws guaranteed by the Fourteenth Amendment" (495). He announced that a reargument case (known today as *Brown* II) would consider the complex questions of class action relief for segregated students the following year (495–96).

Two key rhetorical considerations mark this case. First, the rhetorical labor of overruling was effectively divided among a string of precedent cases that built upon one another over several decades. That was not the court's doing, but largely the LDF's strategy in bringing cases to court at the right time—deploying what the ancient rhetorical theorists called kairos.[55] Experience with the cases allowed the court to eventually focus on concerns involving educational equality that were "intangible" but well understood by those on the high court, particularly those cases involving law school education.

Second, the court protects its own institutional integrity by not calling the *Plessy* justices out for their blatant racism and rejection of social realities that they surely understood, but by emphasizing the less-enlightened age in which they wrote. Social science had discovered new things about social groups and the psychological impacts of segregation. There is an implication that if the former court had known what the court knew in 1954, they might have reached a different conclusion.

The chief justice does not address any concerns over the allegiance owed to the doctrine of stare decisis. Indeed, the opinion does not even mention the term *precedent*.

LAWRENCE V. TEXAS AND GAY RIGHTS

In 1982 an Atlanta police officer was serving a warrant on Michael Hardwick for failing to pay a fine for drinking in public. Another tenant answered Hardwick's door and let the officer in to see if he was at home. The officer walked in on Hardwick giving oral sex to another man in his bedroom. The officer arrested the two men for violating Georgia's antisodomy statute, which defines sodomy as "any sexual act involving the sex organs of one person and the mouth or anus of another."[56] Although the district attorney declined to prosecute the case, Hardwick challenged the Georgia statute in US District Court and won. A divided Eleventh Circuit Court panel overruled the lower court and Hardwick appealed to the US Supreme Court in *Bowers v. Hardwick*.[57] The high court backed the appeals court ruling, finding that Georgia could outlaw sodomy.

Seventeen years later, the court entertained a challenge to *Bowers* in *Lawrence v. Texas*.[58] This case also involved police entering a private residence, this time to respond to a weapons disturbance, where they discovered John Geddes Lawrence and Tyron Garner engaged in anal sex (562–63). They arrested both men under a statute that criminalized homosexual sodomy, as "deviate sexual intercourse," unlike the *Bowers* statute which criminalized sodomy for those of any sexual orientation (563). The two men were tried and convicted under Section 21.06(a) of the Texas Penal Code and fined over three hundred dollars each for the violation. The Texas Court of Appeals rejected the constitutional arguments of the men, relying on *Bowers* (563). The US Supreme Court granted certiorari to reconsider *Bowers*'s holding.

Justice Kennedy authored the 6-3 majority opinion striking down the Texas statute and overruling *Bowers*. He accuses the *Bowers* court of misreading the history of antisodomy legislation and of framing the constitutional question too narrowly. He also notes that post-*Bowers* rulings by the court had changed the landscape regarding gay rights and, indeed, that public opinion had changed as well.

Justice White's majority opinion in *Bowers* had made a sweeping historical claim: "Proscriptions against [homosexual sodomy] have ancient roots" (192). He insisted that such conduct was condemned in ancient times, criminalized by British and American common law, and prohibited by US statutes in the eighteenth, nineteenth, and twentieth centuries, citing dozens of statutes (192–94). Justice Kennedy acknowledged the antisodomy laws referenced by White, but reassessed what exactly they prohibited, drawing on several recent studies that critiqued White's historical claims (567–68).

Kennedy denies that there was a "longstanding history in this country of laws directed at homosexual conduct as a distinct matter," tracing the origins of an antisodomy tradition in Anglo-American law to a 1533 Reformation Parliament law that "was understood to include relations between men and women as well as relations between men and men" (568). Scrutinizing the surviving records of early prosecutions, he noted that the laws primarily punished "predatory acts against those who could not or did not consent, as in the case of a minor or the victim of an assault"; by contrast, he argues, "laws prohibiting sodomy do not seem to have been enforced against consenting adults acting in private" (569). The lack of the latter prosecutions was partly explained by the difficulty of prosecuting such private acts, where participants could not give testimony against their partners because they were considered accomplices to the crime (569).

Although antisodomy statutes in the United States flourished in the last third of the twentieth century, prosecutions often involved sexual conduct in public places (570). And despite the large number of such statutes, Kennedy notes, only nine applied to homosexual sodomy specifically (570). The fact that such statutes came late was unsurprising since no distinct category of "homosexual" emerged until the latter part of the nineteenth century (568). In any case, a large number of state antisodomy statutes had been ignored or removed from state statute books (570). Thus does Kennedy problematize White's simple story of ancient and continuous criminalization of homosexual sodomy.

Justice White had framed the constitutional question as "whether the Federal Constitution confers a fundamental right upon homosexuals to engage in sodomy" (*Bowers* 190). Justice Kennedy insisted that the question at issue involved what individuals are allowed to *be*, with the intimate role of sex as one part of that self-definition, urging: "When sexuality finds overt expression in intimate conduct with another person, the conduct can be but one element in a personal bond that is more enduring. The liberty protected by the Constitution allows homosexual persons the right to make this choice" (567). Analogizing this liberty to those enjoyed by heterosexuals, he insists: "To say that the issue in *Bowers* was simply the right to engage in certain sexual conduct demeans the claim the individual put forward, just as it would demean a married couple were it to be said marriage is simply about the right to have sexual intercourse" (567).

Kennedy draws upon *Griswold v. Connecticut* to show that the court had recognized a zone of privacy within the home and extends that to "[homosexual] adults [who] may choose to enter upon this relationship in the confines of their homes and their own private lives and still retain their dignity as free persons" (567).[59] The addition of "their own private lives" pushes the spatial protection of "homes" further by making individuals' lives themselves a sort of private space.

Two cases decided since *Bowers* were cited to show that the court had recognized a substantive liberty interest that supported the protection of gays and lesbians in this case. The abortion case of *Planned Parenthood of Southeastern Pennsylvania v. Casey* confirmed the privacy protections that *Griswold* and its progeny recognized regarding "personal decisions relating to marriage, procreation, contraception, family relationships, child rearing, and education" (574).[60] A second case was even more on point: *Romer v. Evans*.[61] Colorado had passed an amendment to its constitution that specifically made the state's antidiscrimination laws inapplicable to people who were gay, lesbian, or bisexual. The US Supreme Court invalidated the amendment on equal protection grounds, concluding that the law was "born of animosity toward the class of persons affected" and "had no rational relation to a legitimate governmental purpose" (634).

Justice Kennedy rejects the option of holding the Texas statute invalid under *Romer*, not wishing to encourage states to draw up new statutes that might avoid its equal protection violations (e.g., as *Bowers* had, by prohibiting sodomy by anyone) (574–75). Instead, Kennedy wants to consider the substantive due process rights at issue, the recognition of which "demand[s] respect for conduct [so] protected" (575). Texas's statute undermined such respect by declaring homosexual conduct "criminal," which "in and of itself is an invitation to subject homosexual persons to discrimination both in the public and in the private spheres" (575). Indeed, *Bowers* "continuance as precedent [also] demeans the lives of homosexual persons" (575).

It was a novel conclusion that the right of homosexuals to engage in intimate conduct and, in Kennedy's construction, to define themselves was protected by the due process clause of the Fourteenth Amendment of the Constitution. Kennedy is keenly aware that such novel interpretations could be construed as judicial lawmaking of the kind conservatives particularly claim to abhor.[62] He gestures to this concern by claiming that the liberties protected by the Due Process Clause are "manifold" (578) but not fully known. Recent changes in attitudes revealed "an emerging awareness that liberty gives substantial protection to adult persons in deciding how to conduct their private lives in matters pertaining to sex" (572). Even the *Bowers* court should have recognized this, Kennedy insists, since as early as 1955 the Model Penal Code rejected "criminal penalties for consensual sexual relations conducted in private."[63] He specifically rejects the *Bowers* majority's exclusive reliance on history and tradition in determining such constitutional rights, quoting himself in a concurring opinion insisting that "history and tradition are the starting point but not in all cases the ending point of the substantive due process inquiry."[64]

When Kennedy considers the constraints stare decisis might place on his overruling, he begins with some of the most-oft quoted sources on this point, including the 1940 overruling case of *Helvering v. Hallock*, which more recently has often been channeled through the 1991 overruling of *Payne v. Tennessee*, as: "Stare decisis is not an inexorable command; rather, it 'is a principle of policy and not a mechanical formula of adherence to the latest decision.'"[65] But Kennedy balances that consideration against *Casey*'s distinction for overruling in cases involving constitutional liberty interests, which requires the court to consider that "individual or societal reliance on the existence of that liberty cautions with particular strength against reversing course."[66] The *Casey* court was loath to overturn the right to abortion announced in *Roe v. Wade*, warning:

"Liberty finds no refuge in a jurisprudence of doubt."[67] There was heavy public reliance on abortion rights that counseled the *Casey* court against overruling abortion rights. But Kennedy distinguishes the reliance interests in the *Lawrence* case: "The holding in *Bowers,* however, has not induced detrimental reliance comparable to some instances where recognized individual rights are involved. Indeed, there has been no individual or societal reliance on *Bowers* of the sort that could counsel against overturning its holding once there are compelling reasons to do so. *Bowers* itself causes uncertainty, for the precedents before and after its issuance contradict its central holding" (577).

Overall, Kennedy offers strong reasons for overruling *Bowers.* He claims the case was wrong on the law because it misread the history of antisodomy laws, which primarily were used to convict predatory sex acts against women and minors. White had framed the constitutional issue too narrowly, focusing on the sexual act of sodomy rather than the prohibition for homosexuals to define their own relationships and lives in private. Besides, Kennedy notes, *Casey* and *Romer* had taken substantive due process in a new direction, particularly the latter, which prohibited the state from opening up homosexuals to discrimination and stigmatization, as the Texas statute in this case had done. The world and most states were acknowledging that the intimate relations of homosexuals were among the manifold aspects of liberty protected by the Constitution. Finally, without any reliance interests to consider in overruling *Bowers,* there was no barrier to ignoring stare decisis in this case.

CONCLUSION

While the Revolution of 1937 swiftly recognized broad powers enjoyed by the states and federal government to address economic problems, the court moved more slowly toward constraining states' encroachment on personal liberties and realizing the "full-blown jurisprudence" that lay in Justice Stone's caveat in the *Carolene Products* case regarding "statutes directed at particular religions, national or racial minorities."[68] In economic matters, the court was riding the tide of public sentiment as the nation sought to dig out from the Great Depression. In the matter of personal liberties, the court offered a shield against a majority that threatened those with little political power.

All three cases concerned harms state legislation was doing to minorities and two balanced the minimal "harms" that the state sought to avoid. For *Barnette,* the majority offered a correlative between those strongly protected in their speech by the First Amendment to Jehovah's Witnesses *compelled* to speak something they did not believe, who also deserved constitutional protection. Justice Jackson analogized the flag salute requirement's effort to assure national unity to similar efforts by authoritarian governments. Taking that analogy further, Jackson complained that the state did not even allege the harm "that remaining passive during a flag salute ritual creates a clear and present danger that would justify an effort even to muffle expression" (634). In any case, the "threat" only involved "a handful of children" (636), making the state's means to assure unity appear as unnecessary overkill.

Although Justice Jackson could have easily cited examples of the effects of flag salute hysteria during the height of World War II on innocent Witnesses, he did not do so. However, he did show that the United States Congress believed the issue important enough to weigh in on the controversy and recognize passivity during the flag ceremony as respectful.

Chief Justice Warren did not entertain the idea that forcing white students to integrate with Black students involved a "harm" to be balanced against the good of ensuring equality (though undoubtedly a racist southern population did). Instead, he used social scientific evidence to show the harm segregation itself caused to minority school children.

Justice Kennedy explained that the criminalization of homosexual sodomy involved more than a constraint on sexual activity; it constrained people from forming relationships (which the intimacy of sex helped secure) and from defining themselves. Like the Black children in *Brown*, antisodomy statutes stigmatized homosexuals and invited "discrimination both in the public and in the private spheres" (575). Kennedy did not speculate about whatever the state might imagine its reliance interests were in marginalizing LGBTQ individuals—there were none to be considered, he concluded.

In justifying overruling a precedent, each of these three cases took different approaches. The *Barnette* majority simply noted that the court had frequently overruled itself, so that a reconsideration was appropriate, especially since the prior decision was wrong in underestimating the First Amendment rights at stake. The *Brown* court does not review the *Plessy* court's argument that racial segregation was common and approved by courts in the nineteenth century.[69] Nonetheless, the chief justice insisted that, given the primitive state of prior schools, the question of approval at the time of the Fourteenth Amendment's passage was "inconclusive." Warren was able to build on the work of the LDF in establishing that intangible qualities had to be considered in issues of educational equality. Finally, he contended that the *Plessy* court was uninformed about the harms it allowed because of the state of psychological knowledge then. Justice Kennedy rejected the precedent's account of the history of antisodomy law, relied on additional developments in the law, and insisted that liberty interests were evolving with the Law's (or public's or legal scholar's) growing awareness.

CHAPTER 7

Dobbs v. Jackson and the Decline of Stare Decisis in the Roberts Court

ON MAY 2, 2022, *POLITICO* published a leaked draft of the majority opinion in *Dobbs v. Jackson Women's Health Organization,* with the explosive title "Supreme Court Has Voted to Overturn Abortion Rights, Draft Opinion Shows."[1] The draft included a routing list on the top-right corner of the document showing that the February 10, 2022, opinion draft by Justice Samuel Alito was to be circulated among the justices in order of seniority after going to the chief justice. Despite the furor that arose over the revelation that the high court was taking away a right that American women had enjoyed for a half century, and over the unprecedented leak of an internal Supreme Court document, Justice Alito changed very little in his draft other than adding responses to the concurrence and dissents written criticizing the opinion following its circulation in the court.[2]

The decision in *Dobbs v. Jackson Women's Health Organization,* handed down on June 24, 2022, is the most egregious overruling in the US Supreme Court's history, as I will show in this chapter.[3] It is a fitting focus for this concluding chapter because it indicates where stare decisis stands in the high court today and what kind of overrulings may follow from the conservative majority's attitude toward that central pillar of American jurisprudence. Because Justice Alito's majority opinion justifies overruling *Roe v. Wade* by claiming it is following the practice of previous particular overrulings by the court—many of which are analyzed in this book—my examination of this decision will provide a synoptic review of those prior overrulings and an opportunity to contrast them with what the court did in *Dobbs*. Thus, this final chapter provides a review of much of what has come before, as well as a critique of what the Roberts court did in

Dobbs and may do in future cases. I end with a warning about the implications of this new trend for the standing of the high court and its place in our democratic system. I begin with a history of the sudden reconfiguration of the Roberts court's personnel that led to *Dobbs*.

THE REPUBLICAN TAKEOVER OF THE SUPREME COURT

The US Supreme Court has generally moved in a more conservative direction ever since the Warren court (1953–1969) was replaced by the Burger court (1969–1986). Democrat appointees had dominated the court in the second half of the Hughes court (1930–1941). President Roosevelt replaced every detractor from his New Deal by the time of his death, with the exception of Justice Owen Roberts who held on through all but the last year of the Stone court (1941–1946), when only Democrats occupied the High Bench. The Vinson court (1946–1953) was completely run by Democratic nominees during its seven years. President Eisenhower's five nominees—including the surprisingly liberal Chief Justice Earl Warren—made the Warren court Republican-dominated, though not conservative. President Kennedy's replacement of Justice Whittaker with Justice White made the Democrats dominant on the Warren court once again. In 1970, in the second year of the Burger court, Nixon nominee Harry Blackmun replaced Justice Fortas, ending Democratic majorities up until the present.

Republicans were able to hold the majority of the court for these fifty-two years (through 2022) because President Carter did not appoint any justices to the court, while Republican presidents Nixon, Ford, Reagan, and George H. W. Bush amassed eleven appointments in a row. Since President Nixon's first term, Republican presidents have appointed sixteen members of the Supreme Court, while Democrats have appointed only five. President Reagan's first appointment was the first woman on the court, Justice Sandra Day O'Connor, and the last appointment to the Burger court. Her appointment gave the Republican majority a 7-2 supermajority. That was increased to 8-1 briefly when civil rights champion Justice Thurgood Marshall was replaced with the extremely conservative Justice Clarence Thomas five years into the Rehnquist court (1986–2005).

Justice White was the only Democratic appointee to the court still seated when President Clinton replaced him with Justice Ginsburg in 1993 and clawed back a Democratic justice by replacing Justice Blackmun with Justice Breyer the next year. The centrist Republican Justice O'Connor was replaced by President George W. Bush with the much more conservative Justice Alito in the second year of the Roberts court (2005–present), keeping the 7-2 political dominance until President Obama replaced two moderate Republicans (Souter and Stevens) with more liberal Democrats. This 5-4 split in favor of Republican appointees is the most power the Democrats have enjoyed since 1970. President

Trump's three appointments, discussed at length below, pushed the Republican advantage back to 7-2, although President Biden's replacement of Justice Breyer with Justice Ketanji Brown Jackson, beginning in the 2022/2023 term, brought that back to 6-3. This strongly conservative leaning in the court was brought about in the last thirty years despite the fact that Democrats won the popular vote in seven of the last eight presidential elections.[4]

Of course party affiliation does not ensure the ideological bent of justices, though recent appointees have tended to be right or left rather than centrist.[5] Chief Justice Warren's liberal leanings upset his nominator, President Eisenhower.[6] Justice Blackmun, the author of *Roe v. Wade,* was appointed by President Nixon.[7] Justice Stevens, appointed by President Ford, was liberal on civil rights and moderate on other issues.[8] Justice Kennedy, appointed by President Reagan, was a conservative who became a liberal swing vote on issues such as gay rights and capital punishment.[9] Overall, however, it is fair to say, Republican presidents have tended to make the court more conservative, and Democratic presidents have tended to make it more liberal. Unfortunately for Democrats, since Republicans had more than three times the number of appointments, they have been able to move the court considerably to the right.

The Warren court had moved as strongly against the authority of governments to discriminate against minorities and criminals as the Hughes court had moved to favor the authority of governments in regulating economic activity. While the Burger court handed down some progressive decisions regarding affirmative action and, most famously, in its decision recognizing a right to abortion in *Roe v. Wade,* it gutted many progressive decisions of the Warren court, not to mention holding the record for overruling the greatest number of decisions by another court by overruling nineteen of its predecessors, decisions (as noted in chapter 2).[10]

The Rehnquist court was the second most frequent overruler of Warren court decisions and was the first court to rule against congressional legislation relying on the Commerce Clause since the early Hughes court.[11] While it allowed states to place a number of restrictions on abortion, it explicitly refused to overrule *Roe v. Wade* in the 1992 case of *Planned Parenthood v. Casey.*[12] It reversed a Burger court decision that allowed states to outlaw homosexual sodomy.[13] In its most controversial decision, the Rehnquist court ended a recount in Florida in the 2000 presidential election when Democrat Al Gore was only 154 votes behind Republican George W. Bush, effectively handing him the election.[14]

The Roberts court famously ruled that homosexuals have a right to marry, in *Obergefell v. Hodges.*[15] It also rejected two Republican efforts to scuttle the Obama administration's Affordable Care Act.[16] However, in *District of Columbia v. Heller* it announced for the first time that individuals have a right to keep and bear arms, under the Second Amendment, outside of their participation in a state militia.[17] Two years later, in *Citizens United v. Federal Election Commission,* it overruled two precedents to hold that corporations could make unlimited contributions supporting political campaigns, opening the floodgates to spending on elections by corporations via new "super-PACs."[18] In *Burwell v. Hobby Lobby,* the Roberts court found that closely held, for-profit corporations had religious freedoms that allowed them to refuse to follow regulations that offended their religious sensibilities if more tailored regulations would avoid the infringement.[19] The court dealt a severe blow to the Voting Rights Act of 1965 in *Shelby County v. Holder,* leading southern states to create more obstacles for voters.[20] And, of course, in 2022 they declared, contrary to the court's 1973 ruling in *Roe v. Wade,* that women do not have a constitutional right to abortion.[21] This last ruling was particularly troubling given the political history of recent Republican appointments.

ABORTION AND RECENT REPUBLICAN NOMINEES TO THE SUPREME COURT

Republicans have not always opposed abortion. Republican nominee for president in 1964, Senator Barry Goldwater, supported abortion rights. First Lady Betty Ford commented on *Roe v. Wade* to *60 Minutes* two years after the decision was handed down: "I feel very strongly that it was the best thing in the world when the Supreme Court voted to legalize abortion, and, in my words, bring it out of the back woods and put it in the hospitals where it belongs. I thought it was a great, great decision."[22]

But that all changed with the nomination of Ronald Reagan in 1980. The GOP had been luring southern conservatives away from the Democratic Party at least since President Lyndon B. Johnson signed the Civil Rights Act of 1964. Former Vice President Richard Nixon launched a "southern strategy" in his victorious presidential election campaign in 1968, aided by advisers to Senator Strom Thurmond, who had run for president on a segregationist platform in 1948. Nixon pledged to move slowly on civil rights issues and quietly encouraged what political adviser Kevin Phillips called the "Negrophobe whites" to flee a Democratic Party flooded with new Black members after the 1965 Voting Rights Act put a halt to systematic voter suppression in the South.[23]

Reagan increased and consolidated gains in the South by appealing to the huge swath of evangelical voters there by announcing his opposition to abortion. He joined forces with a politically active religious movement, the Moral Majority. In 1987, Reagan nominated Judge Robert Bork to the Supreme Court, a "strict constructionist" of the Constitution who had criticized *Roe v. Wade* and even *Brown v. Board of Education.*[24] The Democrats' defeat of Bork led to recriminations that continue to reverberate, contributing to the highly politicized Supreme Court nomination process we have today.[25]

Reagan's success in his two-term presidency, as well as the changing membership in the Republican Party he helped make possible, led his Republican successors to embrace the antiabortion position and align with new incarnations of the religious right: George H. W. Bush courted the Christian Coalition, his son courted Focus on the Family, and Trump sidled up to Franklin Graham, the politically powerful evangelical leader and son of Billy Graham.[26]

Donald Trump, a billionaire playboy who once was a pro-choice Democrat, seems an odd standard bearer for antiabortion evangelicals.[27] But he adapted well to his Republican constituency and promised during his 2016 presidential campaign to appoint antiabortion justices to the Supreme Court to finally overrule *Roe v. Wade*. Indeed, in his third debate with Democratic presidential candidate Hillary Clinton, he went so far as to claim that, given his appointment of two to three justices to the high court, the overturning of *Roe v. Wade* would "happen automatically, in my opinion, because I am putting pro-life justices on the court."[28]

Trump ended up appointing three pro-life justices to the court, thanks to political machinations by Senate Majority Leader Mitch McConnell. When the extremely conservative Justice Antonin Scalia died suddenly in February 2016, McConnell announced that he would not hold hearings on a nominee from President Obama to replace him, citing a flimsy excuse about not considering Supreme Court nominations in a presidential election year. President Obama's nomination of Judge Merrick Garland for the court was ignored, and Scalia's seat was filled more than a year later by President Trump's nominee, Neil Gorsuch. McConnell's "rule" proved a ruse when days before the 2020 presidential election the Senate rushed through the confirmation of Amy Coney Barrett to replace the stalwart defender of women's right to choose, Justice Ruth Bader Ginsburg, after she succumbed to cancer.[29] Between these two appointments, the swing vote on abortion and gay rights, Justice Kennedy, was replaced by the much more conservative Brett Kavanaugh after a controversial hearing involving allegations of rape when Kavanaugh was a teenager, and a razor-thin 50-48 vote.[30]

McConnell's hypocritical use of Senate power and the seating of the controversial Kavanaugh tainted the high court. President Trump's repeated promise that he would appoint justices to overturn *Roe v. Wade* made any decision by the court to do so appear to be a matter of politics, rather than of law. Nevertheless, the new conservative majority quickly plowed ahead, first ignoring clear violations of *Roe* in Texas, and then accepting an appeal from a fifteen-week abortion ban in Mississippi, disregarding the consequences for the court's credibility.

ROE V. WADE

Roe v. Wade was a Solomonic decision, seeking to find a middle ground between the competing interests of women seeking to control their bodies and the state seeking to protect their health and the life of the unborn.[31] The majority opinion was written by Justice Harry Blackmun, former counsel for the Mayo Clinic, who spent the summer prior to reargument in the case reviewing medical material related to abortion.[32]

The case involved Jane Roe, a single, pregnant woman from Dallas County, Texas who wished to procure an abortion, but was prevented by the state's penal code, which made procuring an abortion a crime unless it was to save the life of the mother.[33] Roe was joined by an abortion doctor concerned about criminal liability when treating his patients and a married couple who worried that the wife might suffer injury because of a medical condition should she become pregnant.

A three-judge panel of the US District Court for the Northern District of Texas heard the case, which was brought against Henry Wade, the district attorney for Dallas County.[34] The brief, per curiam decision recognized the standing of Roe and the doctor (1220). They drew upon the "right to privacy" recognized in *Griswold v. Connecticut* and extrapolated that right's previous application to "family, marriage and sex matters" to abortion (1222).[35] They noted that "freedom to choose in the matter of abortions has been accorded the status of a 'fundamental' right in every case coming to the attention of this Court where the question has been raised," citing decisions in another district court and in two state courts (1222).[36] They situated the right to abortion among the unenumerated rights recognized as "retained by the people" in the Ninth Amendment, made applicable to the states through the Fourteenth Amendment, as *Griswold* had (1221).

The Texas criminal code trampled on this right, notably, by being vague and overbroad. By prohibiting *all* abortions, except those to save the life of the mother, the state was not only ignoring women's right to privacy in deciding on whether to have an abortion, but also leaving doctors unclear about the conditions required for granting the state's exception to save the life of the mother (1223). While the district court found the Texas criminal statute unconstitutional, for technical reasons they declined to issue an injunction against the enforcement of the law (1224). The plaintiffs appealed this refusal to issue an injunction to the US Supreme Court.

Unlike the relatively brief district court opinion, Justice Blackmun's majority opinion in *Roe* was extensively argued over fifty-two pages. It was heard with a companion case, *Doe v. Bolton,* which involved a Georgia antiabortion statute.[37] The *Roe* opinion considers the court's authority to hear the appeal, the standing and justiciability of the case, the history of abortion law and the statute in the present case, and the constitutional sources and reach of the right to privacy. It develops a trimester framework for weighing the interests of pregnant women against those of the state.

Unlike the district court, Blackmun dismisses the standing of Dr. Hallford because, although he had been arrested in the past for performing abortions, he was not presently under "any substantial and immediate threat to any federally protected right that cannot be asserted in his defense against the state prosecutions" (126). Blackmun agrees with the district court that the married couple's concern over future pregnancy and a denial of access to abortion was "speculative," denying them standing in the case (127–28).

Jane Doe was a more complicated matter. Her district court case had been decided in 1970—three years before the *Roe* decision was handed down. Obviously, she was no longer pregnant. Based upon that fact, a crabby argument by a dissenting Justice Rehnquist would have denied her standing to sue because the case was moot.[38] Blackmun explains that such a dismissal would be unfair and unwise since pregnancy is a common condition, yet "the normal 266-day human gestation period is so short that the pregnancy will come to term before the usual appellate process is complete," making Roe's situation "'capable of repetition, yet evading review'" (125, quoting *Southern Pacific Terminal Co. v. ICC*, 219 U.S. 498, 515 [1911]). With a justiciable case established, Blackmun turns to consider the history of abortion from ancient times to the present.

Summarizing the history of abortion and the laws or customs governing it since the days of classical Greece is more art than science and, unsurprisingly, pro-choice and pro-life advocates characterize things quite differently.[39] Ideally, supporters of choice could provide a credible account to show that abortion was not generally criminalized in 1791 when the Bill of Rights was ratified or in 1868 when the Fourteenth Amendment was ratified. In other words, while the Founding Fathers and the Fourteenth Amendment's authors were writing into law that the government had to provide "due process of law" to their citizens, perhaps they assumed that the freedoms enjoyed by its citizens—that are not to be infringed by the federal or state governments without good reason—would have included access to abortion. That "originalist" way of interpreting those liberties need not be the end of the matter, but it certainly helps make the case for choice.

Blackmun offers an extensive review of laws and customs since ancient Greece, as well as a review of English common law (which was inherited by the colonies and still may be invoked today) and of the laws of US states. He concludes "that the restrictive criminal abortion laws in effect in a majority of States today are of relatively recent vintage" rather than "ancient" or from the common law, "deriv[ing] from statutory changes effected, for the most part, in the latter half of the 19th century" (129). That meant, ironically, that throughout most of the nineteenth century "a woman enjoyed a substantially broader right to terminate a pregnancy than she does in most States today" (141). What happened later in the nineteenth century was a result of lobbying by a medical profession seeking to professionalize its ranks and capitalize on a rise in antiabortion sentiment, Blackmun explains (141).

Before his Solomonic solution, Blackmun considers the source of the right to privacy, which he admits is not mentioned in the Constitution. However, as early as the 1891 case of *Union Pacific Railway Co. v. Botsford,* he finds recognition of a right to privacy.[40] Although he does not detail that case, a brief consideration of its language explains the citation. In a civil case involving a personal injury, a defendant asked the court to order a surgical examination of the plaintiff to assess her injuries (251). Justice Gray denied the lower court's authority to order such an examination, insisting: "No right is held more sacred or is more carefully guarded by the common law than the right of every individual to the possession and control of his own person, free from all restraint or interference of others unless by clear and unquestionable authority of law" (251). To support this claim, he does not cite the Constitution but rather a book on torts by Judge Thomas M. Cooley, insisting: "The right to one's person may be said to be a right of complete immunity; to be let alone" (251).[41]

Blackmun does admit a limitation on privacy rights—which Justice Alito will stress in *Dobbs*—"that only personal rights that can be deemed 'fundamental' or 'implicit in the concept of ordered liberty,' *Palko v. Connecticut,* 302 U.S. 319, 325 (1937), are included in this guarantee of personal privacy" (152). But the inclusion of abortion as "fundamental" is supported by noting "that the right has some extension to activities relating to marriage, *Loving v. Virginia,* 388 U.S. 1, 12 (1967); procreation, *Skinner v. Oklahoma,* 316 U.S. 535, 541–42 (1942); contraception, *Eisenstadt v. Baird,* 405 U.S. at 453–54; id. at 460, 463–65 (WHITE, J., concurring in result); family relationships, *Prince v. Massachusetts,* 321 U.S. 158, 166 (1944); and childrearing and education, *Pierce v. Society of Sisters,* 268 U.S. 510, 535 (1925), *Meyer v. Nebraska,* supra" (152–53). That is, privacy is notably implicated in sex and family planning, offering an opening to add abortion to the list. Without further argument, Blackmun concludes that "this right of privacy, whether it be founded in the Fourteenth Amendment's concept of personal liberty and restrictions upon state action, as we feel it is, or, as the District Court determined, in the Ninth Amendment's reservation of rights to the people, is broad enough to encompass a woman's decision whether or not to terminate her pregnancy" (153). This somewhat hasty conclusion is bolstered by a consideration of the possible personal, physical, psychological, social, and economic harms is at stake for pregnant women if this privacy right is not recognized (153).

Unfortunately, this privacy right was connected to physician-patient privacy concerns. That fit well with the analogy to the previously cited *Griswold v. Connecticut,* where the state forbade physicians and their patients to discuss birth control. Indeed, it was the fined physicians who brought the action rather than the patients, though they brought it *on behalf* of their married patients.[42] Like *Griswold*, *Roe* emphasized a paternalistic relationship that has earned criticism from feminists and others.[43] As Harvard Law professor Noah Feldman notes, *Roe* is "an opinion that transfers responsibility for the woman's decision from the state to the physician—with the woman's control over her own body almost an afterthought by the end of the opinion."[44] Indeed, even abortion champion Justice Ruth Bader Ginsburg said in a lecture to the University of Chicago Law School that the precedent had the emphasis wrong: "It's about a doctor's freedom to practice his profession as he thinks best. . . . It wasn't woman centered. It was physician centered."[45]

The role of the physician continues when Blackmun offers a trimester framework for assessing when various interests become "compelling." He notes that "the state's interest in regulating abortion procedures becomes compelling in the second trimester, when the risk of abortion exceeds the risk of childbirth," and a state may regulate the procedure for "the preservation and protection of maternal health" (163). Before that, in the first trimester, the woman may have an abortion without state interference (163). It is only in the third trimester, Blackmun insists, when the state's interest in protecting potential life becomes compelling, arguing: "This is so because the fetus then presumably has the capability of meaningful life outside the mother's womb. State regulation protective of fetal life after viability thus has *both logical and biological justifications*. If the State is interested in protecting fetal life after viability, it may go so far as to proscribe abortion during that period, except when it is necessary to preserve the life or health of the mother" (163–64; emphasis added). What Blackmun found as "logical and biological" in justifying the third trimester as compelling for the state's interest in fetal life, Alito would dismiss as arbitrary.

Blackmun justifies his overall position concisely: "This holding, we feel, is consistent with the relative weights of the respective interests involved, with the lessons and examples of medical and legal history, with the lenity of the common law, and with the demands of the profound problems of the present day" (165). Alito would question his weighing of interests, the lessons of medical and legal history, the position of the common law, and the demands of the day.

Justice White dissented along with Justice Rehnquist, downplaying the significance of a woman's choice of abortion over childbirth as based upon "convenience, whim, or caprice," as against "the life or potential life of the fetus."[46] He "finds nothing in the language or history of the Constitution to support the Court's judgment" and characterizes their decision as "an exercise of raw judicial power" (*Doe* 221–22). In addition to rejecting standing for Roe, Justice Rehnquist announces that he would apply a low-level "rational relation" test to the statute and allow the state's criminal statute to stand, a standard adopted by Alito in *Dobbs*.

ABORTION CASES AFTER *ROE*

In the Supreme Court cases following *Roe*, the influx of conservatives slowly whittled away at the 7-2 majority supporting abortion in that case. Ten years after *Roe*, in *Akron v. Akron Center for Reproductive Health*, two moderate Republican appointees had replaced one moderate Republican appointee and one liberal Democratic appointee.[47] The first woman appointed to the court, Justice Sandra Day O'Connor did not join the six justices who reaffirmed *Roe v. Wade*. Instead, she wrote an opinion joined by Justices Rehnquist and White dissenting from the majority's invalidation of a an Ohio requirement that all second-trimester abortions be performed in a hospital (despite contrary recommendations from the American Public Health Association) and another that required all minors fifteen and younger to have written permission from one parent or from a court to allow them to receive an abortion (with no opportunity for the minor to demonstrate that she is mature enough to make the decision without a parent). She criticized the trimester framework and the standard by which state regulations of abortion were judged.

The majority lost another vote in reaffirming *Roe* three years later in *Thornburgh v. American College of Obstetricians*, not because of new personnel but because of new line-drawing by Chief Justice Burger.[48] Pennsylvania had passed an "informed consent" statute that required physicians to present several items of information to an abortion patient, notably including possible complications from the procedure, the anatomical stages of fetal development, legal requirements for support from the father, alternatives for state support for raising a child or giving up a child for adoption, and a plea from the state to reconsider the abortion decision (763–65). The majority found the forced speech was "an outright attempt to wedge the Commonwealth's message discouraging abortion into the privacy of the informed consent dialogue between the woman and her physician" (762). The required information also was not tailored to the patient; for example, a woman raped by an unidentified man must be told about the father's financial obligations (764). There were also reporting requirements for the abortion doctor, including details that might allow identification of the patient in these documents that are not "public" but could be copied by anyone who wants to collect them (764–67). Burger defended such a requirement as providing "accurate medical information" about abortion risks (783). He insists his position did not change, but rather the court did in "the distance [it] traveled" away from *Roe* (784).

Three years later when a Missouri statute tried to regulate second-trimester abortions, the composition on the court had shifted against full support for *Roe*. Chief Justice Burger retired and was replaced by Justice Rehnquist, elevated by President Reagan to lead the court. Justice Scalia, one of the most fervent opponents of abortion, took Rehnquist's associate seat. Justice Powell, who had voted for *Roe*, was replaced by Justice Kennedy. Nevertheless, a majority of the court in *Webster v. Reproductive Health Services* either reaffirmed *Roe* or declined to reconsider its standing on the right to abortion, though it gave the state more leeway in regulating abortion.[49]

If the increasingly antiabortion court was reluctant to rally support for overturning *Roe*, the 1992 case of *Planned Parenthood v. Casey* would bring the issue to a head.[50] It would offer a new standard for judging the constitutionality of state regulations of abortion. It would provide one of the most thorough considerations of the role of stare decisis in judicial decision-making in the history of the court. It would also secure *Roe*'s standing for another thirty years. One personnel change did not change the split over abortion. The liberal Republican-appointed Justice Brennan was replaced by the more centrist Republican-appointed Justice Souter.

In a show of unusual solidarity, the majority opinion was jointly authored by Justices O'Connor, Kennedy, and Souter. That unity perhaps was meant to put to rest the unending attempts to challenge the *Roe* precedent, which the trio notes had been tried "in five other cases in the last decade" (844). Foreshadowing their determination to stop the unending statutory maneuvers from states hoping to eradicate the right to abortion, they warn in the very first line of their opinion: "Liberty finds no refuge in a jurisprudence of doubt" (844). They reiterated the woman's and the state's strong rights in the first and third trimesters, respectively, but added that "the State has legitimate interests from the outset of the pregnancy in protecting the health of the woman and the life of the fetus that may become a child" (846). This addition marks a departure from the trimester system which the plurality finds problematic. It opened the door to more state regulations meant to support its interest in "the life of the fetus," including in the first trimester, even if states could not completely ban abortion before viability.

The biggest innovation of the plurality decision is the establishment of a new standard to judge whether a state's regulation of abortion unconstitutionally interferes with the exercise of that right. Justice O'Connor had long pushed a standard giving more deference to states, and here her view wins a plurality of the court. States could regulate abortion so long as they did not impose "an undue burden" on a woman's ability to make this crucial decision (873). This *undue burden* standard replaced *Roe's strict scrutiny* standard for assessing abortion regulations.[51]

The trio provided an extensive consideration of why stare decisis needed to be respected in upholding *Roe*. They began by citing Justice Cardozo on the centrality of following precedent to a working legal system, because "no judicial system could do society's work if it eyed each issue afresh in every case that raised it" (854). "Indeed," they insist, following Justice Powell, "the very concept of the rule of law underlying our own Constitution requires such continuity over time that a respect for precedent is, by definition, indispensable" (854). On the other hand, they admit, following Justice Brandeis, "the rule of *stare decisis* is not an 'inexorable command'" (854). Deciding whether to overrule, thus, must be a thoughtful balancing act that weighs "a series of prudential and pragmatic considerations designed to test the consistency of overruling a prior decision with the ideal of the rule of law, and to gauge the respective costs of reaffirming and overruling a prior case" (854).

The majority offers a list of such considerations that will be familiar to readers at this point in the book: "Thus, for example, we may ask whether the rule has proven to be intolerable simply in defying practical workability; whether the rule is subject to a kind of reliance that would lend a special hardship to the consequences of overruling and add inequity to the cost of repudiation; whether related principles of law have so far developed as to have left the old rule no more than a remnant of abandoned doctrine; or whether facts have so changed, or come to be seen so differently, as to have robbed the old rule of significant application or justification" (854–55; citations omitted).

This standard list of reasons for overruling provide a template for the majority to examine the *Roe* precedent: "So in this case we may enquire whether *Roe*'s central rule has been found unworkable; whether the rule's limitation on state power could be removed without serious inequity to those who have relied upon it or significant damage to the stability of the society governed by it; whether the law's growth in the intervening years has left *Roe*'s central rule a doctrinal anachronism discounted by society; and whether *Roe*'s premises of fact have so far changed in the ensuing two decades as to render its central holding somehow irrelevant or unjustifiable in dealing with the issue it addressed" (855). The majority addresses each consideration seriatim.

Given the opposition to *Roe* that precipitated numerous state attempts to regulate abortion to the point of erasing the right, one might think the ruling is difficult to apply or even unworkable. This is not the case, insists the majority, because the necessary "judicial assessment of state laws affecting the exercise of the choice guaranteed against government infringement," which continues, "fall[s] within judicial competence" (855). The *Dobbs* majority would reach the opposite conclusion.

Although *reliance interests* weighed in judicial decisions are often connected to commercial interests, "where advance planning of great precision is most obviously a necessity" (856), the court notes that not even the Pennsylvania government respondents and their supporters in the case "*in so many words* deny that the abortion right invites some reliance prior to its actual exercise" (856; emphasis added). The *Dobbs* majority would deny such reliance explicitly, so the argument in *Casey* deserves particular notice for its contrast.

Unlike the precision of commercial planning, "abortion is customarily chosen as an *unplanned response* to the consequence of *unplanned activity* or to the *failure of conventional birth control* and except on the assumption that no intercourse would have occurred but for *Roe*'s holding, such behavior may appear to justify no reliance claim" (856; emphasis added). Furthermore, the court suggests "the argument might run, any reliance interest would be *de minimis* . . . [because] reproductive planning could take virtually immediate account of any sudden restoration of state authority to ban abortions" (856). Those who would make this argument (as *Dobbs* does), "refuse to face the fact that for two decades of economic and social developments, people have organized intimate relationships and made choices that define their views of themselves and their places in society, in reliance on the availability of abortion in the event that contraception should fail. The ability of women to participate equally in the economic and social life of the Nation has been facilitated by their ability to control their reproductive lives" (856). So, even if "the effect of reliance on *Roe* cannot be exactly measured, neither can the certain cost of overruling *Roe* for people who have ordered their thinking and living around that case be dismissed" (856). Though the court's argument undoubtedly downplays the outrage that supporters of women's choice should justifiably feel when property interests get more consideration than the independence and bodily integrity of half the body politic that this reliance argument implicates, the opinion's emphasis on the long-term ordering of women's personal, sexual, and economic lives conveys the enormity of this "noncommercial" reliance.

That *Roe* stands on a solid and fairly unchanged legal ground is not in doubt, the court insists: "No evolution of legal principle has left *Roe*'s doctrinal footings weaker than they were in 1973. No development of constitutional law since the case was decided has implicitly or explicitly left *Roe* behind as a mere survivor of obsolete constitutional thinking" (857). The majority ties it to two strong lines of precedent: First, the "right to privacy" line that began with *Griswold* and covered "intimate relationships, the family, and decisions about whether or not to beget or bear a child" (857). But *Roe* also exemplifies "a rule (whether or not mistaken) of personal autonomy and bodily integrity, with doctrinal affinity to cases recognizing limits on governmental power to mandate medical treatment or to bar its rejection" (857). And even if *Roe* were considered standing alone, its central premise has stood and been reaffirmed in a series of cases that the court lists (858) and I documented in the previous section. Although the court does not use the terminology here, the implication seems to be that the consistent support for *Roe* in the face of repeated challenges makes it something of a "super-precedent."[52]

The majority insists that *Roe* exists on a "rational continuum" rather than "a series of isolated points," and stretches out before *Griswold* supporting the idea that privacy includes a liberty "interest in independence in making certain kinds of important decisions."[53] Ominously, the majority says that any error in *Roe*'s assessment of competing interests in abortion might involve "the strength of the state interest in fetal protection" (858); however, they explain how a strong liberty interest has thwarted problems which should horrify pro-life proponents:

> If indeed the woman's interest in deciding whether to bear and beget a child had not been recognized as in *Roe*, the State might as readily restrict a woman's right to choose to carry a pregnancy to term as to terminate it, to further asserted state interests in population control, or eugenics, for example. Yet *Roe* has been sensibly relied upon to counter any such suggestions. E. g., *Arnold v. Board of Education of Escambia County, Ala.*, 880 F. 2d 305, 311 (CA11 1989) (relying upon *Roe* and concluding that government officials violate the Constitution by coercing a minor to have an abortion); *Avery v. County of Burke*, 660 F. 2d 111, 115 (CA4 1981) (county agency inducing teenage girl to undergo unwanted sterilization on the basis of misrepresentation that she had sickle cell trait); see also *In re Quinlan*, 70 N. J. 10, 355 A. 2d 647 (relying on *Roe* in finding a right to terminate medical treatment), cert. denied sub nom. *Garger v. New Jersey*, 429 U.S. 922 (1976)). (859)

Nor had the factual terrain changed to make *Roe* anachronistic. Admittedly, medical technology has tweaked Blackmun's original trimester framework in making later abortions safer and in pushing viability into the second trimester, the court admits, "but these facts go only to the scheme of time limits on the realization of competing interests, and the divergences from the factual premises of 1973 have no bearing on the validity of *Roe*'s central holding, that viability marks the earliest point at which the State's interest in fetal life is constitutionally adequate to justify a legislative ban on nontherapeutic abortions" (860). In short, "no change in *Roe*'s factual underpinning has left its central holding obsolete, and none supports an argument for overruling it" (860).

The majority believes it has made its case against overruling "for any less significant case"; however, the court concedes, "the sustained and widespread debate *Roe* has provoked calls for some comparison between that case and others of comparable dimension that have responded to national controversies and taken on the impress of the controversies addressed" (861). So the majority draws analogies to two prominent overrulings "of comparable dimensions that have responded to national controversies and taken on the impress of the controversies addressed" (861), *West Coast Hotel v. Parrish* (chapter 5) and *Brown v. Board of Education* (chapter 6): "*West Coast Hotel* and *Brown* each rested on facts, or an understanding of facts, changed from those which furnished the claimed justifications for the earlier constitutional resolutions. Each case was comprehensible as the Court's response to facts that the country could understand, or had come to understand already, but which the Court of an earlier day, as its own declarations disclosed, had not been able to perceive" (864). *Casey*, on the other hand, could not claim any such change in the facts or the legal landscape to justify overruling and, the court warned, "to overrule prior law for no other reason than that would run counter to the view repeated in our cases, that a decision to overrule should rest on some special reason over and above the belief that a prior case was wrongly decided" (864). Because of this lack of "some special reason" for overruling, a "terrible price" would be paid for overruling—perhaps by the court, but also the nation, the opinion is strategically ambiguous here. By contrast, a "terrible price . . . would have been paid if the Court had not overruled [*Adkins* and *Plessy*] as it did" (864).

If that "terrible price" was too vague for its audience, the majority provides the broader picture of the role of the court and the source of its power: "The root of American governmental power is revealed most clearly in the instance of the power conferred by the Constitution upon the Judiciary of the United States and specifically upon this Court. As Americans of each succeeding generation are rightly told, the Court cannot buy support for its decisions by spending money and, except to a minor degree, it cannot independently coerce obedience to its decrees. The Court's power lies, rather, in its legitimacy, a product of substance and perception that shows itself in the people's acceptance of the Judiciary as fit to determine what the Nation's law means and to declare what it demands" (865). What the court needs for its legitimacy is both "substance" in its decisions and the public's "perception" that those decisions are rendered by a "fit" judiciary (865). And while "a decision without principled justification would be no judicial act at all," even a "conscientious claim of principled justification" may not be accepted if "the justification claimed" is not "beyond dispute" (865).

This is perhaps the most rhetorically sensitive statement made by the court in the context of pondering an overruling. The majority directly warns that the court must be sensitive not just to offering principled arguments, but also to appearances, "tak[ing] care to speak and act in ways that allow people to accept its decisions on the terms the Court claims for them" (865). Indeed, the majority insists, "the Court's legitimacy depends on making legally principled decisions under circumstances in which their principled character is sufficiently plausible to be accepted by the Nation" (866). As I show below, the *Dobbs* court ignores this warning in overruling *Roe* after a highly politicized reshuffling of the court's personnel that was absolutely deaf to concerns that they "speak and act in ways that allow people to accept its decisions on the terms the Court claims for them."

As this book has noted, overruling is one of the most rhetorically fraught actions the high court can take. The majority in *Casey* recognizes that, while noting that some overrulings will be accepted because: "People understand that some of the Constitution's language is hard to fathom and that the Court's Justices are sometimes able to perceive significant facts or to understand principles of law that eluded their predecessors and that justify departures from existing decisions. However upsetting it may be to those most directly affected when one judicially derived rule replaces another, the country can accept some correction of error without necessarily questioning the legitimacy of the Court" (866). However, acceptance is harder in two circumstances, the majority warns. The first is when the court overrules frequently, a practice that "would overtax the country's belief in the Court's good faith" because "there is a limit to the amount of error that can plausibly be imputed to prior Courts" before "disturbance of prior rulings would be taken as evidence that justifiable reexamination of principle had given way to drives for particular results in the short term" (866). The second is where the court "decides a case in such a way as to resolve the sort of intensely divisive controversy reflected in *Roe* and those rare, comparable cases [such as Brown]" (866). In these rare cases "the Court's interpretation of the Constitution calls the contending sides of a national controversy to end their national division by accepting a common mandate rooted in the Constitution" (867). In settling such a controversy, the opposition will "inevitabl[y]" try "to overturn it and to thwart its implementation" (as the "Massive Resistance" movement in the South did with *Brown*'s desegregation decision).[54] Because of this, the court's "decision requires an equally rare precedential force to counter [this opposition]" (867).

So, the problem is not merely the overruling of a "super-precedent," as some have called *Roe*, though I suggest below that that is problematic as well.[55] For the majority, it is the connection of the case to a national controversy that requires not just good legal justification, not just sensitivity to appearances but something more, because "only the most convincing justification under accepted standards of precedent could suffice to demonstrate that a later decision overruling the first was anything but a surrender to political pressure, and an unjustified repudiation of the principle on which the Court staked its authority in the first instance. So to overrule under fire in the absence of the most compelling reason to reexamine a watershed decision would subvert the Court's legitimacy beyond any serious question" (867). As I have noted earlier, an overruling threatens both the legitimacy of the original decision—which the court itself shows to be wrong—as well as of the overruling decision whose soundness is put in question because of its variance from an earlier judgment. Or, as the majority put it: "The country's loss of confidence in the Judiciary would be underscored by an equally certain and equally reasonable condemnation for another failing [the first being the original decision] in overruling unnecessarily and under pressure" (867).

The *Casey* majority's concern that special reasons are needed in cases involving national controversies is not novel. As noted in chapter 2, a New York appellate judge had warned as early as 1858 that:

> [Courts of last resort] are frequently called upon to decide questions in which, not individuals merely, but the whole people, take an interest, and in regard to which prejudices have become excited and passions inflamed. There must be an arbiter somewhere, to decide such questions, which will command respect, or they will be brought to the abitrament of force; and nothing will contribute so much to secure this respect as a steady uniformity of decision, especially in regard to questions which affect large classes of men, and which lead, therefore, more or less, to the formation of parties. The overthrow of a single decision in a case of that character, unless upon reasons so clear and conclusive as scarcely to admit of controversy, is seriously to be deprecated, as tending to perpetuate an existing conflict of opinion.[56]

The majority warns that should the court suffer a loss of legitimacy, getting it back would be difficult. Unlike politicians, the court does not get to stand in another election and receive a new mandate should it suffer "the loss of its principled character" (868). The court's character is more like that of an individual, and "like the character of an individual, the legitimacy of the Court must be earned over time" (868). Furthermore, it is not merely the standing of the court that is at stake. Because the people of the United States aspire to have a nation based on the rule of law, Americans' "belief in themselves as such a people is not readily separable from their understanding of the Court invested with the authority to decide their constitutional cases and speak before all others for their constitutional ideals. If the Court's legitimacy should be undermined, then, so would the country be in its very ability to see itself through its constitutional ideals. The Court's concern with legitimacy is not for the sake of the Court, but for the sake of the Nation to which it is responsible" (868). I have made the same point recently regarding how the court constructs its own actions in the context of a particular case, noting that "what a court *does* determines *who* that court is in our political system and, who *we as a nation are* that would be governed by such an institution of law. Thus does legal discourse implicate larger issues of political order and legitimacy."[57]

Returning to the *Casey* decision, the majority applies the foregoing to its conclusion that "a decision to overrule *Roe*'s essential holding under the existing circumstances would address error, if error there was, at the cost of both profound and unnecessary damage to the Court's legitimacy, and to the Nation's commitment to the rule of law" (869). The court pulled back from that precipice and reaffirmed *Roe*.

The chief justice and Justices White, Scalia, and Thomas announced that they would overrule *Roe*, which the majority refused to do based on what the chief justice calls "its newly minted variation on *stare decisis*" (944). This "variation," from my reading of the overruling cases to this point, is not a divergence but an eloquent articulation of the foundations of stare decisis as it has developed in our legal system, thrown into relief by the most consequential of overruling decisions. The "variation" takes account of the enhanced scrutiny of what the court says and does in high-profile, controversial overruling and the dire consequences of ignoring the added scrutiny.

The *Casey* decision opened the door to the erosion of the right to abortion as states offered increasingly creative means to make it harder for women to get an abortion, running up to (and often past) the new "undue burden" standard the decision created. However, it apparently served to put to rest for thirty years the hope of states that they could succeed in totally banning abortion. That is until President Trump's "pro-life" appointments to the court offered an opening to those who would take away the right to abortion.

WHOLE WOMAN'S HEALTH V. JACKSON

States whose legislatures opposed abortion were heartened by President Trump's three appointees to the US Supreme Court and began fashioning laws to directly challenge the right to abortion to see if the new conservative majority might finally strike down *Roe v. Wade*. The most inventive legislation, by far, was the Texas Heartbeat Act, signed by Governor Greg Abbott in May 2021. It bans abortions after a fetus's heartbeat is detectable, which is normally around six weeks, before many women even know they are pregnant. It includes no exceptions for rape, incest, or fetal abnormalities.[58] That ban is not what made the law innovative. To avoid judicial review, the act did not allow state officials to bring civil or criminal actions against those who violate the ban; instead, it sets up a "bounty system" that permits private citizens to bring lawsuits seeking injunctions and statutory damage awards of up to $10,000 against those who perform or assist prohibited abortions.[59] That is, those who bring lawsuits can win up to $10,000 in each case against "doctors, nurses, insurance companies, and even the person that provides transportation to the abortion procedure, such as Uber and Lyft drivers."[60] These "bounty hunters" are not even obligated—as they normally would be in a civil case—to pay the defendant's legal costs if they lose the lawsuit![61]

Several organizations sought an injunction to prevent the law from going into effect on September 1, 2021. When Justice Alito responded to an emergency appeal on behalf of the court in *Whole Woman's Health v. Jackson*, he denied relief by essentially allowing Texas's effort to evade judicial review to succeed, insisting: "The applicants now before us have raised serious questions regarding the constitutionality of the Texas law at issue. But their application also presents complex and novel antecedent procedural questions on which they have not carried their burden. For example, federal courts enjoy the power to enjoin individuals tasked with enforcing laws, not the laws themselves. *California v. Texas, 593 U.S.* ___, ___ (2021) (slip op., at 8). And it is unclear whether the named defendants in this lawsuit can or will seek to enforce the Texas law against the applicants in a manner that might permit our intervention. *Clapper v. Amnesty Int'l USA*, 568 U.S. 398, 409 (2013) ("threatened injury must be certainly impending" (citation omitted))."[62] All three liberals, as well as the chief justice, dissented.

Chief Justice Roberts tersely explains the Texas legislature's strategy: "The State defendants argue that they cannot be restrained from enforcing their rules because they do not enforce them in the first place."[63] Unlike the majority, he "would grant preliminary relief to preserve the status quo ante—before the law went into effect—so that the courts may consider whether a state can avoid responsibility for its laws in such a manner" (2). He worries that "both in this particular case and as a model for action in other areas, counsel at least preliminary judicial consideration before the program devised by the State takes effect" (3).

Justice Breyer warns of "imminent and serious harm" that could follow from allowing Texas to use this means to deny women their constitutional rights.[64] Justice Sotomayor calls the majority's decision "stunning" in light of Texas's "flagrantly unconstitutional law engineered to prohibit women from exercising their constitutional rights and evade judicial scrutiny."[65] She charges the majority with "bury[ing] their heads in the sand" and "reward[ing] tactics designed to avoid judicial review and inflict[ing] significant harm on the applicants and on women seeking abortions in Texas" (1). She called the Texas Heartbeat Act "a breathtaking act of defiance—of the Constitution, of this Court's precedents, and of the rights of women seeking abortions throughout Texas" (3). Justice Kagan complains about Justice Alito's use of what has been dubbed a "shadow-docket"—an emergency order or summary judgment without oral argument—here endorsed by the majority, to deny injunctive relief. She complains: "The majority's decision is emblematic of too much of this Court's shadow-docket decisionmaking—which every day becomes more unreasoned, inconsistent, and impossible to defend."[66]

The decision to uphold the Texas Heartbeat Act "generated an unprecedented level of fear and anxiety for both providers and abortion-seekers in the state."[67] The closure of clinics and restrictions placed on their services severely limited access to abortion in the state. One estimate suggests that 85 percent of those seeking abortions in Texas were denied access within the state.[68] But the next abortion case heard that fall by the US Supreme Court would allow such restrictions to be even greater and their impact much wider.

DOBBS V. JACKSON WOMEN'S HEALTH ORGANIZATION

In 2018, Mississippi passed a fifteen-week ban on abortion except in cases of "medical emergency" or "severe fetal abnormality." It included no exceptions for pregnancies resulting from rape or incest. Physicians violating this ban could have their medical licenses revoked, among other sanctions. The only abortion clinic still standing after many previous restrictions passed by the state, Jackson Women's Health Organization, along with one of its physicians, brought suit against Thomas Dobbs, the Mississippi state health officer, to challenge the Gestational Age Act.[69]

The district court struck down the law and the circuit court affirmed that decision, since the law's restriction on previable abortions ran afoul of *Roe v. Wade*'s recognition of a constitutional right to abortion and *Planned Parenthood v. Casey*, which allowed regulations that did not create an "undue burden" on a woman's constitutional right to abortion, but not a per se unconstitutional ban on previability abortion. The Supreme Court granted certiorari "to resolve the question whether 'all pre-viability prohibitions on elective abortions are unconstitutional'" (quoting Mississippi's appeal at 8).

The reason I assess the *Dobbs* decision to overrule *Roe v. Wade* and *Planned Parenthood v. Casey* as the most egregious overruling in the history of the court is its cavalier approach to stare decisis and blind disregard for the damage this overruling would do to the court's legitimacy. As the *Casey* majority rightly noted, that legitimacy concern is "not for the sake of the Court, but for the sake of the Nation to which [the Court] is responsible"—"a Nation of people who aspire to live according to the rule of law" (868). The court had weak justifications for the enormous step it took. First, Alito's majority opinion was poorly argued. Second, the decision flaunted stare decisis and appears to have abandoned it as a principle of judicial decision-making altogether. Third, the decision marks the first time in the court's history that it has taken away a civil right through overruling; worse still, it is a civil right that is broadly popular and widely relied upon, marking its removal as troublingly countermajoritarian. Finally, the court took this aggressive step as the most politicized and activist court since President Franklin Roosevelt's threat to pack the court led to the Revolution of 1937; indeed, its politicization in the abortion area made its actions instantly suspect, so that great caution should have been exercised.

There is no prior overruling that can match *Dobbs* for upending the lives of so many Americans on the basis of such a weak pretext. If this is the new standard for overruling, the country should brace itself for a wholesale change in the law, especially those laws protecting civil rights, minorities, and democracy.

THE DUE PROCESS CLAUSE AND UNENUMERATED RIGHTS

Justice Alito's primary argument is that the *Roe* decision erred when it said that the Constitution confers a right to abortion upon women. His argument against *Roe* enters one of the most complicated and hotly contested areas of constitutional law: substantive due process under the Fourteenth Amendment.[70] What is required by "due process of law" under the Fifth and Fourteenth Amendments' use of that phrase was always complicated, though modern writers have distinguished "procedural" from "substantive" due process, as Ryan C. Williams explains: "An interpretation of the Due Process Clauses can be categorized as 'procedural due process' if it imposes no constraints on governmental deprivations of 'life, liberty, or property' that do not relate to the form of adjudication that must be provided in connection with such deprivations and the procedures that must be observed in connection with such adjudication. By contrast, an interpretation of the Due Process Clauses can be classified as 'substantive due process' if, and only if, it would prohibit governmental actors, in at least some circumstances, from depriving individuals of life, liberty, or property even if those individuals receive an adjudication in which 'even the fairest possible procedure[s]' are observed."[71] Even though these conceptual distinctions are modern, state and federal courts had developed a notion of due process as substantive by 1868 when the Fourteenth Amendment was ratified.[72] Justice Stevens explained why recognizing substantive due process was necessary: "Procedural guarantees are hollow unless linked to substantive interests; and no amount of process can legitimize some deprivations."[73]

During the *Lochner* era that began in 1905, the courts began recognizing "police powers" as a concern for substantive due process.[74] They began assessing the means and ends of legislation to determine whether it fell within the scope of "traditional" police powers. This approach led to the disapproval of many state and federal regulations that infringed on the "liberty" of businesses and workers and, in thirty years, to a confrontation with President Franklin D. Roosevelt's efforts to address the Great Depression. The Revolution of 1937, discussed in chapter 5, signaled the death knell for this approach to substantive due process.[75] As Conkle argues, "when the Supreme Court abandoned *Lochner* in the 1930's, it was widely understood that the Court was abandoning substantive due process generally, and not merely the use of substantive due process in the protection of economic rights."[76]

Thirty years after the demise of the *Lochner* era, the Supreme Court revived substantive due process in the interest of "fundamental rights" in *Griswold v. Connecticut*, overturning a Connecticut statute that banned the use of contraceptives by married people and their doctors' discussion and prescription of them to patients.[77] This "right to privacy" identified in *Griswold* would be extended to the right to marry a person of a different race, the right of unmarried persons to obtain birth control, the right to an abortion, the right to reside with relatives, the right to engage in private, consensual sexual acts (including homosexual sodomy), and the right to marry a person of the same sex.[78] Williams notes that this "fundamental rights" approach, "which is the Court's currently prevailing framework for dealing with substantive due process claims, places principal emphasis on identifying a narrow category of liberty interests that are deemed sufficiently 'fundamental' to warrant heightened scrutiny and 'forbids the government to infringe . . . "fundamental" liberty interests at all . . . unless the infringement is narrowly tailored to serve a compelling state interest.' Rights not deemed sufficiently fundamental to warrant heightened scrutiny are generally treated under a far more relaxed standard requiring only that there be some rational basis for the legislature's decision."[79] The trick, of course, is in determining which rights are "fundamental."

Liberty rights were progressively expanded from *Griswold* through *Casey*. *Casey* builds the liberty interests at stake in choosing to carry a pregnancy to term to a crescendo in one particularly philosophical section of the opinion. The decision begins with the cumulative protections afforded "to personal decisions relating to marriage, procreation, contraception, family relationships, child rearing, and education" (851). The justices note that family planning rights extend to "the individual, married or single" (851). They describe a protected space, "the private realm of family life which the state cannot enter" (851). And then they eloquently explain the significance of these rights: "These matters, involving the most intimate and personal choices a person may make in a lifetime, choices central to personal dignity and autonomy, are central to the liberty protected by the Fourteenth Amendment. At the heart of liberty is the right to define one's own concept of existence, of meaning, of the universe, and of the mystery of human life. Beliefs about these matters could not define the attributes of personhood were they formed under compulsion of the State" (851).

In *Dobbs*, Alito tamps down this expansive view of liberty, insisting: "The Court [in *Casey*] did not claim that this broadly framed right is absolute, and no such claim would be plausible. While individuals are certainly free *to think* and *to say* what they wish about 'existence,' 'meaning,' the 'universe,' and 'the mystery of human life,' they are not always free *to act* in accordance with those thoughts. License to act on the basis of such beliefs may correspond to one of the many understandings of 'liberty,' but it is certainly not 'ordered liberty'" (30–31; emphasis Alito's). This is a direct repudiation of *Casey*, which Alito defends by insisting that "ordered liberty sets limits and defines the boundary between competing interests" (31) And while Alito admits that "*Roe* and *Casey* each struck a particular balance between the interests of a woman who wants an abortion and the interests of what they termed 'potential life,'" he insisted that "the people of the various States may evaluate those interests differently" (31).

So it is not that the *Roe* and *Casey* majorities failed to "set limits and [define] the boundary between competing interests," thereby meeting the requirements of "ordered liberty"; instead, Alito seems to reject *who* sets those limits. But that ignores the *Casey* majority's concern in its opening sentence, that "liberty finds no refuge in a jurisprudence of doubt" (844). Allowing states to determine those limits clearly undermines liberty by making it what it has become after *Dobbs*—a political football. And, as noted in chapter 6, the court warned about other fundamental rights in the *West Virginia State Board of Education v. Barnette,* becoming subject to "the vicissitudes of political controversy."[80]

Alito admits that overturning abortion rights might lead states restrict abortion heavily but insists that it also allows states to "provid[e] even more extensive [abortion access] than the right that *Roe* and *Casey* recognized" (31). This latter point is another sloppy (or purposefully misleading) claim by Alito, since under *Casey* states already had the option to make abortion rights even more expansive, since no state was *required* to prohibit abortions in the third trimester or to set up a gauntlet of obstacles for women seeking abortions. Alito's rhetorical goal here seems to be to make it appear that turning the decision over to the states is balanced—or "neutral," as Kavanaugh's concurrence misleadingly calls turning over the decision to the states (concurring at 2–3).

Despite turning over a determination of the abortion choice to the state, Alito insists he is not "disput[ing] *Casey*'s claim (which we accept for the sake of argument) that 'the specific practices of States at the time of the adoption of the Fourteenth Amendment' do not 'mar[k] the outer limits of the substantive sphere of liberty which the Fourteenth Amendment protects'" (32–33). That seems a necessary assumption if we are to avoid a serious drawback to originalism when it comes to women's rights. The writers of the Constitution and the Fourteenth Amendment shared a patriarchal ideology that relegated women to second-class citizenship. Yet, the *Dobbs*'s dissenters note: "The majority's core legal postulate, then, is that we in the 21st century must read the Fourteenth Amendment just as its ratifiers did. And that is indeed what the majority emphasizes over and over again. If the ratifiers did not understand something as central to freedom, then neither can we. Or said more particularly: If those people did not understand reproductive rights as part of the guarantee of liberty conferred in the Fourteenth Amendment, then those rights do not exist" (14; references omitted). The problem of "what rights . . . those 'people' [had] in their heads at the time," the dissenters note, is that "'people' did not ratify the Fourteenth Amendment. Men did. So it is perhaps not so surprising that the ratifiers were not perfectly attuned to the importance of reproductive rights for women's liberty, or for their capacity to participate as equal members of our Nation" (14). Those men "did not understand women as full members of the community embraced by the phrase 'We the People'" (15). But Alito's cramped reading of unenumerated rights appears to require that we stay yoked to the beliefs of a less enlightened time, like the Taliban who set the apex for women's rights in the seventh century following their reading of their sacred Muslim texts.

While Alito claims to be open to broader rights than a strict originalist might allow, that claim of openness is belied by Alito's strategy of raising the bar for finding unenumerated rights. Alito insists that "any such right must be 'deeply rooted in this Nation's history and tradition' and 'implicit in the concept of ordered liberty,'" citing *Washington v. Glucksberg*.[81] Contrast this approach with that of Justice Kennedy in his majority opinion in *Lawrence v. Texas*, the case overturning homosexual antisodomy laws discussed in chapter 6. There Kennedy insists that "liberty in its manifold possibilities" is something to be discovered over time, rather than something that those who wrote the Constitution and the Fourteenth Amendment already knew about.[82]

Conservatives have worked to tighten the requirements for including unenumerated rights under the Fourteenth Amendment, sometimes by strategically quoting precedents. For example, Chief Justice Rehnquist said in *Glucksberg* that *Moore v. East Cleveland* held that "the Due Process Clause specially protects those fundamental rights and liberties which are, *objectively* 'deeply rooted in this Nation's history and tradition'" (720–21; emphasis added).[83] There is no specific reference to objectivity in *Moore*, but that does not prevent Alito from ignoring the fact that Rehnquist added it and quoting *Glucksberg* to say that those rights and liberties must be "objectively, deeply rooted in this Nation's history and tradition," as if the original *Moore* quotation (which Alito includes elsewhere) carried that modifier.

In his survey of precedents interpreting the requirements for finding these unenumerated rights, Rehnquist also had listed the criteria as an inclusive whole rather than different takes on the requirement, stating that they involved "those fundamental rights and liberties which are, objectively, 'deeply rooted in this Nation's history and tradition,' [*Moore v. East Cleveland*], at 503 (plurality opinion); *Snyder v. Massachusetts*, 291 U.S. 97, 105 (1934) ('so rooted in the traditions and conscience of our people as to be ranked as fundamental'), *and* 'implicit in the concept of ordered liberty,' such that 'neither liberty nor justice would exist if they were sacrificed,' *Palko v. Connecticut*, 302 U.S. 319, 325, 326 (1937)" (720–21; emphasis added). The implication of this "and" is that such standards must *all* be met, rather than one or the other (as, in fact, they had been applied in those separate cases).

Alito follows Rehnquist's lead when he strings together the criteria from *Glucksberg* to say "any such right must be 'deeply rooted in this Nation's history and tradition' *and* 'implicit in the concept of ordered liberty'" (5; emphasis added). Alito tries to construct this "and" as widely accepted by members of the court. For example, eight pages later he cites another case with Rehnquist's additive emphasis: "The Court has long asked whether the right is 'deeply rooted in [our] history and tradition' *and* whether it is essential to our Nation's 'scheme of ordered liberty.' *Timbs v. Indiana*, 586 U.S. ___, ___ (2019) (slip op., at 3)" (13; emphasis added). But Justice Ginsburg's majority opinion in *Timbs* actually said: "A Bill of Rights protection is incorporated, we have explained, if it is 'fundamental to our scheme of ordered liberty,' *or* 'deeply rooted in this Nation's history and tradition'" (3; emphasis added). Indeed, a few pages later Ginsburg reiterates the point: "In considering whether the Fourteenth Amendment incorporates a protection contained in the Bill of Rights, we ask whether the right guaranteed—not each and every particular application of that right—is fundamental *or* deeply rooted" (9; emphasis added).[84]

Alito also selectively quotes *Glucksberg* by leaving out part of its list where that precedent says the unenumerated right must be "'deeply rooted in this Nation's history and tradition,' [*Moore v. East Cleveland*, 431 U.S. 494 (1977)], at 503 (plurality opinion); *Snyder v. Massachusetts*, 291 U.S. 97, 105 (1934) ('so rooted in the traditions and conscience of our people as to be ranked as fundamental'), and 'implicit in the concept of ordered liberty,' such that 'neither liberty nor justice would exist if they were sacrificed,' *Palko v. Connecticut*, 302 U.S. 319, 325, 326 (1937)" (721). Alito's truncated quotation of *Glucksberg* that stresses "deeply rooted . . . history and tradition" allows him to reject abortion as not historically recognized while ignoring other elements to be considered. The excluded reference to the *Snyder* case leaves out the "conscience of our people," which might be broader than historical traditions, particularly if one assumes that what strikes the conscience changes over time. The *Palko* case *Glucksberg* cites adds to the idea that a right is "implicit in the concept of ordered liberty" a concern that without the inclusion of such a right "neither liberty nor justice would exist if they were sacrificed." Given the implications of the state wrestling away women's right to choose and forcing them to give birth, liberty and justice are certainly implicated.

Alito's selective quotation of *Moore* also ignores that case's characterization of the history and tradition as particularly important to its assessment of a municipality's *definition of family* for purposes of housing zoning. The court there said: "Our decisions establish that the Constitution protects the sanctity of the family precisely because *the institution of the family is deeply rooted in this Nation's history and tradition*" (503; emphasis added). For abortion defenders, the deeply rooted institution of the family is connected to family planning and the choice of abortion, bringing it within the larger category of protected rights. Indeed, Moore identifies this connection:

> "This Court has long recognized that freedom of personal choice in matters of marriage and family life is one of the liberties protected by the Due Process Clause of the Fourteenth Amendment." *Cleveland Board of Education v. LaFleur,* 414 U.S. 632, 414 U.S. 639–40 (1974). A host of cases . . . have consistently acknowledged a "private realm of family life which the state cannot enter." *Prince v. Massachusetts,* 321 U.S. 158, 321 U.S. 166 (1944). See, e.g., *Roe v. Wade,* 410 U.S. 113, 410 U.S. 152–53 (1973); *Wisconsin v. Yoder,* 406 U.S. 205, 406 U.S. 231–33 (1972); *Stanley v. Illinois,* 405 U.S. 645, 405 U.S. 651 (1972); *Ginsberg v. New York,* 390 U.S. 629, 390 U.S. 639 (1968); *Griswold v. Connecticut,* 381 U.S. 479 (1965); id. at 381 U.S. 495–96 (Goldberg, J., concurring); id. at 381 U.S. 502–3 (WHITE, J., concurring); *Poe v. Ullman,* 367 U.S. 497, 367 U.S. 542–44, 367 U.S. 549–53 (1961) (Harlan, J., dissenting); cf. *Loving v. Virginia,* 388 U.S. 1, 388 U.S. 12 (1967); May v. Anderson, 345 U.S. 528, 345 U.S. 533 (1953); *Skinner v. Oklahoma ex rel. Williamson,* 316 U.S. 535, 316 U.S. 541 (1942). (499; emphasis added)

In addition to the selective quotation that Alito offers, he fails to note that *Glucksberg,* like *Moore,* cited *Roe* as an example of a protected right. It also cites *Casey* favorably several times.[85] Nancy C. Marcus believes that "it defies logic and the bounds of irony to assert the *Glucksberg* precedent as justification for overruling *Casey* along with *Roe,* when the *Glucksberg* opinion explicitly follows and positively cites *Casey.*"[86] However, *Glucksberg* distinguishes the abortion right from an assisted suicide right that it rejects in that case by implicitly suggesting that *Roe* met the "history and tradition" test along with other right to privacy cases, stating that *Roe* noted "that at the founding and throughout the nineteenth century, 'a woman enjoyed a substantially broader right to terminate a pregnancy'" (727n19). Alito challenges this historical claim later in his opinion, implicitly refuting *Glucksberg* on its inclusion of *Roe.* Implicit refutation serves as a better rhetorical strategy for his argument, since Alito does not want to undermine a precedent which he is relying upon to establish the standard for determining which unenumerated rights deserve protection.

Finally, as the *Dobbs* dissenters (Justices Breyer, Sotomayor, and Kagan) note, Alito ignored a subsequent decision where the purported *Glucksberg* "history" test was rejected. In the case that recognized the right of gays to marry, *Obergefell v. Hodges,* "the Court . . . confronted a claim, based on *Washington v. Glucksberg,* 521 U.S. 702 (1997), that the Fourteenth Amendment 'must be defined in a most circumscribed manner, with central reference to specific historical practices'—exactly the view today's majority follows. *Obergefell* [v. *Hodges,* 576 U.S. 644 (2015)], at 671. And the Court specifically rejected that view. In doing so, the Court reflected on what the proposed, historically circumscribed approach would have meant for interracial marriage [among other privacy concerns]" (16–17).

Obergefell distinguished the issue in *Glucksberg*, noting that "'the *Glucksberg* test . . . may have been appropriate' in considering physician-assisted suicide, but 'is inconsistent with the approach this Court has used in discussing other fundamental rights, including marriage and intimacy.' 576 U.S., at 671" (17n4). *Obergefell* gave several examples concerning how the general "right to marry" had been applied, noting: "*Loving* [*v. Virginia*] did not ask about a 'right to interracial marriage'; *Turner* [*v. Saflly*] did not ask about a 'right of inmates to marry'; and *Zablocki* [*v. Redhail*] did not ask about a 'right of fathers with unpaid child support duties to marry.' Rather, each case inquired about the right to marry in its comprehensive sense, asking if there was a sufficient justification for excluding the relevant class from the right."[87]

Marcus adds another concern over Alito's narrowing of *Glucksberg*: "The opinion is grounded in an interpretation of substantive due process that only recognizes Fourteenth Amendment protections for unenumerated rights when the specific *conduct-framed right* for which protection is sought (i.e., the right to abortion, as opposed to the *broader liberty interest in personal autonomy and privacy*, which encompasses that right) must be 'deeply rooted' in this Nation's history and traditions' and 'implicit in the concept of ordered liberty.'"[88]As I pointed out above, Alito makes abortion as a focus of the right at issue, rather than *Moore*'s broader focus, "the institution of the family," or Marcus's focus on "personal autonomy and privacy." If the historically recognized, unenumerated right involves protecting the family or the individual (in her privacy) from encroachment by the state, then one can meet even Alito's stringent historical test for unenumerated rights and still recognize abortion as a right because it falls within this larger category of protection.

We see a standard rhetorical strategy at work by those who wish to deny an unenumerated right when we compare Alito's narrowing of the right at stake to "abortion" to the homosexual sodomy prohibition at issue in *Bowers v. Hardwick*.[89] Writing for the majority that supported a Georgia ban on this conduct, Justice White framed the constitutional question as "whether the Federal Constitution confers a fundamental right upon homosexuals to engage in sodomy" (190). In the case that overruled it, *Lawrence v. Texas*, Justice Kennedy insisted that the liberty interest at issue was broader than this, involving how individuals were allowed to define themselves, with the intimate role of sex as one part of that self-definition.[90] He offered an analogy: "To say that the issue in *Bowers* was simply the right to engage in certain sexual conduct demeans the claim the individual put forward, just as it would demean a married couple were it to be said marriage is simply about the right to have sexual intercourse" (567). (See chapter 6 for an analysis of this case.)

Alito offers a response to the charge that he unfairly narrows the interest in question: "These attempts to justify abortion through appeals to a broader right to autonomy and to define one's 'concept of existence' prove too much. *Casey*, 505 U.S., at 851. Those criteria, at a high level of generality, could license fundamental rights to illicit drug use, prostitution, and the like. See *Compassion in Dying v. Washington*, 85 F. 3d 1440, 1444 (CA9 1996) (O'Scannlain, J., dissenting from denial of rehearing en banc). None of these rights has any claim to being deeply rooted in history. Id., at 1440, 1445" (32). Alito's slippery slope argument echoes those of anti–gay marriage crusaders who claimed that permitting people of the same sex to marry would lead to people marrying their pets.[91] It also ignores the fact that no such extensions of the arguments made thirty years earlier in *Casey* and repeated in *Lawrence* and elsewhere have, in fact, been used to protect prostitution, illegal drug use, or "the like." That is because judges can properly draw lines that avoid such slippery slopes and also because, as the *Washington Post*'s editorial board argued, "in fact, pregnancy is nothing like those things. It is an intimate decision with few, if any, parallels—one that a constitutional order that prizes personal dignity and autonomy requires individuals be able to make themselves."[92]

Alito's ultimate distinction of abortion from the collection of privacy rights recognized since *Griswold*, and his plucking of abortion out of a broader right to privacy involving family or individual autonomy, turn on the moralization of the abortion question. He opened his opinion by framing abortion in moral terms: "Abortion presents a *profound moral issue* on which Americans hold sharply conflicting views" (1; emphasis added). This "profound moral issue" is what the majority's five (of seven) Catholics on the 2021/2022 court use to differentiate abortion, because abortion "*destroys* what those decisions call 'potential life' and what the law at issue in this case regards as the life of an 'unborn human being'" (32; emphasis added).[93]

In characterizing abortion as a destructive act, Alito does not concede that abortion is first and foremost a moral question *for some people*. He does not acknowledge a diversity of opinion on the issue as Justice Blackmun's original decision had, when he acknowledged "the sensitive and emotional nature of the abortion controversy, . . . the vigorous opposing views, even among physicians, and . . . the deep and seemingly absolute convictions that the subject inspires" (116). Alito implicitly rejects any thinking that does not acknowledge the "absolute [conviction]" that abortion is a moral question and implicitly one requiring a judgment that it is an immoral practice. He ignores those who would stress the economic, personal, or pragmatic elements of the decision to have an abortion over and against any moral element. On the contrary, he appears to take for granted that the immorality of abortion is accepted by all when he insists: "Abortion is nothing new. It has been addressed by lawmakers for centuries, and the fundamental moral question that it poses is ageless" (33). He adds, strangely, that "defenders of *Roe* and *Casey* do not claim that any new scientific learning *calls for a different answer to the underlying moral question*" (33; emphasis added). Different from what? Alito implies there is *an answer* to the "moral question" of abortion, though he does not say what it is because that would reveal his "absolute conviction," which ultimately appears to have been determinative for him and his conservative, religious colleagues.

Stressing the moral element could backfire rhetorically on Alito. If the central issue is moral, in our American tradition that would seem to place it in the hands of the individual decision-maker rather than the government. We live in a country that constitutionally separates church and state. Yet even the "Protestant" outlook that has so shaped our country generally leaves questions of moral conscience to the individual. Denying women a right to make this decision and leaving it up to states to decide whether they want to be the decision-makers is an odd choice if the issue is a moral one. Indeed, the court has addressed such moral decision-making by the state before when Texas outlawed homosexual sodomy in the *Lawrence* case. *Lawrence* concluded that "the fact a State's governing majority has traditionally viewed a particular practice as immoral is not a sufficient reason for upholding a law prohibiting the practice" (577). Marcus admonishes the court for "disregarding that traditional approach to judicial review of unconstitutional laws."[94]

Of course, Alito's moralization of the issue and apparent lack of concern over handing moral issues over to states fits within a tendency of conservative majorities on the court since the early 1990s to erode the separation between church and state.[95] The *Dobbs* decision can be seen as of a piece with this spate of reversals.

REREADING THE HISTORY OF ABORTION

After arguing that the only unenumerated rights we should recognize are those that are "'deeply rooted in this Nation's history and tradition' and 'implicit in the concept of ordered liberty,'" following his truncated and problematic reference to *Glucksberg*, Alito makes a historical argument that "by the time of the adoption of the Fourteenth Amendment [in 1868], three-quarters of the States had made abortion a crime at any stage of pregnancy, and the remaining States would soon follow" (16). Alito tries to show that the law had long criminalized abortion, beginning with British common law, which was adopted by the American colonies and, later, the states. As noted above, the *Roe* majority read this history much differently.

Roe built its case on the common-law rule that abortions are illegal only if they are done after quickening—that is, after the fetus begins to move around the sixteenth week. Alito questions the post-quickening rule as common law and makes claims about nineteenth-century statutory laws on abortion that have been challenged. He insists that "*Roe* either ignored or misstated this history [of abortion law], and *Casey* declined to reconsider *Roe*'s faulty historical analysis" (16). For an originalist like Alito, much turns on this dispute. He wants to dismiss any notion that women had unfettered access to abortion at any stage, refuting *Roe*'s claim that abortion was something women traditionally could access, particularly in the early stages of pregnancy.

Such historical disputes are crucial to originalists, such as Michael W. McConnell, who claims that individuals may "challenge the denial of any right that has been recognized by a sufficiently large number of states for a sufficiently long period of time so that it can truly be said to be part of the fabric of American liberty."[96] Professor Aaron Tang of the University of California–Davis School of Law argues that "the right to pre-quickening abortion fits comfortably within that definition [by McConnell because] it was respected by every single state at the founding, and by a supermajority when the 14th Amendment was ratified."[97] I focus on Tang's arguments because they are recent enough to be directly responsive to the historical claims made in *Dobbs*.[98]

Because Tang's historical claims directly contradict Alito's, I want to carefully consider the case each makes about two historical periods: (1) The common-law period through the Constitution's founding, and (2) the period of the Fourteenth Amendment's ratification. During the colonial period and early decades of the republic, English common law was relied upon in areas where states had not passed statutes governing activities such as abortion. Tang notes that there were no statutes governing abortion when the Constitution was ratified. Connecticut passed the first abortion statute in 1821.[99] So, the only governing law on abortion before that time was the common law.

Alito admits that under the common law "abortion was a crime at least after 'quickening'" (16). He also admits that Blackstone, upon whom he (and most of the early legal community) relies upon heavily, only categorized post-quickening abortion as "a heinous misdemeanor," an offense lower than a felony that is often punished by a fine or a light prison sentence.

Following this common-law rule punishing only post-quickening abortions would permit 96 percent of abortions performed today, so Alito's position allowing states to ban all abortions sought to make his own common-law generalization less relevant.[100] He does so by highlighting a few pre-Founding cases where it was not clear whether an abortion conviction was for pre- or post-quickening, where abortionists who treated women who died because of an abortion attempt were convicted of murder (unconvincingly implying that the charge covered both the mother and fetus) (18–20), and where judges use words like "pernicious" to describe abortion (18).[101]

Alito must have recognized the weakness of his cherry-picked examples because he then reverts to a strategy of "turning the tables," insisting: "Although a pre-quickening abortion was not itself considered homicide, it does not follow that abortion was *permissible* at common law—much less that abortion was a legal *right*" (18; emphasis in original). This is a strange argument since Alito generally admits that pre-quickening abortions were not banned under the common law. He seems to want to require *positive* support for abortion—permissibility—rather than acquiescence. Of course, common-law rules do not give "permission" to engage in activities that are not otherwise governed by the law.

After admitting that the common law at the time of the Founding and for decades after punished only post-quickening abortion, Alito questions the distinction between pre- and post-quickening abortions. He notes: "The original ground for drawing a distinction between pre- and post-quickening abortions is not entirely clear, but some have attributed the rule to the difficulty of proving that a pre-quickening fetus was alive" (21). He quotes an 1872 New York case where the court notes that "foetal movements are the first clearly marked and well defined *evidences of life*" (21; emphasis Alito's). He suggests that because of the primitive nature of early medicine "there were no scientific methods for detecting pregnancy in its early stages" (21). Of course, even if medical science could not detect pregnancy "in its early stages," that does not mean that women (and their doctors) were unaware of their pregnancies until quickening, the stage at issue here. The argument begs the question of what will count as unborn "life" that the law might defend, since awareness of a growing fetus before quickening was obvious to all.

While originalists such as Alito often consider what was known or believed in historical times to determine what the law was then, Alito finds it useful to imply that, given more advanced medical technology, the common law might have found "life" earlier than quickening. Indeed, he notes criticism from a medical professional in 1857 that "quickening" is an arbitrary line to begin criminalizing abortion, despite an 1872 case Alito cites relying upon that demarcation (22). While Alito offers enlightenment from the common law's future to the reconsider the past on fetal development and abortion, he does not offer to inject the same enlightenment regarding women's equality and status today into an understanding of what rights women had then or, with more enlightenment, *should have had.*

There is little disagreement between Alito's and Tang's account of abortion under the common law. As Tang notes: "Quickening mattered at common law because abortions performed after it were generally recognized as a punishable offense."[102] Indeed, he admits that *Roe*'s limitation on state abortion bans to the third trimester was out of line with this common-law standard, since there are several weeks between quickening (sixteen to eighteen weeks) and viability (twenty-four weeks).[103] Although Alito tries to muddy the waters on how firm or reasonable that quickening line was, they both concede that quickening is the most recognized milestone for punishing abortion.[104] Contrary to Alito's insistence that the common law did not make pre-quickening abortion "permissible," Tang insists flatly that "an abortion performed before 'quickening' . . . was not punishable by law." [105]

Both Alito and Tang agree that efforts by the medical community and public concerns over abortion led states to begin banning abortion by 1868 when the Fourteenth Amendment was ratified. They differ on the extent and nature of those bans. Alito claims that by 1868 "three-quarters of the States, 28 out of 37, had enacted statutes making abortion a crime even if it was performed before quickening" (23). Alito provides an appendix listing the texts of state abortion laws (79–108).

Mississippi's brief only listed twenty-seven states banning abortion by 1868, to which Tang originally responded (while quickly adding Rhode Island as the twenty-eighth state).[106] Tang admits that "it is no exaggeration to say that the 27 states claim is among the most consequential historical arguments in modern constitutional law," because that fact would give "an originalist Supreme Court . . . good cause to conclude that the Constitution protects no right to an abortion at any point in a person's pregnancy."[107] However, Tang insists that the twenty-seven- or twenty-eight-state number "is false" because "substantial evidence exists suggesting that as many as 12 of the 28 states on the majority's list actually continued the centuries-old, common-law tradition of permitting pre-quickening abortions."[108] He argues that only sixteen states, including Rhode Island, departed from the common-law rule and outlawed pre-quickening abortions; thus, in twenty-one of thirty-seven states pre-quickening abortions were lawful.[109] Tang explains that the discrepancy in the counts is because Alito and Mississippi mischaracterized the abortion statutes in twelve states.[110]

Tang's position is not uncontroversial. Even the amicus brief by the American Historical Association in support of the abortion clinic contends that twenty-six states prohibited abortion at all stages by the time of ratification of the Fourteenth Amendment.[111] However, they rely on a 1961 essay by Eugene Quay that does not scrutinize the language of the abortion statutes in question but appears to take their facial language and meaning for granted, which Tang examines closely.[112]

Tang claims that eight states that outlawed abortion at all stages punished pre-quickening abortion less harshly than post-quickening abortions, apparently acknowledging a difference in quality reflected in the common law.[113] Eight other states criminalized abortion at all stages with no distinction between punishments for pre- or post-quickening abortions.[114] For nine states there is no dispute from either side that they permitted pre-quickening abortions.[115] For nine other states—Alabama, Florida, Louisiana, Nebraska, New Jersey, Oregon, Texas, Virginia, and West Virginia—Tang offers "specific historical evidence [that] undermines [*Dobbs*'s] conclusion that the respective states prohibited abortion throughout pregnancy."[116] For three other states—California,

Illinois, and Nevada—he offers circumstantial evidence that pre-quickening abortion was permitted.[117]

In reviewing laws in the twelve states that he seeks to contest, Tang begins with Alabama, where "the *Dobbs* majority assumed, without analysis, that the language used to describe the object of the statute—'any pregnant woman'—applied regardless of whether the person's pregnancy had quickened."[118] Tang looks at linguistic practices of the day and an 1857 Alabama Supreme Court case that interpreted the abortion statute in a defamation case brought against a woman another accused of having an abortion. The court insisted: "'Unless the words [used by the defendant] convey th[e] imputation' that 'the woman was "quick with child,"' they 'do not charge an offense punishable by law.'"[119] This and related cases suggest that in this Alabama statute "any pregnant woman" meant "any *quickened* pregnant woman." Indeed, James C. Mohr's 1979 book, *Abortion in America,* agreed that in the Alabama statute, "pregnant meant quickened."[120]

Florida, which had been counted among those prohibiting abortion *before* the Fourteenth Amendment's ratification, actually approved it only *after* ratification, late in 1868.[121] Louisiana, Nebraska, and New Jersey "prohibited only certain *methods* of abortion that were known to be dangerous, while leaving safer procedures untouched."[122] Although Oregon's 1864 revision to its abortion statute replaced coverage from a woman "pregnant with a quick child" by removing the word "quick," seemingly expanding coverage, that change did not keep the state itself from arguing before its highest state court in a 1909 case that under that 1864 statute that "unnecessary abortion is not a crime . . . unless it results in the death of the mother, *or of a quick fœtus.*"[123] An 1858 Texas statute covering a pregnant woman was revised in 1907, according to the Texas Court of Criminal Appeals, because of a fear "that the courts of this state" would continue abiding by the common-law standard that covered only post-quickening abortion. Tang takes this to mean that "pregnant woman" was interpreted to mean a woman quick with child, as he shows in other state statutes.[124]

Tang finds specific evidence that Virginia and West Virginia should not have been included in Alito's count of twenty-eight states banning all abortions and that they "likely, but not definitively, permitted abortion prior to quickening."[125] He treats the cases together because Virginia's 1849 law was virtually identical to West Virginia's—unsurprising since the two states split in 1863. The 1849 law had replaced an 1848 law, eliminating a two-tier system with different punishments for pre- and post-quickening abortions and also, oddly, eliminating a provision covering slaves who performed or aided abortions.[126] Tang considers mixed evidence, including (1) a footnote in a legislative staffer's report on the revision of Virginia's abortion law that seemed to support a full abortion ban, (2) commentary in a medical journal complaining that the revised law did not cover pre-quickening abortions, (3) the single regimen of punishment that did not distinguish between pre- and post-quickening abortions, (4) the fact that slaves aiding abortions would face no penalties under this statute but only under the common law (which had no pre-quickening penalties), and (5) the fact that post-quickening female prisoners could not be executed while pre-quickening females could.[127]

California, Illinois, and Nevada banned abortion on "any woman then being with child" or "any pregnant woman," and Tang could find no commentary or court ruling that clarified what that meant.[128] However, based on circumstantial evidence Tang believes that we should read this as meaning "a woman quick with child." He offers three reasons for this interpretation: First, these states did not use language, as other states had, that specified that the ban applied before quickening, to mark the change from long-standing common law.[129] Second, other states with similar language interpreted "pregnant woman" to mean "post-quickening pregnant woman."[130] Third, these states imposed stringent punishments that other states reserved for post-quickening abortions. Tang notes: "These stringent sentencing provisions create a strong inference that the laws only applied to the most culpable kind of abortion procedures: those performed on a quickened fetus."[131] Finally, there were no recorded cases of any pre-quickening prosecutions in any of the three states.[132] Mohr notes of the Illinois statute in particular that its apparent application at all stages of a pregnancy probably did not matter for prosecutions because the state had to prove intent, which was only possible if a woman was late enough in her pregnancy that she was pregnant "beyond any doubt." Thus, even without language specifying application to later pregnancies, "the quickening distinction was taken for granted."[133]

Tang draws out the implications of his historical assessment for Alito's claims in *Dobbs*: "For an opinion that claims *Roe* was 'egregiously wrong' in its own historical conclusions, it is extremely troubling that the 'most important historical fact' the *Dobbs* majority believed it had proven [that 28 of 37 states banned all abortions in 1868] was no fact at all. At a minimum, it is much harder to claim that *Roe* was egregiously wrong on the bottom-line existence of a deeply rooted history and tradition of permitting abortion when in fact, a majority of states at the Fourteenth Amendment's ratification embraced exactly that tradition."[134]

Tang also thinks it is reasonable to give less regard to the sixteen states that banned abortion from pre-quickening because they were influenced by motives we would reject today: First was a view of women as second-class citizens whose primary role in society was as mothers. The newly formed American Medical Association (AMA), whose leaders spearheaded the antiabortion drive, "argued that a woman who obtains an abortion 'becomes unmindful of the course marked out for her by Providence [and] overlooks the duties imposed on her by the marriage contract.'"[135] The leader of the crusade, Horatio Storer, warned that women would make impulsive decisions about abortion because a "woman's mind is prone to depression, and indeed, to temporary actual derangement."[136] The AMA also was concerned about the dangers of abortion, and likely exaggerated these in their campaign to end the practice. Obviously, those dangers are almost completely removed today, undermining any rationale based upon safety.[137]

The American Historical Association's amicus brief in the *Dobbs* case details another unacceptable motive of those crusading against abortion: anti-Catholic and racist sentiments. Storer warned against the flood of new Catholic immigrants into the United States, whose "large families were poised to overwhelm the white Protestant 'American' population," because of what Storer calls "the watchful protection exercised by the Catholic church over foetal life."[138]

Alito challenges the imputation of these leaders' motives to those of the legislatures that passed the laws. He also implies that the court has typically viewed such motives as irrelevant to determining what the law is (28–29). The rhetoric of legal argument allows arguments on both sides of such questions, stressing or ignoring motives, often in light of their support or detriment to a given position. However, I would argue that it is a difference in quality, not in kind, to impute motives to federal lawmakers based upon what state lawmakers have done—such as concluding that they did not recognize a woman's right to pre-quickening abortion. State legislatures engage in a provincial political dynamic that is different from their federal counterparts. Those elected to federal offices often have broader outlooks than those at the state level, or at least gain them as the work requires. Yet, it is a matter of quick legal inference to go from what states think and do to what their federal counterparts think and do; even Tang accepts this.

Aside from the argument over laws, the American Historical Association's amicus brief notes that the centuries-long common-law rule concerning pre-quickening abortion apparently persisted in the public mind into the late nineteenth century: "Thus even while abortion became more stringently criminalized, the ultimate object of the physicians' campaign was foiled by persistent popular belief that not all abortions were criminal and decision-making over terminating pregnancies belonged to pregnant women."[139] Given this public sentiment, perhaps it is not as remarkable as Tang believes that a large majority of states continued to allow women to access abortion before quickening "in the face of rampant discrimination against (and disfranchisement of) women as well as a factually disproven assessment of medical risk."[140] He asserts that "some state law consensuses speak more loudly than others, precisely because of the obstacles they surmounted" and that "originalism need not blind itself to this reality."[141]

In its amicus brief, the United States adds another reason to give less weight to these nineteenth-century antiabortion statutes: "In most States, women could not even vote for the legislators who enacted those laws," making it "particularly inappropriate to treat the laws of the late 1800s as controlling," especially since "this Court's interpretation of the Due Process Clause has never been controlled by the state of the law when the Fourteenth Amendment was adopted."[142]

The twenty-seven (or twenty-eight) state claim that Tang argues is false has been bandied about by at least five scholars and the legal representatives of two states (23n130). Alito wields it carelessly, not like a serious originalist who should scrutinize more than the facial language of state statutes. Of course, he can still point to the minority of states that banned abortion at all stages in 1868 to show that they had not been *blocked* from doing so by federal intervention. In any event, Tang's historical correction weakens what already was a weak argument by Alito for overturning precedent on account of error.

Although Tang's analysis provides a thorough and balanced rebuke of Alito's historical argument, the *Dobbs* majority concludes that "an unbroken tradition of prohibiting abortion on pain of criminal punishment persisted from the earliest days of the common law until 1973" (25).[143] Alito strategically (and deceptively) blurs the historical record here as a setup to his holding that states may prohibit abortion *from conception* if they so choose. His "unbroken tradition of prohibiting abortion" should more accurately be stated as an "unbroken tradition of prohibiting *post-quickening* abortion" or even as a "centuries-long tradition of allowing early abortions." Obviously, the history of abortion law is highly contested and there is no unassailable proof for either side's 1868 numbers.[144] But, even if we take Alito's history as the correct one, we cannot allow him to gloss over that history and suggest that all abortions have always been outlawed as a justification for allowing states to do so today.

IGNORING THE CONSEQUENCES OF THE COURT'S READING OF THE FOURTEENTH AMENDMENT

Despite the fact that reason, ideology, and judicial philosophy have proven inadequate in preventing results-oriented decisions by the high court, there is one brake on such decisions that is hard to get around: in deciding what "the Law" is, the justices have to live with what they say. This is my point about rhetorical consequentialism in chapter 1, that words come back to haunt rhetors. In the case of judicial decisions, precedents are set that, even if they are not always followed, sit around like a "loaded weapon" to be used in the future, as Justice Jackson warned in the Japanese internment case.[145] That does not mean that justices do not try to skirt the implications of what they do while they are loading the weapon.

Justice Thomas is the only justice still on the court to have joined the majority in perhaps the most notorious case—until now—to attempt to skirt such consequences of a decision. *Bush v. Gore* ended the recount in the election of 2000 and effectively handed the election to Republican Governor George W. Bush.[146] The cobbled-together majority of five Republicans who ruled in favor of Bush argued that there was a violation of equal protection in the recount. It is rare for conservative justices like these five to support equal protection arguments—they more often have rejected or restricted them.[147] Unsurprisingly, the conservative majority did not want to live with this precedent, so they offered one of the most disingenuous arguments in Supreme Court history. Their holding was clear enough: that election recounts in a state's different counties must use the same standard for determining what counts as a "vote" to avoid violating the Equal Protection Clause. Yet, the court insisted that its ruling in *Bush v. Gore* was "limited to present circumstances, for the problem of equal protection in election processes generally presents many complexities."[148] Conservative and liberal scholars savaged that statement as unprincipled.[149] Alan Dershowitz offered a caustic translation: "In future election cases, don't try to hold the Court to what it said in *this* case, because it decided this case not on general principles applicable to all cases, but on a principle that has never before been recognized by any court and that will never again be recognized by this court."[150]

Alito faced a similar problem of precedent-setting in this case. As noted in the previous section, he drew out of a selective quotation of *Glucksberg* a rule that unenumerated liberty rights under the Fourteenth Amendment "must be 'deeply rooted in this Nation's history and tradition' and 'implicit in the concept of ordered liberty.'" (5). The problem with following this rule is obvious: many other unenumerated liberty rights previously recognized would fail this test. As the dissenters noted, for example, "the Fourteenth Amendment's ratifiers did not think it gave black and white people a right to marry each other" (17). So, *Loving v. Virginia*'s protection of interracial marriage would seem to be in peril.[151] The same goes for sex between homosexuals, gay marriage, and even the right to use contraceptives. Indeed, based on the *Dobbs* ruling, Justice Thomas's concurrence insisted, "in future cases, we should reconsider all of this Court's substantive due process precedents, including *Griswold, Lawrence,* and *Obergefell*" (3). The African American justice, who is married to a white woman, conveniently left the interracial marriage case off this list.

Alito tries to allay fears about these precedents, announcing: "And to ensure that our decision is not misunderstood or mischaracterized, we emphasize that our decision concerns the constitutional right to abortion and no other right. Nothing in this opinion should be understood to cast doubt on precedents that do not concern abortion" (66). He reiterates the point in directly responding to the dissenters four pages later, insisting: "Rights regarding contraception and same-sex relationships are inherently different from the right to abortion because the latter (as we have stressed) uniquely involves what *Roe* and *Casey* termed 'potential life'" (71).

Those are hollow reassurances, given Thomas's eagerness to build on *Dobbs* to do just what Alito insists does not follow from this decision. But we should see this as a rhetorical strategy in the vein of the *Bush v. Gore* decision, as an effort to evade the consequences of one's ruling. And he must pretend to evade those consequences to avoid the brake it would apply to this controversial overruling. Of course, one also could read this strategy as a *first step* to overruling those other precedents, despite his protestations that he does not wish to do so.

Justice Kavanaugh, who joined the majority, was even more adamant about protecting these nonabortion precedents. In his concurring opinion, he insists that Alito is correct in denying any implications of this decision for "*Griswold v. Connecticut*, 381 U.S. 479 (1965); *Eisenstadt v. Baird*, 405 U.S. 438 (1972); *Loving v. Virginia*, 388 U.S. 1 (1967); and *Obergefell v. Hodges*, 576 U.S. 644 (2015)" (10). (Note that *he* includes the interracial marriage precedent, *Loving*.) He insists: "Overruling *Roe* does not mean the overruling of those precedents, and does not threaten or cast doubt on those precedents" (10).

Both Alito and Kavanaugh identify larger categories of liberties that have been historically recognized to provide a safe harbor for these precedents. Alito labels this category "rights regarding contraception and same-sex relationships" (oddly ignoring interracial marriage) (71). Kavanaugh calls it the "marriage and contraception" series of cases that are protected as a group (10). But, while marriage might fit historically into that tradition, contraception does not. Just five years after the Fourteenth Amendment was ratified, the Comstock Act (17 Stat. 598), "an Act for the Suppression of Trade in, and Circulation of, Obscene Literature and Articles of Immoral Use," made it a crime to distribute contraceptives or information about them. And Kavanaugh cannot easily collapse contraception into a larger marriage category either, since the *Eisenstadt* decision protects the distribution of contraceptives to nonmarried people.[152]

But, unlike Kavanaugh, Alito does not argue about a larger protected category so much as he distinguishes abortion as destructive. For him the key distinction is that "the exercise of the rights at issue in *Griswold*, *Eisenstadt*, *Lawrence*, and *Obergefell* does not destroy a 'potential life,' but an abortion has that effect" (38). But that still does not explain how those prior cases are protected under Alito's "history and tradition" standard for determining unenumerated liberty rights, or why their future demise in the wake of this ruling is an "unfounded fear" (38).

Potentially undermining the other precedents, which Alito (and especially Kavanaugh, but not Thomas) appears to want to protect, should have given Alito pause in reaching his decision. Indeed, *that* is the way a judge's balancing of past, present, and future considerations is supposed to work (see chapter

1). Alito should have thought: "I'd like to overrule *Roe*, but I really can't do it without sacrificing other precedents that most Americans take for granted and which I respect." But, obviously, he is willing to risk loading this weapon. What should have doubled that pause is that this is an overruling case and requires a strong argument, preferably free of the threat to the future that this precedential baggage brings.

RETURNING CHOICE TO THE STATES

Having discarded *Roe*'s constitutional grounding and assured his audience that other decisions based upon that grounding were somehow safe from sharing *Roe*'s fate, Alito faced the question of what this ungrounding meant for abortion rights. The chief justice, who concurred in the result but not in overruling *Roe*, argued that the case should be narrowly decided on the basis of the Mississippi statute challenged, allowing states to ban abortions after fifteen weeks, urging "adherence to a simple yet fundamental principle of judicial restraint: If it is not necessary to decide more to dispose of a case, then it is necessary not to decide more" (2). He agreed with Alito that only allowing states to prohibit abortions after the second trimester "never made any sense" (1).

Eliminating the "sense" behind the nonviable/viable line was crucial to Alito's justification to give the states a wide berth in prohibiting abortion. But his argument against this line was built upon a lie. He stated: "Although the [*Roe*] Court acknowledged that States had a legitimate interest in protecting 'potential life,' it found that this interest could not justify any restriction on pre-viability abortions. *The Court did not explain the basis for this line*, and even abortion supporters have found it hard to defend *Roe*'s reasoning" (2; emphasis added). Alito references *Roe* from page 163 on the "potential life" point. On that same page, as I note above, Justice Blackmun said: "With respect to the State's important and legitimate interest in potential life, the 'compelling' point is at viability. This is so because the fetus then presumably has the capability of meaningful life outside the mother's womb. State regulation protective of fetal life after viability thus has both *logical and biological justifications*" (*Roe*, 163; emphasis added). Even if Alito is not impressed by Blackmun's "logical and biological justifications" for viability as the line, he should have at least quoted Blackmun and engaged his claims. Those justifications obviously turn on the idea that when a fetus reaches the point at which it can survive without relying upon the mother's direct biological support, it has something of an independent existence that we associate with individual human life.[153] Prior to that, a pregnant woman may be said to literally be "giving herself" biologically to the fetus which, in some cases, also detracts from her own physical needs and health; that is why carrying a fetus to term can be dangerous, even without the perils of the birthing process itself. The United States' amicus brief argues that

Mississippi (and now Alito) "find that line '[un]persuasive' (Br. 40) only because they discount the woman's interests. When those interests are considered, viability reasonably 'reconcile[s] . . . the liberty of the woman' and the State's regulatory interests."[154]

Blackmun's trimester framework revolves around "compelling" moments in pregnancy, from the point at which abortion is more dangerous than childbirth (in the second trimester), justifying more state regulation, to the point where the fetus is viable and the state's interest in "potential life" becomes pressing. But both Alito and Roberts see no "sense" in this viability line. So, Alito feels no compunction about erasing it altogether.

Alito announces the majority's decision that, because there is no constitutional right to abortion, "States may regulate abortion for legitimate reasons" and, when challenged, must meet only a "rational relation" standard—the lowest possible bar for states to clear (77). As Alito explains: "A law regulating abortion, like other health and welfare laws, is entitled to a 'strong presumption of validity.' It must be sustained if there is a rational basis on which the legislature could have thought that it would serve legitimate state interests. These legitimate interests include respect for and preservation of prenatal life at all stages of development; the protection of maternal health and safety; the elimination of particularly gruesome or barbaric medical procedures; the preservation of the integrity of the medical profession; the mitigation of fetal pain; and the prevention of discrimination on the basis of race, sex, or disability" (77–78; citations omitted). Permitting regulations "at all stages of development" means that states can ban abortions from conception. That standard could be used to justify prohibitions on certain kinds of birth control that prevent the implantation of fertilized eggs ("prenatal life" under this standard), as well as in vitro fertilization techniques, which normally begin with more fertilized eggs than are used.

It is ironic that this standard means that states may prohibit abortions that American women in the eighteenth century could have enjoyed and that women under British common law enjoyed for hundreds of years before that. To call this ruling regressive, then, is an understatement. As an *overruling*, it presents significant problems.

ALITO ADDRESSES STARE DECISIS

As the majority opinion in *Planned Parenthood v. Casey* noted, "a decision to overrule should rest on some special reason over and above the belief that a prior case was wrongly decided" (864). Indeed, with the exception of rehearing cases that lead to overrulings, there are almost no overrulings that fail to adhere to that rule and certainly none of significance.[155] As with his efforts to rewrite the standard for identifying unenumerated rights under the Due Process Clause of the Fourteenth Amendment, Alito tries to lower the standard for overruling. He offers an extensive list of reasons for overruling, making even weaker arguments than he had in the first part of the opinion and then, in effect, insisting that a weakened standard for ignoring stare decisis is all that is required. He provides analogies to prior overrulings to suggest that the court's overruling of *Roe* and *Casey* is not unusual, though these analogies have serious problems.

He begins with a standard list of reasons for following stare decisis before turning to standard justifications for overruling (39–40). He repeats the virtually required line that stare decisis is "not an inexorable command" (39), notes that constitutional decisions are hard to correct through political processes (40), lists three important Supreme Court decisions that were overrulings (40–41), and provides a long list of overrulings in a footnote (41–43n48). He urges that overruling "is not a step that should be taken lightly" and references two recent cases that detail considerations for overruling without reviewing those details (43). Instead, he lists "five factors [that] weigh strongly in favor of overruling *Roe* and *Casey*: the nature of their error, the quality of their reasoning, the 'workability' of the rules they imposed on the country, their disruptive effect on other areas of the law, and the absence of concrete reliance." These five factors are not strong, making his insistence that such a step should not be taken lightly more performative than serious.

I have already discussed the weaknesses of Alito's own arguments for his interpretation of the Fourteenth Amendment and its application to this case. Mostly his arguments for the errors of *Roe* and *Casey* involve characterizations. He says *Roe* was like *Plessy v. Ferguson*, "egregiously wrong and deeply damaging" (44). He claims that "*Roe*'s constitutional analysis was" not merely wrong but "far outside the bounds of any reasonable interpretation of the various constitutional provisions to which it vaguely pointed" (44). "*Casey* perpetuated [*Roe*'s] errors," using "nothing but 'raw judicial power,'" to "[usurp] the [people's] power to address a question of profound moral and social importance," taking sides in a "national controversy" (44). He even has the audacity to complain that *Casey* did not respect "the large number of Americans who dissented [from *Roe*]" (44), even as he ignores widely publicized polls showing that his opinion overruling *Roe* disrespects almost two-thirds of Americans who support the right to abortion![156]

Roe also was poorly reasoned, Alito urged, "fail[ing] to ground its decision in text, history, or precedent." It developed a trimester framework that "resemble[d] the work of a legislature" (47). *Casey* "reaffirm[ed] *Roe*'s central holding, [while] pointedly refrain[ing] from endorsing most of its reasoning," replacing the trimester framework "with an arbitrary 'undue burden' test" and developing "an exceptional version of *stare decisis* that . . . this Court had never before applied and has never invoked since" (46). Alito quotes several scholars critical of

Roe's reasoning (53–54) and complains about the state regulations of abortion that the court rejected under *Roe* (54).

As part of his questioning of the quality of *Roe*'s reasoning, Alito spends several pages (50–53) scrutinizing *Roe*'s viability line, arguing that "the most obvious problem with any such argument is that viability is heavily dependent on factors that have nothing to do with the characteristics of a fetus" (51). For example, having better neonatal facilities can make a fetus's survival outside the womb much better. He doubts that such a judgment about viability could be made by the state and is wary of leaving "these difficult questions . . . entirely to the individual 'attending physician on the particular facts of the case before him'" (53). The argument reflects standard problems with any statute involving such line drawing, such as determining an age when someone may buy alcohol, which must ignore very mature teenagers and very immature twenty-somethings. Nonetheless, drawing this line makes it easy for legislatures and courts to follow.[157]

In his "workability" section, Alito insists that *Casey*'s "undue burden" test is too vague to be workable (57), despite the fact that thirty years of rulings have served to clarify that standard. Many other standards in law, such as "reasonable doubt" and "probable cause" are also vague, or more properly "general," in order to capture the complexities of various real-world situations. The dissenters make the same point, noting that "general standards, like the undue burden standard, are ubiquitous in the law, and particularly in constitutional adjudication," and they need to be flexible so they "can be applied case-by-case to a myriad of unforeseeable circumstances" (33). Indeed, "the Court asks about undue or substantial burdens on speech, on voting, and on interstate commerce" (33). In a previous case, Chief Justice Roberts noted that the issue of what counts as "a substantial obstacle" is "the sort of inquiry familiar to judges across a variety of contexts."[158] The amicus brief from the ABA warned that "it is the dismantling of *Roe* and its progeny that would prove unworkable, replacing a clear understanding of how states may not regulate, with confusion and disarray."[159]

By far the most minor argument for overruling is the effect the abortion precedents have had on other areas of the law. Alito complains that "*Roe* and *Casey* have led to the distortion of many important but unrelated legal doctrines, and that effect provides further support for overruling those decisions" (62). For example, First Amendment law has been "distorted" because the court allowed a city to protect women seeking abortion from being accosted by antiabortion protestors by not allowing them to come closer than eight feet of the women (63). Alito does not explain how the high court's 2000 decision in *Hill v. Colorado* undermined larger doctrines of First Amendment law but cites a dissenting Justice Scalia disagreeing with the majority that this is "a minor place restriction on an extremely broad category of communications with unwilling listeners."[160]

The most insulting argument concerns whether women have any "reliance interests" that weigh against overruling the right to abortion. Alito notes that *Casey* admitted that "traditional" reliance interests, such as those involving precise business planning (such as taking account of existing interpretations of tax laws), were not present for abortion, which normally involves an unplanned pregnancy (64). *Casey* had argued for what Alito calls a more "intangible" form of reliance, which he contrasts with "a concrete reliance interest" (64). But what *Casey* described as a reliance on abortion rights was hardly intangible. As I noted above, the *Casey* opinion emphasized that "for two decades of economic and social developments, people have organized intimate relationships and made choices that define their views of themselves and their places in society, in reliance on the availability of abortion in the event that contraception should fail. The ability of women to participate equally in the economic and social life of the Nation has been facilitated by their ability to control their reproductive lives" (856). Of course, by the time of *Dobbs* that reliance was a half-century old. Almost all women living in the United States today enjoyed access to abortion during all or part of their reproductive years following *Roe*.[161]

Alito claims that courts are not equipped to assess such intangible reliance interests:

> When a concrete reliance interest is asserted, courts are equipped to evaluate the claim, but assessing the novel and intangible form of reliance endorsed by the *Casey* plurality is another matter. That form of reliance depends on an empirical question that is hard for anyone—and in particular, for a court—to assess, namely, the effect of the abortion right on society and in particular on the lives of women. The contending sides in this case make impassioned and conflicting arguments about the effects of the abortion right on the lives of women. The contending sides also make conflicting arguments about the status of the fetus. This Court has neither the authority nor the expertise to adjudicate those disputes. (65; references to briefs excluded)

Because Alito—in what should be counted as one of the most disrespectful passages in the Supreme Court's recent history—does not even consider the effects his decision would have on women, he can reduce the concern to a disagreement involving "beliefs." That ignores social science studies, referenced in amicus briefs, showing the *demonstrable* economic harm forced births can cause. For example, the ABA notes that "studies predicated on the data generated by the groundbreaking Turnaway Study confirm that women who are denied abortions suffer a significant and persistent increase in financial hardship and instability for years following the denial. Women denied abortions had significantly higher odds of poverty than women who obtained abortions."[162]

It takes little imagination—which Alito is unwilling to expend—to consider the implications of people of childbearing age in a post-*Roe* world, as the ABA brief concisely explains: "Men and women—not all, but many—have envisioned and planned their futures against the background that they can control whether and when to have children and how many they will have, and need not fear that an error, accident, or misfortune will require them to abandon their plans and aspirations. To deny the existence of that widespread and pervasive reliance on the protections of *Roe* ignores the reality of modern American society."[163] Because accidents such as failed contraception cannot be entirely eliminated, Alito must assume that Americans could take into account the limitations that, say, Texas places on their ability to terminate an unwanted pregnancy (no longer *relying* on the right) and simply *stop having sex*! But eliminating this activity so as not to rely on a right Alito and his colleagues are taking away adds another effect to be considered in choosing to overrule.

Alito might counter that those supporting abortion rights have too little imagination concerning the "death" of "potential life" abortion causes, leading them to leave out of the reliance balance sheet a consideration of such "losses." Of course, *Roe* considered those losses also and gave states authority to outlaw abortions in the third trimester. Perhaps they did not give them the weight that Alito would—as something of a holocaust of aborted children—which is one of the contested "beliefs" that Alito uses to plead judicial inadequacy to consider. But Alito ignores the fact that economic, psychological, and physical harms faced by women are not subject to "beliefs" such as when life begins but are objective factors that all must acknowledge, making them available to be weighed by the court. Yet Alito brushes everything into the same value-laden, contested pile to move it beyond the judicial reach.

In *Lawrence v. Texas*, Justice Scalia ruminated on the overturning of *Roe* in discussing reliance interests in his dissent. He insisted that even states that prohibited abortion would not cause a real problem of reliance because "the choice would not have been between abortion and childbirth, but between abortion nearby and abortion in a neighboring State."[164] Of course, this is a view that ignores the economic situation of poorer Americans who cannot afford to travel, to miss work, or to pay for day care for other children while they are traveling. As the dissenters note, "above all others, women lacking financial resources will suffer from today's decision," that is, until "some States [consider] block[ing] women from traveling out of State to obtain abortions, or even from receiving abortion medications from out of State" (3). And, in any case, Alito argues, women who want to retain their abortion rights have the option of "seek[ing] to affect the legislative process by influencing public opinion, lobbying legislators, voting, and running for office" (65).

Ultimately, Alito rejects any reliance interests in abortion rights because they are not like property interests: "*Casey*'s notion of reliance thus finds little support in our cases, which instead emphasize very concrete reliance interests, like those that develop in 'cases involving property and contract rights.'"[165] However, the Supreme Court has recognized other kinds of reliance interests before. Justice Scalia thought that a standing precedent itself created reliance: "It is my view, in short, that reliance upon a square, unabandoned holding of the Supreme Court is *always* justifiable reliance (though reliance alone may not always carry the day)."[166] For example, when the court considered overruling precedents requiring Miranda warnings for criminal suspects, they considered as a reliance interest the fact that "*Miranda* has become embedded in routine police practice to the point where the warnings have become part of our national culture."[167] In a statutory interpretation case, Scalia found a completely different source of reliance that called for adhering to stare decisis: "The reliance of Congress upon an unrepudiated decision central to the procedural scheme it was creating."[168]

Two years before *Dobbs*, Justice Alito himself dissented bitterly about the majority's decision to overturn a precedent that allowed states to win criminal convictions with nonunanimous jury verdicts as low as 10-2 (rather than 12-0).[169] He complained: "The doctrine of *stare decisis* gets rough treatment in today's decision. Lowering the bar for overruling our precedents, a badly fractured majority casts aside an important and long-established decision with little regard for the enormous reliance the decision has engendered. If the majority's approach is not just a way to dispose of this one case, the decision marks an important turn" (Slip op., 1). Such reliance had nothing to do with property or contracts, but rather with previous criminal convictions under the 10-2 standard which might now be appealed. Alito is purposefully unimaginative in dismissing reliance in *Dobbs*.

Alito turns from his five factors for overruling to consider *Casey*'s warning about overruling cases involving national controversies without especially strong arguments since, as Alito paraphrases it, "the American people's belief in the rule of law would be shaken if they lost respect for this Court as an institution that decides important cases based on principle, not 'social and political pressures'" (66). Alito's response to this problem is to offer an above-the-political-fray argument that ignores the very problem introduced in *Casey*, insisting: "We cannot exceed the scope of our authority under the Constitution, and we cannot allow our decisions to be affected by any extraneous influences such as concern about the public's reaction to our work" (67). He condemns *Casey* for trying to settle the national controversy over abortion once and for all, warning: "The Court has no authority to decree that an erroneous precedent is *permanently* exempt from evaluation under traditional *stare decisis* principles" (68).

Alito's posture of ignoring politics extends to a feigned blindness about the implications of his ruling in claiming: "We do not pretend to know how our political system or society will respond to today's decision overruling *Roe* and *Casey*. And even if we could foresee what will happen, we would have no authority to let that knowledge influence our decision. We can only do our job, which is to interpret the law, apply longstanding principles of *stare decisis*, and decide this case accordingly" (69). Of course, the *Casey* court was only doing its job also. That Alito would evoke such a myth of objective judicial decision-making in this high-charged case is all the more craven given the political machinations that brought him three new colleagues to back this overruling. I will consider this further at the end of the chapter.

Three years before *Dobbs*, Alito offered a standard for overruling that is more in line with the history I review in this book. In *Gamble v. United States*, he said:

> But even in constitutional cases, a departure from precedent "demands special justification." *Arizona v. Rumsey*, 467 U.S. 203, 212 (1984). This means that something more than "ambiguous historical evidence" is required before we will "flatly overrule a number of major decisions of this Court." *Welch v. Texas Department of Highways and Public Transportation*, 483 U.S. 468, 479 (1987). And the strength of the case for adhering to such decisions grows in proportion to their "antiquity." *Montejo v. Louisiana*, [13] 556 U.S. 778, 792 (2009). Here, as noted, Gamble's historical arguments must overcome numerous "major decisions of this Court" spanning 170 years. In light of these factors, Gamble's historical evidence must, at a minimum, be better than middling.[170]

Yet he seems to have abandoned the "special justification" rule in overruling *Roe*. He is unworried about what Tang shows to be "ambiguous historical evidence" or with the relative "antiquity" of *Roe*. Although he listed lots of reasons for the overruling, he practically admits that really he had only one—*Roe*'s error—when he responds to the dissent's complaint that he has ignored stare decisis. He considers their claim for stare decisis, that "recognition that the cases they overruled were egregiously wrong on the day they were handed down was not enough" (69). Although, as I have argued above, that is the correct standard because, otherwise, the admonition not to disturb settled law would have little force, since one court's "good argument" (e.g., *Roe*'s) is another court's "egregious error." Yet Alito tells the dissenters that "the Court has never adopted this strange new version of *stare decisis*—and with good reason" (69–70). Instead of giving a good reason, he gives an example meant to cow liberal pretensions with a "straw person" argument: "Does the dissent really maintain that overruling *Plessy* was not justified until the country had experienced more than a half-century of state-sanctioned segregation and generations of Black schoolchildren had suffered all its effects?" (70). Alito throws in the Flag Salute Cases as a relevant example as well. Those two cases and others that were or might have been invoked to justify Alito's overruling deserve a more thorough examination and I will use it as an opportunity for a final review of what I have argued about those cases in earlier chapters, distinguishing what Alito is doing in *Dobbs*, and explain what the history of overruling in Supreme Court has been, what it may be, and what it should be.

DOBBS AS ANOMALOUS AMONG SUPREME COURT OVERRULINGS

The most important characteristic of a Supreme Court overruling is that it convinces its various audiences—other justices and judges, lawyers, legal scholars, and the public—that it is based on several good arguments, evincing sound legal reasoning that clearly follows the law rather than caprice or the personal or political preferences of the judges. Ideally, it would be unanimous, an agreement of all justices on the outcome and reasoning. It would look even better if those overruling justices had been appointed by presidents of different parties and had diverse beliefs about and approaches to the law, suggesting that the decision was acceptable even to those who otherwise might disagree. The case should have been argued fully and thoughtfully by able counsel on both sides. The justices should have had time to consider the arguments, reach defensible conclusions, and explain them clearly in writing. Those arguments would show ideally that the overruled opinion was wrong on the law, that facts to which the law had applied had changed, and that the law itself had taken a new direction requiring the overruling to maintain its consistency. Weaknesses in the overruled decision would support the case, such as that it was a split decision, that it was poorly argued by weak counsel, and that the written majority opinion was unclear and was not supported with good evidence and arguments. However, at some point undermining a prior court can redound negatively upon views of the current court, so perhaps the ideal case for overruling would not be completely untethered from its legal moorings. Nonetheless, the prior decision might have caused problems because it is unclear, hard to apply, led to injustice or other kinds of problems. It would be useful if the overruling decision supported the interests and feelings of coordinate branches of the government, of a large percentage of the public, and of the legal community. Positive coverage by news media across the spectrum would help. Ideally, the overruling decision would offer a clear and cogent understanding of the law and provide justice for the litigants before the court and for similarly situated people in the future. And it would help if no one had relied heavily on the prior decision and that the overruling decision actually yielded positive benefits.

The world is too messy to yield such rhetorically potent circumstances and outcomes in overruling. The overruling decisions analyzed in this book generally fall short of this ideal, but not nearly as short as the *Dobbs* decision, as comparisons between it and early overrulings will show.

Alito invokes *Brown v. Board of Education* (chapter 6) as a decision that was justified because *Plessy v. Ferguson* had always been wrong and caused great harm to African Americans. *Brown* had many features that made it convincing and different from *Dobbs*. It was unanimous, whereas *Dobbs* was split at 5-4 (on the overruling). Although the *Brown* court was heavily dominated by Democratic appointees, the opinion was written by a chief justice appointed by a Republican; whereas *Dobbs* was written and supported by only Republican appointees and opposed by all Democratic appointees. The *Brown* decision came on the heels of forty years of Supreme Court decisions scrutinizing *Plessy*'s "separate but equal" standard for judging racially segregated accommodations in public transportation and public education and recognizing "intangible" elements of inequality that would be invoked in *Brown*. While *Dobbs* could cite criticism of the trimester framework, the leading case of *Casey* already had considered every argument *Dobbs* raised and rejected them, loudly reaffirming the right to abortion. Alito tries to claim the change to an "undue burden" standard was problematic, but his arguments for this were strained. *Brown* could cite the new and expansive role states had taken in public education, as well as new psychological data showing that segregation was harmful to African Americans, to justify a change. There were no relevant changes in abortion that Alito could cite, other than advances in medicine that made abortion and birth safer, but did not alter *Casey*'s reiteration of *Roe*'s "compelling points" for different interests.

The one thing that *Brown* and *Dobbs* had in common that made them difficult to justify was the reliance of others. Racial segregation had a vast machinery of legislation and practices aimed at keeping the races separate. The southern psyche was steeped in the idea of white supremacy and its "rightful" subjugation of African Americans. This reliance was racist, abhorrent, and contrary to American values, but it was ensconced in a warped way of life so deeply entrenched that Virginia closed down all its public schools to prevent race mixing. Alito might feel the decision to end "abortion on demand" (for many states) put the court on the right side of history from his moral perspective, ending the destruction of "the unborn." But there is a difference between the harm of southerners having to grapple with a racism which most of the country could not stomach and women—over half the US population—losing control of their bodies and their futures. In any case, *Brown* had the legal and factual changes, most of the public's support, an unequivocal appeal to justice, and a unanimous verdict that helped it weather the storm of the overruling, while *Dobbs* did not.

Alito compares his decision to the Flag Salute Cases, noting that *Barnette* overruled *Gobitis* "a bare three years after it was handed down" (70). If *Dobbs* did not have changes to justify its reversal, Alito implies, neither did *Barnette*: "The *Barnette* Court did not claim that its reexamination of the issue was prompted by any intervening legal or factual developments" (70). As I noted in chapter 6, only the concurring opinion obliquely referenced the widespread and horrendous persecution of Jehovah's Witnesses and said nothing about the proliferation of draconian state laws enforcing the flag salute ceremony in schools. However, the movement against this religious minority was widely reported and loomed in the background of the decision. Alito also ignores the fact that Congress weighed in on the issue by revising the standards for showing respect to the flag to include standing silently. But the biggest difference between *Dobbs* and *Barnette* is that the latter was brought about by a *change of heart* in three justices, while the former was brought about by a *change in personnel* involving three justices on the court, specifically, involving appointments that the nominating president said were chosen for their opposition to *Roe*. The *Barnette* justices who changed their minds undoubtedly were moved by what they had wrought, seeking to correct the wrong they had done. The new *Dobbs* justices appeared to be following their political inclinations. A small minority were directly involved in the flag salute persecutions, so the overruling did not inspire resistance. The *Dobbs* verdict was countermajoritarian, made against the widely documented preferences of a large majority of Americans who wanted to maintain a woman's right to choose. *Barnette* ended state persecutions of a religious minority; *Dobbs* allowed state restrictions on women's control of their bodies. And, of course, *Barnette* overruled a three-year-old case, not a forty-nine-year-old case that ensconced a right enjoyed by almost all women living today.

West Coast Hotel v. Parrish, which Alito cites for comparison, bears many similarities to *Dobbs*. FDR was threatening to pack the Supreme Court because it kept finding his New Deal legislation unconstitutional, so any decisions involving the New Deal were politicized, just as President Trump blatantly politicized his appointments by stressing that they would be judges who opposed *Roe*. Like *Dobbs*, the court's decision was 5-4. Unlike *Dobbs*, where the core of *Roe* had been repeatedly supported in multiple cases (most notably in *Casey*), by the time *Parrish* was decided in 1937 the Hughes court had already begun to question the laissez-faire approach of the Lochner era. For example, as I noted in chapter 5, cases in 1934 permitted states to intervene to stop rampant foreclosures and even to regulate the price of milk.[171] But until *Parrish* the court continued to flip-flop in New Deal cases with Justice Owen and Chief Justice Hughes providing the swing votes between the liberals and conservatives. Unlike *Dobbs*, the "revolution" of *Parrish* was brought about not by personnel changes but by a change of heart by Justice Owen.[172] Unlike *Dobbs*, the overruled cases in *Parrish* were fourteen years old and one year old, compared to the half century of reliance enjoyed by *Roe*.

Perhaps the most significant difference between *Dobbs* and *Parrish* is one that goes straight to the heart of public support for the court and its perceived legitimacy. *Dobbs*'s overruling of *Roe* was widely unpopular: 80 percent of Americans believe abortion should be legal in some circumstances, while *Dobbs* allows states to ban abortion outright.[173] By contrast, the overruling in *Parrish* had widespread, bipartisan support.[174] The Depression was raging and the public wanted strong government action to save the country. FDR celebrated a landslide reelection victory in 1936, winning forty-six of forty-eight states while his party won control of more than three-quarters of both houses of Congress. In short, FDR had a strong mandate to push New Deal policies, even if the public did not support his court-packing plan. President Trump, by contrast, did not win the popular vote in the 2016 election that allowed him to radically change the court with Senate Majority Mitch McConnell's disgraceful political maneuvers.

One overruling case that is not cited by anyone for comparison raises many of the same legitimacy concerns that *Dobbs* does. I discuss the Legal Tender Cases of 1870 in chapter 3.[175] That case overruled a sixteen-month-old precedent that had invalidated the Legal Tender Act, a Civil War measure used to raise money by allowing printed greenbacks to serve as official currency, rather than gold or silver coins.[176] The 5-4 ruling reversed a 5-3 precedent solely because of personnel changes that were heavily influenced by politics. The reasons for the personnel changes in the Legal Tender Cases are complicated. The Republican-controlled Congress did not like President Lincoln's Democratic successor, Vice President Andrew Johnson, and prevented him from making appointments to the Supreme Court by reducing its size from ten members to seven—a number to be reached through retirements. Shortly after President Grant was elected, Congress raised the number to nine and the new president appointed two new associates.[177] With one retirement, the seating of those new associates changed the vote on the Legal Tender Act. Unlike with President Trump in *Dobbs*, President Grant did not pledge to appoint someone specifically to overrule a precedent, though any Republican appointee was likely to support the Legal Tender Act.

Because of the quickness of the overruling, there was a public recognition that the precedent decision might be relitigated, as Cormack notes: "The country had been put upon notice so soon after the earlier decision that the question would be reconsidered that the reversal did not have the effect that it otherwise would have had."[178] The decision in *Dobbs* did not follow *Roe* closely, nor was it expected. Even though the Republicans had been pushing for an end to *Roe*, the decision hit the country like a bombshell.[179]

The decision in the Legal Tender Cases had very little impact on the country or its citizens as a whole. It affected only contracts that were almost a decade old or older, which the majority insisted were a small portion of debts in the country.[180] Obviously, this is a stark contrast to a decision potentially affecting more than half of the US population.

Finally, the original 5-3 decision in *Hepburn* was problematic because the aged Justice Grier—who died a few months after the decision was announced—was obviously not well. Initially, he voted with the minority, making a 4-4 decision that would leave the lower court's ruling standing. But when the court heard a related case, he seemed to take the opposite position; when this was pointed out, he changed his *Hepburn* vote.[181] Chief Justice Salmon, who wrote the overruled opinion, had to assure the audience on the day the decision was handed down that Grier was on his side.

The overruling in the Legal Tender Cases hurt the standing of the nineteenth-century Supreme Court. As Charles Fairman noted, "the Court's authority as expositor of the Constitution was seriously impaired by this unfortunate business."[182] But it was not nearly so problematic and was likely less damaging than the *Dobbs* overruling of *Roe*.

No other overruling in the Supreme Court's history has taken away a widely enjoyed constitutional right. Indeed, overrulings are often "rights-conferring."[183] When the Supreme Court simply allowed more regulation of abortion by Missouri in 1989, *Roe*'s author, Justice Blackmun, worried about the future of abortion rights and insisted: "Of the aspirations and settled understandings of American women, of the inevitable and brutal consequences of what [the Court] is doing, the tough-approach plurality utters not a word. This silence is callous. It is also profoundly destructive of this Court as an institution. To overturn a constitutional decision is a rare and grave undertaking. To overturn a constitutional decision that secured a fundamental personal liberty to millions of persons would be unprecedented in our 200 years of constitutional history."[184] It is indeed unprecedented; I cannot name a single overruling decision that withdrew a right shared by a significant number of Americans.[185] This makes the Dobbs decision one of a kind in its egregiousness.

Alito's opinion in *Dobbs* cannot be defended as neutrally following some judicial philosophy. I noted in chapter 1 that these philosophies speak to the past, the present, and the future, often sacrificing the judicial duty to one in service to the temporal emphasis of the philosophy. But Alito's opinion does not embody a coherent philosophy and it features temporal problems on every front.

Alito's arguments in *Dobbs* rely heavily on a focus on the past. This is unsurprising since he was assumed to be an originalist in the mold of Justice Scalia when he joined the court.[186] In his confirmation hearing he said: "In interpreting the Constitution, I think we should look to the text of the Constitution, and we should look to the meaning that someone would have taken from the text of the Constitution at the time of its adoption."[187] His argument against *Roe* relied on the lack of any mention of abortion in the Constitution and upon a historical argument that women under Anglo-American law never enjoyed the right to abortion. His historical argument was weak in attempting to deny the widely recognized access women enjoyed to pre-quickening abortion under the common law. He was on stronger ground in arguing that when the Fourteenth Amendment was ratified most states had outlawed most or all abortions, though Tang even throws doubt upon that taken-for-granted position.

In emphasizing *Roe*'s "error" in accounting for the legal history of abortion, we see Justice Alito leaning on the past to justify his position, almost promoting a declarative theory of law that insists that *Roe* was wrong respecting what the law was. And, although he admits that unenumerated substantive liberty rights are not limited to those that follow "specific practices of States at the time of the adoption of the Fourteenth Amendment" (33), his emphasis on limiting the recognition of rights to those "deeply rooted in . . . history and tradition" looks to the past as guide for what we today may recognize as rights.

Alito's attempt to discern "positive" law from the Founders is layered with a concern closer to natural law philosophy that emphasizes the *moral* dimension of the legal question of abortion. He does, after all, decide that states can do what they wish on abortion. In this way he puts distance between himself and the legal positivists who keep morality out of judicial judgments. Yet, he does not go so far to say that allowing choice in abortion runs against moral law—an argument that would open him to charges of blurring the lines between religion and the state. Instead, he seems to endorse the position that states may inject their moral judgments into legislative enactments concerning abortion—a position rejected in *Lawrence v. Texas* (as I explain in chapter 6). Leaving such judgments to the states is consistent with the originalist idea of leaving lawmaking to lawmakers and eschewing it in judicial opinions.

Constructing abortion as a moral question also serves another purpose in Alito's argument that emphasizes the future: the implied "immorality" of abortion frames his assessment of the damage wrought by recognizing it as a right. *Because* abortion "destroy[s]" what he terms "unborn human being[s]," and unfettered access to abortion will allow this carnage to continue, Alito can weigh such future "losses" against women's interest in controlling their own bodies. In this sense, we can say that Alito's argument is like that of a legal pragmatist who considers what is best for society in reaching his judicial conclusions about abortion rights. However, he is less clear than legal pragmatists in calculating the "good" that will follow from allowing states to ban abortion. He does clearly count as a "good" the deference to legislatures to decide what women's abortion rights will be.

While Alito leans heavily on the judicial commitment to the past and implicates concerns about the future, he says almost nothing about the present and the justice of his decision for the litigants before the court. They are an afterthought in Alito's rush to redirect the law of the land on abortion. On the other hand, he may feel he is defending the rights of an ignored group—the unborn. But he does not take on the rhetorical work of establishing fetuses as rights holders, relying instead on an acknowledgment since *Roe* that states have an "interest" in the unborn of its residents and visitors. That interest has not been scrutinized beyond *Casey*'s warning that state control of procreation could cut the other way and allow the state to mandate abortions. Future scholarship should scrutinize this state interest to discern what it actually involves. My guess is that moral judgment will be primary and that the lives saved will be less of an interest than preventing a *practice* disparaged by many. States that oppose abortion have often been the worst in supporting pregnant women and children.[188]

Rhetorically, Alito emphasizes his strongest argument in challenging *Roe* on the history of abortion regulation, though there are serious problems with that. The rest of his arguments require him to tread carefully so as to avoid rhetorical minefields. Pushing too far on the morality issue could make him look like a Catholic justice rather than an objective adjudicator. Insisting too strongly that states can exercise their moral judgments in passing antiabortion legislation might require him to explain this departure from *Lawrence*. And making "history and tradition" the ultimate standard for liberty rights could endanger a series of precedents (regarding interracial and gay marriage, contraception, child-rearing, etc.) that he wants to steer clear of lest they put the brakes on his overruling of *Roe*. Indeed, this last treading was too heavy, making even concurring justices reassure the Supreme Court's audiences that pulling the abortion thread would not unravel other widely respected liberties under the due process clause.

In the arguments he makes primary, Alito seeks to uphold the past as an originalist or some kind of positivist. In spirit, he comes across as a natural-law jurist, injecting a moral element into his look at the past. His secondary arguments turn morality into a concern for avoiding bad things in the future—a weighing that excludes any concern for women's health and lives—making him a legal pragmatist with a cleric's assessment of what is good for society. Overall, the legal philosophy of *Dobbs* comes across as inconsistent as Alito navigates the contradictions of his position. His respect for the past is belied by his casual dismissal of stare decisis. His respect for the future is belied by his rejection of any concern for the potentially significant impact of his decision on half the population. And he does not even feign respect for the present or those who appealed to the court. The judicial concern for each time orientation is badly compromised.

CONCLUSION

Mitch McConnell packed the court by stealing two seats, preventing what might have been the first majority of Democratic appointees in fifty years. Donald Trump promised to appoint justices to these stolen seats who would realize the forty-year dream of Republicans to overrule *Roe*, and they did so, even though some of them indicated they would not.[189] The conservatives did not wait until they had a convincing supermajority to support this controversial overruling but took the step as soon as they had five justices willing to sign on to it, ignoring pleas from their chief justice to take care and consider the court's standing. In doing so, they followed the trend of the Roberts court in using the raw power of a 5-4 advantage in 92 percent of all its overrulings, something no other court comes close to approaching for its brazenness.

To pull off such an overruling while maintaining its credibility, the court needed an exceptionally strong justification. It had none. Alito offered only the claim that *Roe* was "egregiously wrong." He argued that abortion was always a crime, ignoring the fact that for most of the Anglo-American tradition it was not a crime before quickening. He insisted that the Fourteenth Amendment was passed when most states banned all abortions, although Tang brings considerable evidence to throw that claim into doubt. He admitted that unenumerated rights are not limited to what was actually recognized by those in the nineteenth century and assured his audience that his cramped approach to recognizing those rights would not impact the right to contraceptives, interracial marriage, or gay sexual relations and marriage. But, like the *Bush v. Gore* court, he wanted draw attention away from the implications of his argument, which even Justice Thomas acknowledged set those other right-to-privacy precedents up for overruling. Alito used overruling to take away a significant right for the first time in American history.

Alito rejected any concern over women's reliance on the right to abortion, even though childbirth has perhaps the greatest impact of any life event on a woman's health, finances, and career. Alito allows states to invade the bodily integrity of women and force them to bear children, with all that entails. He insists that he is simply protecting "unborn children," but his rejection of *Roe* as a compromise that also protects the unborn (through permitted state regulations and third-trimester bans) is unconvincing. His decision is clearly based upon a moral judgment about abortion that is not shared by the large majority of Americans who support abortion rights. Alito thinks that he has cleared the bar for "traditional *stare decisis* factors" to justify the overruling (66). He has not.

Casey had warned that overruling Roe by claiming it was wrong would cause "profound and unnecessary damage to the Court's legitimacy, and to the Nation's commitment to the rule of law" (869). It warned that when the court delves into national controversies in overruling a case, it needed an exceptionally strong argument—a position that Alito rejects as "novel" (56). It is not novel, as I have noted, but rather an eloquent articulation of the foundations of stare decisis as it has developed in our legal system, thrown into relief by the most consequential of overruling decisions. Indeed, this position was recognized by a New York court in 1858 that warned: Courts of last resort "are frequently called upon to decide questions in which, not individuals merely, but the whole people, take an interest, and in regard to which prejudices have become excited and passions inflamed. There must be an arbiter somewhere, to decide such questions, which will command respect, or they will be brought to the arbitrament of force; and nothing will contribute so much to secure this respect as a steady uniformity of decision, especially in regard to questions which affect large classes of men, and which lead, therefore, more or less, to the formation of parties. The overthrow of a single decision in a case of that character, unless upon reasons so clear and conclusive as scarcely to admit of controversy, is seriously to be deprecated, as tending to perpetuate an existing conflict of opinion."[190]

After a draft of the *Dobbs* decision was leaked, polling found that Americans wanted to retain the protections under *Roe* by a two-to-one margin.[191] Overall, approval of the court sank to all-time lows, though the impact of *Dobbs* was politically polarized. While Democrats and Republicans were roughly even in their pre-*Dobbs* approval of the court, after the decision Republican approval increased 29 percent to 74 percent, while Democratic approval plummeted 23 percent to 13 percent.[192] Almost two-thirds of eighteen-to-twenty-nine-year-olds had an unfavorable view of the court.[193] Linda Greenhouse remarked that "the depth of disenchantment revealed in these recent polls represents a crisis for the Supreme Court."[194]

The chief justice reacted to the fall of the court's standing by publicly insisting that "simply because people disagree with an opinion is not a basis for criticizing the legitimacy of the Court."[195] But, as Greenhouse astutely noted: "People aren't criticizing the Court's legitimacy; they are criticizing the Court's behavior—the behavior that has led to a loss of legitimacy."[196] Justice Kagan took this view when she warned publicly that judges "undermine their legitimacy when they don't act so much like courts and when they don't do things that are recognizably law, and when they instead stray into places where it looks like they're an extension of the political process, or where they're imposing their own personal preferences."[197]

The majority in *Dobbs* seems oblivious or uncaring about the standing of the court or its implications for our democracy. Ultimately, that is what makes it the worst overruling in the high court's history. If they had cared about the court or the country, they would not have dismissed such an important precedent so incautiously.

If the current conservative majority is willing to sacrifice so much of its standing to overrule *Roe*, we should expect more of this "damn the torpedoes" approach to decision-making. After all, Justice Alito rejected the idea that engaging national controversies requires the court to tread lightly to protect its legitimacy. The *Dobbs* dissenters warn of the future in light of the majority's reckless dismissal of stare decisis: "So how does that approach prevent the 'scale of justice' from 'waver[ing] with every new judge's opinion'? 1 Blackstone 69. It does not. It makes radical change too easy and too fast, based on nothing more than the new views of new judges. The majority has overruled Roe and Casey for one and only one reason: because it has always despised them, and now it has the votes to discard them. The majority thereby substitutes a rule by judges for the rule of law" (33). Our highly polarized political environment has led to the appointment of highly political justices who seem to want to exercise power in support of their politics, ignoring the fact that their power is rhetorical only, supported by institutional ethos rather than a purse or a military, and subject to diminution. Unfortunately, such diminution impacts more that the Supreme Court; it threatens our democratic system and its reliance on a credible notion that we live under "rule of law."

The US Supreme Court must change course from time to time because old decisions sometimes cannot withstand changes in law and society over the long run. But those changes ought to be guided by a prudent and respected court as our navigator. For most of our history, we have had justices who understand that. May that continue to be the case.

APPENDIX A: US SUPREME COURT OVERRULING AND OVERRULED CASES

THE CHART BELOW LISTS ALL the cases I have identified, using a variety of sources, as overruling and overruled cases in the US Supreme Court. It is a chronological list of all such cases I have identified, along with the sources that identify them as overruling and overruled. Appendix B lists a small number of cases identified by one source as overruling that I have reviewed and omitted from this list. The sources identifying overrulings are associated with the codes listed on the key. They include comprehensive sources from Harold J. Spaeth et al., *2020 Supreme Court Database,* Version 2021, Release 01; Congressional Research Service, "Table of Supreme Court Decisions Overruled by Subsequent Decisions," *Constitution Annotated: Analysis and Interpretation of the U.S. Constitution,* US Congress website; and *Supreme Court Decisions Overrruled by Subsequent Decision,* GovInfo (Washington, DC: Government Publishing Office, 2017). Others sources include the following scholarly publications: William O. Douglas, "Stare Decisis," *Columbia Law Review* 49, no. 6 (June 1949): 735–58; Albert P. Blaustein and Andrew H. Field, "'Overruling' Opinions in the Supreme Court," *Michigan Law Review* 57, no. 2 (1958): 152–94; William M. Eskridge Jr. "Overruling Statutory Precedents," *Georgetown Law Review* 76 (April 1988): 1361–1426; Michael Gerhardt, "The Role of Precedent in Constitutional Decisionmaking and Theory," *George Washington Law Review* 60, no. 1 (1991): 68–159; Michael H. LeRoy, "Death of a Precedent: Should Justices Rethink Their Consensus Norms?" *Hofstra Law Review* 43, no. 2 (Winter 2014): 377–415; and Jon D. Noland, "Stare Decisis and the Overruling of Constitutional Decisions in the Warren Years," *Valparaiso University Law Review* 4, no. 1 (1969): 101–35. Two notable cases that include lists of overrulings are the "Brandeis brief" in *Burnet v. Coronado Oil & Gas Co.,* 285 U.S. 393, 406 (1932) (Brandeis, J., dissenting); and the appendix in the dissenting opinion of Justices Breyer, Sotomayor, and Kagan in *Dobbs v. Jackson Women's Health Organization,* 597 U.S. ___ (2022) (slip op., 61–66).

Table 5. Overruling Cases in the United States Supreme Court

Key to Source Abbreviations		
B	"'Overruling' Opinions"	Blaustein & Field
Br	Dissent in *Burnet v Coronado*	Brandeis
D	"Stare Decisis"	Douglas
C	*Supreme Court Decisions Overrruled by Subsequent Decisions*	GPO
E	"Overruling Statutory Precedents"	Eskridge
G	"Role of Precedent"	Gerhardt
J	*Dobbs v. Jackson*	USSC
L	"Death of a Precedent"	LeRoy
N	"Stare Decisis"	Noland
S	*2020 Supreme Court Database*	Spaeth et al.
T	"Supreme Court Decisions"	Congressional Research Service

Overruling Case	Overruled Case(s)	Identified by
Hudson v. Guestier, 10 U.S. (6 Cr.) 281 (1810)	Rose v. Himley, 8 U.S. (4 Cr.) 241 (1808)	B, Br, C, D, L, S, T
Gordon v. Ogden, 28 U.S. (3 Pet.) 33 (1830)	Wilson v. Daniel, 3 U.S. (3 Dall.) 401 (1798)	B, Br, C, L, S, T
Green v. Lessee of Neal, 31 U.S. (6 Pet.) 291 (1832)	Patton v. Easton, 14 U.S. (1 Wheat.) 476 (1816); Powell's Lessee v. Harman, 27 U.S. (2 Pet.) 241 (1829)	B, C, L, S, T
Louisville, Cincinnati & Charleston Railroad v. Letson, 43 U.S. (2 How.) 497 (1844)	Commercial and Railroad Bank v. Slocomb, 39 U.S. (14 Pet.) 60 (1840); Strawbridge v. Curtiss, 7 U.S. (3 Cr.) 267 (1806); and qualifying, Bank of the United States v. Deveaux, 9 U.S. (5 Cr.) 61 (1809)	B, Br, C, L, S, T
The Propeller *Genessee Chief* v. Fitzhugh, 53 U.S. (12 How.) 443 (1851)	The *Thomas Jefferson*, 23 U.S. (10 Wheat.) 428 (1825); The *Orleans* v. Phoebus, 36 U.S. (11 Pet.) 175 (1837)	B, Br, C, G, L, S, T
Gazzam v. Lessee of Phillips, 61 U.S. (20 How.) 372 (1858)	Brown's Lessee v. Clements, 44 U.S. (3 How.) 650 (1845)	B, Br, C, L, S, T
Suydam v. Williamson, 65 U.S. (24 How.) 427 (1861)	Williamson v. Berry, 49 U.S. (8 How.) 495 (1850); Williamson v. Irish Presbyterian Congregation, 49 U.S. (8 How.) 565 (1850); Williamson v. Ball, 49 U.S. (8 How.) 566 (1850)	B, C, L, S, T

Overruling Case	Overruled Case(s)	Identified by
Mason v. Eldred, 73 U.S. (6 Wall.) 231 (1868)	Sheehy v. Mandeville, 10 U.S. (6 Cr.) 253 (1810)	B, Br, C, D, L, S, T
The Belfast, 74 U.S. (7 Wall.) 624 (1869)	Allen v. Newberry, 62 U.S. (21 How.) 244 (1858) (in part)	B, Br, C, D, L, S, T
Knox v. Lee (Legal Tender Cases), 79 U.S. (12 Wall.) 457 (1871)	Hepburn v. Griswold, 75 U.S. (8 Wall.) 603 (1870)	B, Br, C, D, G, L, S, T
Trebilcock v. Wilson, 79 U.S. (12 Wall.) 687 (1871)	Roosevelt v. Meyer, 68 U.S. (1 Wall.) 512 (1863)	B, C, D, L, S, T
Hornbuckle v. Toombs, 85 U.S. (18 Wall.) 648 (1874)	Noonan v. Lee, 67 U.S. (2 Black) 499 (1863); Orchard v. Hughes, 68 U.S. (1 Wall.) 73, 77 (1864); Dunphy v. Kleinsmith, 78 U.S. (11 Wall.) 610 (1871)	B, Br, D, C, E, L, S, T
Union Pacific Railway v. McShane, 89 U.S. (22 Wall.) 444 (1874)	Kansas Pacific Railway v. Prescott, 83 U.S. (16 Wall.) 603 (1873) (in part)	B, C, D, L, S, T
County of Cass v. Johnston, 95 U.S. 360 (1877)	Harshman v. Bates County, 92 U.S. 569 (1875)	B, C, D, L, S, T
Fairfield v. County of Gallatin, 100 U.S. 47 (1879)	Town of Concord v. Portsmouth Savings Bank, 92 U.S. 625 (1875)	B, Br, C, D, L, S, T
Tilghman v. Proctor, 102 U.S. 707 (1880)	Mitchell v. Tilghman, 86 U.S. (19 Wall.) 287 (1873)	B, C, D, L, S, T
Kilbourn v. Thompson, 103 U.S. 168 (1881)	Anderson v. Dunn, 19 U.S. (6 Wheat.) 204 (1821)	B, Br, C, D, G, L, S, T
United States v. Phelps, 107 U.S. 320 (1883)	Shelton v. The Collector, 72 U.S. (5 Wall.) 113 (1867)	B, Br, C, D, L, S, T
Kountze v. Omaha Hotel Co., 107 U.S. 378 (1883)	Stafford v. The Union Bank of Louisiana, 57 U.S. (16 How.) 135 (1853)	B, Br, C, D, L, S, T
Morgan v. United States, 113 U.S. 476 (1885)	Texas v. White, 74 U.S. (7 Wall.) 700 (1869)	B, Br, C, D, L, S, T
Wabash, St. Louis & Pacific Railway Co. v. Illinois, 118 U.S. 557 (1886)	Peik v. Chicago & Northwestern Railway Co., 94 U.S. 164 (1877)	B, C, D, S
Philadelphia Steamship Co. v. Pennsylvania, 122 U.S. 326 (1887)	State Tax on Railway Gross Receipts, 82 U.S. (15 Wall.) 284 (1873)	B, Br, C, D, G, S, T
In re Ayers, 123 U.S. 443 (1887)	Osborn v. Bank of the United States, 22 U.S. (9 Wheat.) 738 (1824)	B, C, D, G, S, T
Leloup v. Port of Mobile, 127 U.S. 640 (1888)	Osborne v. City of Mobile, 83 U.S. (16 Wall.) 479 (1873)	B, Br, C, D, G, L, S, T

Overruling Case	Overruled Case(s)	Identified by
Leisy v. Hardin, 135 U.S. 100 (1890)	Peirce v. New Hampshire, 46 U.S. (5 How.) 504 (1846); Thurlow v. Massachusetts, 46 U.S. (5 How.) 504 (1847) (also known as the License Cases)	B, Br, C, D, G, L, S, T
Brenham v. German-American Bank, 144 U.S. 173 (1892)	Rogers v. Burlington, 10 U.S. (3 Wall.) 654 (1866); Mitchell v. Burlington, 71 U.S. (4 Wall.) 270 (1867)	B, Br, C, L, S, T
Roberts v. Lewis, 153 U.S. 367 (1894)	Giles v. Little, 104 U.S. 291 (1881)	B, Br, C, L, S, T
Pollock v. Farmers' Loan & Trust Co., 158 U.S. 601 (1895)	Hylton v. United States, 3 U.S. (3 Dall.) 171 (1796)	B, Br, C, S
Minnesota Rate Case, 230 U.S. 352 (1913)	Peik v. Chicago & Northwestern Railway Co., 94 U.S. 164 (1877)	S, T
Garland v. Washington, 232 U.S. 642 (1914)	Crain v. United States, 162 U.S. 625 (1896)	B, Br, C, G, L, S, T
United States v. Nice, 241 U.S. 591 (1916)	Matter of Heff, 197 U.S. 488 (1905)	B, Br, C, G, L, S, T
Motion Picture Patents Co. v. Universal Film Manufacturing Co., 243 U.S. 502 (1917)	Henry v. A. B. Dick Co., 224 U.S. 1 (1912)	B, Br, L, S, T
Pennsylvania Railroad Co. v. Towers, 245 U.S. 6 (1917)	Lake Shore & Michigan Southern Railway Co. v. Smith, 173 U.S. 684 (1899) (in part)	B, Br, C, G, L, S, T
Boston Store v. American Graphophone Co., 246 U.S. 8 (1918)	Henry v. A. B. Dick Co., 224 U.S. 1 (1912)	S, T
Rosen v. United States, 245 U.S. 467 (1918)	United States v. Reid, 53 U.S. (12 How.) 361 (1851)	B, Br, C, L, S, T
Terral v. Burke Constr. Co., 257 U.S. 529 (1922)	Doyle v. Continental Ins. Co., 94 U.S. 535 (1877); Security Mut. Life Ins. Co. v. Prewitt, 202 U.S. 246 (1906)	B, Br, C, G, L, S, T
Lee v. Chesapeake & Ohio Railway, 260 U.S. 653 (1923)	Ex parte Wisner, 203 U.S. 449 (1906); In re Moore, 209 U.S. 490 (1908) (in part)	B, Br, C, L, S, T
Alpha Cement Co. v. Massachusetts, 268 U.S. 203 (1925)	Baltic Mining Co. v. Massachusetts, 231 U.S. 68 (1913)	B, Br, C, G, L, S, T
Chesapeake & Ohio Railway v. Leitch, 276 U.S. 429 (1928) (rehearing)	Chesapeake & Ohio Railway v. Leitch, 275 U.S. 507 (1927)	B, Br, C
Gleason v. Seaboard Railway, 278 U.S. 349 (1929)	Friedlander v. Texas & Pac. Railway, 130 U.S. 416 (1889) (in part)	B, Br, C, L, S, T

Overruling Case	Overruled Case(s)	Identified by
Farmers Loan Co. v. Minnesota, 280 U.S. 204 (1930)	Blackstone v. Miller, 188 U.S. 189 (1903)	B, Br, C, G, L, S, T
East Ohio Gas Co. v. Tax Commission, 283 U.S. 465 (1931)	Pennsylvania Gas Co. v. Public Serv. Commission, 252 U.S. 23 (1920)	B, Br, C, G, L, S, T
Fox Film Corp. v. Doyal, 286 U.S. 123 (1932)	Long v. Rockwood, 277 U.S. 142 (1928)	B, C, G, L, S, T
Chicago & E.I.R.R. v. Industrial Commission, 284 U.S. 296 (1932)	Erie Railroad v. Collins, 253 U.S. 77 (1920); Erie Railroad v. Szary, 253 U.S. 86 (1920)	B, Br, C, G, L, S, T
Funk v. United States, 290 U.S. 371 (1933)	Stein v. Bowman, 38 U.S. (13 Pet.) 209 (1839) (in part); Hendrix v. United States, 219 U.S. 79 (1911); Logan v. United States, 144 U.S. 263 (1892); Jin Fuey Moy v. United States, 254 U.S. 189 (1920)	B, C, S, T
New York ex rel. Northern Finance Corp. v. Lynch, 290 U.S. 601 (1933)	Macallen Co. v. Massachusetts, 279 U.S. 620 (1929)	C
United States v. Hastings, 296 U.S. 188 (1935)	United States v. Stevenson, 215 U. S. 190 (1909)	S
West Coast Hotel Co. v. Parrish, 300 U.S. 379 (1937)	Adkins v. Children's Hospital, 261 U.S. 525 (1923); Morehead v. New York ex rel. Tipaldo, 298 U.S. 587 (1936)	B, C, G, L, S, T
Railroad Commission v. Pacific Gas Co., 302 U.S. 388 (1938) (rehearing)	Railroad Commission v. Pacific Gas Co., 301 U.S. 669 (1937)	B, C, S
Helvering v. Producers Corp., 303 U.S. 376 (1938)	Gillespie v. Oklahoma, 257 U.S. 501 (1922); Burnet v. Coronado, Oil & Gas Co. 285 U.S. 393 (1932)	B, C, D, G, L, S, T
Helvering v. Bankline Oil Co., 303 U.S. 362 (1938).	Burnet v. Coronado Oil & Gas Co., 285 U. S. 393	S
Erie Railroad Co. v. Tompkins, 304 U.S. 64 (1938)	Swift v. Tyson, 41 U.S. (16 Pet.) 1 (1842)	B, C, D, G, L, S, T
Graves v. New York ex rel. O'Keefe, 306 U.S. 466 (1939)	Dobbins v. Commissioners of Erie County, 41 U.S. (16 Pet.) 435 (1842); Collector v. Day, 78 U.S. (11 Wall.) 113 (1871); New York ex rel. Rogers v. Graves, 299 U.S. 401 (1937); Brush v. Commissioners, 300 U.S. 352 (1937)	B, C, D, G, L, S, T
Rochester Telephone Corp. v. United States, 307 U.S. 125 (1939)	Procter & Gamble v. United States, 225 U.S. 282 (1912)	B, C, L, S, T

Overruling Case	Overruled Case(s)	Identified by
O'Malley v. Woodrough, 307 U.S. 277 (1939)	Evans v. Gore, 253 U.S. 245 (1920); Miles v. Graham, 268 U.S. 501 (1925)	B, C, D, G, S, T
Madden v. Kentucky, 309 U.S. 83 (1940)	Colgate v. Harvey, 296 U.S. 404 (1935)	B, C, D, G, L, S, T
Helvering v. Hallock, 309 U.S. 106 (1940)	Helvering v. St. Louis Trust Co., 296 U.S. 39 (1935); Becker v. St. Louis Trust Co., 296 U.S. 48 (1935)	B, C, D, G, L, S, T
Tigner v. Texas, 310 U.S. 141 (1940)	Connolly v. Union Sewer Pipe Co., 184 U.S. 540 (1902)	B, C, D, G, L, S, T
Delaware River Joint Toll Bridge Commission v. Colburn, 310 U.S. 419 (1940)	People v. Central Railroad, 79 U.S. (12 Wall.) 455 (1870)	S
United States v. Darby, 312 U.S. 100 (1941)	Hammer v. Dagenhart, 247 U.S. 251 (1918); Carter v. Carter Coal Co., 298 U.S. 238 (1936) (in part)	B, C, D, G, L, S, T
United States v. Chicago, M., St. P. & P.R.R., 312 U.S. 592 (1941)	United States v. Lynah, 188 U.S. 445 (1903) (in part); United States v. Heyward, 250 U.S. 633 -1919	B, C, D, E, G, S, T
Nye v. United States, 313 U.S. 33 (1941)	Toledo Newspaper Co. v. United States, 247 U.S. 402 (1918)	B, C, D, L, S, T
California v. Thompson, 313 U.S. 109 (1941)	Di Santo v. Pennsylvania, 273 U.S. 34 (1927)	B, C, D, G, L, S, T
United States v. Classic, 313 U.S. 299 (1941)	Newberry v. United States, 256 U.S. 232 (1921)	B, C, S
Olsen v. Nebraska ex rel. Western Reference and Bond Association, 313 U.S. 236 (1941)	Ribnik v. McBride, 277 U.S. 350 (1928)	B, C, D, G, L, S, T
Alabama v. King & Boozer, 314 U.S. 1 (1941)	Panhandle Oil Co. v. Knox, 277 U.S. 218 (1928); Graves v. Texas Co., 298 U.S. 393 (1936)	B, C, D, G, L, S, T
Toucey v. N.Y. Life Ins. Co., 314 U.S. 118 (1941)	Supreme Tribe of Ben-Hur v. Cauble, 255 U.S. 356 (1921)	B, C, L, S, T
Edwards v. California, 314 U.S. 160 (1941)	City of New York v. Miln, 36 U.S. (11 Pet.) 102 (1837)	B, C, S, T
Graves v. Schmidlapp, 315 U.S. 657 (1942)	Wachovia Bank & Trust Co. v. Doughton, 272 U.S. 567 (1926)	S, T
State Tax Commission v. Aldrich, 316 U.S. 174 (1942)	First National Bank v. Maine, 284 U.S. 312 (1932)	B, C, D, G, L, S, T
Williams v. North Carolina, 317 U.S. 287 (1942)	Haddock v. Haddock, 201 U.S. 562 (1906)	B, C, D, G, L, S, T

Overruling Case	**Overruled Case(s)**	**Identified by**
Brady v. Roosevelt Steamship Co., 317 U.S. 575 (1943)	Johnson v. Fleet Corp., 280 U.S. 320 (1930)	B, C, D, L, S, T
Jones v. Opelika, 319 U.S. 103 (1943) (rehearing)	Jones v. Opelika, 316 U.S. 584 (1942)	B, C, D, G, S, T
Murdock v. Pennsylvania, 319 U.S. 105 (1943)	Jones v. Opelika, 316 U.S. 584 (1942)	S, T
Oklahoma Tax Commission v. United States, 319 U.S. 598 (1943)	Childers v. Beaver, 270 U.S. 555 (1926)	B, C, D, G, L, S, T
West Virginia State Board of Education v. Barnette, 319 U.S. 624 (1943)	Minersville School District v. Gobitis, 310 U.S. 586 (1940)	B, C, D, G, L, S, T
FPC v. Hope Natural Gas Co., 320 U.S. 591 (1944)	United Railways v. West, 280 U.S. 234 (1930) (in part)	B, C, D, L, S, T
Mercoid Corp. v. Mid-Continent Co., 320 U.S. 661 (1944)	Leeds & Catlin Co. v. Victor Talking Machine Co. (No. 2), 213 U.S. 325 (1909) (limited)	B, C, D, S, T
Mahnich v. Southern Steamship Co., 321 U.S. 96 (1944)	Plamals v. Pinar Del Rio, 277 U.S. 151 (1828) (in part)	B, C, D, L, S, T
Smith v. Allwright, 321 U.S. 649 (1944)	Grovey v. Townsend, 295 U.S. 45 (1935)	B, C, D, G, L, S, T
United States v. South-Eastern Underwriters Association, 322 U.S. 533 (1944)	Paul v. Virginia, 75 U.S. (8 Wall.) 168 (1869)	B, C, D, L, S, T
Girouard v. United States, 328 U.S. 61 (1946)	United States v. Schwimmer, 279 U.S. 644 (1929); United States v. Macintosh, 283 U.S. 605 (1931); United States v. Bland, 283 U.S. 636 (1931)	B, C, D, G, L, S, T
Halliburton Co. v. Walker, 329 U.S. 1 (1946) (rehearing)	Halliburton Co. v. Walker, 326 U.S. 696 (1946)	B, C, S
MacGregor v. Westinghouse Co., 329 U.S. 402 (1947) (rehearing)	MacGregor v. Westinghouse Co., 327 U.S. 758 (1946)	B, C, S
Angel v. Bullington, 330 U.S. 183 (1947)	David Lupton's Sons v. Automobile Club of America, 225 U.S. 489 (1912)	B, C, D, G, S, T
Zap v. United States, 330 U.S. 800 (1947) (rehearing)	Zap v. United States, 328 U.S. 624 (1946)	B, C
Thibaut v. Car and General Insurance Corp., 332 U.S. 828 (1947) (rehearing)	Thibaut v. Car and General Insurance Corp., 332 U.S. 751 (1947)	B, C
Sherrer v. Sherrer, 334 U.S. 343 (1948)	Andrews v. Andrews. 188 U.S. 14 (1903) (in part)	B, C, D, S, T

Overruling Case	Overruled Case(s)	Identified by
Lincoln Fed. Labor Union v. Northwestern Iron & Metal Co., 335 U.S. 525 (1949)	Adair v. United States, 208 U.S. 161 (1908); Coppage v. Kansas, 236 U.S. 1 (1915)	C, D, G, S, T
Commissioner v. Estate of Church, 335 U.S. 632 (1949)	May v. Heiner, 281 U.S. 238 (1930)	B, C, D, L, S, T
Ott v. Mississippi Barge Line, 336 U.S. 169 (1949)	St. Louis v. Ferry Company, 78 U.S. (11 Wall.) 423 (1870); Old Dominion Steamship Co. v. Virginia, 198 U.S. 299 (1905); Ayer & Lord Co. v. Kentucky, 202 U.S. 409 (1906)	B, C, S
Oklahoma Tax Commission v. Texas Co., 336 U.S. 342 (1949)	Choctaw & Gulf Railroad v. Harrison, 235 U.S. 292 (1914); Indian Oil Co. v. Oklahoma, 240 U.S. 522 (1916); Howard v. Gipsy Oil Co., 247 U.S. 503 (1918); Large Oil Co. v. Howard, 248 U.S. 549 (1919); Oklahoma v. Barnsdall Corp., 296 U.S. 521 (1936)	B, C, D, G, L, S, T
Cosmopolitan Co. v. McAllister, 337 U.S. 783 (1949)	Hust v. Moore-McCormack Lines, 328 U.S. 707 (1946)	B, C, L, S, T
United States v. Rabinowitz, 339 U.S. 56 (1950)	Trupiano v. United States, 334 U.S. 699 (1948); McDonald v. United States, 335 U.S. 451 (1948)	B, C, G, L, S, T
Darr v. Burford, 339 U.S. 200 (1950)	Wade v. Mayo, 334 U. S. 672 (1948)	S
Standard Oil Co. v. Peck, Tax Commissioner, et al., 342 U.S. 382 (1951)	Ayer & Lord Tie Co. v. Kentucky, 202 U.S. 409 (1906); Old Dominion Steamship Co. v. Virginia, 198 U.S. 299 (1905); St. Louis v. The Ferry Co., 78 U.S. (11 Wall.) 423 (1870)	S, T
Joseph Burstyn, Inc. v. Wilson, 343 U.S. 495 (1952)	Mutual Film Corp. v. Ohio Indus. Commission, 236 U.S. 230 (1915)	B, C, G, L, S, T
Brown v. Board of Education, 347 U.S. 483 (1954)	Cumming v. County Board of Education, 175 U.S. 528 (1899); Gong Lum v. Rice, 275 U.S. 78 (1927); Plessy v. Ferguson, 163 U.S. 537 (1896)	C, L, S
In re Isserman, 348 U.S. 1 (1954) (on rehearing)	In re Isserman, 345 U.S. 286 (1953)	B, C, S
Carroll v. Lanza, 349 U.S. 408 (1955)	Bradford Electric Light Co. v. Clapper, 286 U.S. 145 (1932)	N, T, S
Gayle v. Browder, 352 U.S. 903 (1956)	Plessy v. Ferguson, 163 U.S. 537 (1896)	B, C, N, S
Reid v. Covert, 354 U.S. 1 (1957)	Kinsella v. Krueger, 351 U.S. 470 (1956); Reid v. Covert, 351 U.S. 487 (1956)	B, C, N, S, T

Overruling Case	Overruled Case(s)	Identified by
Vanderbilt v. Vanderbilt, 354 U.S. 416 (1957)	Thompson v. Thompson, 226 U.S. 551 (1913); United States v. Reese, 92 U.S. 214 (1876)	C, L, S, T
Green v. United States, 355 U.S. 184 (1957)	Trono v. United States, 199 U.S. 521 (1905)	N
Ladner v. United States, 358 U.S. 169 (1958) (rehearing)	Ladner v. United States, 355 U.S. 282 (1958)	C, S
United States v. Raines, 362 U.S. 17 (1960)	United States v. Reese, 92 U.S. 214 (1876)	C, S, T
Elkins v. United States, 364 U.S. 206 (1960)	Weeks v. United States, 232 U.S. 383 (1914) (in part); Center v. United States, 267 U.S. 575 (1925); Byars v. United States, 273 U.S. 28, 33 (1927) (in part); Feldman v. United States, 322 U.S. 487 (1944) (in part)	C, G, L, N, S
James v. United States, 366 U.S. 213 (1961)	Commissioner v. Wilcox, 327 U.S. 404 (1946)	C, E, L, S, T
Mapp v. Ohio, 367 U.S. 643 (1961)	Wolf v. Colorado, 338 U.S. 25 (1949) (in part); Irvine v. California, 347 U.S. 128 (1954) (in part)	C, G, L, N, S, T
Baker v. Carr, 369 U.S. 186 (1962)	Colegrove v. Green, 328 U.S. 549 (1946) (in part)	C, S
Glidden Co. v. Zdanok, 370 U.S. 530 (1962)	Ex parte Bakelite Corp., 279 U.S. 438 (1929); Williams v. United States, 289 U.S. 553 (1933)	N
Smith v. Evening News Association, 371 U.S. 195, 199 (1962)	Westinghouse Employees v. Westinghouse Corp., 348 U.S. 437 (1955) (in part)	C, E, L, S, T
Construction Laborers v. Curry, 371 U.S. 542 (1963)	Building Union v. Ledbetter Co., 344 U.S. 178 (1952) (in part)	C, E, J, L, S
Townsend v. Sain, 372 U.S. 293 (1963)	Brown v. Allen, 344 U.S. 443 (1953)	T
Gideon v. Wainwright, 372 U.S. 335 (1963)	Betts v. Brady, 316 U.S. 455 (1942)	C, L, G, N, S, T
Gray v. Sanders, 372 U.S. 368 (1963)	Cook v. Fortson, 329 U.S. 675 (1946); Turman v. Duckworth, 329 U.S. 675 (1946); South v. Peters, 339 U.S. 276 (1950); Hartsfield v. Sloan, 357 U.S. 916 (1958)	C, S
Fay v. Noia, 372 U.S. 391 (1963)	Darr v. Burford, 339 U.S. 200 (1950) (in part)	C, E, L, S, T
Ferguson v. Skrupa, 372 U.S. 726 (1963)	Adams v. Tanner, 244 U.S. 590 (1917)	C, G, L, S, T

Overruling Case	Overruled Case(s)	Identified by
Wesberry v. Sanders, 376 U.S. 1 (1964)	Colegrove v. Barrett, 330 U.S. 804 (1947)	C, N, S, T
Schneider v. Rusk, 377 U.S. 163 (1964)	Mackenzie v. Hare, 239 U.S. 299 (1915)	C, S
Williams v. Florida, 399 U.S. 78 (1970)	Thompson v. Utah, 170 U.S. 343 (1898) (in part); Rassmussen v. United States, 197 U.S. 516 (1905) (in part)	C, G, L, S, T
Blonder-Tongue Labs v. University of Ill. Found., 402 U.S. 313 (1971)	Triplett v. Lowell, 297 U.S. 638 (1936)	C, E, L, S, T
Perez v. Campbell, 402 U.S. 637 (1971)	Kesler v. Department of Public Safety, 369 U.S. 153 (1962); Reitz v. Mealey, 314 U.S. 33 (1941)	C, G, L, S, T
Griffin v. Breckenridge, 403 U.S. 88 (1971)	Collins v. Hardyman, 341 U.S. 651 (1951) (in part)	C, E, L, S, T
Dunn v. Blumstein, 405 U.S. 330 (1972)	Pope v. Williams, 193 U.S. 621 (1904)	C, G, L, S
Illinois v. City of Milwaukee, 406 U.S. 91 (1972)	Romero v. International Terminal Operating Co., 358 U. S. 354 (1959)	S
Andrews v. Louisville & Nashville Railroad, 406 U.S. 320 (1972)	Moore v. Illinois Central Railroad, 312 U.S. 630 (1941)	C, E, L, S, T
Lehnhausen v. Lake Shore Auto Parts Co., 410 U.S. 356 (1973)	Quaker City Cab Co. v. Pennsylvania, 277 U.S. 389 (1928)	C, G, L, S, T
Braden v. 30th Judicial Circuit Court, 410 U.S. 484 (1973)	Ahrens v. Clark, 335 U.S. 188 (1948)	C, E, L, S, T
Miller v. California, 413 U.S. 15 (1973)	A Book Named "John Cleland's Memoirs of a Woman of Pleasure" v. Attorney General, 383 U.S. 413 (1966)	C, G, S, T
In re Griffiths, 413 U.S. 717 (1973)	Clarke v. Deckebach, 274 U.S. 392 (1927)	L
North Dakota State Board of Pharmacy v. Snyder's Drug Stores, 414 U.S. 156 (1973)	Liggett Co. v. Baldridge, 278 U.S. 105 (1928)	C, G, L, S, T
Edelman v. Jordan, 415 U.S. 651 (1974)	Shapiro v. Thompson, 394 U.S. 618 (1969) (in part); State Department of Health & Rehabilitative Services v. Zarate, 407 U.S. 918 (1972); Sterrett v. Mothers' & Children's Rights Org., 409 U.S. 809 (1973); Wyman v. Bowens, 397 U.S. 49 (1970)	C, G, L, S, T
Mitchell v. W. T. Grant Co., 416 U.S. 600 (1975)	Fuentes v. Shevin, 407 U.S. 67 (1972) (in part)	C, J, S

Overruling Case	Overruled Case(s)	Identified by
Taylor v. Louisiana, 419 U.S. 522 (1975)	Hoyt v. Florida, 368 U.S. 57 (1961)	C, G, L, S, T
United States v. Reliable Transfer Co., 421 U.S. 397 (1975)	The Schooner *Catherine* v. Dickinson, 58 U.S. (17 How.) 170 (1854)	C, L, S, T
Michelin Tire Corp. v. Wages, 423 U.S. 276 (1976)	Low v. Austin, 80 U.S. (13 Wall.) 29 (1872)	C, G, L, S, T
Dove v. United States, 423 U.S. 325 (1976)	Durham v. United States, 401 U.S. 481 (1971)	C, L, S, T
Hudgens v. NLRB, 424 U.S. 507 (1976)	Amalgamated Food Employees Union v. Logan Valley Plaza, 391 U.S. 308 (1968)	C, G, L, S, T
Virginia Board of Pharmacy v. Virginia Citizens Consumer Council, 425 U.S. 748 (1976)	Valentine v. Chrestensen, 316 U.S. 52 (1942)	C, G, L, S, T
National League of Cities v. Usery, 426 U.S. 833 (1976)	Maryland v. Wirtz, 392 U.S. 183 (1968); National Bellas Hess, Inc. v. Department of Revenue, 386 U.S. 753 (1967)	C, G, L, S, T
Machinists & Aerospace Workers v. WERC, 427 U.S. 132 (1976)	UAW v. WERB, 336 U.S. 245 (1949)	C, E, L, S, T
City of New Orleans v. Dukes, 427 U.S. 297 (1976)	Morey v. Doud, 354 U.S. 457 (1957)	C, G, L, S, T
Gregg v. Georgia, 428 U.S. 153 (1976)	McGautha v. California, 402 U.S. 183 (1971)	C, S, T
Standard Oil Co. of California v. United States, 429 U.S. 17 (1976)	In re Potts, 166 U. S. 263 (1897)	S
Craig v. Boren, 429 U.S. 190 (1976)	Goesaert v. Cleary, 335 U.S. 464 (1948)	C, G, J, L, S, T
Oregon ex rel. State Land Board v. Corvallis Sand & Gravel Co., 429 U.S. 363 (1977)	Bonelli Cattle Co. v. Arizona, 414 U.S. 313 (1973)	C, G, L, S, T
Califano v. Sanders, 430 U.S. 99 (1977)	Citizens to Preserve Overton Park v. Volpe, 401 U. S. 402 (1971); Abbott Laboratories v. Gardner, 387 U. S. 136 (1967); Rusk v. Cort, 369 U. S. 367 (1962)	L
Complete Auto Transit, Inc. v. Brady, 430 U.S. 274 (1977)	Spector Motor Serv. v. O'Connor, 340 U.S. 602 (1951)	C, G, L, S, T
Trimble v. Gordon, 430 U.S. 762 (1977)	Labine v. Vincent, 401 U. S. 532 (1971)	L

Overruling Case	Overruled Case(s)	Identified by
Continental T. V. v. GTE Sylvania, 433 U.S. 36 (1977)	United States v. Arnold Schwinn & Co., 388 U.S. 365 (1967)	C, E, L, S, T
Wainwright v. Sykes, 433 U.S. 72 (1977)	Fay v. Noia, 372 U.S. 391 (1963) (in part)	L, S
Shaffer v. Heitner, 433 U.S. 186 (1977)	Pennoyer v. Neff, 95 U.S. 714 (1878)	C, G, L, S, T
Department of Revenue v. Washington Stevedoring Cos., 435 U.S. 734 (1978)	Puget Sound Stevedoring Co. v. State Tax Commission, 302 U.S. 90 (1937); Joseph v. Carter & Weekes Stevedoring Co., 330 U.S. 422 (1947)	C, G, L, S, T
Monell v. New York City Department of Social Services, 436 U.S. 658 (1978)	Monroe v. Pape, 365 U.S. 167 (1961) (in part); City of Kenosha v. Bruno, 412 U.S. 507 (1973) (in part); Moor v. County of Alameda, 411 U.S. 693 (1973) (in part); Aldinger v. Howard, 427 U.S. 1 (1976)	C, E, L, S, T
Burks v. United States, 437 U.S. 1 (1978)	Bryan v. United States, 338 U.S. 552 (1950) (in part); Sapir v. United States, 348 U.S. 373 (1955) (in part); Yates v. United States, 354 U.S. 298 (1957) (in part); Forman v. United States, 361 U.S. 416 (1960) (in part)	C, L, S, T
United States v. Scott, 437 U.S. 82 (1978)	United States v. Jenkins, 420 U.S. 358 (1975)	C, G, L, S, T
Hughes v. Oklahoma, 441 U.S. 322 (1979)	Geer v. Connecticut, 161 U.S. 519 (1896)	C, L, S, T
Trammel v. United States, 445 U.S.40 (1980)	Hawkins v. United States, 358 U.S. 74 (1958)	C, E, G, L, S, T
United States v. Salvucci, 448 U.S. 83 (1980)	Jones v. United States, 362 U.S. 257 (1960)	C, G, L, S, T
Thomas v. Washington Gas Light Co., 448 U.S. 261 (1980)	Magnolia Petroleum Co. v. Hunt, 320 U. S. 430 (1943)	S
Commonwealth Edison Co. v. Montana, 453 U.S. 609 (1981)	Heisler v. Thomas Colliery Co., 260 U.S. 245 (1922)	C, G, L, S, T
United States v. Ross, 456 U.S. 798 (1982)	Robbins v. California, 453 U.S. 420 (1981)	C, G, L, S, T
Sporhase v. Nebraska ex rel. Douglas, 458 U.S. 941 (1982)	Hudson County Water Co. v. McCarter, 209 U.S. 349 (1908)	C, G, S, T
Illinois v. Gates, 462 U.S. 213 (1983)	Aguilar v. Texas, 378 U.S. 108 (1964); Spinelli v. United States, 393 U.S. 410 (1969)	C, G, L, S, T

Overruling Case	Overruled Case(s)	Identified by
Bob Jones Univ. v. United States, 461 U.S. 574 (1983)	Plessy v. Ferguson, 163 U.S. 537 (1896)	S, T
Michigan v. Long, 463 U.S. 1032 (1983)	Lynch v. New York ex rel. Pierson, 293 U. S. 52 (1934)	S
Pennhurst State School & Hospital v. Halderman, 465 U.S. 89 (1984)	Rolston v. Missouri Fund Comm'rs, 120 U.S. 390 (1887) (in part); Siler v. Louisville & Nashville Railroad, 213 U.S. 175 (1909) (in part); Atchison, T. & S.F. Railway v. O'Connor, 223 U.S. 280 (1912) (in part); Greene v. Louisville & Interurban Railroad, 244 U.S. 499 (1917) (in part); Johnson v. Lankford, 245 U.S. 541 (1918) (in part); Numerous other cases fall more or less under the Pennhurst doctrine. See 465 U.S. 109–111 nn.17–21, 117–121 (maj.op.), and id. at 130–37, 159–163, 165–166 nn.50 & 52 (dissent) (listing 28 cases)	C, G, S, T
United States v. One Assortment of 89 Firearms, 465 U.S. 354 (1984)	Coffey v. United States, 116 U.S. 436 (1886)	C, E, G, L, S, T
Limbach v. Hooven & Allison Co., 466 U.S. 353 (1984)	Hooven & Allison Co. v. Evatt, 324 U.S. 652 (1945)	C, G, L, S, T
Copperweld Corp. v. Independence Tube Corp., 467 U.S. 752 (1984)	United States v. Yellow Cab Co., 332 U.S. 218 (1947); Kiefer-Stewart Co. v. Jos. E. Seagram & Sons, 340 U.S. 211 (1951)	C, E, L, S, T
Brown v. Department of Law & Pub. Safety, 468 U.S. 491 (1984)	Hill v. Florida ex rel. Watson, 325 U.S. 538 (1945)	E, S
Garcia v. San Antonio Metro. Transit Auth., 469 U.S. 528 (1985)	National League of Cities v. Usery, 426 U.S. 833 (1976)	C, G, S, T
United States v. Miller, 471 U.S. 130 (1985)	Ex parte Bain,121 U.S. 1 (1887) (in part)	C, G, S, T
Daniels v. Williams, 474 U.S. 327 (1986)	Parratt v. Taylor, 451 U.S. 527 (1981) (in part)	C, G, L, S, T
United States v. Lane, 474 U.S. 438 (1986)	McElroy v. United States, 164 U.S. 76 (1896)	C, E, S
Batson v. Kentucky, 476 U.S. 79 (1986)	Swain v. Alabama, 380 U.S. 202 (1965) (in part)	C, G, L, S, T
Puerto Rico v. Branstad, 483 U.S. 219 (1987)	Kentucky v. Dennison, 65 U.S. (24 How.) 66 (1861)	C, E, G, L, S, T

Overruling Case	Overruled Case(s)	Identified by
Tyler Pipe Indus., Inc. v. Washington State Department of Revenue, 483 U.S. 232 (1987)	General Motors Corp. v. Washington, 377 U.S. 436 (1964)	L, S, T
Solorio v. United States, 483 U.S. 435 (1987)	O'Callahan v. Parker, 395 U.S. 258 (1969)	C, G, L, S, T
Welch v. Texas Department of Highways and Transportation, 483 U.S. 468 (1987)	Parden v. Terminal Railway, 377 U.S. 184 (1964)	C, E, G, L, S, T
Gulfstream Aerospace Corp. v. Mayacamas Corp., 485 U.S. 271 (1988)	Enelow v. New York Life Ins. Co., 293 U.S. 379 (1935); Ettelson v. Metropolitan Life Ins. Co., 317 U.S. 188 (1942)	C, L, S, T
South Carolina v. Baker, 485 U.S. 505 (1988)	Pollock v. Farmers' Loan & Trust Co., 157 U.S. 429 (1895)	C, G, L, S, T
Thornburgh v. Abbott, 490 U.S. 401 (1989)	Procunier v. Martinez, 416 U.S. 396 (1974) (in part)	C, G, L, S, T
Rodriguez de Quijas v. Shearson/American Express, 490 U.S. 477 (1989)	Wilko v. Swann, 346 U.S. 427 (1953)	C, L, S, T
Alabama v. Smith, 490 U.S. 794 (1989)	Simpson v. Rice, 395 U.S. 711 (1969); North Carolina v. Pearce, 395 U.S. 711 (1969)	C, G, L, S, T
Healy v. The Beer Institute, 491 U.S. 324 (1989)	Joseph E. Seagram & Sons v. Hostetter, 384 U.S. 35 (1966)	C, G, L, S, T
W. S. Kirkpatrick & Co. v. Environmental Tectonics Corp., 493 U.S. 400 (1990)	American Banana Co. v. United Fruit Co., 213 U.S. 347 (1909)	C, L, S, T
Collins v. Youngblood, 497 U.S. 37 (1990)	Kring v. Missouri, 107 U.S. 221 (1883); Thompson v. Utah, 170 U.S. 343 (1898)	C, G, L, S, T
Arizona v. Fulminante, 499 U.S. 279 (1991)	Chapman v. California, 386 U.S. 18 (1967) (in part)	C, S
California v. Acevedo, 500 U.S. 565 (1991)	Arkansas v. Sanders, 442 U.S. 743 (1979)	C, G, L, S, T
Exxon Corp. v. Central Gulf Lines, Inc., 500 U.S. 603 (1991)	Minturn v. Maynard, 58 U.S. (17 How.) 476 (1855)	C, L, S, T
Coleman v. Thompson, 501 U.S. 722 (1991)	Fay v. Noia, 372 U.S. 391 (1963)	C, S, T
Payne v. Tennessee, 501 U.S. 808 (1991)	Booth v. Maryland, 482 U.S. 496 (1987); South Carolina v. Gathers, 490 U.S. 805 (1989)	C, G, L, S, T

Overruling Case	Overruled Case(s)	Identified by
Keeney v. Tamayo-Reyes, 504 U.S. 1 (1992)	Townsend v. Sain, 372 U.S. 293 (1963) (in part)	C, L, S, T
Quill Corp. v. North Dakota, 504 U.S. 298 (1992)	National Bellas Hess Inc. v. Department of Revenue, 386 U.S. 753 (1967) (in part)	C, S, T
Planned Parenthood of Southeastern Pennsylvania v. Casey, 505 U.S. 833 (1992)	City of Akron v. Akron Center for Reproductive Health, 462 U.S. 416 (1983) (in part); Thornburgh v. American College of Obstetricians and Gynecologists, 476 U.S. 747 (1986) (in part)	C, L, S, T
United States v. Dixon, 509 U.S. 688 (1993)	Grady v. Corbin, 495 U.S. 508 (1990)	C, L, S, T
Nichols v. United States, 511 U.S. 738 (1994)	Baldasar v. Illinois, 446 U.S. 222 (1980)	C, S, T
Director, Office of Workers' Compensation Programs v. Greenwich Collieries, 512 U.S. 267 (1994)	NLRB v. Transportation Management Corp., 462 U. S. 393 (1983) (in part)	S
Hubbard v. United States, 514 U.S. 695 (1995)	United States v. Bramblett, 348 U.S. 503 (1955)	C, S, T
Adarand Constructors, Inc. v. Pena, 515 U.S. 200 (1995)	Metro Broadcasting Inc. v. FCC, 497 U.S. 547 (1990); Fullilove v. Klutznick, 448 U.S. 448 (1990) (in part)	C, L, S, T
United States v. Gaudin, 515 U.S. 506 (1995)	Sinclair v. United States, 279 U.S. 263 (1929)	C, L, S, T
Fulton Corp. v. Faulkner, 516 U.S. 325 (1996)	Darnell v. Indiana, 226 U.S. 390 (1912)	C, S, T
Seminole Tribe of Florida v. Florida, 517 U.S. 44 (1996)	Pennsylvania v. Union Gas Co., 491 U.S. 1 (1989)	C, L, S, T
44 Liquormart, Inc. v. Rhode Island, 517 U.S. 484 (1996)	California v. LaRue, 409 U.S. 109 (1972) (in part); New York State Liquor Authority v. Bellanca, 452 U.S. 714 (1981) (in part); City of Newport v. Iacobucci, 479 U.S. 92 (1986) (in part)	C, S, T
Lewis v. Casey, 518 U.S. 343 (1996)	Flast v. Cohen, 392 U. S. 83, 101 (1968); Bounds v. Smith, 430 U. S. 817 (1977) (in part)	S
Agostini v. Felton, 521 U.S. 203 (1997)	Aguilar v. Felton, 473 U.S. 402 (1985); Grand Rapids School District v. Ball, 473 U.S. 373 (1985) (in part)	C, J, L, S, T
State Oil Co. v. Khan, 522 U.S. 3 (1997)	Albrecht v. Herald Co., 390 U.S. 145 (1968)	C, L, S, T
Hudson v. United States, 522 U.S. 93 (1997)	United States v. Halper, 490 U.S. 435 (1989)	C, S, T

Overruling Case	Overruled Case(s)	Identified by
Hohn v. United States, 524 U.S. 236 (1998)	House v. Mayo, 324 U.S. 42 (1945)	C, L, S, T
Minnesota v. Mille Lacs Band of Chippewa Indians, 526 U.S. 172 (1999)	Ward v. Race Horse, 163 U.S. 504 (1896) (in part)	C, S, T
College Savings Bank v. Florida Prepaid Postsecondary Educ. Expense Bd., 527 U.S. 666 (1999)	Parden v. Terminal Railway, 377 U.S. 184 (1964) (in part)	C, S, T
Mitchell v. Helms, 530 U.S. 793 (2000)	Meek v. Pittenger, 421 U.S. 349 (1975); Wolman v. Walter, 433 U.S. 229 (1977)	C, L, S, T
United States v. Hatter, 532 U.S. 557 (2001)	Evans v. Gore, 253 U.S. 245 (1920)	C, L, S, T
Lapides v. Board of Regents, 535 U.S. 613 (2002)	Ford Motor Co. v. Department of Treasury of Indiana, 323 U.S. 459 (1945)	C, L, S, T
Atkins v. Virginia, 536 U.S. 304 (2000)	Penry v. Lynaugh, 492 U.S. 302 (1989)	C, S, T
United States v. Cotton, 535 U.S. 625 (2002)	Ex parte Bain, 121 U.S. 1 (1887) (in part)	L, S, T
Ring v. Arizona, 536 U. S. 584 (2002)	Walton v. Arizona, 497 U.S. 302 (1989)	C, J, L, S, T
Lawrence v. Texas, 539 U.S. 558 (2003)	Bowers v. Hardwick, 478 U.S. 186 (1986)	C, L, S, T
Crawford v. Washington, 541 U.S. 36 (2004)	Ohio v. Roberts, 448 U.S. 56 (1980)	C, L, S, T
Roper v. Simmons, 543 U.S. 551 (2005)	Stanford v. Kentucky, 492 U.S. 361 (1989)	C, S, T
Central Virginia Community College v. Katz, 546 U.S. 356 (2006)	Hoffman v. Connecticut Department of Income Maintenance, 492 U.S. 96 (1989)	C, S, T
Illinois Tool Works, Inc. v. Independent Ink, Inc., 547 U.S. 28 (2006)	International Salt Co. v. United States, 332 U. S. 392 (1947); United States v. Loew's Inc., 371 U. S. 38, 46 (1962)	S
Gonzales v. Carhart, 550 U.S. 124 (2007)	Stenberg v. Carhart, 530 U.S. 914 (2000)	C, S
Bell Atlantic Corp. v. Twombly, 550 U.S. 544 (2007)	Conley v. Gibson, 355 U. S. 41, 47 (1957)	S
Bowles v. Russell, 551 U.S. 205 (2007)	Harris Truck Lines, Inc. v. Cherry Meat Packers, Inc., 371 U. S. 215 (1962) (per curiam); Thompson v. INS, 375 U. S. 384 (1964) (per curiam)	S

Overruling Case	Overruled Case(s)	Identified by
Parents Involved in Community Schools v. Seattle School District No. 1, 551 U.S. 701 (2007)	School Comm. of Boston v. Board of Education, 389 U. S. 572 (1968) (per curiam); Swann v. Charlotte-Mecklenburg Bd. of Ed., 402 U. S. (1971)	C, S
Leegin Creative Leather Prods., Inc. v. PSKS, Inc., 551 U.S. 877 (2007)	Dr. Miles Med. Co. v. John D. Parks & Sons Co., 220 U.S. 373 (1911)	L, S, T
Pearson v. Callahan, 555 U.S. 223 (2009)	Saucier v. Katz, 533 U.S. 194 (2001)	C, J, S, T
Montejo v. Louisiana, 556 U.S. 778 (2009)	Michigan v. Jackson, 475 U.S. 625 (1986)	C, L, S, T
Citizens United v. FEC, 558 U.S. 310 (2010)	Austin v. Michigan State Chamber of Commerce, 494 U.S. 652 (1990); McConnell v. Federal Election Commission, 540 U.S. 93 (2003).	C, L, S, T
McDonald v. Chicago, 561 U.S. 742 (2010)	United States v. Cruikshank, 92 U.S. 542 (1876); Presser v. Illinois, 116 U.S. 252 (1886); Miller v. Texas, 153 U.S. 535 (1894)	C, S
Bond v. United States, 564 U.S. 211 (2011)	Tennessee Elec. Power Co. v. TVA, 306 U. S. 118 (1939)	S
Alleyne v. United States, 570 U.S. 99 (2013)	Apprendi v. New Jersey, 530 U.S. 466 (2000)	C, J, S, T
Obergefell v. Hodges, 576 U.S. 644 (2015)	Baker v. Nelson, 409 U.S. 810 (1972)	C, S, T
Johnson v. United States, 576 U.S. 591 (2015)	James v. United States, 550 U.S. 192 (2007); Sykes v. United States, 564 U.S. 1(2011)	C, S, T
Hurst v. Florida, 136 S. Ct. 616 (2016)	Spaziano v. Florida, 468 U.S. 447 (1984); Hildwin v. Florida, 490 U.S. 638 (1989)	C, S, T
Trump v. Hawaii, No. 17-965 (U.S. June 26, 2018)	Korematsu v. United States, 323 U.S. 214 (1944)	S, T
South Dakota v. Wayfair, No. 17-494 (U.S. June 21, 2018)	National Bellas Hess v. Department of Revenue of Illinois, 386 U.S. 753 (1967); Quill Corp. v. North Dakota, 504 U.S. 298 (1992)	J, S, T
Janus v. American Federation of State, County, & Municipal Employees, Council 31, No. 16-1466 (U.S. June 27, 2018)	Abood v. Detroit Board of Education, 431 U.S. 209 (1977)	S, T
Rucho v. Common Cause, No. 18-422 (U.S. June 27, 2019)	Davis v. Bandemer, 478 U.S. 109 (1986)	S, T
Rucho v. Common Cause, No. 18-422 (U.S. June 27, 2019)	Davis v. Bandemer, 478 U.S. 109 (1986)	S, T

Overruling Case	Overruled Case(s)	Identified by
Knick v. Township of Scott, No. 17-647 (U.S. June 21, 2019)	Williamson County Regional Planning Commission v. Hamilton Bank of Johnson City, 473 U.S. 172 (1985) (in part)	S, T
Herrera v. Wyoming, No. 17-532 (U.S. May 20, 2019).	Ward v. Race Horse, 163 U.S. 504 (1896).	S, T
Franchise Tax Board of California v. Hyatt, No. 17-1299 (U.S. May 13, 2019).	Nevada v. Hall, 440 U.S. 410 (1979).	J, S, T
Ramos v. Louisiana, No. 18-5924 (U.S. Apr. 20, 2020)	Apodaca v. Oregon, 406 U.S. 404 (1972) (plurality opinion); Johnson v. Louisiana, 406 U.S. 404 (1972)	S, T
Edwards v. Vannoy, 593 U.S. ___ (2021)	Teague v. Lane, 489 U.S. 288 (1989)	S
Dobbs v. Jackson Women's Health Organization, No. 19-1391 (U.S. June 24, 2022)	Planned Parenthood of Southeastern Pennsylvania v. Casey, 505 U.S. 833 (1992); Roe v. Wade, 410 U.S. 113 (1973)	T

APPENDIX B: CASES EXCLUDED FROM OVERRULING LIST

THE CHART BELOW LISTS CASES identified by a single source as overruling that I have reviewed and rejected for the reasons noted. The two sources cited are *Supreme Court Decisions Overruled by Subsequent Decisions*, GovInfo (Washington, DC: Government Publishing Office, 2017) (C); and Michael H. LeRoy, "Death of a Precedent: Should Justices Rethink their Consensus Norms?" *Hofstra Law Review* 43, no. 2 (Winter 2014): 377–415 (L) (see appendix A).

Table 6. Excluded Cases in the United States Supreme Court Identified as Overruling

Overruling Case	Overruled Case	Source	Explanation for Exclusion
United States v. City of Detroit, 355 U.S. 466 (1958)	United States v. Allegheny City, PA, 322 U.S. 174 (1944)	L	The court says: "In urging that the tax assessed here be struck down, the appellants rely primarily on *United States v. Allegheny County*, 322 U. S. 174, but we do not think that case is at all controlling" (471).
Gold v. DiCarlo 380 U.S. 520 (1965)	Tyson & Bro. v. Banton 273 U.S. 418 (1927)	C	The overruling opinion is a single line that doesn't mention *Tyson*.
G.M. Leasing Corp. v. United States, 429 U.S. 338 (1977).	Boyd v. United States, 116 U.S. 616 (1886)	L	The Court says: "We do not find in *Boyd* any direct holding that the warrant protections of the Fourth Amendment do not apply to invasions of privacy in furtherance of tax collection. Insofar as language in Boyd might be read so to state, we decline to follow those dicta into rejection of the basic governing principle that has shaped Fourth Amendment law" (356). Because the majority is clarifying "dicta," and no dissent disputes this, I assume this case did not overrule a "holding."

Overruling Case	Overruled Case	Source	Explanation for Exclusion
Duren v. Missouri, 439 U.S. 357 (1978)	Hoyt v. Florida, 368 U.S. 57 (1961)	C	According to *The Oxford Companion to the Supreme Court*, *Hoyt* was, in effect, overturned by *Taylor v. Louisiana*, though the majority there distinguished it by insisting it involved a different constitutional provision. In *Duren*, the majority doesn't even mention *Hoyt*. The lone dissenter, Justice Rehnquist, mentions *Hoyt* but doesn't say it was overruled.

NOTES

Chapter 1

1. Julia Malone, "The President in Atlanta: Campaign Finance: As Bush Quietly Signs Limits, Opponents Swing into Action," *Atlanta Journal-Constitution*, March 28, 2002, A14.

2. "Campaign Finance Bill Likely Dead for the Year," *CNN* (online), February 26, 1998.

3. Malone, "President in Atlanta."

4. Citizens United v. Federal Election Commission, 558 U.S. 310 (2010). Citations to this case will be made in the text.

5. The conservative bloc included Chief Justice Roberts and Justices Kennedy, Scalia, Thomas, and Alito.

6. McConnell v. Federal Election Commission, 540 U.S. 93 (2003).

7. Quoted in *Citizens United v. Federal Election Commission*, 558 U.S. 310, 456 (2003) (Stevens, J., dissenting).

8. Austin v. Michigan Chamber of Commerce, 494 U.S. 652 (1990).

9. Quoting *Vasquez v. Hillery*, 474 U.S. 254, 265 (1986) at 414.

10. Neil Nagraj, "Justice Alito Mouths 'Not True' When Obama Blasts Supreme Court Ruling in State of the Union Address," *Daily News*, January 28, 2010.

11. Stephen A. Smith, "Citizens Undone: Freedom of Speech, Political Discourse, and the Import of *Citizens United v. Federal Election Commission*," in Rountree, *Venomous Speech* (Westport, CT: Praeger, 2013), 149.

12. Smith, "Citizens Undone," 158–59.

13. Smith, "Citizens Undone," 158.

14. The legal realists were among the first to challenge law as a set of logically consistent rules and principles that allowed judges to reach determinate outcomes through a value-neutral process. They began writing around 1920 and were led by Karl Llewellyn, Walter Wheeler Cook, Jerome Frank, Herman Oliphant, and Underhill Moore. See Yosal Rogat, "Legal Realism," in *Encyclopedia of Philosophy* (New York: Macmillan, 1967), 420. The quotation is taken from Clarke Rountree, *Judging the Supreme Court: Constructions of Motives in* Bush v. Gore, Rhetoric & Public Affairs (East Lansing: Michigan State University Press, 2007), 3.

15. Michigan v. Bay Mills Indian Community, 572 U.S. ___, ___ (2014) (slip op., at 15). Akron v. Akron Center for Reproductive Health, 462 U.S. 416, 420 (1983).

16. The next chapter will explain the varied sources of these estimates.

17. Raymond S. Rodgers, "Absolutism and Natural Law Argument: William O. Douglas on Freedom of Expression," *Southern Speech Communication Journal* 48, no. 1 (1982): 23–26.

18. Frederick G. Kempin Jr., "Precedent and Stare Decisis: The Critical Years, 1800–1850," *American Journal of Legal History* 3, no. 1 (1959): 33.

19. Ovid C. Lewis, "The High Court: Final . . but Fallible," *Case Western Reserve Law Review* 19, no. 3 (1968): 540.

20. Quoted in Lewis, "High Court," 540.

21. Lewis, "High Court," 540.

22. Swift v. Tyson, 41 U.S. (16 Pet.) 1, 18 (1842).

23. Southern Pacific Co. v. Jensen, 244 U.S. 205, 222 (1917).

24. Quoted in C. Sumner Lobingier, "Precedent in Past and Present Legal Systems," *Michigan Law Review* 44, no. 6 (1946): 969.

25. "The Status of the Rule of Judicial Precedent," *University of Cincinnati Law Review* 14 (1940): 223.

26. Quoted in Peter Wesley-Smith, "Theories of Adjudication and the Status of Stare Decisis," in *Stare Decisis*, ed. Lawrence Goldstein (New York: Oxford University Press, 1987), 78.

27. Quoted in Kempin, "Precedent and Stare Decisis," 33.

28. Quoting *Butler v. Van Wyck*, 1 Hill 438 (1841) in William Green, "Stare Decisis," *American Law Review* 14 (September 1880): 636.

29. H. Campbell Black, "Principle of Stare Decisis," *American Law Register* 25 (December 1886): 749.

30. Quoted in Gerald J Postema, "Some Roots of Our Notion of Precedent," in *Precedent in Law*, ed. Lawrence Goldstein (New York: Oxford University Press, 1987), 9.

31. Southern Pacific Co. v. Jensen, 244 U.S. 205, 222 (1917).

32. H. L. A. Hart, "Positivism and the Separation of Law and Morals," *Harvard Law Review* 71, no. 4 (1958): 593–629.

33. Hart, "Positivism and the Separation," 607.

34. The metaphor of *penumbra* here comes from astronomy, where during the waning or eclipse of the moon the shadowed or "penumbral" area hides (darkened) lunar features from clear view. Hart refers to the unclear, dark, or hidden parts of law, places where what the law requires is not clear.

35. Hart, "Positivism and the Separation," 615.

36. Hart, "Positivism and the Separation," 614.

37. Karl N. Llewellyn, "Some Realism about Realism," in *Jurisprudence: Realism in Theory and Practice*, ed. Karl N. Llewellyn (Chicago: University of Chicago Press, 1962), 56, 58.

38. Llewellyn, "Some Realism," 55.

39. Thomas F. Cotter, "Legal Pragmatism and the Law and Economics Movement," *Georgetown Law Journal* 84, no. 6 (June 1996): 2072.

40. Gary Minda, "The Jurisprudential Movements of the 1980s," *Ohio State Law Journal* 50, no. 3 (Summer 1989): 609.

41. Minda, "Jurisprudential Movements," 609.

42. Edward Cantu, "Posner's Pragmatism and the Turn Toward Fidelity," *Lewis & Clark Law Review* 16, no. 69 (Spring 2012): 70.

43. Nelson argues that you can find an early form of instrumentalism, which involved "an explicit consideration of the 'prospective consequences of the rule' being formulated," from 1820–1850 when American judges supported "general expediency," particularly regarding economic development. William E. Nelson, "The Impact of the Antislavery Movement upon Styles of Judicial Reasoning in Nineteenth Century America," *Harvard Law Review* 87, no. 3 (1974): 514. I exclude consideration of the critical legal studies movement because their skepticism leads them to offer only deconstructions of existing legal theories and practices, rather than a normative theory for how it might best be done. See, for example, Marouf A. Hasian Jr., "Critical Legal Rhetorics: The Theory and Practice of Law in a Postmodern World," *Southern Communication Journal* 60, no. 1 (1994): 44–56.

44. Here I draw primarily upon his seminal legal work, *Taking Rights Seriously*. Ronald Dworkin, *Taking Rights Seriously* (Cambridge, MA: Harvard University Press, 1978).

45. As Dworkin puts it elsewhere, "a judge should regard the law he mines and [in deciding a particular case] as embedded in a much larger system" Ronald Dworkin, "'Natural' Law Revisited," *University of Florida Law Review* 34, no. 2 (Winter 1982): 166. Of course, that could lead laws to be read "against the grain" by judges trying to find good in them, or to be declared unconstitutional where the principles of that document collide with legislation.

46. Dworkin, *Taking Rights Seriously*, 22.

47. Dworkin, "'Natural' Law Revisited," 165.

48. Dworkin, *Taking Rights Seriously*, 116–17.

49. For example, in discussing fairness in the tort case of *MacPherson v. Buick Motor Co.*, 217 N.Y. 382 (1916), Dworkin insists "the main force of the underlying argument of fairness is forward-looking, not backward-looking. The gravitational force of Mrs. MacPherson's case depends not simply on the fact that she recovered for her Buick, but also on the fact that the government proposes to allow others in just her position [of being harmed by a defective product] to recover in the future." Dworkin, *Taking Rights Seriously*, 118.

50. Dworkin, *Taking Rights Seriously*, 81 (emphasis added).

51. Dworkin, *Taking Rights Seriously*, 87.

52. Riggs v. Palmer, 115 N.Y. 506 (1889).

53. Rountree, *Judging the Supreme Court*, 16.

54. Josina M. Makau, "The Supreme Court and Reasonableness," *Quarterly Journal of Speech* 70, no. 4 (1984): 381.

55. Michael R. Hagan, "*Roe v. Wade*: The Rhetoric of Fetal Life," *Central States Speech Journal* 27, no. 3 (1976): 192.

56. Gerald B. Wetlaufer, "Rhetoric and Its Denial in Legal Discourse," *Virginia Law Review* 76 (1990): 1552.

57. James L. Golden and Josina M. Makau, "Perspective on Judicial Reasoning," in *Explorations in Rhetoric: Studies in Honor of Douglas Ehninger*, ed. Ray McKerrow (Glenview, IL: Scott, Foresman, 1982), 173.

58. On the strategic use of language, see, for example, John M. Conley and William M. O'Barr, *Just Words: Law, Language, and Power*, Language and Legal Discourse (Chicago: University of Chicago Press, 1998); Joseph W. Dellapenna and Kathleen Farrell, "Law and the Language of Community: On the Contribution of James Boyd White," *Rhetoric Society Quarterly* 21, no. 3 (1991): 38–58; Peter Goodrich, "Law and Language: An Historical and Critical Introduction," *Journal of Law and Society* 11 (1984): 173–206; Alyson Sprafkin, "Language Strategy and Scrutiny in the Judicial Opinion and the Poem," *Cardozo Studies in Law and Literature* 13, no. 2 (2001): 271–98; James Boyd White, *When Words Lose Their Meaning: Constitutions and Reconstitutions of Language, Character, and Community* (Chicago: University of Chicago Press, 1984); Paul Stob, "Louis Brandeis and the Rhetoric of Transactional Morality," *Rhetoric & Public Affairs* 14, no. 2 (Summer 2011): 261–90; and M. Jack Parker, "The Unique Role of Language in the Judicial Process: After-the-Fact Classification of Human Behavior," in *Dimensions of Argument: Proceedings of the Second Alta Conference on Argument*, ed. George Ziegelmueller and Jack Rhodes (Annandale, VA: Speech Communication Association, 1981), 207–12. On metaphors, see, for example, Haig Bosmajian, *Metaphor and Reason in Judicial Opinions* (Carbondale: Southern Illinois University Press, 1992); Haig Bosmajian, "Fire, Snakes, and Poisons: Metaphors and Analogues in Some Landmark Free Speech Cases," in *Free Speech Yearbook* 20, no. 1 (1981): 16–22; Milner S. Ball, *Lying Down Together: Law, Metaphor, and Theology*, Rhetoric of the Human Sciences (Madison: University of Wisconsin Press, 1985); Anél Boshoff, "Law and Its Rhetoric of Violence," *International Journal for the Semiotics of Law* 26, no. 2 (June 2013): 425–37. On narratives, see, for example, William Lewis, "Of Innocence, Exclusion, and the Burning of Flags: The Romantic Realism of the Law," *Southern Communication Journal* 60, no. 1 (1994): 4–21; Marouf A. Hasian Jr., "In Search of 'Ivan the Terrible': John Demjanjuk and the Judicial Use of Ironic Argumentation," *Argumentation and Advocacy* 39, no. 4 (2003): 231–53; Peter Brooks and Paul Gewirtz, eds., *Law's Stories: Narrative and Rhetoric in the Law* (New Haven, CT: Yale University Press, 1996); L. H. LaRue, *Constitutional Law as Fiction: Narrative in the Rhetoric of Authority* (University Park: Pennsylvania State University Press, 1995); Mysty S. Clapton, "*Murdoch v. Murdoch*: The Organizing Narrative of Matrimonial Property Law Reform," *Canadian Journal of Women and the Law* 20, no. 2 (2008): 199–230. On the construction of persons and actions, see, for example, Rountree, *Judging the Supreme Court*; Clarke Rountree, "Instantiating 'The Law' and Its Dissents in *Korematsu v. United*," *Quarterly Journal of Speech* 87 (February 2001): 1–24; Glenda Conway, "Inevitable Reconstructions: Voice and Ideology in Two Landmark U.S. Supreme Court Opinions," *Rhetoric & Public Affairs* 6, no. 3 (2003): 487–508; and Lewis, "Of Innocence." Arrangement is central to the storytelling of narratives but also of the details. See, for example, my analysis of the case's history of *Bush v. Gore* in Rountree, *Judging the Supreme Court*, 34–37. On appeals to pathos, see, for example, Jamal Greene, "Pathetic Argument in Constitutional Law," *Columbia*

Law Review 113, no. 6 (2013): 1389. For a fairly comprehensive overview of the various types of supporting materials constructed by courts, see Rountree, *Judging the Supreme Court*, 7–10. Many other scholars have examined legal arguments in decisions. For example, Peter Odell Campbell, "The Procedural Queer: Substantive Due Process, *Lawrence v. Texas*, and Queer Rhetorical Futures," *Quarterly Journal of Speech* 98, no. 2 (May 2012): 203–29; Rodgers, "Absolutism and Natural Law Argument"; Carrie Crenshaw, "The Normality of Man and Female Otherness: (Re)Producing Patriarchal Lines of Argument in the Law and the News," *Argumentation & Advocacy* 32, no. 4 (Spring 1996): 170–84; Colin Starger, "Constitutional Law and Rhetoric," *University of Pennsylvania Journal of Constitutional Law* 18, no. 5 (May 2016): 1347–79; Bosmajian, *Metaphor and Reason*; and Robert Danisch, "Aphorisms, Enthymemes, and Oliver Wendell Holmes, Jr. on the First Amendment," *Rhetoric Review* 27, no. 3 (2008): 219–35.

59. On hegemonic ideology in judicial opinions generally, see, for example, Laura Nader, *Harmony Ideology and the Construction of the Law: Justice and Control in a Zapotec Mountain Village* (Palo Alto, CA: Stanford University Press, 1990); and Conway, "Inevitable Reconstructions." On patriarchal ideology, see, for example, Joyce W. Warren, *Women, Money and the Law: Nineteenth-Century Fiction, Gender, and the Courts* (Iowa City: University of Iowa Press, 2005); Angela G. Ray and Cindy Koenig Richards, "Inventing Citizens, Imagining Gender Justice: The Suffrage Rhetoric of Virginia and Francis Minor," *Quarterly Journal of Speech* 93, no. 4 (November 2007): 375–402; Katie L. Gibson, "Judicial Rhetoric and Women's 'Place': The United States Supreme Court's Darwinian Defense of Separate Spheres," *Western Journal of Communication* 71, no. 2 (April 2007): 159–75; and Katie L. Gibson, "In Defense of Women's Rights: A Rhetorical Analysis of Judicial Dissent," *Women's Studies in Communication* 35, no. 2 (January 2012): 123–37. On racist ideology, see, for example, Marouf Hasian Jr., "The Aesthetics of Legal Rhetoric: The Ambiguities of 'Race' in *Adarand v. Peña* and the Beginning of the End of 'Affirmative Action,'" *Howard Journal of Communication* 8, no. 1 (January 1997): 113–27; Cecil J. Hunt II, "The Color of Perspective: Affirmative Action and the Constitutional Rhetoric of White Innocence," *Michigan Journal of Race and Law* 11, no. 2 (2006): 477–555; Jason Edward Black, "Plenary Rhetoric in Indian Country: The *Lone Wolf v. Hitchcock* Case and the Codification of a Weakened Native Character," *Advances in the History of Rhetoric* 11/12 (2008/2009): 59–80; Marouf A. Hasian Jr., Celeste Michelle Condit, and John Louis Lucaites, "The Rhetorical Boundaries of 'The Law': A Consideration of the Rhetorical Culture of Legal Practice and the Case of the 'Separate But Equal' Doctrine," *Quarterly Journal of Speech* 82, no. 4 (1996): 323–42; and Clarke Rountree, ed., Brown v. Board of Education *at Fifty: A Rhetorical Perspective* (Lanham, MD: Lexington Books, 2004). On economic ideology, see, for example, Jessica Reyman, *The Rhetoric of Intellectual Property: Copyright Law and the Regulation of Digital Culture*, Routledge Studies in Rhetoric and Communication (New York: Routledge, 2010); and Marouf Hasian Jr. and Megan D. McFarlane, "A Critique of Jim Aune's Rhetoric, Legal Argumentation, and Historical Materialism," *Argumentation & Advocacy* 50, no. 4 (2014): 210–27.

60. See especially, White, *When Words Lose Their Meaning.*

61. Wetlaufer, "Rhetoric and Its Denial"; Lewis, "Of Innocence," 19n7 (quoting Stanley Fish); Rountree, Judging the Supreme Court, 3; Hasian and McFarlane, "Critique of Jim Aune," 212.

62. Marin Roger Scordato, "Reflections on the Nature of Legal Scholarship in the Post-Realist Era," *Santa Clara Law Review* 48, no. 2 (2008): 370.

63. Scordato, "Reflections," 371.

64. Golden and Makau, "Perspective on Judicial Reasoning," 161. The universal audience is a conception of an ideal audience of reasonable women and men, first introduced in Chaim Perelman and Lucie Olbrechts-Tyteca, *The New Rhetoric: A Treatise on Argumentation,* trans. John Wilkinson and Purcell Weaver (Notre Dame, IN: Notre Dame University Press, 1969), 31–35.

65. Golden and Makau, "Perspective on Judicial Reasoning," 170.

66. Walter Ulrich, "The Creation of a Legacy: Brandeis' Concurring Opinion in Whitney v. California," *Southern Speech Communication Journal* 50, no. 2 (Winter 1985): 143.

67. Thurman Arnold, "Professor Hart's Theology," *Harvard Law Review* 73, no. 7 (1960): 1312.

68. Quoted in Raymond S. Rodgers, "Generic Tendencies in Majority and Non-Majority Supreme Court Opinions: The Case of Justice Douglas," *Communication Quarterly* 30, no. 3 (1982): 232.

69. Golden and Makau, "Perspective on Judicial Reasoning," 171.

70. Scholars from Chancellor Kent to Stephen Toulmin have referred to precedents as having presumption. On Kent, see Christopher G. Tiedeman, "The Doctrine of Stare Decisis, and a Proposal for Modification of Its Practical Application, in the Evolution of the Law," *University Law Review* 3 (January 1896): 13; on Toulmin, see Golden and Makau, "Perspective on Judicial Reasoning," 165.

71. Edward H. Levi, "An Introduction to Legal Reasoning," *University of Chicago Law Review* 15, no. 3 (1948): 1–4.

72. Rountree, *Judging the Supreme Court,* 10.

73. Bush v. Gore, 531 U.S. 98, 109 (2000).

74. Rountree, *Judging the Supreme Court,* 157–58.

75. I developed the theory of rhetorical consequentialism in the following series of publications: Clarke Rountree, "Prospective Argument : Constraining and Licensing Future Arguments," in *Argument and Critical Practices: Proceedings of the Fifth SCA/AFA Conference on Argumentation,* ed. Joseph W. Wenzel (Annandale, VA: Speech Communication Association, 1987), 207–13; "Reversing *Roe v. Wade* Through the Courts: The Rhetorical Strategy of *Americans United for Life,*" paper presented at the National Communication Association Convention, San Francisco, 1989; "Prospective Argument II: Laying the Ground for Future Argument," in *Argument in Controversy: Proceedings of the Seventh SCA/AFA Conference on Argumentation,* ed. Donn W. Parson (Annandale, VA: Speech Communication Association, 1991), 58–63; "Building up to War: Bush's 'Administrative Rhetoric' in the Persian Gulf Conflict," *Speech*

Communication Annual 10 (Spring 1996): 5–19; "Setting the Stage for *Brown v. Board of Education*: The NAACP's Litigation Campaign against the 'Separate but Equal' Doctrine," in Brown v. Board of Education *at Fifty*, 49–90.

76. Quoted in Rodgers, "Generic Tendencies," 232.

77. Quoted in Rodgers, "Generic Tendencies," 232.

78. Burwell v. Hobby Lobby, 573 U.S. ___ (2014); Erin J. Rand, "Fear the Frill: Ruth Bader Ginsburg and the Uncertain Futurity of Feminist Judicial Dissent," *Quarterly Journal of Speech* 101, no. 1 (2015): 74.

79. Newman argues that Scalia's dissents were so fierce as to be damaging. Stephen A Newman, "Political Advocacy on the Supreme Court: The Damaging Rhetoric of Antonin Scalia," *New York Law School Law Review* 51 (2006/2007): 907–26.

80. Daniel Mangis, "Dissent as Prophecy: Justice John Marshall Harlan's Dissent in *Plessy v. Ferguson* as the Religous Rhetoric of Law," in Rountree, Brown v. Board of Education *at Fifty*, 23.

81. The challenge is to agree with an outcome while disagreeing about the best reasons for that outcome or, at least, feeling that something additional needs to be said about the case or at least by the concurring justice. For an early study of a concurring opinion by a rhetorical scholar, see Ulrich, "Creation of a Legacy." See also my analysis of Rehnquist's concurrence in *Bush v. Gore* in Rountree, *Judging the Supreme Court*, 49–56.

82. Lewis, "Of Innocence," 4.

83. Respectively, I am paraphrasing *Payne v. Tennessee*, 501 U.S. 808 (1991); *Brown v. Board of Education*, 349 U.S. 294, 301 (1955); *Bowers v. Hardwick*, 478 U.S. 186 (1986); and *Citizens United v. Federal Election Commission*, 558 U.S. 310 (2010).

84. Chisholm v. Georgia, 2 U.S. 419 (1793).

85. United States v. Nixon, 418 U.S. 683 (1974).

86. Especially important in establishing federal supremacy were *Martin v. Hunter's Lessee*, 1 Wheat. 304 (1816); *McCulloch v. Maryland*, 14 U.S. (4 Wheat.) 316 (1819); *Dartmouth College v. Woodward*, 4 Wheat. 518 (1819); *Cohens v. Virginia*, 6 Wheat. 264 (1821); *Osborn v. Bank of the United States*, 9 Wheat. 738 (1824).

87. NAACP v. Alabama, 357 U.S. 449 (1958).

88. NAACP v. Alabama, 360 U.S. 240, 243–44 (1959).

89. NAACP v. Alabama, 360 U.S. 245 (1959).

90. Quoted in C. Steven Bradford, "Following Dead Precedent: The Supreme Court's Ill-Advised Rejection of Anticipatory Overruling," *Fordham Law Review* 59, no. 1 (1990): 42. A district court had ignored this position in the Flag Salute Cases in the 1940s. See chapter 6 for details on this anticipatory overruling.

91. Scordato, "Reflections," 376.

92. Quoted in Lewis, "Of Innocence," 5.

93. Hasian, "Ivan the Terrible," 236.

94. Edward B. Whitney, "Doctrine of Stare Decisis," *Michigan Law Review* 3, no. 2 (December 1904): 100.

95. Warren E. Wright, "Judicial Rhetoric: A Field for Research," *Speech Monographs* 31, no. 1 (1964): 71.

96. "Status of the Rule," 235.

97. Rule 3.3(a)(2) of the American Bar Association (ABA) Model Rules of Professional Conduct states that a lawyer shall not knowingly "fail to disclose to the tribunal legal authority in the controlling jurisdiction known to the lawyer to be directly adverse to the position of the client and not disclosed by opposing counsel." Rule 3.3(a)(1) states that a lawyer shall not knowingly "make a false statement of fact or law to a tribunal or fail to correct a false statement of law previously made to the tribunal by the lawyer." Quoted in Elaine Bucklo, "The Temptation Not to Disclose Adverse Authority," *Litigation* 40, no. 2 (Winter 2014): 1–4.

98. The case was *Butler & Barker v. Van Wyck*, 1 Hill 438; 1841 NY Lexis 97 (1841), quoted in James Ram and John Townshend, *The Science of Legal Judgment* (New York: Baker, Voorhis, 1871), 228.

99. Mahnich v. Southern Steamship Co., 321 U.S. 96, 112–113 (1944).

100. Rountree, *Judging the Supreme Court*, 171.

101. Jack Crittenden, "Law School Faculties 40% Larger Than 10 Years Ago," *The National Jurist*, March 9, 2010.

102. Law Journals: Submissions and Rankings, 2007–2014, Washington & Lee University Law Library, Lexington, VA.

103. A search of *Books in Print* for titles under only the general term "law" yielded about three thousand books in 2020.

104. I would imagine that literary scholars who study Shakespeare might come close to the intense scrutiny given to the high court, though unlike the Supreme Court, the bard is no longer producing new things to analyze. Likewise, plenty of mathematicians and scientists have scrutinized the writings of Newton, philosophers the writings of Aristotle, and physicists the writings of Einstein. But these are finished oeuvres.

105. Ella Govshtein, "Justice Scalia and His Meta-Canon of Absurdity," *Hofstra Law Review* 35, no. 3 (2007): 1595.

106. Perelman and Olbrechts-Tyteca, *New Rhetoric*, 31–35.

107. Wright, "Judicial Rhetoric," 71.

108. Charles F. Stafford, "The Public's View of the Judicial Role," *Judicature* 52, no. 2 (1968): 73.

109. See Rountree, *Judging the Supreme Court*, chap. 5.

110. Whitney, "Doctrine of Stare Decisis," 101–2.

111. Michael Gerhardt, "The Role of Precedent in Constitutional Decisionmaking and Theory," *George Washington Law Review* 60, no. 1 (1991): 77.

112. Richard Posner, *How Judges Think* (Cambridge, MA: Harvard University Press, 2008), 274.

113. Posner, *How Judges Think*, 274, citing *Newdow v. United States Congress*, 292 F.3d 597, 612 (9th Cir. 2002).

114. Quoting Holmes's *The Common Law* in Henry Paul Monaghan, "Stare Decisis and Constitutional Adjudication," *Columbia Law Review* 88, no. 4 (May 1988): 751n162.

115. Charles P. Curtis, "A Modern Supreme Court in a Modern World," *Vanderbilt Law Review* 4, no. 3 (1951): 445.

116. Scordato, "Reflections," 365–66.

117. Scordato, "Reflections," 366.

118. See, for example, Catherine L. Langford, *Scalia v. Scalia: Opportunistic Textualism in Constitutional Interpretation* (Tuscaloosa: University of Alabama Press, 2008).

119. I discuss the legitimacy functions of the formalist form in Clarke Rountree, "On the Rhetorical Analysis of Judicial Discourse and More: A Response to Lewis," *Southern Communication Journal* 61, no. 2 (Winter 1995): 166–73.

Chapter 2

1. Aside from differences noted below, a key difference, of course, is the fact that courts in England do not exercise judicial review; the country has an unwritten constitution that is interpreted by Parliament as well as the courts, and, until recently, the highest court in England was the upper house of the parliament. As Kocourek notes: "There is a difference here between the United States and England explainable on the ground of difference in location of law's center of gravity. In England that center is in Parliament; in the United States the center is in the highest courts." Albert Kocourek, "Retrospective Decisions and Stare Decisis: A Proposal," *American Bar Association Journal* 17, no. 3 (1931): 181.

2. C. Sumner Lobingier, "Precedent in Past and Present Legal Systems," *Michigan Law Review* 44, no. 6 (1946): 955–56.

3. Lobingier, "Precedent in Past," 956–57, 956–57nn5–10.

4. Lobingier, "Precedent in Past," 960.

5. Lobingier, "Precedent in Past," 960.

6. Clive M. Schmitthoff, "Should Precedents Be Binding?" *Journal of Business Law* (1982): 291.

7. Quoted in Barbara A. Singer, "The Reason of the Common Law," *University of Miami Law Review* 37, no. 3 (1983): 814.

8. Singer, "Reason of the Common Law," 815.

9. Lobingier, "Precedent in Past," 961n34.

10. Lobingier, "Precedent in Past," 960n29.

11. Schmitthoff, "Should Precedents Be Binding?" 295.

12. Quoted in T. Ellis Lewis, "The History of Judicial Precedent IV," *Law Quarterly Review* 190 (April 1932): 246.

13. Quoted in Peter Wesley-Smith, "Theories of Adjudication and the Status of Stare Decisis," in *Stare Decisis*, ed. Lawrence Goldstein (New York: Oxford University Press, 1987), 78.

14. Schmitthoff, "Should Precedents Be Binding?" 294–95.

15. The Constitutional Reform Act of 2005 provided for this change.

16. Chisholm v. Georgia, 2 U.S. (2 Dall.) 419, 441 (1793).

17. Ex Parte Crane, 30 U.S. 190, 222 (1831) (Baldwin, J., dissenting).

18. Cook v. Moffat, 46 U.S. 295, 309 (1847).

19. The Propeller *Genesee Chief* v. Fitzhugh, 53 U.S. 443, 458 (1851).

20. This case, *Knox v. Lee*, 79 U.S. (12 Wall.) 457, 553 (1871), is discussed in the next chapter. It does involve a constitutional question of Congress's authority to print

money and make it a legal tender, but the impact on contracts (and therefore on property) was notable.

21. Craig Joyce, "The Rise of the Supreme Court Reporter: An Institutional Perspective on Marshall Court Ascendancy," *Michigan Law Review* 83, no. 5 (April 1985): 1347.

22. Joyce, "Supreme Court Reporter," 1308.

23. Joyce, "Supreme Court Reporter," 1304, 1319, 1327.

24. Denis P. Duffey Jr., "Genre and Authority: The Rise of Case Reporting in the Early United States," *Chicago-Kent Law Review* 74, no. 1 (1998): 267.

25. Edward B. Whitney, "Doctrine of Stare Decisis," *Michigan Law Review* 3, no. 2 (December 1904): 95.

26. Karl Llewellyn, *The Bramble Bush: On Our Law and Its Study* (New York: Oceana, 1951), 68.

27. Max Radin, "Case Law and Stare Decisis: Concerning *Prajudizienrecht in Amerika*," *Columbia Law Review* 33, no. 2 (1933): 210.

28. Roscoe Pound, "What of Stare Decisis?" *Fordham Law Review* 10, no. 1 (January 1941): 8.

29. Edward H. Levi, "An Introduction to Legal Reasoning," *University of Chicago Law Review* 15, no. 3 (1948): 501.

30. Kelo v. City of New London, 545 U.S. 469 (2005). Further references to this case will be made in the text.

31. Levi, *An Introduction to Legal Reasoning*, 3.

32. Justice Brandeis includes *The Belfast* in his list of Supreme Court overrulings in *Burnet v. Coronado Oil Gas Co.*, 285 U.S. 393, 407 n.2 (1932). Justice Douglas also includes this case in his list. William O Douglas, "Stare Decisis," *Columbia Law Review* 49, no. 6 (June 1949): 756. Blaustein and Field exclude this case. Albert P. Blaustein and Andrew H. Field, "'Overruling' Opinions in the Supreme Court," *Michigan Law Review* 57, no. 2 (1958): 184. I include *The Belfast* in my list of overrulings in appendix A. The cases are *The Belfast*, 74 U.S. (7 Wall.) 624 (1868); and *Allen v. Newberry*, 62 U.S. (21 How.) 244 (1858). The quotation is found at *The Belfast*, 641.

33. Albert W. Alschuler, "Rediscovering Blackstone," *University of Pennsylvania Law Review* 145, no. 1 (November 1996): 1–55.

34. Quoted in Lewis F. Powell Jr., "Stare Decisis and Judicial Restraint," *Vital Speeches of the Day* 56, no. 3 (1989): 71.

35. Powell, "Stare Decisis," 72. Bradford argues to the contrary that stare decisis renders decisions much more important (since they must be followed) and, therefore, more time must be spent getting it right; furthermore, more work is required in distinguishing those binding precedents in future cases. C. Steven Bradford, "Following Dead Precedent: The Supreme Court's Ill-Advised Rejection of Anticipatory Overruling," *Fordham Law Review* 59, no. 1 (1990): 80.

36. Powell, "Stare Decisis," 71.

37. Thomas M. Cooley, *A Treatise on Constitutional Limitations Which Rest upon the Legislative Power of the States of the American Union* (Boston: Little, Brown, 1868), 50.

38. "Stare Decisis," *Albany Law Journal* 6 (November 16, 1872): 329.

39. Screws v. United States, 325 U.S. 91, 112 (1945).

40. Mahnich v. Southern Steamship Co., 321 U.S. 96, 113 (1944) (Roberts, J., dissenting).

41. Smith v. Allwright, 321 U.S. 649, 666 (1944) (Roberts, J., dissenting).

42. Rogers v. Goodwin, 2 Mass 475, 477–78 (1807).

43. James Ram, *The Science of Legal Judgment* (Philadelphia: John S. Littell, 1835), 75 (citations omitted).

44. Leavitt v. Blatchford, 17 N.Y. 521, 543 (1858).

45. Kimble et al. v. Marvel Entertainment, LLC, 576 U.S. ___ (2015) (slip op. at 9).

46. Kimble et al. v. Marvel Entertainment, LLC (slip op. at 10).

47. "Stare Decisis," 329.

48. Burnet v. Coronado Oil & Gas Co., 285 U.S. 393, 406 (1932) (Brandeis, J., dissenting).

49. United States v. South-Eastern Underwriters Association, 322 U.S. 533, 580 (1944) (Stone, J., dissenting).

50. Kimble et al. v. Marvel Entertainment, LLC (slip op. at 8).

51. Emmet H. Wilson, "Stare Decisis, Quo Vadis? The Orphaned Doctrine in the Supreme Court," *Georgetown Law Journal* 33, no. 2 (March 1945): 278.

52. I reviewed early efforts to undermine *Roe* in Clarke Rountree, "Reversing *Roe v. Wade* through the Courts: The Rhetorical Strategy of *Americans United for Life*," paper presented at the National Communication Association Convention, San Francisco, 1989. The case overruling *Roe v. Wade* will be examined at length in chapter 7.

53. Bradford, "Following Dead Precedent," 75. The four key policy concerns he identifies are (1) predictability, certainty, and reliability; (2) fairness and uniformity of treatment; (3) judicial economy; and (4) protecting the public image of the courts.

54. James J. Eisenhower III, "Four Theories of Precedent and Its Role in Judicial Decision," *Temple Law Review* 61, no. 3 (1988): 871.

55. Quoting Justice Smith's opinion in *Pratt v. Brown*, 3 Wis., 603 in Christopher G. Tiedeman, "The Doctrine of Stare Decisis, and a Proposal for Modification of Its Practical Application, in the Evolution of the Law," *University Law Review* 3 (January 1896): 13.

56. Robert H. Jackson, "Decisional Law and Stare Decisis," *American Bar Association Journal* 30 (1944): 334.

57. Mahnich v. Southern Steamship Co., 331 U.S. 96, 112 (1944) (Roberts, J., dissenting).

58. The Legal Tender Cases, 79 U.S. (12 Wall.) 457 (1871), overruled *Hepburn v. Griswold*, 75 U.S. (8 Wall.) 603 (1870). This case is discussed in chapter 3.

59. Quoted in Douglas, "Stare Decisis," 740.

60. Webster v. Reproductive Health Services, 492 U.S. 490, 111 (Blackmun, J., dissenting).

61. Mitchell v. W. T. Grant Co., 416 U.S. 600, 634 (1974) (Stewart, J., dissenting).

62. I will elaborate on the overruling records of all Supreme Courts below.

63. Quoted in Harold J. Spaeth and Jeffrey A. Segal, *Majority Rule or Minority Will:*

Adherence to Precedent on the U.S. Supreme Court (New York: Cambridge University Press, 1999), 12.

64. For example, in the midst of the Burger court's record-breaking overruling spree, Maltz made this complaint. Earl M. Maltz, "Some Thoughts on the Death of Stare Decisis in Constitutional Law," *Wisconsin Law Review* 1980 (1980): 467–96.

65. Planned Parenthood of Southeastern Pennsylvania v. Casey, 505 U.S. 833, 866 (1992).

66. George Edward Sullivan, "The Correct Doctrine of Stare Decisis," *Central Law Journal* 55, no. 19 (1902): 365.

67. Quoting *Leavitt v. Blatchford,* 17 N.Y. 521 (1858) in William Green, "Stare Decisis," *American Law Review* 14 (September 1880): 639.

68. Ann M. Gill, "The Supreme Court's Rhetoric of Legitimization," in Rountree, Brown v. Board of Education *at Fifty*, 153; Richard Kluger, *Simple Justice: The History of* Brown v. Board of Education *and Black America's Struggle for Equality.* (New York: Alfred A. Knopf, 1976). As I will explain in chapter 6, *Brown* did not explicitly overrule *Plessy*, though it rejected the "separate but equal" doctrine and can be said to at least have overruled it "in part." It did explicitly overrule a couple of other cases.

69. Gill, "Supreme Court's Rhetoric," 153.

70. See, for example, Ann E. Burnette, "The Rhetoric of Virginia's Massive Resistance Movement," in Rountree, Brown v. Board of Education *at Fifty*, 119–41.

71. Sullivan, "Correct Doctrine," 374.

72. "The Status of the Rule of Judicial Precedent," *University of Cincinnati Law Review* 14 (1940): 287.

73. Pound, "What of Stare Decisis?" 5–6.

74. This is my own estimate based upon a review of eleven sources that have attempted to account for all, or a particular subset of overrulings, on the date they were published. The most comprehensive sources are ongoing databases, from Harold J. Spaeth et al., *2020 Supreme Court Database*, Version 2021, Release 01; Congressional Research Service, "Table of Supreme Court Decisions Overruled by Subsequent Decisions," *Constitution Annotated: Analysis and Interpretation of the U.S. Constitution*, US Congress website; and *Supreme Court Decisions Overrruled by Subsequent Decision*, GovInfo (Washington, DC: Government Publishing Office, 2017). An early attempt to list all overrulings came from Blaustein and Field, "Overruling Opinions." Other sources include Douglas, "Stare Decisis"; William M. Eskridge Jr., "Overruling Statutory Precedents," *Georgetown Law Review* 76 (April 1988): 1361–1426; Michael Gerhardt, "The Role of Precedent in Constitutional Decisionmaking and Theory," *George Washington Law Review* 60, no. 1 (1991): 68–159; Michael H. LeRoy, "Death of a Precedent: Should Justices Rethink Their Consensus Norms?" *Hofstra Law Review* 43, no. 2 (Winter 2014): 377–415; Jon D. Noland, "Stare Decisis and the Overruling of Constitutional Decisions in the Warren Years," *Valparaiso University Law Review* 4, no. 1 (1969): 101–35; the "Brandeis brief" in *Burnet v. Coronado Oil & Gas Co.,* 285 U.S. 393, 406 (1932) (Brandeis, J., dissenting); and the appendix in the dissenting opinion of Justices Breyer, Sotomayor, and Kagan in *Dobbs v. Jackson Women's Health Organization*, 597 U.S. ___ (2022) (slip op., 61–66).

I include in appendix A all cases identified as overruled by at least two of my eleven sources. In cases where a single source has identified a case as overruling, I have examined the case and come to my own conclusions about whether to include it. I have excluded four such excluded cases, identified in appendix B. As I note below, overrulings often do not explicitly state that they are overruling a case, leading to differences of opinion about whether a case actually overruled another. Nevertheless, as this list demonstrates, there is a substantial history of overruling in the United States Supreme Court.

75. Quoting *McDowell v. Oyer*, 9 Harris' Reports, 423 [21 Pa. 317, 423] (1853) in F. R Aumann, "Judicial Law Making and Stare Decisis," *Kentucky Law Journal* 21, no. 2 (1933): 161n28.

76. Blaustein and Field, "Overruling Opinions," 168.

77. Monell v. New York City Department of Social Services, 436 U.S. 658, 708 (1978) (Powell, J., concurring).

78. Gordon v. Ogden, 28 U.S. (3 Pet.) 33, 34 (1830).

79. Mahnich v. Southern Steam Ship Co., 321, U.S. 96, 105 (1944). Cited in Blaustein and Field, "Overruling Opinions," 168–69.

80. United States v. Darby, 312 U.S. 100, 116–17 (1941).

81. Blaustein and Field call this a "virtual" overruling in "Overruling Opinions," 168. For use of "sub silentio," see "Precedents—Sub Silentio: The Lurking Problem," *New York University Law Review* 29 (May 1954): 1122–31. For "stealth," see, for example, Barry Friedman, "The Wages of Stealth Overruling (with Particular Attention to Miranda v. Arizona)," *Georgetown Law Journal* 99 (November 2010): 1–63.

82. Friedman, "Wages of Stealth Overruling," 4.

83. Douglas, "Stare Decisis," 747.

84. Smith v. Evening News Association, 371 U.S. 195, 199 (1962).

85. Green v. United States, 355 U.S. 184 (1957). Further references to this case will be made in the text.

86. The precedent in question is *Trono v. United States*, 199 U.S. 521 (1905).

87. Richard M. Re, "Narrowing Precedent in the Supreme Court," *Columbia Law Review* 114, no. 7 (November 2014): 1865.

88. Re, "Narrowing Precedent," 1864. With the seating of a solid majority of conservative justices during the Trump presidency and the surprising overruling of *Roe v. Wade* in 2022, the court may be in a new phase where they are not so coy. See chapter 7 for more discussion of this change.

89. Blaustein and Field, "Overruling Opinions," 169–70.

90. The cases were *Patton's Lessee v. Easton*, 14 U.S. (1 Wheat.) 476 (1816), and *Powell's Lessee v. Harmon*, 27 U.S. (2 Pet.) 241 (1829).

91. *Green v. Lessee of Neal*, 31 U.S. (6 Pet.) 291 (1832).

92. Gelpeke v. Dubuque, 68 U.S. (1 Wall.) 175 (1863); cited in H. Campbell Black, "Principle of Stare Decisis," *American Law Register* 25 (December 1886): 753.

93. Gelpeke v. Dubuque, 68 U.S. (1 Wall.) 175, 205 (1863).

94. Douglass v. Pike County, 101 U.S. 677, 687 (1879). This case did not require the high court to reverse itself, as it drew a distinction between *Douglass* and the precedent case.

95. Regarding "obvious error," see Blaustein and Field, "'Overruling' Opinions in the Supreme Court," 168. Blackstone is quoted in Wesley-Smith, "Theories of Adjudication," 78.

96. W. M Lile, "Some Views on the Rule of Stare Decisis," *Virginia Law Review* 4, no. 2 (1916): 100.

97. Helvering v. Hallock, 309 U.S. 106, 122 (1940).

98. Nye v. United States, 313 U.S. 33, 48 (1941).

99. Powell, "Stare Decisis," 72.

100. Kimble et al. v. Marvel Entertainment, LLC, 576 U.S. ___ (2015) (slip op. at 11; citations omitted).

101. Kimble et al. v. Marvel Entertainment, LLC, 576 U.S. ___ (2015) (citations omitted) (Alito, J., dissenting; slip op. at 7).

102. Passenger Cases, 48 U.S. (7 How.) 283, 470 (1849).

103. Burnet v. Coronado Oil & Gas Co., 285 U.S. 393, 405 (1932) (Brandeis, J., dissenting).

104. Maltz, "Some Thoughts," 468.

105. Williams v. United States, 289 U.S. 554, 592 (1933).

106. Smith v. Allwright, 321 U.S. 649, 665 (1944).

107. Douglas, "Stare Decisis," 736.

108. James Ram, *Science of Legal Judgment*, 73.

109. Williams v. Florida, 399 U.S. 78, 127 (1970) (Harlan, J., dissenting).

110. Quoted in Spaeth and Segal, *Majority Rule*, 16.

111. James William Moore and Robert Stephen Oglebay, "The Supreme Court, Stare Decisis and Law of the Case," *Texas Law Review* 21 (May 1943): 523. Their reference to "horse and buggy" days undoubtedly gains meaning from a speech by President Franklin D. Roosevelt, given five years before their essay was published, criticizing the high court in just these terms. See chapter 5 for a detailed description of this criticism.

112. Change in such areas, nonetheless, has been slower than one might imagine. See, for example, Theresa Glennon, "Somebody's Child: Evaluating the Erosion of the Marital Presumption of Paternity," *Virginia Law Review* 102, no. 3 (Spring 2000): 547–605.

113. Rudolf H. Heimanson, "Overruling—an Instrument of Social Change?" *New York Law Forum* 7 (1961): 170.

114. Pound, "What of Stare Decisis?" 11.

115. Quoted in Bradford, "Following Dead Precedent," 70n168.

116. Kenneth Burke, *Language as Symbolic Action* (Berkeley: University of California Press, 1966), 16–20.

117. Vincent M. Barnett Jr., "The Political Philosophy of the New Supreme Court," *Journal of Social Philosophy & Jurisprudence* 7, no. 2 (1942): 116.

118. Noland, "Stare Decisis," 128–29.

119. Swift & Co. v. Wickham, 382 U.S. 111, 116 (1965).

120. Powell, "Stare Decisis," 71.

121. Richard Posner, *How Judges Think* (Cambridge, MA: Harvard University Press, 2008), 276–77.

122. Alleyne v. United States, 133 S. Ct. 2151, 2166 (2013) (Sotomayor, J., concurring).

123. Citizens United v. Federal Election Commission, 558 U.S. 310, 414 (2010) (Stevens, J., dissenting).

124. Knox v. Lee (Legal Tender Cases), 79 U.S. (12 Wall.) 457, 572 (1871), (Chase, C. J., dissenting).

125. Michigan, Petitioner v. Bay Mills Indian Community et al., 134 S. Ct. 2024, 2045 (2014).

126. Union Pacific Railway v. McShane, 89 U.S. (22 Wall.) 444, 461 (1874).

127. Wabash, St. Louis & Pacific Railway Co. v. Illinois, 118 U.S. 557, 568 (1886).

128. Tilghman v. Proctor, 102 U.S. 707 (1880), overruling *Mitchell v. Tilghman*, 86 U.S. (19 Wall.) 287 (1873). Further references to *Proctor* will be made in the text.

129. With the sudden death of Justice Antonin Scalia on February 13, 2016, and the Republican Senate's refusal to let President Obama replace him, the court remained 4-4 for more than a year, bringing this issue to the public's attention. See, for example, Robert Barnes, "Evenly Balanced Court Undercuts Conservative Hopes for Sweeping Wins," *Washington Post*, February 15, 2016, A1.

130. Afroyim v. Rusk, 387 U.S. 253, 255 (1967).

131. Collins v. Youngblood, 497 U.S. 37, 48 (1990).

132. Knox v. Lee (Legal Tender Cases), 79 U.S. (12 Wall.) 457, 553–54 (1871).

133. Noland, "Stare Decisis," 109.

134. Regarding interests of a state, see, for example, *Ramos v. Louisiana*, 590 U.S. ___ (2020) (Alito, J., dissenting at slip op. 2). Regarding interests of the nation, see, for example, *Dickerson v. United States*, 530 U.S. 428, 443 (2000) (a later case clarified that *Dickerson* "was referring not to police reliance on a rule requiring them to provide warnings but to the broader societal reliance on that individual right."); *Arizona v. Gant*, 556 U.S. 332, 350 (2009). Of the public, see, for example, *Planned Parenthood of Southeastern Pennsylvania v. Casey*, 505 U.S. 833, 856 (1992); and of legislators, see, for example, *Hubbard v. United States*, 514 U.S. 695, 714 (1995).

135. Ram, *Science of Legal Judgment*, 69–70.

136. Quoted in Noland, "Stare Decisis," 103.

137. Erie Railroad Co. v. Tompkins, 304 U.S. 64, 74 (1938).

138. North Dakota State Board of Pharmacy v. Snyder's Drug Stores, 414 U.S. 156, 164 (1973).

139. Payne v. Tennessee, 501 U.S. 808, 849 (1991) (Marshall, J., dissenting).

140. Swift & Co. v. Wickham, 382 U.S. 111, 116 (1965).

141. Douglas, "Stare Decisis," 740.

142. Knox v. Lee (Legal Tender Cases), 79 U.S. (12 Wall.) 457, 570 (1871) (Bradley, J., concurring).

143. South Carolina v. Gathers, 490 U.S. 805, 824 (1989) (Scalia, J., dissenting).

144. James Ram and John Townshend, *Science of Legal Judgment*, 201.

145. Genessee Chief v. Fitzhugh, 53 U.S. (12 How.) 443, 456 (1851).

146. Knox v. Lee (Legal Tender Cases), 79 U.S. (12 Wall.) 457, 634 (1871) (Field, J., dissenting).

147. Noland, "Stare Decisis," 128–29.

148. Monell v. New York City Department of Social Services, 436 U.S. 658, 709, note 6 (1978) (Powell, J., concurring).

149. Lile, "Some Views," 100.

150. June Medical Services, LLC v. Russo, 140 S. Ct. at 2134 (2020) (Roberts, C.J., concurring in the judgment).

151. Kimble et al. v. Marvel Entertainment, LLC, 576 U.S. 446, 455 (2015).

152. Vasquez v. Hillery, 474 U.S. 254, 266 (1986) (emphasis added).

153. Arizona v. Rumsey, 467 U.S. 203, 212 (1984) (emphasis added).

154. Garcia v. San Antonio Metropolitan Transit Authority, 469 U.S. 528, 559 (1985) (Powell, J., dissenting); Welch v. Texas Department of Highways and Public Transportation, 483 U.S. 468, 479 (1987); Adarand Constructors, Inc. v. Peña, 515 U.S. 200, 231 (1995); Payne v. Tennessee, 501 U.S. 808, 849 (1991) (Marshall, J., dissenting); United States v. Dixon, 509 U.S. 688, 759 (1993). (Souter, J., dissenting); United States v. International Business Machines Corp., 517 U.S. 843, 856 (1996); Dickerson v. United States, 530 U.S. 428, 443 (2000); Citizens United v. Federal Election Commission, 558 U.S. 310, 377 (2010) (Roberts, C.J., concurring); Halliburton Co. v. Erica P. John Fund, Inc., 573 U.S. 258, 266 (2014); Alleyne v. United States, 570 U.S. 99, 118 (2013) (Sotomayor, J., concurring); Gamble v. United States, 139 S. Ct. 1960, 1969 (2019); Michigan v. Bay Mills Indian Community, 572 U.S. ____, (2014) (slip op. at 15); Allen v. Cooper, 140 S. Ct. 994, 1003 (2020).

155. This is my own estimate based upon a review of eleven sources that have attempted to account for all, or a particular subset of overrulings, on the date they were published. The most comprehensive sources are ongoing databases, from Spaeth et al., *2020 Supreme Court Database*; Congressional Research Service, "Supreme Court Decisions"; and *Supreme Court Decisions Overrruled by Subsequent Decision*. Other sources include the following scholarly publications: Douglas, "Stare Decisis"; Blaustein and Field, "'Overruling' Opinions"; Eskridge, "Overruling Statutory Precedents"; Gerhardt, "Role of Precedent"; LeRoy, "Death of a Precedent"; and Noland, "Stare Decisis." Two notable cases that include lists of overrulings are the "Brandeis brief" in *Burnet v. Coronado Oil & Gas Co.*, 285 U.S. 393, 406 (1932) (Brandeis, J., dissenting); and the appendix in the dissenting opinion of Justices Breyer, Sotomayor, and Kagan in *Dobbs v. Jackson Women's Health Organization*, 597 U.S. ____ (2022) (slip op., 61–66).

156. Knox v. Lee (Legal Tender Cases) 79 U.S. (12 Wall.) 457, 553 (1871).

157. Lee v. Chesapeake & Ohio Railway, 260 U.S. 653, 659–60 (1923), overruling *Ex parte Wisner*, 203 U.S. 449 (1906).

158. Peyton v. Rowe, 391 U.S. 54, 60 (1968), overturning *McNally v. Hill*, 293 U.S. 131 (1934).

159. Mitchell v. Helms, 530 U.S. 793, 835 (2000), overruling *Meek v. Pittenger*, 421 U.S. 349 (1975) and *Wolman v. Walter*, 433 U.S. 229 (1977).

160. Alpha Cement Co. v. Massachusetts, 268 U.S. 203, 218 (1925).

161. Craig v. Boren, 429 U.S. 190, 210n23 (1976), overruling *Goesaert v. Cleary*, 335 U.S. 464 (1948).

162. Escobedo v. Illinois, 378 U.S. 478, 492 (1964), overruling *Crooker v. California*, 357 U.S. 433 (1958) and *Cicenia v. Lagay*, 357 U.S. 504 (1958).

163. Taylor v. Louisiana, 419 U.S. 522, 537 (1975), overruling *Hoyt v. Florida*, 368 U.S. 57 (1961).

164. Ferguson v. Skrupa, 372 U.S. 726, 731 (1963), overruling *Adams v. Tanner*, 244 U.S. 590 (1917).

165. Federal Power Commission v. Hope Natural Gas Co., 320 U.S. 591, 606–7 (1944), overruling *United Railways v. West* 280 U.S. 234 (1930).

166. 44 Liquormart, Inc. v. Rhode Island, 517 U.S. 484, 516 (1996), overruling *California v. LaRue* 409 U.S. 109 (1972).

167. Gazzam v. Lessee of Phillips, 61 U.S. (20 How.) 372, 378 (1858), overruling *Brown's Lessee v. Clements*, 44 U.S. (3 How.) 650 (1845).

168. Griffin v. Breckenridge, 403 U.S. 88, 95–96 (1971), referring to *Collins v. Hardyman*, 341 U.S. 651 (1951). Further references to *Griffin* will be made in the text.

169. See appendix A for a list of which sources support listing particular cases as overruled.

170. Construction Laborers v. Curry, 371 U.S. 542 (1963). Further references to this case are made in the text.

171. Those eleven sources are listed at the beginning of appendix A.

172. Pennhurst State School & Hospital v. Halderman, 465 U.S. 89 (1984). The dissent makes its accusations at 159, 165n50, and 166n52. The majority opinion rejects those accusations at 111n21. I list only the five clearly identified overruled cases for this case in appendix A.

173. Hylton v. United States, 3 U.S. (3 Dall.) 171 (1796), overruled by *Pollock v. Farmers' Loan & Trust Co.*, 158 U.S. 601 (1895), which was subsequently overruled by *South Carolina v. Baker*, 485 U.S. 505 (1988).

174. Darr v. Burford, 339 U.S. 200 (1950), overruled in part in *Fay v. Noia*, 372 U.S. 391 (1963), which was overturned by *Wainwright v. Sykes*, 433 U.S. 72 (1977).

175. Trupiano v. United States, 334 U.S. 699 (1948), and McDonald v. United States, 335 U.S. 451 (1948), overruled by *United States v. Rabinowitz*, 339 U.S. 56 (1950), which was subsequently overruled by *Chimel v. California*, 395 U.S. 752 (1969).

176. Maryland v. Wirtz, 392 U.S. 183 (1968), overruled by *National League of Cities v. Usery*, 426 U.S. 833 (1976), which was subsequently overruled by *Garcia v. San Antonio Metropolitan Transit Authority*, 469 U.S. 528 (1985). Further references to this case will be made in the text.

177. Some of these changes were brought about by the Warren court itself through ensuring equality in electing members of the house through Warren-era decisions that hold out an ideal "one man–one vote" standard.

178. Garcia v. San Antonio Metropolitan Transit Authority, 469 U.S. 528, 557 (1985).

179. Garcia v. San Antonio Metropolitan Transit Authority, 469 U.S. 528, 580 (1985) (Rehnquist, J., dissenting).

180. *United States v. Lopez*, 514 U.S. 549 (1995).

181. Public Law 99-150, passed November 13, 1985.

182. David M. O'Brien, "Business of the Court," in *The Oxford Companion to the*

Supreme Court of the United States, ed. Kermit L. Hall (New York: Oxford University Press, 1992), 106–10.

183. Kenneth W. Moffett et al., "Strategic Behavior and Variation in the Supreme Court's Caseload over Time," *Justice System Journal* 37, no. 1 (January–March 2016): 21.

184. Hudson v. Guestier, 10 U.S. (6 Cr.) 281 (1810).

185. On the origins of this phrase, see Barry Friedman, "The History of the Countermajoritarian Difficulty: Part Four: Law's Politics," *University of Pennsylvania Law Review* 148, no. 4 (April 2000): 974n9.

186. West Coast Hotel Co. v. Parrish, 300 U.S. 379 (1937), overruling *Adkins v. Children's Hospital*, 261 U.S. 525 (1923), and *Morehead v. New York ex rel. Tipaldo*, 298 U.S. 587 (1936).

187. Table 1 rounds up the averages. The Stone court averaged 3.4 overrulings per year, while the Warren court averaged 3.375, making Stone second and Warren third, after the Burger court.

188. Re, "Narrowing Precedent," 1864 The overruling of *Roe v. Wade* in 2022, following President Trump's appointment of three very conservative justices, may mark a change in this reluctance to overrule. Chapter 7 discusses this case in detail.

189. The number of decided cases was drawn from Spaeth et al., *2020 Supreme Court Database*. This database lists all cases argued before the Supreme Court. However, they exclude rulings handed down without argument (often per curiam decisions). Some of the rehearing cases included here as overrulings are among those excluded from this count of total cases. No particular count of the cases decided by the high court will be uncontested, though I believe this database is the most complete and accurate source for those counts.

190. Planned Parenthood of Southeastern Pennsylvania v. Casey, 505 U.S. 833 (1992).

191. William Henry Moody, appointed associate justice in 1906 and serving just under four years, is the lone twentieth-century justice to never join an overruling decision.

192. These justices who never voted in an overruling case include John Jay, John Rutledge, William Cushing, James Wilson, John Blair, James Iredell, Thomas Johnson, William Paterson, Samuel Chase, Oliver Ellsworth, Alfred Moore, Robert Trimble, Phillp P. Barbour, Levi Woodbury, and Rufus W. Peckham. Washington and Chase were on the court when it handed down its first overruling in 1810, but they are not recorded as voting.

193. This number has risen to 118 now that Justice Ketanji Brown Jackson was seated in fall 2022.

194. This ranking does not include cases where justices concurred in part and dissented in part.

195. For example, *Oklahoma Tax Commission v. Texas Co.* 336 U.S. 342 (1949); *Lee v. Chesapeake & Ohio Railway* 260 U.S. 653 (1923); *Joseph Burstyn, Inc. v. Wilson*, 343 U.S. 495 (1952); *Leloup v. Port of Mobile*, 127 U.S. 640 (1888); *East Ohio Gas Co. v. Tax Commission*, 283 U.S. 46 (1931); *Fairfield v. County of Gallatin*, 100

U.S. 47 (1879); *United States v. Phelps*, 107 U.S. 320 (1883); *Union Pacific Railway v. McShane*, 89 U.S. (22 Wall.) 444 (1874); *Roberts v. Lewis*, 153 U.S. 367 (1894); *Brady v. Roosevelt Steamship Co.*, 317 U.S. 575 (1943).

196. On the rise of partisanship in Supreme Court nominations, see generally Trevor Parry-Giles, *The Character of Justice: Rhetoric, Law, and Politics in the Supreme Court Confirmation Process*, Rhetoric and Public Affairs Series (East Lansing: Michigan State University Press, 2006).

197. Charles Fairman, *Reconstruction and Reunion, 1864–88, Part One*, vol. 4 of *History of the Supreme Court of the United States* (New York: Macmillan, 1971), 678.

198. Dobbs v. Jackson Women's Health Organization, No. 19-1391 (U.S. June 24, 2022). Although Chief Justice Roberts concurred in the decision, he would not have overturned *Roe*, making the overruling a 5-4 split.

199. Hylton v. United States, 3 U.S. (3 Dall.) 171 (1796), overruled by *Pollock v. Farmers' Loan & Trust Co.*, 158 U.S. 601 (1895).

200. Sykes v. United States, 564 U.S. 1 (2011), overruled by *Johnson v. United States*, 35 S. Ct. 2551 (2015).

201. Between the two courts they only decided twenty cases, so this is not a surprising record.

202. Green v. Lessee of Neal, 31 U.S. (6 Pet.) 291 (1832), overruled *Powell's Lessee v. Harman*, 27 U.S. (2 Pet.) 241 (1829), and *Patton's Lessee v. Easton*, 14 U.S. (1 Wheat.) 476 (1816).

203. Reid v. Covert (rehearing), 354 U.S. 1 (1957), overruled *Reid v. Covert*, 351 U.S. 487 (1956) and *Kinsella v. Krueger*, 351 U.S. 470 (1956). Further references to the overruling case will be made in the text.

204. Ladner v. United States (rehearing), 358 U.S. 169 (1958), overruled *Ladner v. United States*, 355 U.S. 282 (1958). Further references to the rehearing case will be made in the text.

205. Justice Stewart replaced Justice Burton in the short time between the two cases, so he obviously could not have "switched."

206. Frankfurter did vote with the court in *Brown v. Board of Education*, so he was not uniformly opposed to expanding civil rights.

207. Donald M. Roper, "Goldburg, Arthur Joseph," in Hall, *Oxford Companion*, 340.

208. Roper, "Goldberg, Arthur Joseph," 341.

209. Laura Kalman, "Fortas, Abe," in Hall, *Oxford Companion*, 308–9; Roper, "Goldburg, Arthur Joseph."

210. Escobedo v. Illinois, 378 U.S. 478 (1964), overruled *Crooker v. California*, 357 U.S. 433 (1958) and *Cicenia v. Lagay*, 357 U.S. 504 (1958).

211. Miranda v. Arizona, 384 U.S. 436, 479n48 (1966).

212. Harris v. United States, 382 U.S. 162 (1965), overruling *Brown v. United States*, 359 U.S. 41 (1959).

213. Spevack v. Klein, 385 U.S. 511 (1967), overruling *Cohen v. Hurley*, 366 U.S. 117 (1961).

214. Camara v. Municipal Court, 387 U.S. 523 (1967), overruling *Frank v. Maryland*, 359 U.S. 360 (1959). Justice White replaced Justice Whittaker.

215. Afroyim v. Rusk, 387 U.S. 253 (1967), overruling *Perez v. Brownell,* 356 U.S. 44 (1958).

216. Afroyim v. Rusk, 387 U.S. 253 (1967), quoting Brennan at 255n5, from *Kennedy v. Mendoza-Martinez,* 372 U.S. 144, 187.

217. Carafas v. LaVallee, 391 U.S. 234 (1968), overruled *Parker v. Ellis,* 362 U.S. 574 (1960). Justice Marshall's change was from Justice Clark's support for *Parker* to his absence of a vote in *Carafas.*

218. Quoting *Parker v. Ellis,* 362 U.S. 574, 585 (Warren, C.J., dissenting opinion) at 239.

219. Smith v. Evening News Association, 371 U.S. 195, 199 (1962) overruled *Westinghouse Employees v. Westinghouse Corp.,* 348 U.S. 437 (1955) in part. Further references to *Smith* will be made in the text.

220. Justice White did not immediately succeed Justice Reed; Justice Whittaker had a short term between the two. Nonetheless, White's support in *Smith* opposes Reed's support for *Westinghouse.*

221. Westinghouse Employees v. Westinghouse Corp., 348 U.S. 437, 465 (1955) (Douglas, J., dissenting).

222. Smith v. Evening News Association, 371 U.S. 195, 203 (1962) (Black, J., dissenting).

223. Swift & Co. v. Wickham, 382 U.S. 111 (1965), overruling *Kesler v. Department of Public Safety,* 369 U.S. 153 (1962). Further references to *Swift* are made in the text.

224. Justice Goldberg served in Justice Frankfurter's seat immediately before Justice Fortas, so Fortas was not reversing his immediate predecessor.

225. Justice Black dissented in both *Kesler* and *Swift,* as well as in *Westinghouse* and *Smith.* Justice Douglas dissented in both *Kesler* and *Swift.*

226. Delli Paoli v. United States, 352 U.S. 232 (1957), overruled by *Bruton v. United States,* 391 U.S. 123 (1968). Further references to these cases will be made in the text.

227. Quoting *Krulewitch v. United States,* 336 U.S. 440, 453 (1949) (Jackson, J., concurring) at 129.

228. *Bonelli Cattle Co. v. Arizona,* 414 U.S. 313 (1973) was overruled by *Oregon ex rel. State Land Board v. Corvallis Sand & Gravel Co.,* 429 U.S. 363 (1977). Further references to the *Oregon* case will be made in the text.

229. United States v. Scott, 437 U.S. 82 (1978), overruled *United States v. Jenkins,* 420 U.S. 358 (1975). Further references to the *Scott* case will be made in the text.

230. Michigan, Petitioner v. Bay Mills Indian Community et al., 134 S. Ct. 2024, 2045 (2014).

231. *Parratt v. Taylor,* 451 U.S. 527 (1981) was overruled by *Daniels v. Williams,* 474 U.S. 327 (1986). Further references to these cases will be made in the text.

232. Another change between the 1975 and 1984 decisions described below was the replacement of Justice Stewart with Justice O'Connor. However, the latter took the same position as her predecessor.

233. National League of Cities v. Usery, 426 U.S. 833 (1976).

234. Garcia v. San Antonio Metropolitan Transit Authority, 469 U.S. 528, 538 (1985).

235. Robbins v. California, 453 U.S. 420 (1981), overruled by *United States v. Ross,* 456 U.S. 798 (1982). Further references to *Ross* are made in the text.

236. Later appointments that reversed the ideological approach of justices include the replacement of the liberal Justice Thurgood Marshall with the conservative Justice Thomas in 1991, and the replacement of the conservative Justice White with the liberal Justice Ginsburg in 1993. Justice Breyer replaced a similarly progressive Justice Blackman in 1994, yielding a court that would continue until Chief Justice Rehnquist's death in 2005.

237. Payne v. Tennessee, 501 U.S. 808 (1991); South Carolina v. Gathers, 490 U.S. 805 (1989); Booth v. Maryland, 482 U.S. 496 (1987). Further references to *Payne* will be made in the text.

238. Cases involving double jeopardy: Hudson v. United States, 522 U.S. 93 (1997), overruling *United States v. Halper,* 490 U.S. 435 (1989); United States v. Dixon, 509 U.S. 688 (1993), overruling *Grady v. Corbin,* 495 U.S. 508 (1990). Cases involving the death penalty: Atkins v. Virginia, 536 U.S. 304 (2002), overruling *Penry v. Lynaugh,* 492 U.S. 302 (1989); Roper v. Simmons, 543 U.S. 551 (2005), overruling *Stanford v. Kentucky,* 492 U.S. 361 (1989); and Ring v. Arizona, 536 U.S. 584 (2002), overruling *Walton v. Arizona,* 497 U.S. 639 (1990). Case involving sovereign immunity of states: Seminole Tribe of Florida v. Florida, 517 U.S. 44 (1996), overruling *Pennsylvania v. Union Gas Co.,* 491 U.S. 1 (1989). Case involving affirmative action: Adarand Constructors, Inc. v. Peña, 515 U.S. 200 (1995), overruling *Metro Broadcasting, Inc. v. Federal Communications Commission,* 497 U.S. 547 (1990).

239. Roper v. Simmons, 543 U.S. 551 (2005); Ring v. Arizona, 536 U.S. 584 (2002).

240. Helvering v. Mountain Producers Corp., 303 U.S. 376 (1938), overruling *Burnet v. Coronado Oil & Gas Co.,* 285 U.S. 393 (1932); Madden v. Commissioner, 309 U.S. 83 (1940), overruling *Colgate v. Harvey,* 296 U.S. 404 (1935); Helvering v. Hallock, 309 U.S. 106 (1940), overruling *Becker v. St. Louis Union Trust Co.,* 296 U.S. 48 (1935), and *Helvering v. St. Louis Union Trust Co.,* 296 U.S. 39 (1935); Railroad Commission v. Pacific Gas Co., 302 U.S. 388 (1938) (rehearing), overruling *Railroad Commission v. Pacific Gas Co.,* 301 U.S. 669 (1937). Retirements of those supporting the overruled cases began after the 1936–37 term. See chapter 5 for details about this change.

241. Justices Harlan and Woods were appointed by President Hayes, Justice Matthews by President Garfield, and Justices Gray and Blatchford by President Cleveland over this period. A sixth appointment, Justice Lamar, came near the end of that court in 1888.

242. Tilghman v. Proctor, 102 U.S. 707 (1880), overruling *Mitchell v. Tilghman,* 86 U.S. (19 Wall.) 287 (1873); County of Cass v. Johnston, 95 U.S. 360 (1877), overruling *Harshman v. Bates County,* 92 U.S. 569 (1875); Fairfield v. County of Gallatin, 100 U.S. 47 (1879), overruling *Town of Concord v. Portsmouth Savings Bank,* 92 U.S. 625 (1875); Wabash, St. Louis & Pacific Railway Co. v. Illinois, 118 U.S. 557 (1886), overruling *Peik v. Chicago & Northwestern Railway Co.,* 94 U.S. 164 (1877).

243. Darr v. Burford, 339 U.S. 200 (1950), overruling *Wade v. Mayo,* 334 U.S.

672 (1948); United States v. Rabinowitz, 339 U.S. 56 (1950), overruling *Trupiano v. United States*, 334 U.S. 699 (1948); and Thibaut v. Car and General Insurance Corp., 332 U.S. 828 (1947) (rehearing), overruling *Thibaut v. Car and General Insurance Corp.*, 332 U.S. 751 (1947).

244. Marshall Court: Hudson v. Guestier, 10 U.S. (6 Cr.) 281 (1810), overruling *Rose v. Himely*, 8 U.S. (4 Cr.) 241 (1808); Green v. Lessee of Neal, 31 U.S. (6 Pet.) 291 (1832), overruling *Powell's Lessee v. Harman*, 27 U.S. (2 Pet.) 241 (1829), and *Patton's Lessee v. Easton*, 14 U.S. (1 Wheat.) 476 (1816); Taney Court: Gazzam v. Lessee of Phillips, 61 U.S. (20 How.) 372 (1857), overruling *Brown's Lessee v. Clements*, 44 U.S. (3 How.) 650 (1845); Suydam v. Williamson, 65 U.S. (24 How.) 427 (1861), overruling *Williamson v. Ball*, 49 U.S. (8 How.) 566 (1850), *Williamson v. Irish Presbyterian Congregation*, 49 U.S. (8 How.) 565 (1850), and *Williamson v. Berry*, 49 U.S. (8 How.) 495 (1850).

245. White court: Motion Picture Patents Co. v. Universal Film Manufacturing Co., 243 U.S. 502 (1917), and Boston Store of Chicago v. American Graphophone Co., 246 U.S. 8 (1918), both overruling *Henry v. A.B. Dick Co.*, 224 U.S. 1 (1912); Stone court: Murdock v. Pennsylvania, 319 U.S. 105 (1943), and Jones v. Opelika (rehearing), 319 U.S. 103 (1943), overruling *Jones v. Opelika*, 316 U.S. 584 (1942). Note that the Stone court cases were companion cases decided together.

246. Knox v. Lee, 79 U.S. (12 Wall.) 457 (1871), overruling *Hepburn v. Griswold*, 75 U.S. (8 Wall.) 603 (1870). Chesapeake & Ohio Railway. v. Leitch (rehearing), 276 U.S. 429 (1928), overruling *Chesapeake & Ohio Railway v. Leitch*, 275 U.S. 507 (1927).

247. Hylton v. United States, 3 U.S. (3 Dall.) 171 (1796), overruled by *Pollock v. Farmers' Loan & Trust Co.*, 158 U.S. 601 (1895).

248. South Carolina v. Baker, 485 U.S. 505 (1988).

249. Sykes v. United States, 564 U.S. 1, 180 L. Ed. 2d 60 (2011), was overruled by *Johnson v. United States*, 576 U.S. 591 (2015).

250. The calculations in this section were drawn from an analysis of the Supreme Court Database, with my own slight corrections and additions in a few cases.

251. Melvin I. Urofsky, "Brandeis, Louis Dembitz," in Hall, *Oxford Companion*, 85.

252. In this calculation of overruled cases, I am including only the oldest overruled case for each overruling decision, since many later cases simply follow the earliest precedents.

253. Exxon Corp. v. Central Gulf Lines, Inc., 500 U.S. 603 (1991), overruling *Minturn v. Maynard*, 58 U.S. (17 How.) 476 (1855).

254. These include *Chesapeake & Ohio Railway v. Leitch*, 276 U.S. 429 (1928) (rehearing), overruling *Chesapeake & Ohio Railway v. Leitch*, 275 U.S. 507 (1927); *Jones v. Opelika*, 319 U.S. 103 (1943) (rehearing), overruling *Jones v. Opelika*, 316 U.S. 584 (1942); *Murdock v. Pennsylvania*, 319 U.S. 105 (1943), overruling *Jones v. Opelika*, 316 U.S. 584 (1942); *Halliburton Co. v. Walker*, 329 U.S. 1 (1946) (rehearing), overruling *Halliburton Co. v. Walker*, 326 U.S. 696 (1946); *MacGregor v. Westinghouse Co.*, 329 U.S. 402 (1947) (rehearing), overruling *MacGregor v. Westinghouse Co.*, 327 U.S. 758 (1946); *Zap v. United States*, 330 U.S. 800 (1947) (rehearing), overruling *Zap*

v. United States, 328 U.S. 624 (1946); *In re Isserman,* 348 U.S. 1 (1954) (rehearing), overruling *In re Isserman,* 345 U.S. 286 (1953); *Reid v. Covert 354,* U.S. 1 (1957), overruling *Reid v. Covert,* 351 U.S. 487 (1956); *Thibaut v. Car and General Insurance Corp.,* 332 U.S. 828 (1947) (on rehearing), overruling *Thibaut v. Car and General Insurance Corp.,* 332 U.S. 751 (1947); *Ladner v. United States,* 358 U.S. 169 (1958) (on rehearing), overruling *Ladner v. United States,* 355 U.S. 282 (1958).

255. Union Pacific Railway v. McShane, 89 U.S. (22 Wall.) 444 (1875), overruling *Kansas Pacific Railway v. Prescott,* 83 U.S. (16 Wall.) 603 (1873). Further references to this overruling case will be made in the text.

256. United States v. Ross, 456 U.S. 798 (1982), overruling *Robbins v. California,* 453 U.S. 420 (1981). Further references to this overruling case are made in the text.

257. Statistics on the legal issues determined in overruling cases is drawn from data in Spaeth et al., *2020 Supreme Court Database.* Richard Posner notes: "The percentage of Supreme Court cases that are primarily constitutional has not exceeded 50 percent in recent years. In fact the Court is deciding a smaller percentage of constitutional cases today than it did in the late 1960s and early 1970s." Posner, *How Judges Think,* 271.

258. Wabash, St. Louis & Pacific Railway Co. v. Illinois, 118 U.S. 557 (1886), overruling *Peik v. Chicago & Northwestern Railway Co.,* 94 U.S. 164 (1877).

259. Edwards v. California, 314 U.S. 160 (1941), overruling *City of New York v. Miln,* 36 U.S. (11 Pet.) 102 (1837).

260. Fulton Corp. v. Faulkner, 516 U.S. 325 (1996), overruling *Darnell v. Indiana,* 226 U.S. 390 (1912).

261. Pennsylvania Railroad Co. v. Towers, 245 U.S. 6 (1917), overruling *Lake Shore & Michigan Southern Railway Co. v. Smith,* 173 U.S. 684 (1899); Ott v. Mississippi Barge Line, 336 U.S. 169 (1949), overruling *St. Louis v. Ferry Company,* 78 U.S. (11 Wall.) 423 (1870), *Old Dominion Steamship Co. v. Virginia,* 198 U.S. 299 (1905), and *Ayer & Lord Co. v. Kentucky,* 202 U.S. 409 (1906); Jackson v. Denno, 378 U.S. 368 (1964), overruling *Stein v. New York,* 346 U.S. 156 (1953).

262. Farmers Loan Co. v. Minnesota, 280 U.S. 204 (1930), overruling *Blackstone v. Miller,* 188 U.S. 189 (1903).

263. Harper v. Virginia Board of Elections, 383 U.S. 663 (1966), overruling *Breedlove v. Suttles,* 302 U.S. 277 (1937), and *Butler v. Thompson,* 341 U.S. 937 (1951). Craig v. Boren, 429 U.S. 190 (1976), overruling *Goesaert v. Cleary,* 335 U.S. 464 (1948); Obergefell v. Hodges, 576 US _ (2015), overruling *Baker v. Nelson,* 409 U.S. 81 (1972).

264. First Amendment cases: West Virginia State Board of Education v. Barnette, 319 U.S. 624 (1943), overruling *Minersville School District v. Gobitis,* 310 U.S. 586 (1940); Jones v. Opelika, 319 U.S. 103 (1943) (rehearing), overruling *Jones v. Opelika,* 316 U.S. 584 (1942); Brandenburg v. Ohio, 395 U.S. 444 (1969), overruling *Whitney v. California,* 274 U.S. 357 (1927); 44 Liquormart, Inc. v. Rhode Island, 517 U.S. 484 (1996), overruling *California v. LaRue,* 409 U.S. 109 (1972) (in part), *New York State Liquor Authority v. Bellanca,* 452 U.S. 714 (1981) (in part), and *City of Newport v. Iacobucci,* 479 U.S. 92 (1986) (in part); Citizens United v. Federal Election

Commission, 558 U.S. 310 (2010), overruling *Austin v. Michigan State Chamber of Commerce,* 494 U.S. 652 (1990), and *McConnell v. Federal Election Commission,* 540 U.S. 93 (2003). Fourth Amendment cases: Mapp v. Ohio, 367 U.S. 643 (1961), overruling *Wolf v. Colorado,* 338 U.S. 25 (1949) (in part), and *Irvine v. California,* 347 U.S. 128 (1954) (in part); Katz v. United States, 389 U.S. 347 (1967), overruling *Olmstead v. United States,* 277 U.S. 438 (1928), and *Goldman v. United States,* 316 U.S. 129 (1942); Chimel v. California, 395 U.S. 752 (1969), overruling *Harris v. United States,* 331 U.S. 145 (1947), and *United States v. Rabinowitz,* 339 U.S. 56 (1950); United States v. Rabinowitz, 339 U.S. 56 (1950), overruling *Trupiano v. United States,* 334 U.S. 699 (1948), and *McDonald v. United States,* 335 U.S. 451 (1948). Fifth Amendment cases: Price v. Georgia, 398 U.S. 323, 329– 330 (1970), overruling *Brantley v. Georgia,* 217 U.S. 284 (1910); Ashe v. Swenson, 397 U.S. 436 (1970), overruling *Hoag v. New Jersey,* 356 U.S. 464 (1958); Burks v. United States, 437 U.S. 1 (1978), overruling *Bryan v. United States,* 338 U.S. 552 (1950) (in part), *Sapir v. United States,* 348 U.S. 373 (1955) (in part), *Yates v. United States* 354 U.S. 298 (1957) (in part), and *Forman v. United States,* 361 U.S. 416 (1960) (in part); United States v. Scott 437 U.S. 82 (1978), overruling *United States v. Jenkins* 420 U.S. 358 (1975); United States v. One Assortment of 89 Firearms, 465 U.S. 354 (1984), overruling *Coffey v. United States,* 116 U.S. 436 (1886); United States v. Dixon, 509 U.S. 688 (1993), overruling *Grady v. Corbin,* 495 U.S. 508 (1990); Hudson v. United States, 522 U.S. 93 (1997), overruling *United States v. Halper,* 490 U.S. 435 (1989); Benton v. Maryland, 395 U.S. 784 (1969), overruling *Palko v. Connecticut,* 302 U.S. 319 (1937); Malloy v. Hogan, 378 U.S. 1, 6 (1964), overruling *Twining v. New Jersey,* 211 U.S. 78 (1908); Murphy v. Waterfront Commission, 378 U.S. 52, 57, 77 (1964), overruling *Adamson v. California,* 332 U.S. 46 (1947), *Jack v. Kansas,* 199 U.S. 372 (1905), *United States v. Murdock,* 284 U.S. 141 (1931), *Feldman v. United States,* 322 U.S. 487 (1944), *Knapp v. Schweitzer,* 357 U.S. 371 (1958), and *Mills v. Louisiana,* 360 U.S. 230 (1959); Marchetti v. United States, 390 U.S. 39 (1967), overruling *United States v. Kahriger,* 345 U.S. 22 (1953); and Spevack v. Klein, 385 U.S. 511 (1967), overruling *Cohen v. Hurley,* 366 U.S. 117 (1961). Sixth Amendment cases: Duncan v. Louisiana, 391 U.S. 145 (1968), overruling *Maxwell v. Dow,* 176 U.S. 581 (1900); Alleyne v. United States, 133 S. Ct. 2151 (2013), overruling *Apprendi v. New Jersey,* 530 U.S. 466 (2000); Hurst v. Florida, 136 S. Ct. 616 (2016), overruling *Spaziano v. Florida,* 468 U.S. 447 (1984), and *Hildwin v. Florida,* 490 U.S. 638 (1989); Williams v. Florida, 399 U.S. 78 (1970), overruling *Thompson v. Utah,* 170 U.S. 343 (1898), and *Rassmussen v. United States,* 197 U.S. 516 (1905) (in part); Gideon v. Wainwright, 372 U.S. 335 (1963), overruling *Betts v. Brady,* 316 U.S. 455 (1942); Nichols v. United States, 511 U.S. 738 (1994), overruling *Baldasar v. Illinois,* 446 U.S. 222 (1980); and Montejo v. Louisiana, 556 U.S. ___, No. 07–1529 (2009), overruling *Michigan v. Jackson,* 475 U.S. 625 (1986); Pointer v. Texas, 380 U.S. 400, 406 (1965), overruling *West v. Louisiana,* 194 U.S. 258 (1904); Bruton v. United States, 391 U.S. 123 (1968), overruling *Delli Paoli v. United States,* 352 U.S. 232 (1957); and Crawford v. Washington, 541 U.S. 36 (2004), overruling *Ohio v. Roberts,* 448 U.S. 56 (1980).

265. Atkins v. Virginia, 536 U.S. 304 (2002), overruling *Penry v. Lynaugh,* 492 U.S.

302 (1989); Roper v. Simmons, 543 U.S. 551 (2005), overruling *Stanford v. Kentucky*, 492 U.S. 361 (1989) (on the execution of minors); In re Ayers, 123 U.S. 443 (1887), overruling *Osborn v. Bank of the United States*, 22 U.S. (9 Wheat.) 738 (1824) (on the execution of the mentally disabled); and on sovereign immunity: Edelman v. Jordan, 415 U.S. 651 (1974), overruling *Shapiro v. Thompson*, 394 U.S. 618 (1969) (in part); *State Department of Health & Rehabilitative Services v. Zarate*, 407 U.S. 918 (1972); *Sterrett v. Mothers' & Children's Rights Org.*, 409 U.S. 809 (1973); and *Wyman v. Bowens*, 397 U.S. 49 (1970); Welch v. Texas Department of Highways and Public Transportation, 483 U.S. 468 (1987), overruling *Parden v. Terminal Railway*, 377 U.S. 184 (1964); Seminole Tribe of Florida v. Florida, 517 U.S. 44 (1996), overruling *Pennsylvania v. Union Gas Co.*, 491 U.S. 1 (1989); Lapides v. Board of Regents, 535 U.S. 613 (2002), overruling *Ford Motor Co. v. Department of Treasury of Indiana*, 323 U.S. 459 (1945).

266. Respectively: McDonald v. Chicago, 561 U.S. 742 (2010), overruling *United States v. Cruikshank*, 92 U.S. 542 (1876), *Presser v. Illinois*, 116 U.S. 252 (1886), and *Miller v. Texas*, 153 U.S. 535 (1894); National League of Cities v. Usery, 426 U.S. 833 (1976), overruling *Maryland v. Wirtz*, 392 U.S. 183 (1968); Smith v. Allwright, 321 U.S. 649 (1944), overruling *Grovey v. Townsend*, 295 U.S. 45 (1935).

267. Admiralty law: Moragne v. States Marine Lines, 398 U.S. 375 (1970), overruling *The Harrisburg*, 119 U.S. 199 (1886); United States v. Reliable Transfer Co., 421 U.S. 397 (1975), overruling *The Schooner* Catherine *v. Dickinson*, 58 U.S. (17 How.) 170 (1854); Exxon Corp. v. Central Gulf Lines, Inc., 500 U.S. 603 (1991), overruling *Minturn v. Maynard*, 58 U.S. (17 How.) 476 (1855). Antitrust: Continental T. V. v. GTE Sylvania, Inc., 433 U.S. 36 (1977), overruling *United States v. Arnold Schwinn & Co.*, 388 U.S. 365 (1967); Copperweld Corp. v. Independence Tube Corp., 467 U.S. 752 (1984), overruling *United States v. Yellow Cab Co.*, 332 U.S. 218 (1947); *Kiefer-Stewart Co. v. Jos. E. Seagram & Sons*, 340 U.S. 211 (1951); State Oil Co. v. Khan, 522 U.S. 3 (1997), overruling *Albrecht v. Herald Co.*, 390 U.S. 145 (1968); Leegin Creative Leather Prods., Inc. v. PSKS, Inc., 551 U.S. 877 (2007), overruling *Dr. Miles Med. Co. v. John D. Parks & Sons Co.*, 220 U.S. 373 (1911). Habeas corpus: Peyton v. Rowe, 391 U.S. 54 (1968), overruling *McNally v. Hill*, 293 U.S. 131 (1934); Carafas v. LaVallee, 391 U.S. 234 (1968), overruling *Parker v. Ellis*, 362 U.S. 574 (1960); Braden v. 30th Judicial Circuit Court, 410 U.S. 484 (1973), overruling *Ahrens v. Clark*, 335 U.S. 188 (1948); Coleman v. Thompson, 501 U.S. 722 (1991), overruling *Fay v. Noia*, 372 U.S. 391 (1963). Labor: Smith v. Evening News Association, 371 U.S. 195 (1962), overruling *Westinghouse Employees v. Westinghouse Corp.*, 348 U.S. 437 (1955) (in part); Construction Laborers v. Curry, 371 U.S. 542 (1963), overruling *Building Union v. Ledbetter Co.*, 344 U.S. 178 (1952) (in part); Boys Markets v. Retail Clerks Union, 398 U.S. 235 (1970), overruling *Sinclair Refining Co. v. Atkinson*, 370 U.S. 195 (1962); Andrews v. Louisville & Nashville Railroad, 406 U.S. 320 (1972), overruling *Moore v. Illinois Central Railroad*, 312 U.S. 630 (1941); Machinists & Aerospace Workers v. WERC, 427 U.S. 132 (1976), overruling *UAW v. WERB*, 336 U.S. 245 (1949); Brown v. Hotel Employees International Union Local 54, 468 U.S. 491 (1984), overruling *Hill v. Florida ex rel. Watson*, 325 U.S. 538 (1945). Patent law:

Tilghman v. Proctor, 102 U.S. 707 (1880), overruling *Mitchell v. Tilghman*, 86 U.S. (19 Wall.) 287 (1873); Motion Picture Patents Co. v. Universal Film Manufacturing Co., 243 U.S. 502 (1917), overruling *Henry v. Dick Co.*, 224 U.S. 1 (1912); Mercoid Corp. v. Mid-Continent Co., 320 U.S. 661 (1944), overruling *Leeds & Catlin Co. v. Victor Talking Machine Co.* (No. 2), 213 U.S. 325 (1909) (limited). Revenue: Helvering v. Hallock, 309 U.S. 106 (1940), overruling *Helvering v. St. Louis Trust Co.*, 296 U.S. 39 (1935); Becker v. St. Louis Trust Co., 296 U.S. 48 (1935); Helvering v. Mountain Producers Corp., 303 U.S. 376 (1938), overruling *Gillespie v. Oklahoma*, 257 U.S. 501 (1922), and *Burnet v. Coronado Oil & Gas Co.*, 285 U.S. 393 (1932); James v. United States, 366 U.S. 213 (1961), overruling *Commissioner v. Wilcox*, 327 U.S. 404 (1946). Judicial Processes: Lee v. Chesapeake & Ohio Railway, 260 U.S. 653 (1923), overruling *Ex parte Wisner*, 203 U.S. 449 (1906), and qualifying, *In re Moore*, 209 U.S. 490 (1908); Toucey v. N.Y. Life Insurance Co., 314 U.S. 118 (1941), overruling *Supreme Tribe of Ben-Hur v. Cauble*, 255 U.S. 356 (1921); Gordon v. Ogden, 28 U.S. (3 Pet.) 33, (1830), overruling *Wilson v. Daniel*, 3 U.S. (3 Dall.) 401 (1798); The Belfast, 74 U.S. (7 Wall.) 624 (1869), overruling *Allen v. Newberry*, 62 U.S. (21 How.) 244 (1858) (in part); Trebilcock v. Wilson. 79 U.S. (12 Wall.) 687 (1871), overruling *Roosevelt v. Meyer*, 68 U.S. (1 Wall.) 512 (1863); Swift & Co. v. Wickham, 382 U.S. 111 (1965), overruling *Kesler v. Department of Public Safety*, 369 U.S. 153 (1962) (in part).

268. Gordon v. Ogden, 28 U.S. (3 Pet.) 33, 34 (1830). Further references to this case are made in the text.

269. *Gordon v. Ogden* has been abrogated by 28 U.S.C. 1332(b), the modern diversity-jurisdiction statute, which makes recovery of less than the jurisdictional amount in controversy no longer fatal to federal court diversity jurisdiction.

270. Copperweld Corp. v. Independence Tube Corp., 467 U.S. 752 (1984). Further references will be made in the text.

271. *Copperweld*, 760, quoting *United States v. Yellow Cab Co.*, 332 U.S. 218, 227 (1947) (emphasis added by *Copperweld* court).

272. Kiefer-Stewart Co. v. Joseph E. Seagram & Sons, 340 U.S. 211 (1951).

273. See my discussion of H. L. A. Hart and the legal positivists in the previous chapter.

274. Hudson v. Guestier, 10 U.S. (6 Cr.) 281 (1810). Further references to this case are made in the text.

275. Rose v. Himley, 8 U.S. (4 Cr.) 241 (1808).

276. Angel v. Bullington, 330 U.S. 183, 189–90 (1947).

277. *Angel*, 191. The overruled case was *David Lupton's Sons v. Automobile Club of America*, 225 U.S. 489 (1912).

Chapter 3

1. See his opinions in Texas v. Chiles, 88 U.S. 488 (1875); Supervisors v. Galbraith, 99 U.S. 214 (1879); National Bank of the Commonwealth v. Mechanics' National Bank, 94 U.S. 437 (1879).

2. Robert W. Gordon, "The Case for (and against) Harvard," Michigan Law Review 93, no. 6 (1995): 1245.

3. W. Burlette Carter, "Reconstructing Langdell," Georgia Law Review 32, no. 1 (Fall 1997): 37.

4. The Thomas Jefferson, 23 U.S. 428 (1825). Further references to this case will be made in the text.

5. U.S. Const., art. III, § 2, para. 1.

6. The Propeller Genesee Chief v. Fitzhugh, 53 U.S. 443; 13 L. Ed. 1058 (1851). Further references to this case will be made in the text.

7. In Hudson v. Guestier, 10 U.S. (6 Cr.) 281 (1810), the court explicitly noted "the principle of that case (Rose v. Himely) is now overruled" (285). Three subsequent reversals were made in Gordon v. Ogden, 28 U.S. (3 Pet.) 33 (1830); Green v. Lessee of Neal, 31 U.S. (6 Pet.) 291 (1832); and Louisville, Cincinnati & Charleston Railroad v. Letson, 43 U.S. (2 How.), 497 (1844), though they did not expressly state that they were overruling. For example, in the Green case, the high court was dealing with a change of state law regarding a statute of limitations on claims to property rights, concluding:

As it appears to this court, that the construction of the statutes of limitations is now well settled, differently from what was supposed to be the rule at the time this court decided the case of Patton's Lessee v. Easton, and the case of Powell's Lessee v. Green; and as the instructions of the circuit court were governed by these decisions, and not by the settled law of the state; the judgment must be reversed, and the cause remanded for further proceedings. (301)

8. Fitzhugh v. Propeller Genesee Chief in *Briefs and Records of the Supreme Court of the United States*, N.P.: Washington, DC, 1851, 253.

9. Ch. 20, 5 Stat. 726–727. The statute is quoted in Joseph C. Sweeney, "The Lexington," *Journal of Maritime Law & Commerce* 39, no. 1 (January 2008): 77n45.

10. Sweeney, "Lexington," 77.

11. Justice Story died on September 10, 1845, seven months after the new Judiciary Act he drafted was passed. Sweeney, "Lexington," 71, 77.

12. Sweeney, "Lexington," 77n45.

13. Taney's position may reflect his general support for states rights against the infringements of the commerce clause power of the federal government. David Currie notes of Taney's long career as chief justice: "When Taney died in 1864, however, . . no one could yet say confidently that the Court had ever found an instance in which [the commerce clause limited state power, even though, theoretically it might]." David P. Currie, "The Constitution in the Supreme Court: Contracts and Commerce, 1836–1864," *Duke Law Journal* 1983, no. 3 (June 1983): 512–13.

14. Kenneth Burke, A Grammar of Motives (Berkeley: University of California Press, 1969), 3.

15. Clarke Rountree, *Judging the Supreme Court: Constructions of Motives in Bush v. Gore, Rhetoric & Public Affairs* (East Lansing: Michigan State University Press, 2007), 5.

16. Graydon S. Staring, "The Lingering Influence of Richard II and Lord Coke in the American Admiralty," *Journal of Maritime Law & Commerce* 41, no. 2 (April 2010): 239.

17. Staring, "Lingering Influence," 239.

18. Staring, "Lingering Influence," 244.

19. Sweeney, "Lexington," 75.

20. Frank H. Dixon, A Traffic History of the Mississippi River System (Washington, DC: US Government Printing Office, 1909), 25.

21. Knox v. Lee (Legal Tender Cases) 79 U.S. (12 Wall.) 457 (1871); Hepburn v. Griswold, Hepburn 75 U.S. (8 Wall.) 603 (1870). Further references to these cases will be made in the text.

22. Charles Fairman, Reconstruction and Reunion, 1864–88, Part One, vol. 4 of History of the Supreme Court of the United States (New York: Macmillan, 1971), 679.

23. Fairman, Reconstruction and Reunion.

24. Fairman, Reconstruction and Reunion, 684.

25. Quoted in Fairman, Reconstruction and Reunion, 685.

26. Quoting Spaulding in Fairman, Reconstruction and Reunion, 685.

27. Quoted in Fairman, Reconstruction and Reunion, 686.

28. Quoted in the Prior History section of Hepburn v. Griswold, 603.

29. There were exceptions in cases where contracts specifically requested payment in gold or other forms. See Hepburn v. Griswold, 606–7.

30. Chase notes that at the lowest point of the greenback's depreciation, $1,000 in gold was worth $2,850 in greenbacks (608).

31. Broderick's Executor v. Magraw, 75 U.S. (8 Wall) 639 (1870).

32. David J. Garrow, "Mental Decrepitude on the U.S. Supreme Court: The Historical Case for a 28th Amendment," University of Chicago Law Review 67, no. 4 (Fall 2000): 1003–4.

33. Garrow, "Mental Decrepitude," 1006.

34. Fairman, Reconstruction and Reunion, 741.

35. The number of Supreme Court justices had been raised to ten by an act of March 3, 1863. But with the death of Justice Cantron and the prospect of more vacancies on the horizon, Congress dropped the number of justices to seven, with that number to be reached by deaths and retirements, to prevent the unpopular President Johnson from getting any appointments. The number only reached eight by Grant's inauguration, when Congress raised the total back to nine (effective in December 1869). Grier retired in January 1870 and Grant's nominees took office two months later. Leon Sachs, "Stare Decisis and the Legal Tender Cases," Virginia Law Review 20, no. 8 (1933): 864–65.

Grant had made two nominations in December 1869, one to replace Grier (who would retire on February 1, 1870) and another to fill a new seat afforded by the expansion of the court to nine members. However, his nomination of E. R. Hoar was rejected by the Senate; and while his nomination of secretary of war Edwin Stanton was confirmed on the same day as the nomination, Stanton died four days later on Christmas Eve. Hepburn was handed down on February 7, 1870, and Grant nominated William Strong and Joseph P. Bradley that same day. Sachs, "Stare Decisis," 865.

36. Fairman, Reconstruction and Reunion, 678.

37. The case is Knox v. Lee.

38. Hepburn dealt only with a case involving a contract before the passage of the act, so the court's decision did not necessarily resolve this issue. Indeed, one of its primary concerns was the violation of expectations for contracts made before the act was passed.

39. Veazie Bank v. Fenno, 75 U.S. 533 (1869) at 543.

40. Fairman, Reconstruction and Reunion, 715.

Chapter 4

1. Judiciary Act of 1789, ch. 20, § 11.

2. Strawbridge v. Curtiss, 7 U.S. (3 Cr.) 267 (1806). Further references to this case will be made in the text.

3. Bank of the United States v. Deveaux, 9 U.S. (5 Cr.) 61 (1809). Further references to this case will be made in the text.

4. See my analyses of the development of corporations as fully capable agents in Clarke Rountree, "Judicial Invention in Cases Contributing to the Development of Corporate Criminal Liability: A Multi-Dimensional Dramatistic Analysis," PhD diss., University of Iowa, 1988.

5. Commercial and Railroad Bank v. Slocomb, 39 U.S. (14 Pet.) 60 (1840). Further references to this case will be made in the text.

6. Louisville, Cincinnati & Charleston Railroad v. Letson, 43 U.S. (2 How.) 497 (1844). Further references to this case will be made in the text.

7. Charles Fairman, *Reconstruction and Reunion, 1864–88, Part One*, vol. 4 of *History of the Supreme Court of the United States* (New York: Macmillan, 1971), 461.

8. Fairman, *Reconstruction and Reunion*, 461.

9. Fairman, *Reconstruction and Reunion*, 462.

10. Fairman, *Reconstruction and Reunion*, 462.

11. Chief Justice Taney was ill, Justice McKinley had missed many sessions, and Justice Thompson had recently died, reducing the participants. Fairman, *Reconstruction and Reunion*, 463–64.

12. Judiciary Act of 1789, § 11 (emphasis added).

13. Reuven S. Avi-Yonah, "The Cyclical Transformations of the Corporate Form: A Historical Perspective on Corporate Social Responsibility," *Delaware Journal of Corporate Law*, 30, no. 3 (2005): 792–94.

14. Marshall v. Baltimore & Ohio Railroad Co., 57 U.S. 314 (1850), 327–28.

15. Avi-Yonah, "Cyclical Transformations," 463.

16. Quoted in Fairman, *Reconstruction and Reunion*, 463.

17. Bank of United States v. Planters' Bank of Georgia, 22 U.S. (9 Wheat.) 904 (1824).

18. Rountree, "Judicial Invention."

19. Citizens United v. Federal Election Commission, 558 U.S. 310 (2010); Burwell v. Hobby Lobby, 573 U.S. 682 (2014).

20. Quoting *Dartmouth College v. Woodward*, 17 U.S. (4 Wheat.) 518, 636 (1819) at 558.

21. An "aggregate" corporation is distinguished from a "corporation sole," which involves a single individual holding an office in succession, such as a sheriff.

22. 28 U.S.C. 1332(a), (c) adopted the complete diversity requirement and defined the citizenship of a corporation as its state of incorporation and its principal place of business, resolving the issues with which these cases grappled.

23. Alexandra Gil, "Breaking the Studios: Antitrust and the Motion Picture Industry," *New York University Journal of Law & Liberty* 3, no. 1 (2008): 10.

24. Gil, "Breaking the Studios," 14.

25. Barak Y. Orbach, "Antitrust and Pricing in the Motion Picture Industry," *Yale Journal on Regulation* 21, no. 2 (Summer 2004): 329.

26. Matthew Josephson, *Edison: A Biography* (New York: McGraw-Hill, 1959), 401.

27. Orbach, "Antitrust and Pricing," 329.

28. Orbach, "Antitrust and Pricing," 330.

29. Orbach, "Antitrust and Pricing," 330; Gil, "Breaking the Studios," 90–91; Scott Kirsner, *Inventing the Movies: Hollywood's Epic Battle between Innovation and the Status Quo, from Thomas Edison to Steve Jobs* (USA: CinemaTech Books, 2008), 10–11.

30. Gil, "Breaking the Studios, 91.

31. Robert Conot, *Streak of Luck* (New York: Simon & Schuster, 1979), 395.

32. Gil, "Breaking the Studios," 18.

33. Gil, "Breaking the Studios," 18.

34. Gil, "Breaking the Studios," 19.

35. Josephson, *Edison*, 401.

36. Gil, "Breaking the Studios," 20.

37. Jon Lewis, *American Film: A History* (New York: W. W. Norton, 2008), 20.

38. Douglas Collins, *The Story of Kodak* (New York: H. N. Abrams, 1990), 143.

39. Collins, *Story of Kodak*, 139. Pathé, which was the largest filmmaker in the world, also had incorporated these innovations into its cameras, but avoided a conflict with Edison by joining the trust and ensuring the American inventor was well remunerated for his patents.

40. Quoted in Charles Musser, *Before the Nickelodeon: Edwin S. Porter and the Edison Manufacturing Company* (Berkeley: University of California Press, 1991), 440.

41. Conot, *Streak of Luck*, 395.

42. Collins, *Story of Kodak*, 143.

43. Collins, *Story of Kodak*, 21–23.

44. Collins, *Story of Kodak*, 144.

45. Josephson, *Edison*, 402.

46. Gil, "Breaking the Studios," 21.

47. "Disney Ends the Historic 20th Century Brand," BBC News (online), August 12, 2020.

48. Kirsner, *Inventing the Movies*, 13–14; Musser, *Before the Nickelodeon*, 437.

49. Motion Picture Patents Co. v. Universal Film Manufacturing Co., 243 U.S. 502 (1917); Henry v. Dick, 224 U.S. 1 (1912). Further references to these cases will be made in the text.

50. He does quote the statute near the end of his opinion nineteen pages later (46) on another issue, but not in making his central argument for a broad right of patentees to control how others use their inventions.

51. Quoting Marshall from *Grant v. Raymond,* 31 U.S. (6 Pet.) 218, 241 (1832) at 27.

52. Quoting *Bloomer v. McQuewan,* 55 (14 How.) 539, 547 (1852) at 28.

53. Quoting the Button Fastener Cases, 77 F. 288 (6th Cir. 1896).

54. Quoting *Bement v. National Harrow Co.,* 186 U.S. 70, 90 (1902) at 29–30.

55. Motion Picture Patents Co. v. Universal Film Manufacturing Co., 243 U.S. 502, 518–519 (1917). While the court noted that the patent under which this case was brought had expired before the unlicensed film was shown (507), it did not use the opinion to quickly reject the MPPC's practice on that obvious ground, but raised the issue of the legality of the entire practice.

56. President Kennedy signed the Equal Pay Act in 1963. President Johnson included sex as a protected category in the Civil Rights Act of 1964 and formed the Equal Employment Opportunity Commission in 1964.

57. Oscar G. Chase and Arlo Monell Chase, "*Monell:* The Story Behind the Landmark," *Urban Lawyer* 31, no. 3 (Summer 1999): 491–92; Monell v. New York City Department of Social Services, 436 U.S. 658 (1978). Further references to this case will be made in the text.

58. Mt. Healthy City School District v. Doyle, 429 U.S. 274, 279 (1977).

59. While race, religion, and a few other categories are considered "suspect" classifications by the federal courts, sex is not. Instead, it is an "intermediate" or "quasi-suspect" classification. See *Mississippi University for Women v. Hogan,* 458 U.S. 718 (1982).

60. Monroe v. Pape, 365 U.S. 167 (1961). Further references to this case are made in the text.

61. Chase and Chase note that "It was the first case in which the Supreme Court held that § 1983 authorized a damage award against police (and by extension, other municipal agents) who violated the constitutional rights of the plaintiff by acts that were unauthorized by local law." Chase and Chase, "*Monell,*" 494.

62. Shellabarger quoting Washington from *Corfield v. Coryell,* 4 Wash. C. C. 371, 380–81 (CC ED Pa. 1825), cited by Brennan at 670.

63. U.S. Const., art. IV, § 2, cl. 2; cl. 3; cl. 1.

64. Prigg v. Pennsylvania, 41 U.S. (16 Pet.) 539 (1842).

65. Citing *Board of Commissioners of Knox County* v. *Aspinwall,* 65 U.S. (24 How.) 376 (1861).

66. Quoting *Collector v. Day,* 79 U.S. (11 Wall.) 113, 127 (1871) at 676.

67. 65 U.S. (24 How.) 66 (1861).

68. The cases include *Prigg, Kentucky v. Dennison,* 65 U.S. (24 How.) 66 (1861), and *Collector v. Day.*

69. He lists *Northwestern Fertilizing Co. v. Hyde Park,* 18 F. Cas. 393 (No. 10,336) (CC ND Ill. 1873); *City of Manchester* v. *Leiby,* 117 F. 2d 661 (CAI 1941); *Hannan* v. *City of Haverhill,* 120 F. 2d 87 (CAl 1941); *Douglas* v. *City of Jeannette,* 319 U.S.

157 (1943); and *Holmes* v. *Atlanta,* 350 U.S. 879 (1955), as examples of cases from which *Monroe* departed (695). He lists the following cases with school boards as defendants: *Milliken v. Bradley,* 433 U.S. 267 (1977); *Dayton Board of Education* v. *Brinkman,* 433 U.S. 406 (1977); *Vorchheimer v. School District of Philadelphia,* 430 U.S. 703 (1977); *East Carroll Parish School Board* v. *Marshall,* 424 U.S. 636 (1976); *Milliken* v. *Bradley,* 418 U.S. 717 (1974); *Bradley* v. *Richmond School Board,* 416 U.S. 696 (1974); *Cleveland Board of Education* v. *LaFleur,* 414 U.S. 632 (1974); *Keyes v. School District No. 1, Denver, Colo.,* 413 U.S. 189 (1973); *San Antonio School District* v. *Rodriguez,* 411 U.S. 1 (1973); *Swann* v. *Charlotte-Mecklenburg Board of Education,* 402 U.S. 1 (1971); *Northcross v. Memphis Board of Education,* 397 U.S. 232 (1970); *Carter v. West Feliciana Parish School Board,* 396 U.S. 226 (1969); *Alexander v. Holmes County Board of Education,* 396 U.S. 19 (1969); *Kramer v. Union Free School District,* 395 U.S. 621 (1969); *Tinker* v. *Des Moines Independent School District,* 393 U.S. 503 (1969); *Monroe v. Board of Commissioners,* 391 U.S. 450 (1968); *Raney* v. *Board of Education,* 391 U.S. 443 (1968); *Green v. New Kent County School Board,* 391 U.S. 430 (1968); *Abington School District v. Schempp,* 374 U.S. 203 (1963); *Goss v. Board of Education,* 373 U.S. 683 (1963); *McNeese v. Board of Education,* 373 U.S. 668 (1963); and *Orleans Parish School Board v. Bush,* 365 U.S. 569 (1961) (663n5).

70. Brennan's opinion touched on *respondeat superior,* though it did not directly argue that the Sherman amendment failed because of a rejection of this doctrine. Rather, he scrutinizes § 1983's language about the *cause* of the injury to reject this possibility *(691–92).*

71. "Policies" here include official written rules and directives, as well as "customs and usages" that involve practices that often are "permanent and well settled." See *Adickes v. S. H. Kress & Co.,* 398 U.S. 144, 167–68 (1970), quoted in Brennan's opinion at 691.

72. Chase and Chase, *"Monell,"* 499.

73. Chase and Chase, *"Monell,"* 499. quoting Jerome Skolnick and James J. Fyfe, *Above the Law: Police and the Excessive Use of Force* (New York: Free Press, 1993), 198.

74. I write this in the wake of the May 25, 2020, killing of George Floyd by Minneapolis police officer Derek Chauvin (who was later criminally convicted for his actions). Sadly, perhaps four decades of municipal liability of this sort has led cities to treat such payouts as the cost of policing cities.

Chapter 5

1. Merlo J. Pusey, *The Supreme Court Crisis* (New York: Macmillan, 1937), 11.

2. National Labor Relations Board v. Jones & Laughlin Steel Corp., 301 U.S. 1 (1937); Steward Machine Co. v. Davis, 301 US. 548 (1937).

3. William E. Leuchtenburg, *The Supreme Court Reborn: The Constitutional Revolution in the Age of Roosevelt* (Oxford: Oxford University Press, 1995), 178.

4. Leuchtenburg, *Supreme Court Reborn,* 177.

5. See chapter 2 on comparative numbers of overrulings by the court. The Stone court would have a much higher rate of overruling at three per year but not surpass the twenty-one total overrulings of the Hughes court.

6. Hammer v. Dagenhart, 247 U.S. 251 (1918). Further references to this case will be made in the text.

7. United States v. E. C. Knight Co., 156 U.S. 1 (1895). See also Barry Cushman, *Rethinking the New Deal Court: The Structure of a Constitutional Revolution* (New York: Oxford University Press, 1998), 142.

8. United States v. E. C. Knight Co., 276.

9. J. Robert Cox notes that the reliance of poor widows and other marginalized families on the income of their working children helped to undermine the passage of the Child Labor Amendment. See J. Robert Cox, "The Rhetoric of Child Labor Reform: An Efficacy-Utility Analysis," *Quarterly Journal of Speech* 60, no. 3 (October 1974): 359–70.

10. Munn v. Illinois, 94 U.S. 113, 126 (1877). Further references to this case will be made in the text.

11. Swift & Co. v. United States, 196 U.S. 375, 398–99 (1905) (emphasis added).

12. Cushman, *Rethinking the New Deal*, 146.

13. Cushman, *Rethinking the New Deal*, 152.

14. Richard H. Pells, "Great Depression," *Encyclopedia Britannica* online, 2021. Additional details of the economic collapse referenced in this paragraph come from this source.

15. Kenneth T. Walsh, "The First 100 Days: Franklin Roosevelt Pioneered the 100-Day Concept," *US News & World Report*, February 12, 2009.

16. Walsh, "First 100 Days."

17. Walsh, "First 100 Days."

18. Home Building & Loan Association v. Blaisdell, 290 U.S. 398 (1934). Further references to this case are made in the text.

19. Justice Sutherland quotes Judge Campbell of the Michigan Supreme Court. Home Building & Loan Association v. Blaisdell, 290 U.S. 398, 451 (1934) (Sutherland, J., dissenting).

20. Nebbia v. New York, 291 U.S. 502 (1934). Further references to this case are made in the text.

21. Cushman, *Rethinking the New Deal*, 90.

22. Cushman, *Rethinking the New Deal*, 90; Laura Kalman, "Law, Politics, and the New Deal(s)," *Yale Law Journal* 108, no. 8 (June 1999): 2186.

23. Panama Refining Co. v. Ryan, 293 U.S. 388 (1935).

24. Neil Reynolds, "There is No 'Peak Oil,'" *Globe and Mail*, June 23, 2010.

25. Panama Refining Co. v. Ryan, 415.

26. Stern suggests this problem with early New Deal legislation in Robert L. Stern, "The Court-Packing Plan and the Commerce Clause," *Yearbook: Supreme Court Historical Society* 1988 (1988): 94.

27. The Gold Clause Cases include *Norman v. Baltimore & Ohio Railroad Co.*, 294 U.S. 240 (1935); *Nortz v. United States*, 294 U.S. 317 (1935); and *Perry v. United States*, 294 U.S. 330 (1935).

28. Perry v. United States, 362 (McReynolds, J., dissenting).

29. Railroad Retirement Board v. Alton Railroad Co., 295 U.S. 330 (1935). Further references to this case will be made in the text.

30. While some have said that Justice Roberts's reference to the "gratitude" and "loyalty" of employees to their employers as reflecting an "almost medieval" conception of management-worker relations, making his later change of heart on government regulation amenable to the charge that he was influenced by Roosevelt's court reform scheme (Kalman, "Law, Politics," 2188), I take his argument here as a response to the government's claim that a retirement program was warranted by the good will it would buy for railroad companies. The dissent rightly notes that such a requirement, which was portable between companies, would not clearly serve that function.

31. Railroad Retirement Board v. Alton Railroad Co., 295 U.S. 330, 376 (1935) (Hughes, C.J., dissenting), citing *The Shreveport Case,* 234 U.S. 342, 234 U.S. 351; *Dayton-Goose Creek Ry. Co. v. United States,* 263 U.S. 456, 263 U.S. 478; *Colorado v. United States,* 271 U.S. 153, 271 U.S. 163–64; and *New York Central Securities Corp. v. United States,* 287 U.S. 12, 287 U.S. 24–25.

32. Leuchtenburg, *Supreme Court Reborn,* 46–47.

33. Leuchtenburg, *Supreme Court Reborn,* 49.

34. Leuchtenburg, *Supreme Court Reborn,* 49.

35. Louisville Bank v. Radford, 295 U.S. 555 (1935); Humphrey's Executor v. United States, 295 U.S. 602 (1935); Schechter Poultry Corp. v. United States, 295 U.S. 495 (1935).

36. Louisville Bank v. Radford, 601–2.

37. Schechter Poultry Corp. v. United States, 295 U.S. 495, 543 (1935). Further references to this case will be made in the text.

38. C. Herman Pritchett, "Schechter Poultry Corp. v. United States," in *The Oxford Companion to the Supreme Court of the United States,* ed. Kermit L. Hall (New York: Oxford University Press, 1992), 757.

39. Roosevelt, Franklin D. Press Conference, Washington, DC, May 31, 1935, American Presidency Project, University of California–Santa Barbara.

40. Roosevelt, Press Conference, May 31, 1935.

41. Roosevelt, Press Conference, May 31, 1935.

42. United States v. Butler et al., 297 U.S. 61, 62 (1936).

43. United States v. Butler et al., 62.

44. United States v. Butler et al., 78–79 (Stone, J., dissenting).

45. Carter v. Carter Coal, 298 U.S. 238 (1936). Further references to this case will be made in the text.

46. James William Moore and Shirley Adelson, "Supreme Court: The 1938 Term," *Virginia Law Review* 26, no. 1 (1939–40): 15.

47. Cushman, *Rethinking the New Deal,* 193–94.

48. Ashton v. Cameron County Water Improvement District No. 1, 298 U.S. 513 (1936).

49. Sanders Shanks Jr., "The Municipal Bankruptcy Act (Sumners-Wilcox Bill)," *American Political Science Review* 28, no. 6 (December 1934): 1072–73.

50. Leuchtenburg, *Supreme Court Reborn,* 215.

51. Ashton v. Cameron County Water Improvement District No. 1, 298 U.S. 513, 532 (1936).

52. John W. Johnson, "Morehead v. New York Ex Rel. Tipaldo," in Hall, *Oxford Companion*, 562.

53. Morehead v. New York ex rel. Tipaldo, 298 U.S. 587 (1936).

54. Morehead v. New York ex rel. Tipaldo, 632 (Stone, J., dissenting).

55. Morehead v. New York ex rel. Tipaldo, 632 (Stone, J., dissenting).

56. Johnson, "Morehead," 562.

57. Leuchtenburg, *Supreme Court Reborn*, 168.

58. Leuchtenburg, *Supreme Court Reborn*, 133.

59. Leuchtenburg, *Supreme Court Reborn*, 105.

60. Donovan Bisbee, "Driving the Three-Horse Team of Government: *Kairos* in FDR's Judiciary Fireside Chat," *Rhetoric & Public Affairs* 21, no. 3 (2018): 485.

61. Michael Nelson, "The President and the Court: Reinterpreting the Court-Packing Episode of 1937," *Political Science Quarterly* 103, no. 2 (Summer 1988): 275.

62. Warner W. Gardner, "Court Packing: The Drafting Recalled," *Journal of Supreme Court History* 15, no. 1 (1990): 99.

63. Barry Cushman, "Court-Packing and Compromise," *Constitutional Commentary* 29, no. 1 (Summer 2013): 1.

64. Nelson, "President and the Court," 279.

65. Gardner, "Court Packing," 99.

66. Valentine v. Great Atlantic & Pacific Tea Co., 299 U.S. 32 (1936); Stewart Dry Goods Co. v. Lewis, 294 U.S. 550 (1935).

67. William G. Ross, "When Did the Switch in Time Actually Occur?: Re-Discovering the Supreme Court's Forgotten Decisions of 1936–1937," *Arizona State Law Journal* 37, no. 4 (Winter 2005): 1205.

68. Chamberlin v. Andrews, 299 U.S. 515 (1936) (per curiam), affirming 2 N.E.2d 22 (1936).

69. Ross, "When Did the Switch," 1162–65.

70. Ross, "When Did the Switch," 1165. Ross says Roberts apparently voted with the liberals because the 4-4 stalemate was per curiam and did not indicate who was on which side, though presumably the Four Horsemen voted as a bloc.

71. Quoted in Ross, "When Did the Switch," 1169.

72. Ross, "When Did the Switch," 1170–71.

73. Ross, "When Did the Switch," 1202.

74. Duke Power Co. v. Greenwood County, 299 U.S. 259 (1936); Ross, "When Did the Switch," 1177.

75. Ross, "When Did the Switch," 1178.

76. Quoted in Ross, "When Did the Switch," 1215.

77. Quoted in Trevor Parry-Giles and Marouf A. Hasian Jr., "Necessity or Nine Old Men: The Congressional Debate over Franklin D. Roosevelt's 1937 Court-Packing Plan," in *American Rhetoric in the New Deal Era, 1932–1945*, vol. 7 of *A Rhetorical History of the United States*, ed. Thomas W. Benson (East Lansing: Michigan State University Press, 2006), 254.

78. Franklin D. Roosevelt, Annual Message to Congress on the State of the Union, January 6, 1937, American Presidency Project.

79. Franklin D. Roosevelt, Annual Budget Message to Congress, January 7, 1937, American Presidency Project.

80. Franklin D. Roosevelt, Press Conference, January 22, 1937, American Presidency Project.

81. Norris v. Alabama, 294 U.S. 587 (1935); De Jonge v. Oregon, 299 U.S. 353 (1937).

82. Ross, "When Did the Switch," 1187.

83. Great Northern Railway Co. v. Washington, 300 U.S. 154 (1937).

84. Homer Cummings, letter to FDR on the need for judicial reform, February 2, 1937, box 165, Franklin D. Roosevelt, Papers as President: The President's Secretary's File (PSF), 1933–1945, Franklin D. Roosevelt Presidential Library & Museum, Hyde Park, NY.

85. Cummings, letter to FDR.

86. Cummings, letter to FDR.

87. Josiah M. Daniel III, "'Here is Where I Cash In': The Instrumental Role of Congressman Hatton Sumners in the Resolution of the 1937 Court-Packing," *UIC John Marshall Law Review* 54, no. 2 (Summer 2021): 406.

88. Parry-Giles and Hasian, "Necessity or Nine," 256.

89. Justin R. Braga, "The Other Switch in Time: How the Opposition Changed the Debate Over the Court-Packing Plan and Won," *Georgetown Journal of Law & Public Policy* 17, no. 2 (Summer 2019): 658.

90. Braga, "Other Switch in Time," 659.

91. Braga, "Other Switch in Time," 659, 660.

92. Leuchtenburg, *Supreme Court Reborn*, 120.

93. Quoted in Leuchtenburg, *Supreme Court Reborn*, 120.

94. Leuchtenburg, *Supreme Court Reborn*, 127, 129.

95. Quoted in Cushman, "Court-Packing and Compromise," 30.

96. Cushman, *Rethinking the New Deal*, 14.

97. Franklin D. Roosevelt, Press Conference, February 5, 1937, American Presidency Project.

98. Parry-Giles and Hasian, "Necessity or Nine," 252.

99. Leuchtenburg, *Supreme Court Reborn*, 134.

100. Hugh S. Johnson, Address over CBS Radio, 3:00 p.m., from NYC, February 7, 1937, Franklin D. Roosevelt, Papers as President, 1.

101. Johnson, Address over CBS Radio, 2.

102. Johnson, Address over CBS Radio, 3.

103. Johnson, Address over CBS Radio, 3–4.

104. Franklin D. Roosevelt, Excerpts from the Press Conference, February 12, 1937, American Presidency Project.

105. Kyle Graham, "A Moment in the Times: Law Professors and the Court-Packing Plan," *Journal of Legal Education* 52, no. 1–2 (2002): 157n40.

106. See, for example, Young B. Smith, "Statement on the Proposal Regarding the Supreme Court before the Senate Judiciary Committee," *American Bar Association Journal* 23, no. 4 (April 1937): 261–64; George G. Bogart, "A Law Teacher's View of

the President's Plan to Enlarge the Supreme Court," *American Bar Association Journal* 23, no. 4 (1937): 251; Walter F. Dodd, "Defense of Our Constitutional System," *American Bar Association Journal* 23, no. 5 (May 1937): 344–46, 363; William J. Donovan, "An Independent Supreme Court and the Protection of Minority Rights," *American Bar Association Journal* 23, no. 4 (April 1937): 254–60, 295–96; "The Supreme Court Issue," *American Bar Association Journal* 23, no. 4 (April 1937): 268–70.

107. Thuman W. Arnold, "A Reply," *American Bar Association Journal* 23, no. 5 (May 1937): 364.

108. Parry-Giles and Hasian, "Necessity or Nine," 259.

109. Parry-Giles and Hasian, "Necessity or Nine," 259.

110. Parry-Giles and Hasian, "Necessity or Nine," 259–60.

111. Holyoke Water Power Co. v. American Writing Paper Co., 300 U.S. 324 (1937).

112. Holyoke Water Power Co., 340. Ross quotes a legal scholar who notes how the novelty of this argument would shape later arguments on the court regarding regulation. Ross, "When Did the Switch," 1199.

113. Richard D. Friedman, "Chief Justice Hughes' Letter on Court-Packing," *Journal of Supreme Court History* 22, no. 1 (1997): 78.

114. Franklin D. Roosevelt, Fireside Chat, March 9, 1937, American Presidency Project.

115. Roosevelt, Fireside Chat, March 9, 1937.

116. Daniel, "Where I Cash In," 407.

117. Bisbee, "Three-Horse Team," 506.

118. Daniel, "Where I Cash In," 407.

119. Ross, "When Did the Switch," 1215.

120. Parry-Giles and Hasian, "Necessity or Nine," 262.

121. Parry-Giles and Hasian, "Necessity or Nine," 262.

122. Parry-Giles and Hasian, "Necessity or Nine," 263.

123. Graham, "Moment in the Times," 159.

124. Parry-Giles and Hasian, "Necessity or Nine," 264.

125. Parry-Giles and Hasian, "Necessity or Nine," 264.

126. Braga, "Other Switch in Time," 661.

127. "Dorothy Thompson." *Encyclopedia Britannica* online, July 5, 2021.

128. Parry-Giles and Hasian, "Necessity or Nine," 265.

129. Parry-Giles and Hasian, "Necessity or Nine," 263; Nelson, "President and the Court," 282.

130. Parry-Giles and Hasian, "Necessity or Nine," 264.

131. Pusey, *Supreme Court Crisis*, v.

132. Pusey, *Supreme Court Crisis*, vi.

133. Braga, "Other Switch in Time," 662.

134. Braga, "Other Switch in Time," 663.

135. Stephen Early, Confidential Memorandum for the President, February 8, 1937, single page letter, Franklin D. Roosevelt, Papers as President.

136. Daniel, "Where I Cash In," 392.

137. Cushman, "Court-Packing and Compromise," 5.

138. Cushman, "Court-Packing and Compromise," 5.

139. Daniel, "Where I Cash In," 392.

140. Daniel, "Where I Cash In," 380. As Daniel explains, most histories of Sumners's statement report that he said "Here is where I cash in my chips." But in fall 1937 Sumners responded to a letter from a constituent (who would later run against him for Congress) asking about his comment, and Sumners corrected the quotation and said that he said "Here is where I cash in."

141. Daniel, "Where I Cash In," 380. Daniel draws upon a *Saturday Evening Post* article on the court fight written by Joseph Alsop and Turner Catledge, "The Supreme Court Fight," September 18, 1937, 9, 93–98. (Daniel mislabels the first page as "8.") The quotation is indeed found at page 94.

142. Early, Confidential Memorandum for the President.

143. Early, Confidential Memorandum for the President.

144. Daniel, "Where I Cash In," 381; Hatton W. Sumners, Letter to T. B. Love, 1937, box 2.325/M18b, Hatton Sumners Papers, Dolph Briscoe Center for American History, University of Texas–Austin.

145. Daniel, "Where I Cash In," 427.

146. Daniel, "Where I Cash In," 405.

147. Daniel, "Where I Cash In," 407.

148. Cushman, "Court-Packing and Compromise," 17.

149. Daniel, "Where I Cash In," 402.

150. Daniel, "Where I Cash In," 411, 383–84.

151. Daniel, "Where I Cash In," 419.

152. Daniel, "Where I Cash In," 406.

153. Ross, "When Did the Switch," 1219.

154. Daniel, "Where I Cash In," 407.

155. Ross, "When Did the Switch," 1184.

156. Cushman, "Court-Packing and Compromise," 14–15.

157. Cushman, "Court-Packing and Compromise," 25–26.

158. Heller Brothers Co. v. Lind, 86 F.2d 862 (D.C. Cir. 1936), cert. denied, 300 U.S. 672 (1937); Brush v. Commissioner, 300 U.S. 352 (1937).

159. Highland Farms Dairy v. Agnew, 300 U.S. 608 (1937).

160. Virginian Railway Co. v. Railway Employees, 300 U.S. 515 (1937); Sonzinsky v. United States, 300 U.S. 506 (1937); Wright v. Vinton Branch of Mountain Trust Bank of Roanoke, 300 U.S. 440 (1937).

161. Morehead v. New York ex rel. Tipaldo, 298 U.S. 587 (1936). Further references to this case are made in the text.

162. Adkins v. Children's Hospital, 261 U.S. 525 (1923). Additional references to this case appear in the text.

163. Cushman, *Rethinking the New Deal*, 99.

164. Leuchtenburg, *Supreme Court Reborn*, 105.

165. West Coast Hotel Co. v. Parrish, 300 U.S. 379 (1937); Cushman, *Rethinking the New Deal*, 84. Further References to *West Coast Hotel* will be made in the text.

166. Stern and others have highlighted a justification for Roberts's switch in a Supreme Court memorandum published in 1955 by Felix Frankfurter, with the permission of Justice Roberts, that explained "that Roberts voted against the validity of the New York minimum wage statute in the Morehead case because New York was arguing only that that case was distinguishable from the Court's 1923 decision in Adkins v. Childrens Hospital, 261 U.S. 525, [so] 'that it was unnecessary to overrule the Adkins case in order to sustain' New York's position." Stern, "Court-Packing Plan," 92.

167. Burnet v. Coronado Oil & Gas Co., 285 U.S. 393, 405 (1932) (Brandeis, J., dissenting).

168. Leuchtenburg, *Supreme Court Reborn*, 143; G. Edward White, "*West Coast Hotel*'s Place in American Constitutional History," *Yale Law Journal Forum* 122 (2012–13): 73.

169. Edward L. Carter and Edward E. Adams, "Justice Owen J. Roberts on 1937," *Green Bag 2d* 15, no. 4 (Summer 2012): 382.

170. Carter and Adams, "Justice Owen J. Roberts," 379.

171. Parry-Giles and Hasian, "Necessity or Nine," 266.

172. Parry-Giles and Hasian, "Necessity or Nine," 266.

173. Parry-Giles and Hasian, "Necessity or Nine," 267.

174. That landmark decision, *NLRB v. Jones & Laughlin Steel Corp.*, 301 U.S. 1 (1937), is discussed below; Tinney quoted in John Q. Barrett, "Attribution Time: Cal Tinney's 1937 Quip, 'A Switch in Time'll Save Nine,'" *Oklahoma Law Review* 73, no. 2 (2021): 238.

175. Barrett, "Attribution Time," 239.

176. Barrett, "Attribution Time," 233–34.

177. Barrett, "Attribution Time," 236.

178. Barrett, "Attribution Time," 236.

179. NLRB v. Jones & Laughlin Steel Corp., 301 U.S. 1 (1937). Further references to this case are made in the text.

180. Samuel W. Sawyer, "The Commerce Clause of the Constitution: The Old and the New," *University of Kansas City Law Review* 8, no. 4 (1939–40): 242–43.

181. Quoted in *NLRB v. Jones & Laughlin Steel Corp.*, 27.

182. Kalman, "Law, Politics," 2176–77.

183. Franklin D. Roosevelt, Excerpts from the Press Conference, April 13, 1937, American Presidency Project.

184. Cushman, "Court-Packing and Compromise," 13.

185. Cushman, "Court-Packing and Compromise," 9.

186. Cushman, "Court-Packing and Compromise," 5.

187. Cushman, "Court-Packing and Compromise," 5–6.

188. Franklin D. Roosevelt, Excerpts from the Press Conference, May 18, 1937, American Presidency Project.

189. Cushman, "Court-Packing and Compromise," 6.

190. Nelson, "President and the Court," 290.

191. Daniel, "Where I Cash In," 412.

192. Steward Machine Co. v. Davis, 301 U.S. 548 (1937); Carmichael v. Southern Coal & Coke Co., 301 U.S. 495 (1937).

193. Franklin D. Roosevelt, Excerpts from the Press Conference, May 25, 1937, American Presidency Project.

194. Cushman, "Court-Packing and Compromise," 5–6.

195. Daniel, "Where I Cash In," 413–14.

196. Franklin D. Roosevelt, Press Conference, July 23, 1937, American Presidency Project.

197. Cushman, "Court-Packing and Compromise," 30.

198. Cushman, *Rethinking the New Deal*, 208.

199. A classic treatise on the movement is Karl N. Llewellyn, "Some Realism about Realism," *Harvard Law Review* 44 (1931): 1222–64. I discuss this movement in chapter 1.

200. Concerns over personnel changes that coincide with new rulings by the court were expressed recently. President's Trump replacement of the liberal Justice Ruth Bader Ginsburg with the conservative Justice Amy Coney Barrett—just a few days before the 2020 presidential election was held—led the Supreme Court to allow a six-week Texas abortion ban to remain in place until the court was ready to hear full arguments over the issue and to show receptivity to a Mississippi law banning abortions after eleven weeks. Such changes of judicial attitudes because of personnel changes led Justice Sotomayor ask: "Will this institution survive the stench that this creates in the public perception that the Constitution and its reading are just political acts? I don't see how it is possible." Dareh Gregorian, "Sotomayor Suggests Supreme Court Won't 'Survive the Stench' of overturning Roe v. Wade," *NBC News* (online), December 1, 2021.

201. Railroad Commission v. Pacific Gas Co. (Rehearing), 302 U.S. 388 (1938); Erie Railroad Co. v. Tompkins; Helvering v. Mountain Producers Corp., 303 U.S. 376 (1938); Graves v. New York ex rel. O'Keefe, 306 U.S. 466 (1939); O'Malley v. Woodrough, 307 U.S. 277 (1939). Butler did not author the dissent in *Erie Railroad Co. v. Tompkins*, 304 U.S. 64 (1938). McReynolds was out for the *O'Malley* case.

202. Rochester Telephone Corp. v. United States, 307 U.S. 125 (1939).

203. *Rochester Telephone*, 147–48 (1939) (Butler, J., concurring in part).

204. Helvering v. Mountain Producers Corp., 303 U.S. 376, 390–91 (1938) (Butler, J., dissenting).

205. Graves v. New York ex rel. O'Keefe, 306 U.S. 466, 493 (1939) (Butler, J., dissenting).

206. Railroad Commission v. Pacific Gas Co. (Rehearing), 302 U.S. 388, 418 (1938) (Butler, J., dissenting).

207. O'Malley v. Woodrough, 307 U.S. 277, 299 (1939) (Butler, J., dissenting).

208. Madden v. Commissioner, 309 U.S. 83 (1940); Helvering v. Hallock, 309 U.S. 106 (1940).

209. Graves v. New York ex rel. O'Keefe, 306 U.S. 466, 489 (1939) (Frankfurter, J., concurring), quoting *McCulloch v. Maryland*, 4 Wheat. (17 U.S.) 316, 431 (1819). Further references to Graves are made in the text.

210. Melvin I. Urofsky, "Graves v. New York Ex Rel. O'Keefe," in Hall, *Oxford Companion*, 345.

211. Helvering v. Mountain Producers Corp., 303 U.S. 376 (1938). Further references to this case are made in the text.

212. These were *Gillespie v. Oklahoma*, 257 U.S. 501 (1922), and *Burnet v. Coronado Oil & Gas Co.*, 285 U.S. 393 (1932).

213. O'Malley v. Woodrough, 307 U.S. 277, 280 (1939). The overruled precedents were *Evans v. Gore*, 253 U.S. 245 (1920), and *Miles v. Graham*, 268 U.S. 501 (1925).

214. Madden v. Commissioner, 309 U.S. 83 (1940). Further references to this case are made in the text.

215. Colgate v. Harvey, 296 U.S. 404 (1935).

216. Helvering v. Hallock, 309 U.S. 106 (1940). Further references to this case are made in the text.

217. Klein v. United States, 283 U.S. 231, 234 (1931).

218. Helvering v. St. Louis Union Trust Co., 296 U.S. 39, 41 (1935). Further references to this case are made in the text.

219. Becker v. St. Louis Trust Co., 296 U.S. 48 (1935).

220. Leavitt v. Blatchford, 17 N.Y. 521, 543 (1858).

221. Rochester Telephone Corp. v. United States, 307 U.S. 125 (1939). Further references to this case are made in the text.

222. Railroad Commission v. Pacific Gas Co. (Rehearing), 302 U.S. 388 (1938). Further references to this case are made in the text.

223. Olsen v. Nebraska, 313 U.S. 236, 244 (1941), overruling *Ribnik v. McBride*, 277 U.S. 350 (1928).

224. Tigner v. Texas, 310 U.S. 141, 147 (1940).

225. Clarke Rountree, "Setting the Stage for *Brown v. Board of Education*: The NAACP's Litigation Campaign Against the 'Separate but Equal' Doctrine," in Brown v. Board of Education *at Fifty: A Rhetorical Perspective*, ed. Clarke Rountree (Lanham, MD: Lexington Books, 2004), 49–90. I discuss prospective argument briefly in chapter 1.

226. Roe v. Wade, 410 U.S. 113 (1973); Doe v. Bolton, 410 U.S. 179 (1973).

227. United States v. Classic, 313 U.S. 299 (1941). Further references to this case are made in the text.

228. Newberry v. United States, 256 U.S. 232 (1921).

229. United States v. Darby, 312 U.S. 100 (1941). Further references to this case are made in the text.

230. Swift v. Tyson, 41 U.S. 1, 18 (1842). Further references to this case are made in the text.

231. William M. Wiecek, "Erie Railroad Co. v. Tompkins," in Hall, *Oxford Companion*, 260.

232. Erie Railroad Co. v. Tompkins, 304 U.S. 64 (1938). Further references to this case will be made in the text.

233. The article referenced is Charles Warren, "New Light on the History of the Federal Judiciary Act of 1789," *Harvard Law Review* 37 (1923): 49, 51–52, 81–88, 108.

234. Baltimore & Ohio Railroad Co. v. Baugh, 149 U.S. 368, 149 U.S. 401 (1893).

235. Quoting *Black & White Taxicab Co. v. Brown & Yellow Taxicab Co.*, 276 U.S. 518, 532–36 at 79 (emphasis added).

236. United States v. Butler et al., 297 U.S. 61, 62 (1936).

Chapter 6

1. Richard Danzig, "Justice Frankfurter's Opinions in the Flag Salute Cases: Blending Logic and Psychologic in Constitutional Decisionmaking," *Stanford Law Review* 36, no. 3 (February 1984): 683; United States v. Carolene Products, 304 U.S. 144, 152 (1938).

2. United States v. Carolene Products, 154n44.

3. Danzig, "Justice Frankfurter's Opinions," 686.

4. Dobbs v. Jackson Women's Health Organization, 597 U.S. ___ (2022) (slip op.). This case will be analyzed in chapter 7.

5. West Virginia State Board of Education v. Barnette, 319 U.S. 624 (1943); Minersville School District v. Gobitis, 310 U.S. 586 (1940). Further references to these cases will be made in the text.

6. J. A. Weems, "Religious Freedom and the Jehovah's Witnesses," *Virginia Law Review* 34, no. 1 (January 1948): 77.

7. Weems, "Religious Freedom," 77.

8. See Weems, "Religious Freedom," 78. Among the cases they won were *State v. Morris*, 28 Idaho 599, 155 Pac. 296 (1916); *Lovell v. City of Griffin*, 303 U.S. 444 (1938); *Schneider v. New Jersey*, 308 U.S. 147 (1939); and *Cantwell v. Connecticut*, 310 U.S. 296 (1940).

9. Weems, "Religious Freedom," 78.

10. Weems, "Religious Freedom," 78n16.

11. Leoles v. Landers, 302 U.S. 656 (1937); Hering v. State Board of Education, 303 U.S. 624 (1937); Gabrielli v. Knickerbocker, 306 U.S. 621 (1938); and Johnson v. Deerfield, 306 U.S. 621 (1938).

12. Jones v. Opelika, 316 U.S. 584 (1942). Further references to this case will be cited in the text.

13. Eight justices reversed their positions with a unanimous verdict in *Union Pacific Railway v. McShane*, 89 U.S. 444 (1874), which overruled a unanimous verdict in *Railway Company v. Prescott*, 83 U.S. 603 (1872). They insisted that "a fuller argument and more mature consideration" (461) led to the change. The only new personnel in the overruling case was Chief Justice Waite, who replaced Chief Justice Chase.

14. Francis H. Heller, "A Turning Point for Religious Liberty," *Virginia Law Review* 29, no. 4 (January 1943): 446, 446n24.

15. Heller, "Turning Point," 446.

16. Weems, "Religious Freedom," 81.

17. Weems, "Religious Freedom," 81.

18. Heller, "Turning Point," 446.

19. Harold H. Punke, "The Flag and the Courts in Free Public Education," *Journal of Religion* 24, no. 2 (April 1944): 123.

20. Punke, "Flag and the Courts," quoting a *Nation* essay at 123.
21. Punke, "Flag and the Courts," 123–24.
22. Quoted in Punke, "Flag and the Courts," 123.
23. Punke, "Flag and the Courts," 123.
24. Quoted in Punke, "Flag and the Courts," 124.
25. Heller, "Turning Point," 449.
26. Punke, "Flag and the Courts," 122; Heller, "Turning Point," 449–50.
27. Punke, "Flag and the Courts," 125.
28. Heller, "Turning Point," 449.
29. Heller, "Turning Point," 450.
30. Heller, "Turning Point," 450–51.
31. Heller, "Turning Point," 452.
32. Heller, "Turning Point," 452.
33. Heller, "Turning Point," quoted at 453.
34. Quoted with emphasis added in Punke, "Flag and the Courts," 127.
35. Barnette v. West Virginia State Board of Education, 37 F. Supp. 251, 253 (D. W. Va. 1942), quoted in Danzig, "Justice Frankfurter's Opinions," 678.
36. At note 10 he cites *Helvering v. Griffiths*, 318 U.S. 371, 401, note 52. Justice Brandeis's famous footnote is in *Burnet v. Coronado Oil & Gas Co.*, 285 U.S. 393, 406–8, notes 1 and 2.
37. See Aristotle, *Rhetoric*, 2.23.3.
38. Danzig, "Justice Frankfurter's Opinions," 689.
39. Brown v. Board of Education, 347 U.S. 483 (1954). Further references to this case will be made in the text.
40. Plessy v. Ferguson, 163 US 537 (1896). Further references to this case will be made in the text.
41. Nikole Hannah-Jones, "Segregation Now," *Atlantic*, May 2014. On southern resistance to desegregation, see, for example, Ann E. Burnette, "The Rhetoric of Virginia's Massive Resistance Movement," in Brown v. Board of Education *at Fifty: A Rhetorical Perspective*, ed. Clarke Rountree (Lanham, MD: Lexington Books, 2004), 119–41.
42. Clarke Rountree, "Setting the Stage for *Brown v. Board of Education*: The NAACP's Litigation Campaign Against the 'Separate but Equal' Doctrine," in Brown v. Board of Education *at Fifty*, 49–90.
43. Mark V. Tushnet, *The NAACP's Legal Strategy against Segregated Education, 1925–1950* (Chapel Hill: University of North Carolina Press, 1987), 29. One of the NAACP's early efforts involved hiring New York attorney Nathan Margold to develop a legal strategy to attack these problems. This yielded his "Preliminary Report to the Joint Committee Supervising the Expenditure of the 1930 Appropriation by the American Fund for Public Service to the N.A.A.C.P." Records of the NAACP, group I (1909–1939), series C, box 200, Library of Congress (photocopy).
44. Susan D. Carle, "Race, Class, and Legal Ethics in the Early NAACP (1910–1920)," *Law and History Review* 20, no. 1 (Spring 2002): 97–147.
45. McCabe v. Atchison, Topeka & Santa Fe Railway Co., 235 U.S. 151, 161–62 (1914).

46. Pearson v. Murray, 169 Md. 478, 485–86 (1936). See also Tushnet, *NAACP's Legal Strategy*, 56.

47. Pearson v. Murray, 169 Md. 478, 487.

48. Missouri ex rel. Gaines v. Canada, 308 U.S. 337, 349–50 (1938).

49. Sipuel v. University of Oklahoma, 332 U.S. 631, 633 (1948) (per curiam). Examples of setbacks include *Bluford v. Canada*, 32 F. Supp. 707 (1940); *State ex rel. Bluford v. Canada*, 348 Mo. 298 (1941); *State ex rel. Michael et al. v. Witham et al.*, 179 Tenn. 250 (1942).

50. McLaurin v. Oklahoma State Regents for Higher Education, 339 U.S. 637, 640 (1950).

51. *McLaurin*, 641–42.

52. Sweatt v. Painter, 339 U.S. 629, 633–34 (1950). Further references to this case are made in the text.

53. For example, see R. C. Taylor, "The Demise of Race Distinctions in Graduate Education," *Duke Bar Journal* 1, no. 2 (June 1951): 141.

54. Cumming v. County Board of Education, 175 U.S. 528 (1899); and Gong Lum v. Rice, 275 U.S. 78 (1927).

55. For a review of the ancient concept of *kairos* and its particular application to the LDF's long-term litigation effort, see Clarke Rountree, "Kairos and American Legal Praxis," *Nevada Law Journal* 20, no. 3 (2020): 855–76.

56. John Anthony Maltese, "Bowers v. Hardwick," in *The Oxford Companion to the Supreme Court of the United States*, ed. Kermit L. Hall (New York: Oxford University Press, 1992), 80. The statute at issue is Georgia Code Ann. § 16-6-2 (1984).

57. Bowers v. Hardwick, 478 U.S. 186 (1986). Further references to this case are made in the text.

58. Lawrence v. Texas, 539 U.S. 558 (2003). Further references to this case will be made in the text.

59. Griswold v. Connecticut, 381 U.S. 479 (1965).

60. Planned Parenthood of Southeastern Pennsylvania v. Casey, 505 U.S. 833 (1992).

61. Romer v. Evans, 517 U.S. 620 (1996). Further references to this case will be made in the text.

62. I say that conservatives claim to abhor such innovations because it appears antithetical to what is supported by conservatives who claim to be originalists, or textualists who rely on interpretations of the Constitution by scrutinizing what words meant when its provisions were passed. But the staunchest textualist in recent times was Justice Scalia, who made a novel interpretation of the Second Amendment in *District of Columbia v. Heller*, finding that the provision gives individuals the right to bear arms—the first time this conclusion had been reached in over 200 years since the amendment was approved. The decision gives short shrift to the opening clause about "[a] well-regulated militia" that has informed the preceding interpretations by the high court. On Scalia's notable deviations from his purported philosophy, see Catherine L. Langford, *Scalia v. Scalia: Opportunistic Textualism in Constitutional Interpretation* (Tuscaloosa: University of Alabama Press, 2008).

63. Citing ALI, Model Penal Code § 213.2, comment 2, p. 372 (1980) at 572.

64. Quoting *County of Sacramento v. Lewis,* 523 U.S. 833, 857 (1998) (Kennedy, J., concurring) at 572.

65. Payne v. Tennessee, 501 U.S. 808, 828 (1991), quoting *Helvering v. Hallock,* 309 U.S. 106, 119 (1940), referenced by Kennedy at 577. *Helvering* has been cited regarding stare decisis by at least a half-dozen cases, including *Boys Markets, Inc. v. Retail Clerks Union, Local 770,* 398 U.S. 235 (1970); *Continental T. V., Inc. v. GTE Sylvania, Inc.,* 433 U.S. 36 (1977); *Payne v. Tennessee,* 501 U.S. 808 (1991); *Quill Corp. v. North Dakota,* 504 U.S. 298 (1992); *Adarand Constructors, Inc. v. Peña,* 515 U.S. 200 (1995); *Citizens United v. Federal Election Commission,* 558 U.S. 310 (2010). *Payne* has been cited regarding stare decisis more than a dozen times, including in *Arizona v. Fulminante,* 499 U.S. 279 (1991); *Quill Corp. v. North Dakota,* 504 U.S. 298 (1992); *Planned Parenthood of Southeastern Pennsylvania v. Casey,* 505 U.S. 833 (1992); *United States v. Dixon,* 509 U.S. 688 (1993); *Seminole Tribe of Florida v. Florida,* 517 U.S. 44 (1996); *State Oil Co. v. Khan,* 522 U.S. 3 (1997); *Agostini v. Felton,* 521 U.S. 203 (1997); *Hohn v. United States,* 524 U.S. 236 (1998); *Crawford v. Washington,* 541 U.S. 36 (2004); *Pearson v. Callahan,* 555 U.S. 223 (2009); *Montejo v. Louisiana,* 556 U.S. 778 (2009); *Citizens United v. Federal Election Commission,* 558 U.S. 310 (2010); *Alleyne v. United States,* 570 U.S. 99 (2013); *Johnson v. United States,* 576 U.S. 591 (2015).

66. Planned Parenthood of Southeastern Pennsylvania v. Casey, 505 U.S. 833, 855–56 (1992).

67. Planned Parenthood of Southeastern Pennsylvania v. Casey, 844.

68. Danzig, "Justice Frankfurter's Opinions in the Flag Salute Cases," 686; United States v. Carolene Products, 304 U.S. 144, 154, note 4 (1938).

69. Plessy v. Ferguson, 163 U.S. 537, 544 (1896).

Chapter 7

1. Josh Gerstein and Alexander Ward, "Supreme Court Has Voted to Overturn Abortion Rights, Draft Opinion Shows." *Politico,* May 2, 2022.

2. The *Wall Street Journal* says "the reaction from the left and the media [to the leaked draft] has been apocalypse now." It quotes a press release from Democratic Speaker of the House Nancy Pelosi and Democratic Senate Majority Leader Chuck Schumer saying: "The Republican-appointed Justices' reported votes to overturn *Roe v. Wade* would go down as an abomination, one of the worst and most damaging decisions in modern history." Editorial Board, "The Supreme Court Leak," *Wall Street Journal,* May 4, 2022.

Both sides of the abortion controversy recognized that the leak was unprecedented, though they obviously had different reactions to it. Kate Zernike and Elizabeth Dias, "Demonstrators Flock to the Supreme Court after Leak of Draft Decision," *New York Times* (online), May 3, 2022.

CNN posted a draft of the final decision showing changes from the leaked draft. They were almost all copyediting revisions to the original text to meet formatting guidelines, with responses to dissenters adding 20 percent to the total decision. John Keefe et al., *CNN,* June 27, 2022.

3. Dobbs v. Jackson Women's Health Organization, 597 U.S. ___ (2022).

4. Michael J. Klarman, "The Supreme Court 2019 Term: The Degradation of American Democracy—and the Court," *Harvard Law Review* 134, no. 1 (2020): 250. George W. Bush is the only Republican candidate to win the popular vote in any presidential election since 1992, winning in 2004 largely because of his leadership after the terrorist attacks of September 11, 2001. President Bush (in his 2000 election) and President Trump (in his 2020 election) lost the popular vote but won the Electoral College vote. Bill Clinton won the popular vote in the 1992 election, but not a majority of the total popular vote, because third-party candidate Ross Perot siphoned off almost 19 percent of the vote from the total.

5. For example, President Trump's three appointments to the court voted in 2022 to overturn *Roe v. Wade*, allowing states to criminalize abortions from conception. This overruling will be analyzed at length below.

6. Stephen J. Wermiel, "The Nomination of Justice Brennan: Eisenhower's Mistake? A Look at the Historical Record," *Constitutional Commentary* 11, no. 3 (1995): 515–37.

7. Republican opposition to abortion developed initially during President Nixon's reelection campaign as a means to peel blue-collar Catholics away from the Democratic Party, though he dropped it when he discovered he already attracted that demographic on the issues of Vietnam and race and did not want to offend other voters unnecessarily. Ford took a more moderate position on abortion than religious conservatives wanted. But Ronald Reagan allied with the burgeoning Christian political movement, the Moral Majority, and followed his own preferences in opposing abortion. Neil A. O'Brian, "Before Reagan: The Development of Abortion's Partisan Divide," *Perspectives on Politics* 18, no. 4 (2020): 1041–42. The history of this change is discussed at length below.

8. Richard Y. Funston, "Stevens, John Paul," in *The Oxford Companion to the Supreme Court of the United States*, ed. Kermit L. Hall (New York: Oxford University Press, 1992), 836–37.

9. Justice Kennedy authored the decision in *Lawrence v. Texas*, 539 U.S. 558 (2003), that overturned *Bowers v. Hardwick*, 478 U.S. 186 (1986), a case that allowed states to prosecute homosexual sodomy; he also authored *Obergefell v. Hodges*. 576 U.S. 644 (2015), which made gay marriage legal across the United States. He was on the liberal side in other decisions, such as outlawing capital punishment for the mentally ill and for juveniles in *Atkins v. Virginia*, 536 U.S. 304 (2002), and *Roper v. Simmons*, 543 U.S. 551 (2005), respectively.

10. On affirmative action, see, for example, *Regents of the University of California v. Bakke*, 438 U.S. 265 (1978); and *United Steelworkers of America v. Weber*, 443 U.S. 1993 (1979); *Roe v. Wade*, 410 U.S. 113 (1973).

11. *United States v. Alfonso D. Lopez, Jr.*, 514 U.S. 549 (1995), struck down the Gun-Free School Zones Act, which had relied on the Commerce Clause, establishing a doctrine of new federalism. *United States v. Morrison*, 529 U.S. 598 (2000), struck down the Violence against Women Act that relied on the Commerce Clause as well.

12. Planned Parenthood of Southeastern Pennsylvania v. Casey, 505 U.S. 833

(1992). As an example of allowing states to place restrictions on abortion, see *Hodgson v. Minnesota*, 497 U.S. 417 (1990).

13. Lawrence v. Texas, 539 U.S. 558 (2003).

14. Bush v. Gore, 531 U.S. 98 (2000). When the high court announced a stay of the counting, George W. Bush was (unofficially) ahead by only 154 votes. Clarke Rountree, *Judging the Supreme Court: Constructions of Motives in* Bush v. Gore, Rhetoric & Public Affairs (East Lansing: Michigan State University Press, 2007), 18.

15. Obergefell v. Hodges, 576 U.S. 644 (2015).

16. Chief Justice Roberts joined the liberal justices in a 5-4 decision in *National Federation of Independent Business v. Sebelius*, 567 U.S. 519 (2012), and Justice Kennedy as well in the 6-3 decision of *King v. Burwell*, 576 U.S. 473 (2015).

17. District of Columbia v. Heller, 554 U.S. 570 (2008).

18. Citizens United v. Federal Election Commission, 558 U.S. 310 (2010). On the impact of this decision see Klarman, "Degradation of American Democracy," 203–4.

19. Burwell v. Hobby Lobby, 573 U.S. 682 (2014).

20. Shelby County v. Holder, 570 U.S. 529 (2013); Paul Blumenthal, "8 Years on, John Roberts' Disastrous Voting Rights Ruling is Wreaking Havoc," *HuffPost*, June 25, 2021.

21. Dobbs v. Jackson Women's Health Organization, 597 U.S. ___ (2022).

22. Clarke Rountree, ed., *Venomous Speech: Problems with American Political Discourse on the Right and Left*, 2 vol. (Santa Barbara, CA: Praeger, 2013), 1:xxvii.

23. Clarke Rountree, "Introduction: Strained Voices in American Political Discourse," in *Venomous Speech*, 1:xxv–xxvi.

24. Rountree, "Introduction," xxvii–xxix.

25. Trevor Parry-Giles, *The Character of Justice: Rhetoric, Law, and Politics in the Supreme Court Confirmation Process*, Rhetoric and Public Affairs (East Lansing: Michigan State University Press, 2006), 119–20.

26. Eliza Griswold, "Franklin Graham's Uneasy Alliance with Donald Trump," *New Yorker*, September 11, 2018.

27. Donald Trump told *Meet the Press* in 1999 that he was "very pro-choice." Interview with Donald Trump, October 24, 1999, *Meet the Press*, NBC.

28. Samantha Cooney, "The Mixed-up History of Donald Trump's Abortion Stance(s)," *Time*, October 21, 2016.

29. Carl Hulse, "Mitch McConnell's Court Delivers," *New York Times*, June 27, 2022.

30. "Brett Kavanaugh Confirmation, Victory for Trump in Supreme Court Battle," *BBC News*, October 7, 2018.

31. Roe v. Wade, 410 U.S. 113 (1973). Further references to this case will be made in the text.

32. Mark V. Tushnet, "Roe v. Wade," in Hall, *Oxford Companion*, 740.

33. Jane Roe went public after the case, identifying herself as Norma McCorvey. Tushnet, "Roe v. Wade," 740.

34. Roe v. Wade, 314 F. Supp. 1217 (N.D. Tex. 1970). Further references to this case will be made in the text.

35. Griswold v. Connecticut, 381 U.S. 479 (1965). "Family, marriage and sex matters": quoting *United States v. Vuitch*, 305 F. Supp. 1032, 1035 (D.D.C.1969).

36. Babbitz v. McCann, 312 F. Supp. 725 (E.D. Wis.1970); People v. Belous, 80 Cal. Rptr. 354, 458 P.2d 194 (Cal.1969); State v. Munson, (South Dakota Circuit Court, Pennington County, April 6, 1970).

37. Doe v. Bolton, 410 U.S. 179 (1973). Further references to this case will be made in the text.

38. Rehnquist has two concerns. The first is that the district court failed to indicate the stage of Roe's pregnancy, so that if she had been in her third trimester, the statute could have applied to her even under the court's ruling (since states can prohibit abortions not necessary to preserve the life or health of the mother in the third trimester). The mootness for the Supreme Court's decision is not stated outright, though Rehnquist asserts: "*Even if there were a plaintiff' in this case capable of litigating the issue which the Court decides*, I would reach a conclusion opposite to that reached by the Court" (171–72; emphasis added).

39. For example, see Dennis J. Horan and Thomas J. Balch, "*Roe v. Wade*: No Justification in History, Law, or Logic," in *Abortion and the Constitution: Reversing* Roe v. Wade *Through the Courts*, ed. Dennis J. Horan, Edward R. Grant, and Paige C. Cunningham (Washington, DC: Georgetown University Press, 1987), 57–88. Justice Alito's summary of this history in *Dobbs*, challenging Blackmun's account, will be analyzed below.

40. *Union Pacific Railway Co. v. Botsford*, 141 U.S. 250 (1891). Further references to this case will be made in the text.

41. The reference is apparently to Thomas M. Cooley, *The Elements of Torts* (Chicago: Callahan, 1895), 29.

42. Griswold v. Connecticut, 381 U.S. 479, 480–81 (1965). Further references to this case are made in the text.

43. See, for example, Noah Feldman, "Doctors Have the Right to Perform Abortions," *Washington Post*, May 23, 2016.

44. Feldman, "Doctors Have the Right."

45. Quoted in Jonathan Bullington, "Justice Ginsburg: *Roe v. Wade* not 'Woman-Centered,'" *Chicago Tribune*, May 11, 2013.

46. Justice White's dissent to the twin cases is reported in *Doe* (221).

47. Akron v. Akron Center for Reproductive Health, 462 U.S. 416 (1983). Further references to this case will be made in the text. The replacements involved Justice Stevens succeeding Justice Douglas, and Justice O'Connor succeeding Justice Stewart.

48. Thornburgh v. American College of Obstetricians, 476 U.S. 747 (1986). Further references to this case will be made in the text.

49. Webster v. Reproductive Health Services, 492 U.S. 490 (1989). Further references to this case will be made in the text.

50. Planned Parenthood of Southeastern Pennsylvania v. Casey, 505 U.S. 833 (1992). Further references to this case will be made in the text.

51. In his opinion in *Casey* concurring in part and dissenting in part, Justice Blackmun, who authored the *Roe* majority opinion, held his ground, asserting: "Today, no

less than yesterday, the Constitution and decisions of this Court require that a State's abortion restrictions be subjected to the strictest judicial scrutiny. Our precedents and the joint opinion's principles require us to subject all *non-de-minimis* abortion regulations to strict scrutiny" (926).

52. Dormaan J. Dalal, "The Concept of Super-Precedent," *Bar & Bench*, June 19, 2022. The term gained currency when Pennsylvania Republican Senator Arlen Specter asked John Roberts at his Senate Judiciary Committee hearing to become chief justice if he believed that *Roe* enjoyed a form of "super-stare decisis" because of its repeated reaffirmation.

53. Referencing *Poe v. Ullman*, 367 U.S., at 543 (Harlan, J., dissenting) at 858, and *Carey v. Population Services International*, 431 U.S. 678, 684 (1977) at 859. A pre-*Griswold* decision cited by the court in this rational continuum is *Skinner v. Oklahoma ex rel. Williamson*, 316 U.S. 535 (1942).

54. See, for example, Ann E. Burnette, "The Rhetoric of Virginia's Massive Resistance Movement," in Brown v. Board of Education *at Fifty: A Rhetorical Perspective*, ed. Clarke Rountree (Lanham, MD: Lexington Books, 2004), 119–42.

55. Dalal, "Concept of Super-Precedent."

56. Quoting *Leavitt v. Blatchford*, 17 N.Y. 521 (1858), in William Green, "Stare Decisis," *American Law Review* 14 (September 1880): 639.

57. Clarke Rountree, "Constructing a Free Agent: 'Good Judgment' in Justice Kennedy's *Lawrence v. Texas* Opinion," in *Justice Anthony Kennedy: The Rhetoric of Liberty*, ed. David A. Frank and Francis M. Mootz (University Park: Pennsylvania State University Press, 2023), 98.

58. Kelly Zielinski, "The Implication of Texas Abortion Law SB8 on at-Risk Populations in Texas and Other States," *DePaul Journal of Health Care Law* 23, no. 2 (2022): 61.

59. Zielinski, "Implication of Texas Abortion," 62–63.

60. Zielinski, "Implication of Texas Abortion," 63–64.

61. Zielinski, "Implication of Texas Abortion," 63.

62. Whole Woman's Health v. Jackson, 594 U.S. _____ (2021) (Alito, J., slip op., at 2).

63. Whole Woman's Health v. Jackson, 594 U.S. ____ (2021) (Roberts, C.J., dissenting, slip op., at 2). Further references to this opinion will be made in the text.

64. Whole Woman's Health v. Jackson, 594 U.S. ____ (2021) (Breyer, J., dissenting, slip op., at 1).

65. Whole Woman's Health v. Jackson, 594 U.S. ____ (2021) (Sotomayor, J., dissenting, slip op., at 1). Further references to this opinion will be made in the text.

66. Whole Woman's Health v. Jackson, 594 U.S. ____ (2021) (Kagan, J., dissenting, slip op., at 1–2).

67. Rachel Martin, "The Impact of the Strict New Abortion Law in Texas," *Morning Edition*, NPR, September 20, 2021.

68. Martin, "Strict New Abortion Law."

69. Jeffrey Hannan, "*Dobbs v. Jackson Women's Health Organization* and the Likely End of the *Roe v. Wade* Era," *Duke Journal of Constitutional Law and Public Policy Sidebar* 17 (2021–22): 282.

70. Timothy Sandefur, "In Defense of Substantive Due Process, or the Promise of Lawful Rule," *Harvard Journal of Law and Public Policy* 35, no. 1 (Winter 2012): 350.

71. Ryan C. Williams, "The One and Only Substantive Due Process Clause," *Yale Law Journal* 120, no. 3 (2010): 419.

72. Williams says that they had a different ground for substantive due process that focused on what he calls "vested rights" and "general law" concerns. Williams, "One and Only," 498.

73. McDonald v. City of Chicago, 561 U.S. 742, 862 (2010) (Stevens, J., dissenting).

74. Daniel O. Conkle, "The Second Death of Substantive Due Process," *Indiana Law Journal* 62, no. 2 (1987): 216; Williams, "One and Only," 26. Conkle calls *Lochner v. New York*, 198 U.S. 45 (1905), the "first sustained commitment to the use of substantive due process" by the US Supreme Court (216).

75. Williams, "One and Only," 26–27.

76. Conkle, "Second Death," 218–19 ("When the Supreme Court abandoned *Lochner* in the 1930's, it was widely understood that the Court was abandoning substantive due process generally, and not merely the use of substantive due process in the protection of economic rights").

77. Griswold v. Connecticut, 381 U.S. 479 (1965). Conkle, "Second Death," 218–20.

78. Respectively: Loving v. Virginia, 388 U.S. 1 (1967); Eisenstadt v. Baird, 405 U.S. 438 (1972); Roe v. Wade, 410 U.S. 113 (1973); Moore v. East Cleveland, 431 U.S. 494 (1977); Lawrence v. Texas, 539 U.S. 558 (2003); Obergefell v. Hodges, 576 U.S. 644 (2015).

79. Williams, "One and Only," 427.

80. West Virginia State Board of Education v. Barnette, 319 U.S. 624, 638 (1943).

81. Quoting *Washington v. Glucksberg*, 521 U.S. 702, 721 (1997) at 5. Further references to this case will be made in the text.

82. Lawrence v. Texas, 539 U.S. 558, 578 (2003). I explore this case more fully in Rountree, "Constructing a Free Agent."

83. Moore v. East Cleveland, 431 U.S. 494 (1977).

84. Ginsburg does use the "and" language at one point in the opinion, but it is applied to the specific issue at hand: "Protection against excessive punitive economic sanctions secured by the Clause is, to repeat, both 'fundamental to our scheme of ordered liberty' and 'deeply rooted in this Nation's history and tradition'" (7).

85. *Glucksberg*, 710, 720, 727–28, and note 19.

86. Nancy C. Marcus, "Yes, Alito, There Is a Right to Privacy: Why the Leaked Dobbs Opinion is Doctrinally Unsound," *ConLawNOW* 13, no. 1 (2021–22): 109.

87. *Obergefell*, 18, citing *Loving v. Virginia*, 388 U.S. 1 (1967), *Turner v. Safley*, 482 U.S. 78 (1987), *Zablocki v. Redhail*, 434 U.S. 374 (1978).

88. Marcus, "Yes, Alito," 102. Emphasis added.

89. Bowers v. Hardwick, 478 U.S. 186 (1986). Further references to this case are made in the text.

90. Lawrence v. Texas, 539 U.S. 558 (2003). Further references to this case will be made in the text.

91. Alexander Abad-Santos, "How the Death of DOMA Ended the Right's Fear of a Dog-Marrying Planet," *Atlantic* (online), June 26, 2013.

92. Editorial Board, "The Supreme Court's Radical Abortion Ruling Begins a Dangerous New Era," *Washington Post* (online), June 24, 2022.

93. Leslie C. Griffin, "What Did Those Sixteen Justices Say?" *Wilamette Law Review* 58, no. 2 (Spring 2022): 164. Not all Catholics on the court follow Church doctrine and oppose abortion—Justice Sotomayor is an obvious exception. However, it is curious that 78 percent of the members of the Supreme Court were raised Catholic when they comprise only one-fifth of the US population. Because Republicans have appointed the greatest number of Supreme Court justices and have been committed to overturning the right to abortion, we might surmise that they believed religious affiliation was an indicator of position on the issue. Six of the seven Catholic-raised justices on the court were appointed by Republican presidents, including all three of President Trump's picks.

94. Marcus, "Yes, Alito," 103.

95. Griffin, "Sixteen Justices Say?" 193–250.

96. Aaron Tang, "The Originalist Case for an Abortion Middle Ground," Social Science Research Network, 2021, 3, quoting Michael W. McConnell, "The Right to Die and the Jurisprudence of Tradition," *Utah Law Review* 1997, no. 3 (1997): 696.

97. Aaron Tang, "Op-Ed: The Supreme Court Flunks Abortion History," *Los Angeles Times* (online), May 5, 2022.

98. I draw from three essays by Professor Tang, including an unpublished paper from 2021, an editorial from 2022, and a law review essay from 2023.

99. Tang, "Originalist Case," 15n83.

100. Tang, "Supreme Court Flunks." Since even the common law allowed one to abort a post-quickening fetus to save the life of the mother, this number is probably higher.

101. Alito says that "in the 1732 case mentioned above, the judge said of the charge of abortion (*with no mention of quickening*) that he had 'never met with a case so barbarous and unnatural'" (18; emphasis added).

Tang agrees that an abortionist who kills a pregnant woman through a poison can be convicted of murder. However, that does not mean abortion was a crime, as he explains:

The Court is . . misguided to rely on the common law rule under which an abortion provider may be punished for the mother's murder if the provider prescribes a poison so noxious or performs a procedure so dangerous as to cause the mother's death. This rule does mean something was "not a legal right": namely, the act of killing a patient through a dangerous procedure. But that fact does nothing to impugn the permissibility of performing a safe abortion that produces no such tragic outcome—conduct that the majority concedes was not punishable in any state at the founding.

Tang uses an example of right of parents to educate their children, which cannot be rejected simply because they also might harm them by neglecting their needs. Aaron Tang, "*Dobbs*: History, Tradition, and the Uncertain Future of a Nationwide Abortion Ban," *Stanford Law Review* 75, no. 5 (May 2023): 1116n133.

102. Tang, "Originalist Case," 16. See also Tang, "*Dobbs*," 1097.

103. Tang, "Originalist Case," 17.

104. In his book on abortion in the United States, James C. Mohr claimed: "American women in 1800 were legally free to attempt to terminate a condition that might turn out to be pregnancy until the existence of that pregnancy was incontrovertibly confirmed by the perception of fetal movement." James C. Mohr, *Abortion in America: The Origins and Evolution of National Policy* (New York: Oxford University Press, 1979), 4.

105. Tang, "*Dobbs*," 1096.

106. Tang, "Originalist Case," 23–24.

107. Tang, "Originalist Case," 24.

108. Tang, "*Dobbs*," 1128.

109. Tang, "Originalist Case," 24.

110. Tang, "Originalist Case," 24.

111. Brief for American Historical Association et al. as Amici Curiae, 26–27.

112. Eugene Quay, "Justifiable Abortion—Medical and Legal Foundations" Georgetown Law Journal 49, no. 3 (1961): 395. See especially the brief's reliance in making a list of twenty-six states at 26–28. For example, in discussing the Alabama statute, Quay does not even quote the statute in concluding: "In 1841 Alabama enacted what had by then become something of a standard American abortion statute, forbidding attempts to cause miscarriage by any means unless necessary to preserve the life of the mother, but provided only a three to six months' jail term as punishment. Quay, "Justifiable Abortion," 437. He does include the language of the statute in the appendix but does not question it.

113. Tang, "Originalist Case," 25. These states included Kansas, Michigan, Missouri, New Hampshire, New York, Ohio, Pennsylvania, and Wisconsin.

114. Tang, "Originalist Case," 26–30. These states included Maine, Maryland, Indiana, Vermont, Rhode Island, Connecticut, Iowa, and Massachusetts.

115. Tang, "Originalist Case," 30–31. These states included Delaware, Georgia, Kentucky, North Carolina, South Carolina, Tennessee, Arkansas, Minnesota, and Mississippi. The first six listed here still relied on the common law; the last three had statutes that banned only post-quickening abortions.

116. Tang, "*Dobbs*," 1128.

117. Tang, "*Dobbs*," 1145–49.

118. Tang, "*Dobbs*," 1129.

119. Tang, "*Dobbs*," 1131, quoting *Smith v. Gafford*, 31 Ala. 45, 51 (1857).

120. Mohr, *Abortion in America*, 41.

121. Tang, "*Dobbs*," 1133; Tang, "Originalist Case," 37.

122. Tang, "*Dobbs*," 1135; Tang, "Originalist Case," 39.

123. Tang, "*Dobbs*," 1138, quoting *State v. Dunn*, 53 Or. 304. 315 (1909).

124. Tang, "*Dobbs*," 1138–40. The case was *Gray v. State of Texas*, 178 S.W. 337 (1915), quoted at 338.

125. Tang, "Originalist Case," 49.

126. Tang, "*Dobbs*," 1143.

127. Tang, "*Dobbs*," 1141–42, 1142–43, 1142, 1143, 1144.

128. Tang, "*Dobbs*," 1145.

129. Tang, "*Dobbs*," 1145–46; Tang, "Originalist Case," 46.

130. Tang, "*Dobbs*," 1146–47; Tang, "Originalist Case," 46.

131. Tang, "*Dobbs*," 1147–48; Tang, "Originalist Case," 47.

132. Tang, "*Dobbs*," 1148–49; Tang, "Originalist Case," 48.

133. Mohr, *Abortion in America*, 26.

134. Tang, "*Dobbs*," 1149–50. Tang's "middle ground" recognizes that the common-law standard criminalizing abortions after quickening is earlier than *Roe*'s third trimester be several weeks; thus, he would limit *Roe*'s restriction on abortion bans to the sixteenth week, forging a "middle way." Tang, "Originalist Case," 60–63.

135. Tang, "Originalist Case," 61.

136. Tang, "Originalist Case," 62.

137. Tang, "Originalist Case," 62.

138. Brief for American Historical Association et al. as Amici Curiae, 22.

139. Brief for American Historical Association, 30.

140. Tang, "Originalist Case," 62.

141. Tang, "Originalist Case," 62.

142. Brief for the United States as Amici Curiae Supporting Respondents, *Dobbs v. Jackson Women's Health Organization, et al.*, 597 U.S. _____ (2022), 28.

143. I say "balanced" not because Tang is neutral—he clearly supports abortion rights. Instead, he evinces a scholarly interest in truth. For example, in one paper he admits he was wrong in his prior assessment of Massachusetts abortion law: "My prior treatment of Massachusetts also failed inexcusably to account for the state Supreme Court's decision in *Commonwealth v. Wood*, which held that even the state's 1845 law applied 'to all cases of pregnancy,' including before quickening. With both of these mistakes corrected, I readily confess error. Pro-life advocates are correct to count the state as banning pre-quickening procedures at the relevant time." Tang, "Originalist Case," 30.

144. See, for example, Alito's discussion and references at 26–27.

145. Korematsu v. United States, 323 U.S. 214, 246 (1944) (Jackson, J., dissenting).

146. Rountree, *Judging the Supreme Court*.

147. Rountree, *Judging the Supreme Court*, 113.

148. Bush v. Gore, 121 S.Ct. 525, 532 (2000).

149. Rountree, *Judging the Supreme Court*, 248–50.

150. Quoted in Rountree, *Judging the Supreme Court*, 249–50.

151. This is not to say that the right to interracial marriage could not be defended on other constitutional grounds, such as Equal Protection.

152. Eisenstadt v. Baird, 405 U.S. 438 (1972).

153. That is not to say that an infant, whether premature or not, does not require care or even medical intervention to live. But that care need not be given by the mother—she is no longer a required element in the sustenance of her offspring.

154. Brief for American Bar Association as Amici Curiae Supporting Respondents, *Dobbs v. Jackson Women's Health Organization, et al.*, 597 U.S. _____ (2022), 28, quoting *Casey*, 505 U.S. at 873 (plurality opinion).

155. For example, *Zap v. United States,* 330 U.S. 800 (1947) (rehearing), overruling *Zap v. United States,* 328 U.S. 624 (1946).

156. Linda Greenhouse, "What in the World Happened to the Supreme Court?" *Atlantic* (online), November 14, 2022.

157. In the Brief for States supporting the respondents, they list courts and legislatures following this standard:

Cases from other jurisdictions further demonstrate that the viability rule is workable in practice. Since *Casey,* the courts of appeals that have considered laws prohibiting abortions before viability have had no difficulty applying the rule. *See, e.g., MKB Mgmt. Corp. v. Stenehjem,* 795 F.3d 768, 773 (8th Cir. 2015); *McCormack v. Herzog,* 788 F.3d 1017, 1029 (9th Cir. 2015); *Edwards,* 786 F.3d at 1117; *Isaacson v. Horne,* 716 F.3d 1213, 1231 (9th Cir. 2013); *Jane L. v. Bangerter,* 102 F.3d 1112, 1114, 1117–1118 (10th Cir. 1996); *Guam Soc'y of Obstetricians & Gynecologists v. Ada,* 962 F.2d 1366, 1368–1369, 1372 (9th Cir. 1992); *see also* Resp. Br. 23, 41 n.26.

The experience of the States offers still more evidence of the workability of this rule. Eighteen States—including States on both sides of this case—expressly use "viability" as the point beyond which most abortions are prohibited under state law. *See, e.g.,* Ariz. Rev. Stat. § 36-2301.01; Cal. Health & Safety Code § 123468(b); Conn. Gen. Stat. § 19a-602(b); Del. Code. tit. 24, § 1790(b); Haw. Rev. Stat. § 453-16(b); Idaho Code §§ 18-604, 18-608(3); Ill. Comp. Stat. 55/1-25(a); Me. Rev. Stat. tit. 22, § 1598(4); Md. Code, Health-Gen. § 20-209(b); Minn. Stat. § 145.412(3); Mo. Stat. § 188.030(1); Mont. Code § 50-20-109(1)(b); N.Y. Pub. Health Law § 2599-bb(1); R.I. Gen. Laws § 23-4.13-2(d); Tenn. Code § 39-15-211(b)(1); Utah Code § 76-7-302(b); Wash. Rev. Code §§ 9.02.110, 9.02.120; Wyo. Stat. § 35-6-102. There is no indication that the legislators who drafted those statutes, the courts that apply them, or the physicians and women who are subject to them, have experienced difficulty understanding or applying that line. (*Brief for States et al. as Amici Curiae Supporting Respondents, Dobbs v. Jackson Women's Health Organization, et al.,* 597 U.S. _____ [2022], 10).

158. June Medical Services, LLC v. Russo, 140 S. Ct. 2103, 2136 (2020) (Roberts, C.J., concurring in the judgment).

159. Brief for American Bar Association as Amici Curiae Supporting Respondents, *Dobbs v. Jackson Women's Health Organization, et al.,* 597 U.S. _____ (2022), 30.

160. Hill v. Colorado, 530 U.S. 703, 723 (2000); Scalia's complaint appears at 741–42.

161. A ninety-year-old woman in 2022 would be forty-one in 1973 when *Roe* was handed down, still in her childbearing years. So, only a tiny percentage of women—those somewhat over ninety—would miss this window.

162. Brief for American Bar Association as Amici Curiae Supporting Respondents, *Dobbs v. Jackson Women's Health Organization, et al.,* 597 U.S. _____ (2022), 26, citing Diana Greene Foster, PhD, et al., "Socioeconomic Outcomes of Women Who Receive and Women Who Are Denied Wanted Abortions in the United States," *American Journal of Public Health* 108 (February 2008): 407, 411–12 (Feb. 2018); Sarah Miller et al., "The Economic Consequences of Being Denied an Abortion," *National*

Bureau of Economic Research, Working Paper 26662, 29 (January 2020). The Turnaway Study followed women seeking abortions.

163. Brief for American Bar Association as Amici Curiae Supporting Respondents, *Dobbs v. Jackson Women's Health Organization, et al.*, 597 U.S. ____ (2022), 23.

164. Lawrence v. Texas, 539 U.S. 558, 592 (2003) (Scalia, J., dissenting).

165. Quoting *Payne v. Tennessee*, 501 U.S. 808, 828 (1991) at 64.

166. Quill Corp. v. North Dakota, 504 U.S. 298, 321 (1992).

167. Dickerson v. United States, 530 U.S. 428, 443 (2000). A later case clarified that *Dickerson* "was referring not to police reliance on a rule requiring them to provide warnings but to the broader societal reliance on that individual right." Arizona v. Gant, 556 U.S. 332, 350 (2009).

168. Hohn v. United States, 524 U.S. 236, 261 (1998) (Scalia, J., dissenting).

169. Ramos v. Louisiana, 590 U.S. ___ (2020), overruling *Apodaca v. Oregon*, 406 U.S. 404 (1972) (plurality opinion), and *Johnson v. Louisiana*, 406 U.S. 404 (1972).

170. Gamble v. United States, 587 U.S. ____ (2019), slip op., 11–12.

171. Home Building & Loan Association v. Blaisdell, 290 U.S. 398 (1934); Nebbia v. New York, 291 U.S. 502 (1934).

172. As chapter 5 notes, some claim Roberts changed in position in one year because of a technicality in the *Tipaldo* case. The many overrulings following the 1936/1937 term were supported by the retirement of conservatives and their replacement by FDR.

173. "A Countermajoritarian Difficulty," *Economist*, May 7, 2022, 19.

174. As I noted in chapter 5, even conservatives lambasted the overruled *Tipaldo*, with Herbert Hoover calling for an amendment to restore to the states "the power they thought they already had." William E. Leuchtenburg, *The Supreme Court Reborn: The Constitutional Revolution in the Age of Roosevelt* (Oxford: Oxford University Press, 1995), 105.

175. Knox v. Lee (Legal Tender Cases) 79 U.S. (12 Wall.) 457 (1871). Further references to this case will be made in the text.

176. Hepburn v. Griswold, Hepburn 75 U.S. (8 Wall.) 603 (1870). Further references to this case will be made in the text.

177. See a discussion of these changes in the size of the court and appointments in chapter 3.

178. Joseph M. Cormack, "The Legal Tender Cases. A Drama of American Legal and Financial History," *Virginia Law Review* 16, no. 2 (1929): 143.

179. "Countermajoritarian Difficulty."

180. Knox v. Lee (Legal Tender Cases) 79 U.S. (12 Wall.) 457, 529 (1871).

181. David J. Garrow, "Mental Decrepitude on the U.S. Supreme Court: The Historical Case for a 28th Amendment," *University of Chicago Law Review* 67, no. 4 (Fall 2000): 1003–4.

182. Charles Fairman, *Reconstruction and Reunion, 1864–88, Part One*, vol. 4 of *History of the Supreme Court of the United States* (New York: Macmillan, 1971), 678.

183. Brief for American Bar Association as Amici Curiae Supporting Respondents, *Dobbs v. Jackson Women's Health Organization, et al.*, 597 U.S. ____ (2022), 21.

184. Webster v. Reproductive Health Services, 492 U.S. 490, 558 (1989) (Blackmun, J., dissenting) (emphasis added).

185. The reinstatement of the death penalty in *Gregg v. Georgia,* 428 U.S. 153 (1976), might be characterized as taking away a right not to be executed, but it affects a very small number of people.

186. Epps notes that Alito was nicknamed "Scalito" by some who thought he would follow in his elder colleague's footsteps. Garrett Epps, "The Alito Court: Justice Samuel Alito—Harris v. Quinn," in *American Justice 2014: Nine Clashing Visions on the Supreme Court* (Philadelphia: University of Pennsylvania Press, 2014), 112.

187. Epps, "Alito Court," 112.

188. Brief of Amici Curiae Birth Equity Organizations and Scholars in Support of Respondents, *Dobbs v. Jackson Women's Health Organization, et al.,* 597 U.S. _____ (2022), 28.

189. Paul Kane, "In Confirming Supreme Court Justices, Private Senator Meetings Trump Hearings," *Washington Post* (online), May 7, 2022.

190. Quoting *Leavitt v. Blatchford,* 17 N.Y. 521 (1858), in Green, "Stare Decisis," 639.

191. Linda Greenhouse, "What in the World Happened to the Supreme Court?" *Atlantic* (online), November 14, 2022.

192. Greenhouse, "What in the World."

193. Greenhouse, "What in the World."

194. Greenhouse, "What in the World."

195. Greenhouse, "What in the World."

196. Greenhouse, "What in the World."

197. Greenhouse, "What in the World."

BIBLIOGRAPHY

Alschuler, Albert W. "Rediscovering Blackstone." *University of Pennsylvania Law Review* 145, no. 1 (November 1996): 1–55.

Arnold, Thuman. "Professor Hart's Theology." *Harvard Law Review* 73, no. 7 (1960): 1298–1317.

———. "A Reply." *American Bar Association Journal* 23, no. 5 (May 1937): 364–68, 393–94.

Aumann, F. R. "Judicial Law Making and Stare Decisis." *Kentucky Law Journal* 21, no. 2 (1933): 156–71.

Avi-Yonah, Reuven S. "The Cyclical Transformations of the Corporate Form: A Historical Perspective on Corporate Social Responsibility." *Delaware Journal of Corporate Law* 30, no. 3 (2005): 767–818.

Ball, Milner S. *Lying Down Together: Law, Metaphor, and Theology*. Rhetoric of the Human Sciences. Madison: University of Wisconsin Press, 1985.

Barnett, Vincent M., Jr. "The Political Philosophy of the New Supreme Court." *Journal of Social Philosophy & Jurisprudence* 7, no. 2 (1942): 101–26.

Barrett, John Q. "Attribution Time: Cal Tinney's 1937 Quip, 'A Switch in Time'll Save Nine.'" *Oklahoma Law Review* 73, no. 2 (2021): 229–43.

Bisbee, Donovan. "Driving the Three-Horse Team of Government: Kairos in FDR's Judiciary Fireside Chat." *Rhetoric & Public Affairs* 21, no. 3 (2018): 481–522.

Black, H. Campbell. "Principle of Stare Decisis." *American Law Register* 25 (December 1886): 745–57.

Black, Jason Edward. "Plenary Rhetoric in Indian Country: The *Lone Wolf v. Hitchcock* Case and the Codification of a Weakened Native Character." *Advances in the History of Rhetoric* 11/12 (2008/2009): 59–80.

Blaustein, Albert P., and Andrew H. Field. "'Overruling' Opinions in the Supreme Court." *Michigan Law Review* 57, no. 2 (1958): 152–94.

Bogart, George G. "A Law Teacher's View of the President's Plan to Enlarge the Supreme Court." *American Bar Association Journal* 23, no. 4 (April 1937): 251–53.

Boshoff, Anél. "Law and Its Rhetoric of Violence." *International Journal for the Semiotics of Law* 26, no. 2 (June 2013): 425–37.

Bosmajian, Haig. "Fire, Snakes, and Poisons: Metaphors and Analogues in Some Landmark Free Speech Cases." *Free Speech Yearbook* 20, no. 1 (1981): 16–22.

———. *Metaphor and Reason in Judicial Opinions*. Carbondale: Southern Illinois University Press, 1992.

Bradford, C. Steven. "Following Dead Precedent: The Supreme Court's Ill-Advised Rejection of Anticipatory Overruling." *Fordham Law Review* 59, no. 1 (1990): 39–90.

Braga, Justin R. "The Other Switch in Time: How the Opposition Changed the Debate Over the Court-Packing Plan and Won." *Georgetown Journal of Law & Public Policy* 17, no. 2 (Summer 2019): 653–82.

Brooks, Peter, and Paul Gewirtz, eds. *Law's Stories: Narrative and Rhetoric in the Law*. New Haven, CT: Yale University Press, 1996.

Bucklo, Elaine. "The Temptation Not to Disclose Adverse Authority." *Litigation* 40, no. 2 (Winter 2014): 1–4.

Burke, Kenneth. *A Grammar of Motives*. 1945. Berkeley: University of California Press, 1969.

———. *Language as Symbolic Action*. Berkeley: University of California Press, 1966.

Burnette, Ann E. "The Rhetoric of Virginia's Massive Resistance Movement." In Rountree, Brown v. Board *at Fifty*, 119–41.

Campbell, Peter Odell. "The Procedural Queer: Substantive Due Process, *Lawrence v. Texas*, and Queer Rhetorical Futures." *Quarterly Journal of Speech* 98, no. 2 (May 2012): 203–29.

Cantu, Edward. "Posner's Pragmatism and the Turn toward Fidelity." *Lewis & Clark Law Review* 16, no. 69 (Spring 2012): 69–123.

Carle, Susan D. "Race, Class, and Legal Ethics in the Early NAACP (1910–1920)." *Law and History Review* 20, no. 1 (Spring 2002): 97–147.

Carter, Edward L., and Edward E. Adams. "Justice Owen J. Roberts on 1937." *Green Bag 2d* 15, no. 4 (Summer 2012): 375–88.

Carter, W. Burlette. "Reconstructing Langdell." *Georgia Law Review* 32, no. 1 (Fall 1997): 1–139.

Chase, Oscar G., and Arlo Monell Chase. "*Monell*: The Story Behind the Landmark." *Urban Lawyer* 31, no. 3 (Summer 1999): 491–501.

Clapton, Mysty S. "*Murdoch v. Murdoch*: The Organizing Narrative of Matrimonial Property Law Reform." *Canadian Journal of Women and the Law* 20, no. 2 (2008): 199–230.

Collins, Douglas. *The Story of Kodak*. New York: H. N. Abrams, 1990.

Conkle, Daniel O. "The Second Death of Substantive Due Process." *Indiana Law Journal* 62, no. 2 (1987): 215–42.

Conley, John M., and William M. O'Barr. *Just Words: Law, Language, and Power*. Language and Legal Discourse. Chicago: University of Chicago Press, 1998.

Conot, Robert. *Streak of Luck*. New York: Simon & Schuster, 1979.

Conway, Glenda. "Inevitable Reconstructions: Voice and Ideology in Two Landmark U.S. Supreme Court Opinions." *Rhetoric & Public Affairs* 6, no. 3 (2003): 487–508.

Cooley, Thomas M. *A Treatise on Constitutional Limitations Which Rest upon the Legislative Power of the States of the American Union*. Boston: Little, Brown, 1868.

———. *The Elements of Torts*. Chicago: Callahan, 1895.

Cormack, Joseph M. "The Legal Tender Cases. A Drama of American Legal and Financial History." *Virginia Law Review* 16, no. 2 (1929): 132–48.

Cotter, Thomas F. "Legal Pragmatism and the Law and Economic Movement." *Georgetown Law Journal* 84, no. 6 (June 1996): 2071–141.

Cox, J. Robert. "The Rhetoric of Child Labor Reform: An Efficacy-Utility Analysis." *Quarterly Journal of Speech* 60, no. 3 (October 1974): 359–70.

Crenshaw, Carrie. "The Normality of Man and Female Otherness: (Re)Producing Patriarchal Lines of Argument in the Law and the News." *Argumentation & Advocacy* 32, no. 4 (Spring 1996): 170–84.

Currie, David P. "The Constitution in the Supreme Court: Contracts and Commerce, 1836–1864." *Duke Law Journal* 1983, no. 3 (June 1983): 471–513.

Curtis, Charles P. "A Modern Supreme Court in a Modern World." *Vanderbilt Law Review* 4, no. 3 (1951): 427–45.

Cushman, Barry. "Court-Packing and Compromise." *Constitutional Commentary* 29, no. 1 (Summer 2013): 1–30.

———. *Rethinking the New Deal Court: The Structure of a Constitutional Revolution*. New York: Oxford University Press, 1998.

Daniel, Josiah. M., III. "'Here is Where I Cash In': The Instrumental Role of Congressman Hatton Sumners in the Resolution of the 1937 Court-Packing." *UIC John Marshall Law Review* 54, no. 2 (Summer 2021): 379–428.

Danisch, Robert. "Aphorisms, Enthymemes, and Oliver Wendell Holmes, Jr. on the First Amendment." *Rhetoric Review* 27, no. 3 (2008): 219–35.

Danzig, Richard. "Justice Frankfurter's Opinions in the Flag Salute Cases: Blending Logic and Psychologic in Constitutional Decisionmaking." *Stanford Law Review* 36, no. 3 (February 1984): 675–723.

Dellapenna, Joseph W., and Kathleen Farrell. "Law and the Language of Community: On the Contribution of James Boyd White." *Rhetoric Society Quarterly* 21, no. 3 (1991): 38–58.

Dixon, Frank H. *A Traffic History of the Mississippi River System*. Washington, DC: US Government Printing Office, 1909.

Dodd, Walter F. "Defense of Our Constitutional System." *American Bar Association Journal* 23, no. 5 (May 1937): 344–46, 363.

Donovan, William J. "An Independent Supreme Court and the Protection of Minority Rights." *American Bar Association Journal* 23, no. 4 (April 1937): 254–60, 295–96.

Douglas, William O. "Stare Decisis." *Columbia Law Review* 49, no. 6 (June 1949): 735–58.

Duffey, Denis P., Jr. "Genre and Authority: The Rise of Case Reporting in the Early United States." *Chicago-Kent Law Review* 74, no. 1 (1998): 263–75.

Dworkin, Ronald. "'Natural' Law Revisited." *University of Florida Law Review* 34, no. 2 (Winter 1982): 165–88.

———. *Taking Rights Seriously*. Cambridge, MA: Harvard University Press, 1978.

Eisenhower, James J., III. "Four Theories of Precedent and Its Role in Judicial Decision." *Temple Law Review* 61, no. 3 (1988): 871–77.

Epps, Garrett. "The Alito Court: Justice Samuel Alito—Harris v. Quinn." In *American Justice 2014: Nine Clashing Visions on the Supreme Court*, 109–22. Philadelphia: University of Pennsylvania Press, 2014.

Eskridge, William M., Jr. "Overruling Statutory Precedents." *Georgetown Law Review* 76 (April 1988): 1361–1426.

Fairman, Charles. *Reconstruction and Reunion, 1864–88, Part One*. Vol. 4 of *History of the Supreme Court of the United States*. New York: Macmillan, 1971.

Friedman, Barry. "The History of the Countermajoritarian Difficulty: Part Four: Law's Politics." *University of Pennsylvania Law Review* 148, no. 4 (April 2000): 971–1064.

———. "The Wages of Stealth Overruling (with Particular Attention to *Miranda v. Arizona*)." *Georgetown Law Journal* 99 (November 2010): 1–63.

Friedman, Richard D. "Chief Justice Hughes' Letter on Court-Packing." *Journal of Supreme Court History* 22, no. 1 (1997): 76–86.

Funston, Richard Y. "Stevens, John Paul." In Hall, *Oxford Companion*, 836–37.

Gardner, Warner W. "Court Packing: The Drafting Recalled." *Journal of Supreme Court History* 15, no. 1 (1990): 99–103.

Garrow, David J. "Mental Decrepitude on the U.S. Supreme Court: The Historical Case for a 28th Amendment." *University of Chicago Law Review* 67, no. 4 (Fall 2000): 995–1087.

Gerhardt, Michael. "The Role of Precedent in Constitutional Decisionmaking and Theory." *George Washington Law Review* 60, no. 1 (1991): 68–159.

Gibson, Katie L. "In Defense of Women's Rights: A Rhetorical Analysis of Judicial Dissent." *Women's Studies in Communication* 35, no. 2 (January 2012): 123–37.

———. "Judicial Rhetoric and Women's 'Place': The United States Supreme Court's Darwinian Defense of Separate Spheres." *Western Journal of Communication* 71, no. 2 (April 2007): 159–75.

Gil, Alexandra. "Breaking the Studios: Antitrust and the Motion Picture Industry." *New York University Journal of Law & Liberty* 3, no. 1 (2008): 83–123.

Gill, Ann M. "The Supreme Court's Rhetoric of Legitimization." In Rountree, Brown v. Board *at Fifty*, 143–69.

Glennon, Theresa. "Somebody's Child: Evaluating the Erosion of the Marital Presumption of Paternity." *Virginia Law Review* 102, no. 3 (Spring 2000): 547–605.

Golden, James L., and Josina M. Makau. "Perspective on Judicial Reasoning." In *Explorations in Rhetoric: Studies in Honor of Douglas Ehninger*, edited by Ray McKerrow, 157–77. Glenview, IL: Scott, Foresman, 1982.

Goodrich, Peter. "Law and Language: An Historical and Critical Introduction." *Journal of Law and Society* 11 (1984): 173–206.

Gordon, Robert W. "The Case for (and against) Harvard." *Michigan Law Review* 93, no. 6 (1995): 1231–60.
Govshtein, Ella. "Justice Scalia and His Meta-Canon of Absurdity." *Hofstra Law Review* 35, no. 3 (2007): 1595–1615.
Graham, Kyle. "A Moment in the Times: Law Professors and the Court-Packing Plan." *Journal of Legal Education* 52, no. 1–2 (2002): 151–66.
Green, William. "Stare Decisis." *American Law Review* 14 (September 1880): 609–51.
Greene, Jamal. "Pathetic Argument in Constitutional Law." *Columbia Law Review* 113, no. 6 (2013): 1389–1481.
Griffin, Leslie C. "What Did Those Sixteen Justices Say?" *Wilamette Law Review* 58, no. 2 (Spring 2022): 163–250.
Hagan, Michael R. "*Roe v. Wade*: The Rhetoric of Fetal Life." *Central States Speech Journal* 27, no. 3 (1976): 192–99.
Hannan, Jeffrey. "*Dobbs v. Jackson Women's Health Organization* and the Likely End of the *Roe v. Wade* Era." *Duke Journal of Constitutional Law and Public Policy Sidebar* 17 (2021–22): 281–302.
Hall, Kermit L., ed. *The Oxford Companion to the Supreme Court of the United States.* New York: Oxford University Press, 1992.
Hart, H. L. A. "Positivism and the Separation of Law and Morals." *Harvard Law Review* 71, no. 4 (1958): 593–629.
Hasian, Marouf A., Jr. "The Aesthetics of Legal Rhetoric: The Ambiguities of 'Race' in *Adarand v. Peña* and the Beginning of the End of 'Affirmative Action.'" *Howard Journal of Communication* 8, no. 1 (January 1997): 113–27.
———. "Critical Legal Rhetorics: The Theory and Practice of Law in a Postmodern World." *Southern Communication Journal* 60, no. 1 (1994): 44–56.
———. "In Search of 'Ivan the Terrible': John Demjanjuk and the Judicial Use of Ironic Argumentation." *Argumentation and Advocacy* 39, no. 4 (2003): 231–53.
Hasian, Marouf A. Jr., Celeste Michelle Condit, and John Louis Lucaites. "The Rhetorical Boundaries of 'The Law': A Consideration of the Rhetorical Culture of Legal Practice and the Case of the 'Separate But Equal' Doctrine." *Quarterly Journal of Speech* 82, no. 4 (1996): 323–42.
Hasian, Marouf A., Jr., and Megan D. McFarlane. "A Critique of Jim Aune's Rhetoric, Legal Argumentation, and Historical Materialism." *Argumentation & Advocacy* 50, no. 4 (2014): 210–27.
Heimanson, Rudolf H. "Overruling—an Instrument of Social Change?" *New York Law Forum* 7 (1961): 167–75.
Heller, Francis H. "A Turning Point for Religious Liberty." *Virginia Law Review* 29, no. 4 (January 1943): 440–59.
Horan, Dennis J., and Thomas J. Balch. "*Roe v. Wade*: No Justification in History, Law, or Logic." In *Abortion and the Constitution: Reversing* Roe v. Wade *Through the Courts,* edited by Dennis J. Horan, Edward R. Grant, and Paige C. Cunningham, 57–88. Washington, DC: Georgetown University Press, 1987.

Hunt, Cecil J., II. "The Color of Perspective: Affirmative Action and the Constitutional Rhetoric of White Innocence." *Michigan Journal of Race and Law* 11, no. 2 (2006): 477–555.

Jackson, Robert H. "Decisional Law and Stare Decisis." *American Bar Association Journal* 30, no. 6 (1944): 334–35.

Johnson, John W. "Morehead v. New York Ex Rel. Tipaldo." In Hall, *Oxford Companion*, 562.

Josephson, Matthew. *Edison: A Biography*. New York: McGraw-Hill, 1959.

Joyce, Craig. "The Rise of the Supreme Court Reporter: An Institutional Perspective on Marshall Court Ascendancy." *Michigan Law Review* 83, no. 5 (April 1985): 1291–1391.

Kalman, Laura. "Fortas, Abe." In Hall, *Oxford Companion*, 308–9.

———. "Law, Politics, and the New Deal(s)." *Yale Law Journal* 108, no. 8 (June 1999): 2165–214.

Kempin, Frederick G., Jr. "Precedent and Stare Decisis: The Critical Years, 1800–1850." *American Journal of Legal History* 3, no. 1 (1959): 28–54.

Kirsner, Scott. *Inventing the Movies: Hollywood's Epic Battle between Innovation and the Status Quo, from Thomas Edison to Steve Jobs*. USA: CinemaTech Books, 2008.

Klarman, Michael J. "The Supreme Court 2019 Term: The Degradation of American Democracy—and the Court." *Harvard Law Review* 134, no. 1 (2020): 1–264.

Kluger, Richard. *Simple Justice: The History of Brown v. Board of Education and Black America's Struggle for Equality*. New York: Alfred A. Knopf, 1976.

Kocourek, Albert. "Retrospective Decisions and Stare Decisis: A Proposal." *American Bar Association Journal* 17, no. 3 (1931): 180–82.

Langford, Catherine L. Scalia v. Scalia: *Opportunistic Textualism in Constitutional Interpretation*. Tuscaloosa: University of Alabama Press, 2008.

LaRue, L. H. *Constitutional Law as Fiction: Narrative in the Rhetoric of Authority*. University Park: Pennsylvania State University Press, 1995.

LeRoy, Michael H. "Death of a Precedent: Should Justices Rethink Their Consensus Norms?" *Hofstra Law Review* 43, no. 2 (Winter 2014): 377–415.

Leuchtenburg, William E. *The Supreme Court Reborn: The Constitutional Revolution in the Age of Roosevelt*. Oxford: Oxford University Press, 1995.

Levi, Edward H. "An Introduction to Legal Reasoning." *University of Chicago Law Review* 15, no. 3 (1948): 501–74.

———. *An Introduction to Legal Reasoning*. Chicago: University of Chicago Press, 1949.

Lewis, Jon. *American Film: A History*. New York: W. W. Norton, 2008.

Lewis, Ovid C. "The High Court: Final . . . but Fallible." *Case Western Reserve Law Review* 19, no. 3 (1968): 528–643.

Lewis, T. Ellis. "The History of Judicial Precedent IV." *Law Quarterly Review* 190 (April 1932): 230–47.

Lewis, William. "Of Innocence, Exclusion, and the Burning of Flags: The Romantic Realism of the Law." *Southern Communication Journal* 60, no. 1 (1994): 4–21.

Lile, W. M. "Some Views on the Rule of Stare Decisis." *Virginia Law Review* 4, no. 2 (1916): 95–113.

Llewellyn, Karl N. *The Bramble Bush: On Our Law and Its Study*. New York: Oceana, 1951.

———. "Some Realism about Realism." *Harvard Law Review* 44 (1931): 1222–64.

———. "Some Realism about Realism." In *Jurisprudence: Realism in Theory and Practice*, edited by Karl N. Llewellyn, 53–76. Chicago: University of Chicago Press, 1962.

Lobingier, C. Sumner. "Precedent in Past and Present Legal Systems." *Michigan Law Review* 44, no. 6 (1946): 955–96.

Makau, Josina M. "The Supreme Court and Reasonableness." *Quarterly Journal of Speech* 70, no. 4 (1984): 379–96.

Maltese, John Anthony. "Bowers v. Hardwick." In Hall, *Oxford Companion*, 79–80.

Maltz, Earl M. "Some Thoughts on the Death of Stare Decisis in Constitutional Law." *Wisconsin Law Review* 1980 (1980): 467–96.

Mangis, Daniel. "Dissent as Prophecy: Justice John Marshall Harlan's Dissent in *Plessy v. Ferguson* as the Religious Rhetoric of Law." In Rountree, Brown v. Board *at Fifty*, 23–48.

Marcus, Nancy C. "Yes, Alito, There Is a Right to Privacy: Why the Leaked Dobbs Opinion is Doctrinally Unsound." *ConLawNOW* 13, no. 1 (2021–22): 101–14.

Minda, Gary. "The Jurisprudential Movements of the 1980s." *Ohio State Law Journal* 50, no. 3 (Summer 1989): 599–662.

Moffett, Kenneth W., Forrest Maltzman, Karen Miranda, and Charles R. Shipan. "Strategic Behavior and Variation in the Supreme Court's Caseload over Time." *Justice System Journal* 37, no. 1 (January–March 2016): 20–38.

Mohr, James C. *Abortion in America: The Origins and Evolution of National Policy*. New York: Oxford University Press, 1979.

Monaghan, Henry Paul. "Stare Decisis and Constitutional Adjudication." *Columbia Law Review* 88, no. 4 (May 1988): 723–73.

Moore, James William, and Shirley Adelson. "Supreme Court: The 1938 Term." *Virginia Law Review* 26, no. 1 (1939–40): 1–69.

Moore, James William, and Robert Stephen Oglebay. "The Supreme Court, Stare Decisis and Law of the Case." *Texas Law Review* 21 (May 1943): 514–53.

Musser, Charles. *Before the Nickelodeon: Edwin S. Porter and the Edison Manufacturing Company*. Berkeley: University of California Press, 1991.

Nader, Laura. *Harmony Ideology and the Construction of the Law: Justice and Control in a Zapotec Mountain Village*. Palo Alto, CA: Stanford University Press, 1990.

Nelson, Michael. "The President and the Court: Reinterpreting the Court-Packing Episode of 1937." *Political Science Quarterly* 103, no. 2 (Summer 1988): 267–93.

Nelson, William E. "The Impact of the Antislavery Movement upon Styles of

Judicial Reasoning in Nineteenth Century America." *Harvard Law Review* 87, no. 3 (1974): 513–66.

Newman, Stephen A. "Political Advocacy on the Supreme Court: The Damaging Rhetoric of Antonin Scalia." *New York Law School Law Review* 51 (2006/2007): 907–26.

Noland, Jon D. "Stare Decisis and the Overruling of Constitutional Decisions in the Warren Years." *Valparaiso University Law Review* 4, no. 1 (1969): 101–35.

O'Brian, Neil A. "Before Reagan: The Development of Abortion's Partisan Divide." *Perspectives on Politics* 18, no. 4 (2020): 1031–47.

O'Brien, David M. "Business of the Court." In Hall, *Oxford Companion*, 106–10.

Orbach, Barak Y. "Antitrust and Pricing in the Motion Picture Industry." *Yale Journal on Regulation* 21, no. 2 (Summer 2004): 317–67.

Parker, M. Jack. "The Unique Role of Language in the Judicial Process: After-the-Fact Classification of Human Behavior." In *Dimensions of Argument: Proceedings of the Second Alta Conference on Argument*, edited by George Ziegelmueller and Jack Rhodes, 207–12. Annandale, VA: Speech Communication Association, 1981.

Parry-Giles, Trevor. *The Character of Justice: Rhetoric, Law, and Politics in the Supreme Court Confirmation Process*. Rhetoric and Public Affairs. East Lansing: Michigan State University Press, 2006.

Parry-Giles, Trevor, and Marouf A. Hasian, Jr. "Necessity or Nine Old Men: The Congressional Debate over Franklin D. Roosevelt's 1937 Court-Packing Plan." In *American Rhetoric in the New Deal Era, 1932–1945*, vol 7 of *A Rhetorical History of the United States*, edited by Thomas W. Benson, 245–78. East Lansing: Michigan State University Press, 2006.

Perelman, Chaim, and Lucie Olbrechts-Tyteca. *The New Rhetoric: A Treatise on Argumentation*. Translated by John Wilkinson and Purcell Weaver. Notre Dame, IN: Notre Dame University Press, 1969.

Posner, Richard. *How Judges Think*. Cambridge, MA: Harvard University Press, 2008.

Postema, Gerald J. "Some Roots of Our Notion of Precedent." In *Precedent in Law*, edited by Lawrence Goldstein, 9–33. New York: Oxford University Press, 1987.

Pound, Roscoe. "What of Stare Decisis?" *Fordham Law Review* 10, no. 1 (January 1941): 1–13.

Powell, Lewis F, Jr. "Stare Decisis and Judicial Restraint." *Vital Speeches of the Day* 56, no. 3 (1989): 70–73.

"Precedents—Sub Silentio: The Lurking Problem." *New York University Law Review* 29 (May 1954): 1122–31.

Pritchett, C. Herman. "Schechter Poultry Corp. v. United States." In Hall, *Oxford Companion*, 757.

Punke, Harold H. "The Flag and the Courts in Free Public Education." *Journal of Religion* 24, no. 2 (April 1944): 119–30.

Pusey, Merlo J. *The Supreme Court Crisis*. New York: Macmillan, 1937.

Quay, Eugene. "Justifiable Abortion—Medical and Legal Foundations." *Georgetown Law Journal* 49, no. 3 (1961): 395.

Radin, Max. "Case Law and Stare Decisis: Concerning *Prajudizienrecht in Amerika*." *Columbia Law Review* 33, no. 2 (1933): 199.

Ram, James. *The Science of Legal Judgment*. Philadelphia: John S. Littell, 1835.

Ram, James, and John Townshend. *The Science of Legal Judgment*. New York: Baker, Voorhis, 1871.

Rand, Erin J. "Fear the Frill: Ruth Bader Ginsburg and the Uncertain Futurity of Feminist Judicial Dissent." *Quarterly Journal of Speech* 101, no. 1 (2015): 72–84.

Ray, Angela G., and Cindy Koenig Richards. "Inventing Citizens, Imagining Gender Justice: The Suffrage Rhetoric of Virginia and Francis Minor." *Quarterly Journal of Speech* 93, no. 4 (November 2007): 375–402.

Re, Richard M. "Narrowing Precedent in the Supreme Court." *Columbia Law Review* 114, no. 7 (November 2014): 1861–1911.

Reyman, Jessica. *The Rhetoric of Intellectual Property: Copyright Law and the Regulation of Digital Culture*. Routledge Studies in Rhetoric and Communication. New York: Routledge, 2010.

Rodgers, Raymond S. "Absolutism and Natural Law Argument: William O. Douglas on Freedom of Expression." *Southern Speech Communication Journal* 48, no. 1 (1982): 22–37.

———. "Generic Tendencies in Majority and Non-Majority Supreme Court Opinions: The Case of Justice Douglas." *Communication Quarterly* 30, no. 3 (1982): 232–36.

Rogat, Yosal. "Legal Realism." In *Encyclopedia of Philosophy*, edited by Paul Edwards, 420–21. New York: Macmillan, 1967.

Roosevelt, Franklin D. American Presidency Project. University of California–Santa Barbara.

———. Franklin D. Roosevelt, Papers as President: The President's Secretary's File (PSF), 1933–1945. Franklin D. Roosevelt Presidential Library & Museum, Hyde Park, NY.

Roper, Donald M. "Goldburg, Arthur Joseph." In Hall, *Oxford Companion*, 340–41.

Ross, William G. "When Did the Switch in Time Actually Occur?: Re-Discovering the Supreme Court's Forgotten Decisions of 1936–1937." *Arizona State Law Journal* 37, no. 4 (Winter 2005): 1153–220.

Rountree, Clarke, ed. Brown v. Board of Education *at Fifty: A Rhetorical Perspective*. Lanham, MD: Lexington Books, 2004.

———. "Building up to War: Bush's 'Administrative Rhetoric' in the Persian Gulf Conflict." *Speech Communication Annual* 10 (Spring 1996): 5–19.

———. "Constructing a Free Agent: 'Good Judgment' in Justice Kennedy's *Lawrence v. Texas* Opinion." In *Justice Anthony Kennedy: The Rhetoric of Liberty*, edited by David A. Frank and Francis M. Mootz, 95–109. University Park: Pennsylvania State University Press, 2023.

———. "Instantiating 'The Law' and Its Dissents in *Korematsu v. United States.*" *Quarterly Journal of Speech* 87 (February 2001): 1–24.

———. "Introduction: Strained Voices in American Political Discourse." In *Venomous Speech*, xix-xl.

———. *Judging the Supreme Court: Constructions of Motives in* Bush v. Gore. Rhetoric & Public Affairs. East Lansing: Michigan State University Press, 2007.

———. "Judicial Invention in Cases Contributing to the Development of Corporate Criminal Liability: A Multi-Dimensional Dramatistic Analysis." PhD diss., University of Iowa, 1988.

———. "Kairos and American Legal Praxis." *Nevada Law Journal* 20, no. 3 (2020): 855–76.

———. "On the Rhetorical Analysis of Judicial Discourse and More: A Response to Lewis." *Southern Communication Journal* 61, no. 2 (Winter 1995): 166–73.

———. "Prospective Argument: Constraining and Licensing Future Arguments." In *Argument and Critical Practices: Proceedings of the Fifth SCA/AFA Conference on Argumentation*, edited by Joseph W. Wenzel, 207–13. Annandale, VA: Speech Communication Association, 1987.

———. "Prospective Argument II: Laying the Ground for Future Argument." In *Argument in Controversy: Proceedings of the Seventh SCA/AFA Conference on Argumentation*, edited by Donn W. Parson, 58–63. Annandale, VA: Speech Communication Association, 1991.

———. "Reversing *Roe v. Wade* through the Courts: The Rhetorical Strategy of *Americans United for Life.*" Paper presented at the National Communication Association Convention. San Francisco, 1989.

———. "Setting the Stage for *Brown v. Board of Education*: The NAACP's Litigation Campaign Against the 'Separate but Equal' Doctrine." In Brown v. Board *at Fifty*, 49–90.

———, ed. *Venomous Speech: Problems with American Political Discourse on the Right and Left.* 2 vols. Santa Barbara, CA: Praeger, 2013.

Sachs, Leon. "Stare Decisis and the Legal Tender Cases." *Virginia Law Review* 20, no. 8 (1933): 856–85.

Sandefur, Timothy. "In Defense of Substantive Due Process, or the Promise of Lawful Rule." *Harvard Journal of Law and Public Policy* 35, no. 1 (Winter 2012): 283–350.

Sawyer, Samuel W. "The Commerce Clause of the Constitution: The Old and the New." *University of Kansas City Law Review* 8, no. 4 (1939–40): 229–52.

Schmitthoff, Clive M. "Should Precedents Be Binding?" *Journal of Business Law* (1982), 290–302.

Scordato, Marin Roger. "Reflections on the Nature of Legal Scholarship in the Post-Realist Era." *Santa Clara Law Review* 48, no. 2 (2008): 353–440.

Shanks, Sanders, Jr. "The Municipal Bankruptcy Act (Sumners-Wilcox Bill)." *American Political Science Review* 28, no. 6 (December 1934): 1072–74.

Singer, Barbara A. "The Reason of the Common Law." *University of Miami Law Review* 37, no. 3 (1983): 797–823.

Skolnick, Jerome, and James J. Fyfe. *Above the Law: Police and the Excessive Use of Force.* New York: Free Press, 1993.

Smith, Stephen A. "Citizens Undone: Freedom of Speech, Political Discourse, and the Import of *Citizens United v. Federal Election Commission.*" In Rountree, *Venomous Speech,* 149–65.

Smith, Young B. "Statement on the Proposal Regarding the Supreme Court before the Senate Judiciary Committee." *American Bar Association Journal* 23, no. 4 (April 1937): 261–64.

Spaeth, Harold J., and Jeffrey A. Segal. *Majority Rule or Minority Will: Adherence to Precedent on the U.S. Supreme Court.* New York: Cambridge University Press, 1999.

Spaeth, Harold J., Lee Epstein, Andrew D. Martin, Jeffrey A. Segal, Theodore J. Ruger, and Sara C. Benesh. *2020 Supreme Court Database.* Version 2021, Release 01.

Sprafkin, Alyson. "Language Strategy and Scrutiny in the Judicial Opinion and the Poem." *Cardozo Studies in Law and Literature* 13, no. 2 (2001), 271–98.

Stafford, Charles F. "The Public's View of the Judicial Role." *Judicature* 52, no. 2 (1968): 73–77.

"Stare Decisis." *Albany Law Journal* 6 (November 16, 1872): 329–30.

Starger, Colin. "Constitutional Law and Rhetoric." *University of Pennsylvania Journal of Constitutional Law* 18, no. 5 (May 2016): 1347–79.

Staring, Graydon S. "The Lingering Influence of Richard II and Lord Coke in the American Admiralty." *Journal of Maritime Law & Commerce* 41, no. 2 (April 2010): 239–62.

"The Status of the Rule of Judicial Precedent." *University of Cincinnati Law Review* 14 (1940): 203–355.

Stern, Robert L. "The Court-Packing Plan and the Commerce Clause." *Yearbook: Supreme Court Historical Society* 1988 (1988): 91–97.

Stob, Paul. "Louis Brandeis and the Rhetoric of Transactional Morality." *Rhetoric & Public Affairs* 14, no. 2 (Summer 2011): 261–90.

Sullivan, George Edward. "The Correct Doctrine of Stare Decisis." *Central Law Journal* 55, no. 19 (1902): 362–75.

Supreme Court Decisions Overrruled by Subsequent Decision. GovInfo. Washington, DC: Government Publishing Office, 2017.

"The Supreme Court Issue." *American Bar Association Journal* 23, no. 4 (April 1937): 268–70.

Sweeney, Joseph C. "The Lexington." *Journal of Maritime Law & Commerce* 39, no. 1 (January 2008): 65–80.

Tang, Aaron. "*Dobbs*: History, Tradition, and the Uncertain Future of a Nationwide Abortion Ban." *Stanford Law Review* 75, no 5 (May 2023): 1091–156.

———. "The Originalist Case for an Abortion Middle Ground." Social Science Research Network, 2021.

Taylor, R. C. "The Demise of Race Distinctions in Graduate Education." *Duke Bar Journal* 1, no. 2 (June 1951): 135–69.

Tiedeman, Christopher G. "The Doctrine of Stare Decisis, and a Proposal for Modification of Its Practical Application, in the Evolution of the Law." *University Law Review* 3 (January 1896): 11–26.

Tushnet, Mark V. *The NAACP's Legal Strategy Against Segregated Education, 1925–1950*. Chapel Hill: University of North Carolina Press, 1987.

———. "Roe v. Wade." In Hall, *Oxford Companion*, 739–42.

Ulrich, Walter. "The Creation of a Legacy: Brandeis' Concurring Opinion in Whitney v. California." *Southern Speech Communication Journal* 50, no. 2 (Winter 1985): 143–55.

Urofsky, Melvin I. "Brandeis, Louis Dembitz." In Hall, *Oxford Companion*, 83–85.

———. "Graves v. New York Ex Rel. O'Keefe." In Hall, *Oxford Companion*, 345.

Warren, Joyce W. *Women, Money and the Law: Nineteenth-Century Fiction, Gender, and the Courts*. Iowa City: University of Iowa Press, 2005.

Weems, J. A. "Religious Freedom and the Jehovah's Witnesses." *Virginia Law Review* 34, no. 1 (January 1948): 77–83.

Wermiel, Stephen J. "The Nomination of Justice Brennan: Eisenhower's Mistake? A Look at the Historical Record." *Constitutional Commentary* 11, no. 3 (1995): 515–37.

Wesley-Smith, Peter. "Theories of Adjudication and the Status of Stare Decisis." In *Stare Decisis*, edited by Lawrence Goldstein, 73–87. New York: Oxford University Press, 1987.

Wetlaufer, Gerald B. "Rhetoric and Its Denial in Legal Discourse." *Virginia Law Review* 76 (1990): 1545–97.

White, G. Edward. "*West Coast Hotel*'s Place in American Constitutional History." *Yale Law Journal Forum* 122 (2012–13): 69–84.

White, James Boyd. *When Words Lose Their Meaning: Constitutions and Reconstitutions of Language, Character, and Community*. Chicago: University of Chicago Press, 1984.

Whitney, Edward B. "Doctrine of Stare Decisis." *Michigan Law Review* 3, no. 2 (December 1904): 89–107.

Wiecek, William M. "Erie Railroad Co. v. Tompkins." In Hall, *Oxford Companion*, 259–60.

Williams, Ryan C. "The One and Only Substantive Due Process Clause." *Yale Law Journal* 120, no. 3 (2010): 408–512.

Wilson, Emmet H. "Stare Decisis, Quo Vadis? The Orphaned Doctrine in the Supreme Court." *Georgetown Law Journal* 33, no. 2 (March 1945): 251–78.

Wright, Warren E. "Judicial Rhetoric: A Field for Research." *Speech Monographs* 31, no. 1 (1964): 64–72.

Zielinski, Kelly. "The Implication of Texas Abortion Law SB8 on At-Risk Populations in Texas and Other States." *DePaul Journal of Health Care Law* 23, no. 2 (2022): 52–74.

INDEX